Structural analysis in the social sciences

Political networks: the structural perspective

Structural analysis in the social sciences

Mark Granovetter, editor

Other books in the series

Ronald Breiger, editor, *Social Mobility and Social Structure*

Mark S. Mizruchi and Michael Schwartz, editors, *Intercorporate Relations: The Structural Analysis of Business*

Barry Wellman and S. D. Berkowitz, editors, *Social Structures: A Network Approach*

The series Structural Analysis in the Social Sciences presents approaches that explain social behavior and institutions by reference to *relations* among such concrete social entities as persons and organizations. This contrasts with at least four other popular strategies: (1) reductionist attempts to explain by a focus on individuals alone; (2) explanations stressing the causal primacy of such abstract concepts as ideas, values, mental harmonies and cognitive maps (thus, "structuralism" on the Continent should be distinguished from structural analysis in the present sense); (3) technological and material determinism; and (4) explanations using "variables" as the main analytic concepts (as in the "structural equation" models that dominated much 1970s sociology), where the "structure" is that connecting variables rather than actual social entities.

The "social network" approach is an important example of the strategy of structural analysis; the series also draws on social science theory and research that is not framed explicitly in network terms, but stresses the importance of relations rather than the atomization of reductionism or the determinism of ideas, technology, or material conditions. Though the structural perspective has become extremely popular and influential in all the social sciences, it does not have a coherent identity, and no series yet pulls together such work under a single rubric. By bringing the achievements of structurally oriented scholars to a wider public, the series hopes to encourage the use of this very fruitful approach.

Mark Granovetter

Political Networks
The Structural Perspective

David Knoke
University of Minnesota

CAMBRIDGE
UNIVERSITY PRESS

Published by the Press Syndicate of the University of Cambridge
The Pitt Building, Trumpington Street, Cambridge CB2 IRP
40 West 20th Street, New York, NY 10011-4211, USA
10 Stamford Road, Oakleigh, Melbourne 3166, Australia

© Cambridge University Press 1990

First published 1990
First paperback edition 1994

Printed in the United States of America

Library of Congress Cataloging-in-Publication Data is available.

A catolog record for this book is available from the British Library.

ISBN 0-521-37552-5 hardback
ISBN 0-521-47762-X paperback

To Roberta and Kathryn

Contents

Tables and figures

Tables

Figures

Preface

Structural analysis in its contemporary form is less that two decades old. In that time it has matured from an intellectual social movement to an established specialty spanning several traditional disciplines. Steadily expanding literatures employing the network perspective on social behavior have accumulated. A set of interdisciplinary journals and regular professional meetings in the United States and Europe provide the critical mass to sustain this collective enterprise. Several generations of scholars are concurrently consolidating theoretical and empirical research advances using sophisticated structural analysis concepts, data, and principles. The aim of this book is to enhance the appreciation of structural analysis for improving our knowledge of political phenomena at all levels from primary groups to the world system. The primary audience is other serious scholars who study power with various intellectual tools. We do not assume a great familiarity with sophisticated mathematical techniques, although a brief appendix of technical terms is provided. Rather, we seek to convince our readers at the conceptual level of comprehension and leave to their own discretion how much quantitative depth they wish to acquire from numerous network methodology primers. By making detailed examinations of the roots of structural analysis, its ties to and divergences from alternative theoretical and methodological perspectives, and its contributions to political research, my coauthors and I hope to persuade the members of a wider intellectual community that the network approach to power has much to offer them.

Each substantive chapter focuses on key relational dimensions of political power in a different social institution. After presenting existing alternative approaches, we show how structural principles can be applied to illuminate unexplained features of the phenomena. Recent empirical research writings are reviewed for contributions, and some illustrative analyses of previously unpublished data are presented to demonstrate the power of network power analysis. "Looking Forward" sections at the end of each chapter offer agendas for theory construction and research projects that could make significant contributions to knowledge. Our hope is that both old hands and new converts to the structural analysis perspective will pursue these topics and others of their own devising, thereby advancing the frontiers of our collective understanding.

University of Minnesota
August 1989

Acknowledgments

Anyone who analyzes structural relations for a living realizes how much we owe to other people for ideas, inspiration, and support. This book is no exception, as I have acquired over the years a large network of colleagues who have shaped my perceptions of social theory and research. I have benefited in multiple ways from their advice, papers, articles, book reviews, conference sessions, editorial work, research assistance, data and computer programs, collaboration, criticism, encouragement, and emotional support. I hope I have reciprocated, if not in kind, then in complement. I have never attempted to diagram my egocentric intellectual network for fear that the ramifying threads beyond the first-order zone would be a tangled, indecipherable web. So out of expedience, I merely list here all the direct contacts that I can recall over the years who contributed in some form or another to my development as a network scholar. I praise them all for their unstinting efforts to raise the standards of scholarship to new heights: Mark Abrahamson, Howard Aldrich, Duane Alwin, Steve Berkowitz, Lawrence Bobo, Richard Braungart, Frank Burleigh, Jodi Burmeister-May, Paul Burstein, Ronald Burt, Elisabeth Clemens, James Coleman, Hilda Daniels, James Davis, Bonnie Erickson, Harmut Esser, Roberto Fernandez, William Form, Joseph Galaskiewicz, Mark Granovetter, Miguel Guilarte, Thomas Guterbock, Robert Huckfeldt, Hans Hummell, Naomi J. Kaufman, Arne Kalleberg, Edward Kick, Young-Hak Kim, Bert Klandermans, James Kuklinski, Edward Laumann, Joel Levine, Doug McAdam, Bernard McMullan, J. Miller McPherson, Peter Marsden, Joanne Miller, Nicholas Mullins, Norman Nie, Franz Pappi, Bernice Pescosolido, Walter Powell, David Prensky, Larry Raffalovich, David Rogers, Kay Lehman Schlozman, Thomas Scott, W. Richard Scott, Thomas Smith, Lynn Smith-Lovin, Wolfgang Sodeur, Joe Spaeth, Susan Stephens, Frans Stokman, Sheldon Stryker, Ad Teulings, Michael Useem, Jan van den Bos, Sidney Verba, Stanley Wasserman, David Whetten, Barry Wellman, Douglas White, Harrison White, Robert White, Nancy Wisely, James Wood, Christine Wright-Isak and many anonymous referees and reviewers. I also thank the following organizations for providing financial support and facilities at various data collection, analysis, and writing phases of projects reported herein: the National Science Foundation, the National Institute of Mental Health, the Russell Sage Foundation, the Fulbright Commission, the General Social Survey at the National Opinion Research Center, the University of Chicago, Indiana University, the University of Minnesota, Christian Albrechts Universitaet zu Kiel, and the Cambridge University Press. Finally, but far from least, the continuing bonds with Joann and Margaret are inseparable from the quality of work and love.

Grateful acknowledgment is made for permission to reprint the following quotations:

From Max Weber, 1947. *The Theory of Social and Economic Organization*, translated and edited by A.M. Henderson and Talcott Parsons. Copyright © 1947, renewed 1975 by Talcott Parsons. Reprinted by permission of The Free Press, a division of Macmillan Publishing Co., Inc.

From Peter M. Blau and W. Richard Scott, 1962. *Formal Organizations*, permission granted by Peter Blau.

From Gary S. Becker, 1976. *The Economic Approach to Human Behavior*, permission granted by the University of Chicago Press.

From Herbert A. Simon, 1985. "Human Nature in Politics: The Dialogue of Psychology with Political Science." *American Political Science Review*, Vol. 79, permission granted by the American Political Science Association.

From Mark Granovetter, 1985. "Economic Action and Social Structure: The Problem of Embeddedness." *American Journal of Sociology*, Vol. 91, permission granted by the University of Chicago Press.

From David Knoke, 1983. "Organization Sponsorship and Influence Reputation of Social Influence Associations." *Social Forces*, Vol. 61, permission granted by the University of North Carolina Press.

From Joseph Galaskiewicz, 1979. *Exchange Networks and Community Politics*, permission granted by Joseph Galaskiewicz.

From Thomas Guterbock, 1980. *Machine Politics in Transition: Party and Community in Chicago*, permission granted by the University of Chicago Press.

From Edward Laumann and Franz Urban Pappi, 1976. *Networks of Collective Action: A Perspective on Community Influence Systems*, permission granted by Academic Press and by Edward O. Laumann.

From John Higley and Gwen Moore, 1981. "Elite Integration in the United States and Australia." *American Political Science Review*, Vol. 75, permission granted by the American Political Science Association.

From Michael Useem, 1980. "Which Business Leaders Help to Govern?" in *Power Structure Research*, edited by G. William Domhoff, permission granted by Michael Useem.

From Edward O. Laumann and David Knoke, 1987. *The Organizational State: A Perspective on National Energy and Health Domains*, permission granted by the University of Wisconsin Press.

From Edward O. Laumann, David Knoke, and Yong-Hak Kim, 1985. "An Organizational Approach to State Policymaking: A Comparative Study of Energy and Health Domains." *American Sociological Review*, Vol. 50, permission granted by the American Sociological Association.

From Larry Sabato, 1984. *PAC Power*, permission granted by W.W. Norton & Company, Inc.

From Karl Marx, 1978. "Preface to A Contribution to the Critique of Political Economy" in *The Marx-Engels Reader, 2nd Ed.*, edited by Robert C. Tucker, permission granted by International Publishers, Inc.

From Ray Marshall, 1986. "Working Smarter" in *The Changing American Economy*, edited by David R. Obey and Paul Sarbanes, permission granted by Basil Blackwell, Inc.

From Michael Piore, 1987. "Beyond Social Anarchy" in *The Changing American Economy*, edited by David R. Obey and Paul Sarbanes, permission granted by Basil Blackwell, Inc.

From Paul Kennedy, 1987. *The Rise and Fall of the Great Powers: Economic Change and Military Conflicts from 1500 to 2000*. Copyright © 1987 by Paul Kennedy. Reprinted by permission of Random House, Inc.

From Beth Mintz and Michael Schwartz, 1985. *The Power Structure of American Business*, permission granted by the University of Chicago Press.

From Gareth Morgan, 1988. *Riding the Waves of Change: Developing Managerial Competencies for a Turbulent World*, permission granted by Jossey-Bass Inc., Publishers.

Reprinted from "Empowering Nets of Participation" by Judith R. Blau and Richard D. Alba, published in *Administrative Science Quarterly*, Vol. 27, Number 3 by permission of Administrative Science Quarterly. Copyright © 1982 Cornell University.

From Mary L. Fennell, Christopher O. Ross, and Richard B. Warnecke, 1987. "Organizational Environment and Network Structure." *Research in the Sociology of Organizations*, permission granted by JAI Press, Inc.

From Howard E. Aldrich, 1979. *Organizations and Environments*, permission granted by Howard E. Aldrich.

From Andre G. Frank, 1967. *Capitalism and Underdevelopment in Latin America*. Copyright © 1967 by Andre Gunder Frank. Reprinted by permission of Monthly Review Foundation.

From Christopher Chase-Dunn and Richard Rubinson, 1977. "Toward a Structural Perspective on the World-System." *Politics and Society*, Vol. 7, permission granted by Butterworth Publishers.

From Immanuel Wallerstein, 1974. *The Modern World System, I: Capitalist Agriculture and the Origins of the European World-Economy in the Sixteenth Century*, permission granted by Academic Press and by Immanuel Wallerstein.

From Immanuel Wallerstein, 1982. "The Rise and Future Demise of the World Capitalist System: Concepts for Comparative Analysis" in *Introduction to the Sociology of 'Developing Societies'*, edited by Hamza Alavi and Teodor Shanin. Copyright © 1982 by Hamza Alavi and Teodor Shanin. Reprinted by permission of Monthly Review Foundation.

From Thomas R. Dye, 1986. *Who's Running America: The Conservative Years. Fourth Edition*, permission granted by Simon & Schuster Higher Education Group.

From David Knoke, 1983. "Organization Sponsorship and Influence Reputation of Social Influence Associations." *Social Forces*, Vol. 61, permission granted by University of North Carolina Press.

From Norman Schofield and James Alt, 1983. "The Analysis of Relations in an Organization." *Quality and Quantity*, Vol. 17, permission granted by Elsevier Science Publishing Co., Inc.

From Roger V. Gould and Roberto M. Fernandez, 1987. "Structures of Mediation: A Formal Approach to Brokerage in Transaction Networks." Tucson, AZ: University of Arizona, Department of Sociology, permission granted by Roberto M. Fernandez.

1   *Politics in structural perspective*

Almost all political analysts are unwitting structuralists, because they define social power primarily in relational terms. Power is not a property or attribute that is inherent in an individual or group in the way that an electrical battery stores so many volts of energy. Rather, power is an aspect of the actual or potential interaction between two or more social actors. (*Actor* is a generic term for a unitary social entity, whether an individual person or a larger collectivity, such as a corporation or a nation state.) Most formal definitions of social power explicitly indicate this relational dimension. For example, Bertrand Russell wrote of power as "the production of intended effects" (Russell, 1938: 25), which Wrong modified to "the capacity of some persons to produce intended and foreseen effects on others" (Wrong, 1979: 2). Similarly, Max Weber's two famous definitions of power (*Macht*) underscored the coercive aspect of relationships between two or more actors:

> 'Power' is the probability that one actor within a social
> relationship will be in a position to carry out his own will
> despite resistance, regardless of the basis on which this
> probability rests. (Weber, 1947: 152)

> We understand by 'power' the chance of a man or a number of
> men to realize their own will in a social action even against the
> resistance of others who are participating in the action. (Weber,
> 1968: 962)

Note that Weber allowed for opposition to a power wielder's intended efforts, but he did not require it ("despite resistance" and "even against the resistance"). That is, although force is the ultimate foundation in any power relation, in many situations one actor may comply voluntarily, even eagerly, with the will of another. Assent or consent to commands characterizes many exercises of power. Weber called this subjective acceptance

1

with which the ruled obey their commanders *Herrschaft*, variously translated from German as "domination," "imperative coordination," or "legitimate authority" (Bendix, 1960: 291–92; Weber, 1947: 152, 328ff.).
Whether carried out with force, acquiescence, or enthusiasm, the exercise
of social power in its various forms inevitably requires interaction among
several social actors. Indeed, how any credible conceptualization of power
could be cast in absolutely quantitative terms is impossible to imagine.

Three contemporary treatments of power each echoed the Weberian
theme of overcoming potential opposition within a relationship. Herbert
Simon wrote of actors' causal intentions: "The statement 'A has power over
B' is equivalent to the statement that 'A causes B's behavior'" (Simon,
1957: 5). Robert Dahl expressed his "intuitive idea" of power as "A has
power over B to the extent that he can get B to do something that B would
not otherwise do" (1957: 202–3). And Richard Emerson stated an ex-
change-oriented definition: "The power of actor A over actor B is the
amount of resistance on the part of B which can be potentially overcome
by A" (Emerson, 1962: 32). In these and many similar definitions two
themes recur; power is a relationship of one social actor to another and it
is specific to a situation. Power enjoyed on one occasion may not be
transferable to other sets of conditions. To take a clear if trivial instance,
a policeman who has just been turned down for an automobile loan can
turn around and arrest the bank officer for overdue parking tickets. (A
more interesting interaction would be the patrolman's agreement to fix the
banker's tickets in return for the loan. The potential power obligations
would be quite illuminating.)

Because power is inherently situational, it is dynamic and potentially
unstable. Force, violence, and coercion aside, voluntary compliance may
fluctuate markedly over time, even reversing itself dramatically among the
same set of actors. A corporation's promotion of an underling to a managerial position routinely alters the power relations between the new executive and his former peers. At times, such power shifts can greatly disrupt
work routines and decrease productivity, for example, when women become the bosses of men (Kanter, 1977: 206–42; see also the movie *9 to
5*, in which Dolly Parton, Lily Tomlin, and Jane Fonda prove more adept
than their chauvinistic male supervisor at running the office). If relational
power is a situation-specific continuum – with a probability ranging from
zero to one that an actor's command will be obeyed by another – then it
waxes and wanes in response both to the various characteristics of actors
in power relationships and to external circumstances in which their relationships are embedded. Much political analysis is concerned with trying
to uncover the variables that systematically explain changes in the temporal
magnitudes of power relations.

Fundamental forms of power

Power relationships are asymmetrical actual or potential interactions in which one social actor exerts greater control over another's behavior. But, such generic definitions reveal little about the forms that power relations may take in social life. Many typologies classify the varieties of power (e.g., French and Raven, 1959; Parsons, 1963; Gamson, 1968; Wrong, 1979) and it may be presumptuous to construct yet another. However, some scheme is necessary to order the diversity of political relations. The one presented here specifies all power relationships as combinations of two fundamental dimensions: influence and domination.

Influence occurs when one actor intentionally transmits information to another that alters the latter's actions from what would have occurred without that information (see Gamson, 1968: 60; Parsons, 1963). Influence operates by providing information that changes an actor's perception of the connection between an action and its consequences. Influence is a relational dimension of power because a communication channel must exist between influencer and influencee. To be effective, the target of influence must believe the information to be credible and/or the source to be trustworthy. For example, a physician who advises a patient to avoid a heart attack by giving up smoking and taking up jogging can be said to exercise influence if the patient accepts the recommendation and complies with the advice. The basis of the doctor's influence resides in his expert knowledge of medical matters that the patient finds credible. Similarly, a mayor may persuade her electorate to pass a tax levy because she possesses data about the projected revenue and expenditure needs of the municipal service bureaus. Again, her influence over the voters stems from providing them with information that changes their views of the fiscal situation.

Influence is possible only when communication occurs between social actors; one actor must transmit a message to another, and the second actor must receive, decode, interpret, and react to that message. Rebuttal and counterargument may ensue before final resolution and compliance are reached. This intersubjective aspect of political influence requires that meaningful communication channels be established and maintained among actors. Not only must actors speak a common formal language, but they must share connotative understandings of words and symbols used in political discourse – freedom, equality, justice, peace, country, flag, prosperity. Influence is possible only if perceptions of situations can be framed in ways that are compelling to audiences. The rhetoric of political communication is effective if a reasonable level of agreement about terms and their meanings can be sustained among citizens. When the expression of desires and intentions is distorted as it passes through communication devices, the political community breaks down: "Power is actualized only where word and deed have not parted company, where words are not empty and deeds not brutal, where words are not used to violate and destroy but to establish relations and create new realities" (Arendt, 1958: 200). Influence thus originates in communication structures that link a set of disparate social actors into a genuine community of political discourse. Small wonder that totalitarian regimes first seek to monopolize the means of communication, then to empty the language of all meaningful distinctions, so that war becomes peace, slavery means freedom, and hate is love.

The second fundamental form of power, *domination*, is a relationship in which one actor controls the behavior of another actor by offering or withholding some benefit or harm. In other words, one actor promises or actually delivers a *sanction* (reward or punishment) to an actor in order to gain compliance with commands. Sanctions may be physical events (a salary increase, a new highway, execution at sunrise), but may also involve primarily intangible symbols (a redesigned flag, a benediction, ridicule on the editorial page). Obviously, domination can occur only if the dominee is responsive to the sanction. Even the threat of death may be ineffective in gaining compliance, as in the case of religious and political martyrs. Domination is clearly relational, because it involves one actor exchanging some valued (or abhorred) resource for obedience by another actor.

To use the municipal example again, the mayor dominates her city council when she awards public works contracts to the friends of those council members who support her policies. The classic urban party machines were clearly systems of domination, relying on both rewards and punishments to keep their entourages in line (see further analysis of patron-client relations in Chapter 5). Attempts to dominate in international relations occur often, for example, the Ayatollah Khomeini's threat to sink Persian Gulf oil tankers straying inside his unilateral restriction zone. As with an influence relationship, domination persists only while the dominator's capacity to deliver the promised sanctions are believed to be credible. Note that positive and negative sanctions are asymmetrical in their potency. A promised reward ultimately must be delivered to assure continued compliance. But, a threatened harm need not be carried out so long as the dominee complies with the dominator's commands (Oliver, 1980; Laumann and Knoke, 1987: 153–62). As in poker, however, calling one's political bluff is not unknown.

In every domination relationship the potential for truly evil uses of power inevitably lurks: might, force, coercion, manipulation, violence. The exertion of will by one actor implies the subordination, however apparently willing, of other actors. The capacity to realize one's interests through the application of rewards and punishments is always a temptation for unscrupulous actors to serve their private rather than collective purposes. Whether justified as benefiting the fatherland, racial purity, or the revolutionary proletariat, power relations that originate in domination always risk the destruction of the political community by turning some actors from subjects into mere objects for the achievement of others' desires. The dramatic histories of all nations are replete with horror stories of domination that degenerated into slavery and slaughter. Carried to such extremes, naked forms of domination may be ultimately self-limiting. At some unclear point, resistance to domination is sparked, revolt erupts, and a reconstitution of social power on a more equitable basis will be sought by the oppressed. Superior-subordinate relations rest on precarious foundations: "Ruling classes do not justify their power exclusively by *de facto* possession of it, but try to find a moral and legal basis for it" (Mosca, 1939: 70). Hence, the pure process of domination is usually accompanied by appeals to other grounds for obedience – religious, ethical, or ideological.

Influence and domination are not mutually exclusive processes within a power relation. Indeed, both dimensions comprise a mixed strategy in many real situations. Fig. 1.1 suggests schematically how these two dimensions can accommodate four pure types of power. Although shown and discussed here for convenience as dichotomies, influence and domination should be conceived as continuous concepts varying from entirely absent to present in increasing magnitudes. Strictly speaking, *egalitarian power* is not a form of power at all, because neither actor possesses means to control the other's behavior. Clearly, actors who lack any direct or indirect connection with one another stand in an egalitarian, if vacuous, relationship. *Coercive power*, otherwise known as force and violence, depends solely on threats and applications of negative sanctions. It is not accompanied by information that convinces the recipient of the rightness of the dominator's action. Indeed, coercion requires no acceptance by its victims. Brute force in prisons, concentration camps, invasions, and Kissingerian realpolitik

INFLUENCE

		Absent	Present
DOMINATION	Present	Coercive Power	Authoritative Power
	Absent	Egalitarian "Power"	Persuasive Power

Figure 1.1 Types of power as combinations of influence and domination.

exemplify unadorned coercion. In contrast, *persuasive power* relies only on the informational content of messages, with no ability to invoke sanctions for refusals to comply. Television advertising in electoral campaigns is almost a pure case; media consultants cannot even control people's ability to switch off their sets!

When influence and domination occur simultaneously, power relations take the form of *authoritative power*. Its essence is the issuing of a command with the expectation of uncontested obedience by the recipient (Wrong, 1979: 35). The source of the command rather than its content induces compliance with orders. Although voluntary compliance may be secured at low cost by providing information that appeals to an order-taker's self-interest, the expectation of benefit or the threat of deprivation is never entirely absent from any authority relationship. Authority always seeks to cloak its iron fist in a glove of sweet reason. The bases on which subordinates obey their superiors may be quite diverse, leading to a variety of subtypes of authority. Perhaps the most important special case of authority is Weber's "legitimate power" (Weber, 1947: 325). The legitimation of a command involves a special type of communication, information that justifies obedience to the command on the basis of previously established norms and beliefs. For example, President Reagan's order sending naval escorts to the Persian Gulf was implemented by admirals and sailors because they implicitly believed his command was authorized by the Constitution. In a legitimate power relationship, the subordinate participants strongly believe that their superior's exercise of power is appropriate and acceptable, to the extent that sanctions seldom need to be invoked to assure their compliance with commands. In general, these sentiments are widely shared by the members of a collectivity; indeed, followers may compel one another to comply with their leader's directives because it is "the right thing to do," regardless of latent positive and negative sanctions:

> The group's demand that orders of the superior be obeyed makes obedience partly independent of his coercive power [i.e., domination] or persuasive influence over individual subordinates and thus transforms these other kinds of social control into authority. (Blau and Scott, 1962: 29)

A legitimate power relationship is reciprocal; a ruler issues a command in the expectation of compliance, and obedience to the command is guided by the ruled's subjective beliefs that the orders are legitimate. Weber, of course, was famous for his classification of the bases for claiming legitimate power: traditional, charismatic, and rational-legal (Weber, 1947: 328–9; see Willer [1967] for an argument of a fourth type: ideological authority). But, regardless of the particular grounds for subordinates' beliefs, the legitimate power form of authority ultimately rests on domination com-

bined with influence. The necessity of having both power ba
itimate power relationship was succinctly captured by S/
(1968: 162) notion that ultimately a power-holder can call o/
centers to back up his command with sanctions. The legiti/
the Somoza and the Sandinista regimes depended both on their cap.
persuade the Nicaraguan people of the rightness of their rule *and* on their
ability to use the armed forces to fight against challengers. As tyrants from
Pisistratus to Nicolai Ceausescu have learned, domination without influence in the long run proves ineffective in sustaining an illegitimate
authority in power.

To this point, the abstract discussion of relational power has concentrated on dyads – pairs of social actors. But most power interactions occur
in complex situations. When considering power relations among many
actors in a large political system, the idea of a social network is helpful.

Political systems as social network

The basic units of any complex political system are not individuals, but
positions or roles occupied by social actors and the relations or connections
between these positions. Anthropologists and sociologists conventionally
conceive of *roles* (or *statuses*, the action components of a role) as clearly
articulated bundles of rights, duties, obligations, and expectations that
guide the characteristic conduct of persons assuming such positions in a
social system (e.g., Linton, 1936: 113 ff.; Nadel, 1957: 20–44; Merton,
1957). A role is not merely a shorthand label for a set of appropriate
activities, it also indicates how an incumbent is expected to interact with
other roles under appropriate circumstances. These relationships refer to
constants of behavior and to the particular contents or qualities of the
interaction between people occupying the different role positions (Nadel,
1957: 102). Every social role – whether that of *mother, lawyer, boss,* or
sergeant – exists concretely only in relation to one or more complementary
roles with which it regularly interacts – *daughter, client, employee, private.*
For any given role pair, the rules or norms of behavior typically specify
which actor is more likely to comply with the commands of the other.
Mothers often tell their teenage daughters to straighten up their rooms,
and they occasionally find their instructions obeyed! Every political system
consists of a division of labor among participants that can potentially be
analyzed in terms of its component power relationships.

In many political systems, role incumbents come and go, but the power
configurations among the positions remain fairly stable. Thus, universities
and hospitals experience frequent turnovers in staff and clients, yet the
unequal doctor-patient and teacher-student power relations persist. The

inauguration of a new U.S. president usually leaves unaltered his position's power relations vis-à-vis the Congress, armed forces, civil bureaucracies, and the federated states (but not so in 1860, even before Lincoln was sworn in). Or, the configurations of military alliances among the world's nations remain relatively durable from year to year and decade to decade, despite numerous changes in regime personnel. Because so many political systems are highly stable, they can be analyzed as structures of power relations among their component social positions. The basic idea of a *social structure* is a stable order or pattern of social relations among positions, consisting of the set of direct and indirect connections between the actors occupying these different social positions (Laumann and Pappi, 1976: 6). The primary analytic focus is on the relational connections as such – the ties among the positions – and not on the attributes of the incumbent individuals who occupy these positions. These linkages may be singular or multiple and may vary along numerous dimensions of intensity, frequency, duration, content, affect, and the like. These varied features of structural relations are examined in greater detail elsewhere in this book.

In contrast to the conventional depiction of social role systems as fairly rigid positions, constraining the incumbents' actions in the same way that a script dictates actors' speeches, no claim is made here about the a priori existence of social positions apart from the relationships among them. Indeed, position and relationship are inseparable aspects of a unitary structural phenomenon – the social network. Continually changing interactions among persons or groups occupying a network's social positions can alter role-based performances, allowing new roles to emerge and old roles to be transformed. Thus, the role of the urban political party leader in the United States during the twentieth century was transformed from a dominating boss to a mediating broker when politicians developed personalized resource and information exchange relations with their constituencies under pressures from increasingly media-driven electoral campaigns. By emphasizing that positions must be identified not by descriptive labels, but from careful examinations of actual interactions that take place between actors in multiple networks, structural analysts can adopt a flexible and sensitive stance toward the amount of rigidity and innovation occurring in any particular social system.

Formal representations of social structure place powerful mathematical tools at the disposal of structural analysts. These diverse procedures pass under the general rubric of *social network analysis* (see Berkowitz, 1982; Burt, 1982; Knoke and Kuklinski, 1982; Freeman, White, and Romney, 1988). The two basic components of all network analyses are a set of objects (variously called *nodes, positions,* or *actors*) and a set of relations among these objects (variously called *edges, ties,* or *links*). Network analysts proceed by developing formal models to represent accurately selected features of real-world social behaviors (that is, their models are *isomorphic* with reality). A formal network model permits examination of social structures by rigorously applying mathematical graph and topology principles to the data. Social structures can be displayed as pictorial graphs involving points and lines or, equivalently, as algebraic matrices. By mathematically manipulating these network representations, the structural analyst seeks to uncover the fundamental forms and processes of social and political behavior. The Appendix at the end of the book presents some basic concepts and terms in network analysis. This Appendix should be read to acquire a vocabulary that is useful in understanding many of the ideas in this and later chapters. With these network concepts, new insights into the influence and domination relations of political systems are possible.

The prime directive

Structural analysis is not a unified theory, but an assemblage of loosely connected perspectives on interaction within social networks. If limited just to describing the linkages among political actors in a social system, structural analysis will cause little intellectual ferment. But the structural approach offers an explicit premise of great import: "The structure of relations among actors and the location of individual actors in the network have important behavioral, perceptual, and attitudinal consequences both for the individual units and for the system as a whole" (Knoke and Kuklinski, 1982: 13). Or, in Mitchell's (1969) eloquent phrase, "The patterning of linkages can be used to account for some aspects of behavior of those involved." Both the forms and contents of relations among social positions have significant consequences for the formation of political attitudes and behaviors. Regardless of the particularities of a given structural analysis, virtually all network analysts share the presumption that a complete explanation for some social phenomenon requires knowledge about the relationships among system actors. To ignore structures gives, at best, a deficient explanation and, at worst, an incorrect one.

The basic objective of a structural analysis of politics is to explain the distribution of power among actors in a social system as a function of the positions that they occupy in one or more networks. A position's power – its ability to produce intended effects on the attitudes and behaviors of other actors – emerges from its prominence in networks where valued information and scarce resources are transferred from one actor to another. Positions are stratified according to the dependence of other positions on them for these essential resources. Not only the direct connections are important in determining positional power, but the indirect connections are critical because they comprise limits and opportunities for obtaining desired ends. The local and global structures of alternatives for exchanging resources and information largely determine the relative power of each actor in the network. In general, a position has greater power to the extent that others depend on it for information, goods, and affection that are unavailable elsewhere. A position lacks power when other actors enjoy many alternatives for securing their preferences. Basic principles of social exchange are operative (see Chapter 4). Over time, incumbents of positions that enjoy fewer structural choices must compensate others for the information and resources they receive by agreeing to the exchange terms offered by less-dependent positions (Emerson, 1962). Structurally disadvantaged positions pay their debts by subordinating themselves, complying with the commands of those positions to whom they are indebted (Blau, 1964: 22). Thus, positional power derives from networks of structural relations and it exists apart from actors' knowledge or ignorance about the larger opportunity structures within which their positions are embedded.

The structural approach to power requires that analysts assess a position's prominence by taking account not only of its direct but also its indirect connections in complete networks. Two conceptions of prominence can be distinguished according to the types of exchange relations presumed to make actors' positions visible to system members (Knoke and Burt, 1983: 198). *Centrality* concepts do not differentiate sending from receiving relations, but simply treat all connections as symmetric. The most central positions in a network are those involving many reciprocated ties to other actors. Network stars acquire power because they are close to many system actors, in effect, by lying between positions that must use them to transmit messages and goods (Freeman, 1977, 1979). For example, a parliamentary leader often discusses legislative tactics with his party whips, who are in constant touch with the rank-and-file legislators, and with the opposition leaders who also communicate with *their* parties' members. Thus, centrality prominence is useful for analyzing positional power in symmetric exchange networks, such as communication structures. In contrast, *prestige* concepts preserve the asymmetry of ties among positions so that prominence increases with the extent to which a position receives many relations but does not reciprocate. The quality of ties, not their sheer volume, is crucial; the prominence of a position's contacts determines, in part, its prominence (Knoke and Burt, 1983: 206). The most prestigious positions in an asymmetric exchange network are those receiving strong relations from many actors who are themselves the recipients of strong ties from many actors. Prestige prominence is especially useful in analyzing the power of positions in networks where commands or goods are not reciprocally exchanged. For example, the U.S. president is the target of numerous government and private-sector organizations that seek access to make their pitches for his support; but he is very selective about those to whom he grants audiences, seeing mainly the actors with the most power to help or hurt his agenda (see Chapter 8). Given their different conceptions and operationalizations, both centrality and prestige measures of prominence may prove useful for analyzing power in diverse situations (see the Appendix for more on centrality and prestige measures).

Whether trying to understand how Stalin stole the Russian Revolution from Trotsky and Bukharin (Deutscher, 1966) or to explain why the blueprint and tool attendants are especially powerful workers in factories (Burawoy, 1979), knowing how actors are connected to one another in the overall structural configuration is indispensable. Structural analysis holds the promise of identifying the explicit forms and contents through which power structures and processes produce their effects on network participants.

Influence and domination networks

When analyzing power relations among actors in a large system, influence and domination linkages should not be conflated into a single dimension of power. They must be separately and jointly analyzed because the connections among influence and domination relations each tend to produce distinct structures. As noted above, influence involves transmission of information that changes other actors' behaviors by changing their perceptions. Communication is the main process by which actors determine and express their interests in a political event. Most communication relations involve two-way channels for exchanging messages between pairs of positions, suggesting that centrality is the best way to measure prominence in an influence network.

Communication networks promote attitude similarities through social comparison processes (Erickson, 1988). Any subset of actors that maintains similar structural relations to the other network actors is said to occupy the same position in the network jointly. Indeed, if all their interactions with others are identical, the individuals are indistinguishable on relational grounds and can be treated as a single position in the system. Actors who jointly occupy a position tend to conform to the same viewpoints as a consequence of similar experiences and exposures to the same subsets of network participants. The main concern is whether the members of a jointly occupied position interact among themselves (cohesion) or are unconnected internally (structural equivalence). As described in the Appendix, both cohesive and structurally equivalent network positions encourage actors to model their beliefs and behaviors after one another. But the processes by which conformity arises involve different socializing reference groups. Briefly, cohesive groups involve intense direct relations among all members, whereas structurally equivalent positions have highly similar interactions to other network actors but not necessarily among themselves (Burt, 1987b). Members of a cohesive group or clique are linked directly to one another by many intense mutual ties across which influence communications are transmitted. They are structurally oriented toward their internal reference groups for clues to appropriate thoughts and deeds. In an ambiguous situation, such as deciding to vote for a primary election candidate, people typically turn to others who are similar to themselves in salient respects for advice to clarify uncertainties in their thinking. Within a cohesive clique, the stronger and more frequent the empathic communications, the more likely are clique members to foster similar social and political attitudes in one another. Intense discussions socialize clique participants to a common normative understanding about their collective interests. A consensual evaluation of the meaning of alternative choices results in uniform political opinions and voting decisions among the clique's members (see Chapter 2).

By contrast, structurally equivalent actors may lack direct ties to one another, but maintain highly similar relations with the same set of other system actors (see Appendix). The more similar that a pair of actors are in these relations, the more likely it is that one will adopt any behavior perceived to make the second an attractive source or object of relations (Burt, 1987b: 1291). Highly competitive rivalries for affections and benefits that are dispensed by a third party on a zero-sum basis may induce emulation and conformity of thought and deed among the competitors. For example, a dictator increases his personal security by requiring that his officers deal directly only with him for their military provisions and career advancement. By remaining their sole source of rewards and punishments, the dictator creates a rivalry among the generals for his favors and prevents them from conspiring for his overthrow. By isolating potential opponents in a noncohesive but structurally equivalent position, the dictator can promote the paranoid loyalty and dependency of every subordinate. Because structurally equivalent actors communicate with the same set of third parties, they come to similar understandings – not as a result of dealing directly with one another, but because of their common external reference group. Thus, influence in networks results from communication processes that occur in both cohesive and structurally equivalent groups.

Information exchanges can empower an actor by giving it access to data on conditions, threats, and opportunities. Several well-known political phenomena can be interpreted as consequences of such communication network structures:

1. Communication networks are essential for social contagion and innovation diffusion processes, including the spread of technical innovations (Burt, 1987b), social movement tactical repertoires (Tilly, 1978), electoral campaign techniques, riots, assemblies (McPhail and Miller, 1973), fads, and other forms of collective behavior (Granovetter, 1978).

2. The spread of political publicity and propaganda through impersonal mass media channels is a two-step flow that requires networks of personal communication linking community opinion leaders to followers (Katz and Lazarsfeld, 1955). Marginally positioned individuals serve as bridges between social groups, but "most of the influence flow within a group is carried out by 'centrals,' mainly in a downward, vertical flow" (Weimann, 1982: 769).

3. Systems of interest representation, in which delegates are chosen to vote for public policies favored by constituents, require stable two-way channels for revealing preferences and actions (Eulau, 1986: 179–204). The appearance of a mass polity, such as was alleged of Weimar Germany, stems from the breakdown in mutual communication between elites and masses that constrains expectations and actions (Kornhauser, 1959: Halebsky, 1976).

4. The location and availability of political resources, including potential coalition partners, is identified primarily through communication channels that transmit data along lengthy chains. Mobilization for collective action depends on the timely and trustworthy transmission of information within a domain of interest (Laumann and Knoke, 1987: 206–48).

All these forms of political influence involve information exchange networks that spread messages from one actor to another through chains of varied length. Indeed, in many collective action situations, communication trees are deliberately constructed to spread instructions rapidly throughout the network. For example, the National Association of Realtors and the National Rifle Association can mobilize hundreds or thousands of members in each U.S. congressional district within hours to lobby for or against pending legislation that affects their interests. Of course, some social systems do restrict access to privileged information, particularly antagonistic systems such as legislative bodies. But even here a surprising volume of communication occurs between political opponents (Laumann and Knoke, 1987: 213). Centrality prominence in a communication network is synonymous with influence (see Chapter 6). Actors who are connected to other prominent actors gain power through their positional ability to tap into larger stores of useful political information. Persons on the periphery, or whose direct and indirect ties link them mainly to other marginal actors, will encounter inadequate quantities and qualities of information. They are relegated to uninfluential locations.

Domination relations involve the promised or actual exchange of sanctions. One network position dominates another by providing the latter with scarce resources that are unavailable from alternative suppliers. Imperatively coordinated organizations (bureaucracies) and informal systems of political exchange (patron-client networks) are two general types of political structures based on domination relationships. Hierarchical formal organizations – such as churches, armies, corporations, and governmental agencies – coordinate the actions of their participants by designating some positions to issue commands and others to carry them out (see Chapter 4). The command-givers apply sanctions that reward or punish the command-takers for their obedience or insubordination. Because organizational resources are always scarce, material goods are typically allocated selectively to individuals rather than generally to all participants. In vertical chain-of-command office structures, a superior indirectly commands a subordinate's subordinates. Rewards for good performance – promotions, medals, salary raises, bonuses, perks – cascade unevenly through the hierarchy. Some participants are gainers, others losers. Relatively stable patterns of dominance emerge that reflect these mutually exclusive allocations of sanctions among organizational participants. These resource exchange networks account for significant outcomes in the continual struggles for intraorganizational control (Tichy and Fombrun, 1979; Bacharach and Lawler, 1980: 203–23; Pfeffer, 1982: 271–7).

Similarly, informal political exchange systems – such as party caucuses in legislatures, village brokerage systems (Boissevain, 1974), urban interorganizational networks (Galaskiewicz, 1979b, 1989), and national pressure group systems (Walker, 1983; Salisbury, 1984) – operate on the reciprocity principle that rewards should be proportional to contributions (Gouldner, 1960; Hwang, 1987). Patrons help clients in expectation of return favors, although the inability of resource-poor participants to reciprocate fully results in unequal power distributions over time (Blau, 1964: 113–18). A stable structure emerges in which a patron dominates his constituents through judicious use of the IOUs he controls. Because political exchanges are carried out in the absence of a rigorous accounting system, such as a money economy, trust is the vital ingredient in any informal dominance system (Blau, 1964: 94–9; Luhmann, 1979; Barber, 1983; Heckathorn, 1985; Gambetta, 1988). A power broker willingly incurs obligations that others may never fully repay, because such debts can be invoked in piecemeal chunks that over the long run may exceed the value of the original favor (see Chapter 5). The alleged power of the criminal godfather lies in his ability to put municipal political and police leaders in incriminating petty debts that remain concealed only by tolerating lucrative illegal service activities within their jurisdictions. Less sinister log-rolling systems characterize parliamentary vote-trading blocs (Coleman, 1973; Eulau, 1986). Many political systems blend both formal sanctioning relations and informal exchanges, for example, Mexico's convoluted networks of political brokers inside and outside the official government bureaucracies (Carlos and Anderson, 1981; see also Van Velzen [1973] for a similar analysis of Tanzanian village politics). In every type of formal and informal exchange system, the differential exchanges of sanctions among participants allow some positions to gain dominance over others.

Some theorists argue that exchange networks consisting of positively or negatively connected relations have important implications for an actor's power. A relation between actors *A* and *B* is connected to a relation between *B* and *C* to the extent that the second relation is contingent on the first. The connection is positive "if exchange in one relation is contingent on exchange in the other . . . [and] is negative if exchange in one relation is contingent on nonexchange in the other" (Cook, Emerson, Gillmore, and Yamagishi, 1983: 277). For example, a communication network is positively connected because an actor's information is a direct function of the information available to its contacts. But a commodity exchange network is negatively connected because many ties among one position's trading partners reduces that position's ability to control the terms of trade. These concepts have been applied in laboratory experiments of bargaining networks. Greater profits were obtained by positions that were more central in both positively and negatively connected structures, where a position has higher centrality if its contacts' centralities are higher (Bonacich, 1987). Although the positive-negative distinction seems important for explaining these simple bargaining systems, the contingency concept is not definitionally symmetrical. Nor does the positive-negative distinction have clear relevance to concrete networks, which mostly have mixed characteristics (Cook et al., 1983: 278). At this point, perhaps the most charitable conclusion is that the value of the differential connection concept for political structural analysis remains to be demonstrated (see Chapter 4 for more discussion).

The flexibility and strength of a structural analysis of power lie in its dualistic microanalysis and macroanalysis capabilities. Not only may the influence and domination of individual positions be assessed, but the political system as a whole can be investigated through the structural properties of its participants, while allowing for the emergence of new structural features at a higher level of analysis. For example, in trying to explain why individual voters turn out for elections, an inspection of the reinforcing or conflicting political messages carried in their egocentric political discussion networks is essential (see Chapter 2). This individual-level explanation is the notorious cross-cutting-cleavages hypothesis too often specified simply as attributes of the voter without taking account of interpersonal interactions (but see Dahrendorf, 1959: 267–72; Horan, 1971). At the system level, when trying to explain why some communities have higher election turnout rates than others, the individual-level networks become key data. The density of individual voters' connections to local political activists may be much greater in communities where voter mobilization is more effective.

Theoretical development and empirical research advances in understanding political phenomena require significant research efforts to identify and measure relations of influence and domination. Such structural analyses must proceed simultaneously at microlevels and macrolevels, in other words, at local structures consisting of dyads, triads, and cliques, and with global structures, as well as with the cross-level connections (aggregations).

Other structuralisms

The relational perspective on political structures is only one of several prevalent conceptions of *structuralism*. In their various usages of the term structure, these other approaches seem to connote any underlying regularity or pattern of action or thought in a social system, but not necessarily relations among social positions. Thus, one popular sociology textbook asserted that "all characteristics of groups are social structures" (Stark, 1985: 73), whereas a major theorist argued that organizational structure consists of "the distributions, along various dimensions, of people among social positions that influence the role relations among these people" (Blau, 1974: 12). Talcott Parsons (1970) viewed social structure as the integration of individual motivations with normative cultural values. In linguistics, cognitive psychology, and social anthropology, numerous structuralisms abound that attempt to explain systematic regularities in human consciousness and cultural beliefs (e.g., Saussure, 1966; Hawkes, 1977; Piaget, 1971). The classic exemplar is Lévi-Strauss's (1952) search for a universal, unconscious "deep structure," or logical organization, in primitive kinship and myth systems. Social structures exist not in the ongoing interactions among concrete individuals, but in the intrasubjective principles of social organization that may or may not have empirical manifestations. The mental images of society that people carry around in their heads need have little connection to their actual day-to-day interactions. Lukes saw the common theme in all these structuralisms as the "basic opposition between structure and agency . . . although views differ about what constitute structural factors, about what sort of limits they set upon agency and about whether the limits curtail freedom or provide the condition of its effective exercise" (Lukes, 1977: 8).

Perhaps the most salient of these approaches for readers in the United States is Anthony Giddens' theory of *structuration*. Strongly influenced by Continental hermeneutics and linguistics, he tried to formulate a theory of agency without lapsing into purely subjectivist phenomenology. In Giddens' unique terminology, social systems, as continuous flows of conduct in time and space, are distinguished from social structures, which are defined as rules and roles existing as memory traces that are revealed in actions (Giddens, 1984: 377). Four basic modes of structuration occur:

rules for signification of meaning, rules for normative legitimation of social conduct, authorized resources to command persons (political power), and allocation of resources to command objects (economic property). Giddens' elaborately codified structuration theory links these structural modes to recurrent interactions through a duality of structure and agency (Giddens, 1979; 100). His structuration theory comes closer to the relational structural perspective advocated in this book than do the purely phenomenological structuralisms. However, its usefulness is severely limited by Giddens' failure to specify a research methodology for testing its arcane theoretical formulations.

Marxist structuralisms also seek to penetrate the superficial world of appearances and to uncover the fundamental forces that shape political, economic, and social life. Within such historical modes of production as feudalism and capitalism, the ultimate source of structural reproduction and change lies in the autonomous forces of material production. Perhaps the clearest statement of this position was Marx's own:

> The sum total of these relations of production constitutes the
> economic structure of society, the real foundation, on which
> rises a legal and political superstructure and to which
> correspond definite forms of social consciousness (Marx, 1859
> [1978: 4]).

Foremost among these social relations, of course, is the exploitation of one class by another. For classical Marxists, cultural values, beliefs, and other mental processes are derived from society's fundamental economic structures. In its extreme versions, Marxist structural analysis is detached from any concern with interactions involving flesh-and-blood human beings. In Althusser's abstract, ahistorical structuralism, people disappear entirely as autonomous agents within their social relations (Althusser and Balibar, 1970: 180; see also Poulantzas [1978] for agreement with and Thompson [1978] for criticism of the Althusserian position). The more conventional neo-Marxians recognize that human agents retain some degree of autonomy of choice and action within social institutions. Further, the empirical relationships among economically, politically, and ideologically interacting individuals and collectivities comprise the basic data for explaining historical social change. Thus, Marxist structuralism comes closest to the perspective of this book when it depicts real instances of class conflict, state domination, and imperialism as the result of changing relationships among persons and groups.

Others define the term *structural* as the distribution of social entities into the categories of a variable. For example, the structure of economic opportunity might be equated with the percentages of ethnic group members in various occupations or with their unequal distributions of earned income (e.g., Blau, 1977). Or proletarianization in the class structures of postindustrial society is depicted as the distribution of the labor force into various industry and occupational categories, defined according to their positions within a mode of production (Wright and Singelmann, 1982; Wright and Martin, 1987). These approaches reveal little about the relations among ethnic groups or the ongoing interactions among workers and employers in the division of labor. Others apply econometric methods to highly aggregated data to produce numerous cross-national and time-series analyses of mass political violence, inequality, and democracy, governmental transfers and fiscal expenditures, arms races and the like whose purpose is to estimate "structural equation models" (e.g., Cameron, 1978; Hibbs, 1981; Hicks and Swank, 1984; Griffin, Wallace, and Rubin, 1986). These models are structural only in the sense that their parameter estimates purport to measure stable effects of causal variables. But they are not structural analyses in the relational sense. Given their high degree of data aggregation, these models cannot reveal the interactions among the policymakers, rebel and military forces, or workers and employers that produced the riot deaths, military expenditures, or union memberships. The black box of flesh-and-blood interactions remains closed to view. At best, such aggregate analyses point to important gross relationships that require more refined understanding of how these distributions are created. Thus, aggregated cross-national and time series analysis can best be seen as a low-cost antecedent to detailed structural analysis (see Chapter 7).

To illustrate the contrast, consider two explanations for why an electorate gives its votes to certain political parties. The distributional approach measures the proportions of Democrats, Independents, and Republicans; the relative frequency of minorities; the numbers of working-class and middle-class wage earners. The net and joint influence of these and other factors on voting choices is then estimated through their patterns of covariation with ballots cast. A structural analysis examines instead the two-way flow of political communication between party activists and ordinary voters; the partisan composition of friendship, kinship, and coworker circles; and the impact of persuasion efforts by mass media campaigns as filtered through local opinion makers. The consistent emphasis here is that political choices are formed through dynamic interactions among participants in a concrete electoral system, and not from the static social attributes and political attitudes of individual voters. Chapter 2 takes a closer look at how well these alternative perspectives explain voting behavior at the individual or system levels of analysis.

Alternative paradigms

The structural view of politics is fully embraced today by a minority of political scientists and sociologists. To the extent that their research is theoretically informed at all, most social scientists endorse one of two alternative explanations – normative conformity or objective rationality. These dominant paradigms make radically contrasting assumptions about the social processes that generate political orientations and actions. The *normative conformity* approach emphasizes consensus and deviation from institutionalized societal norms and values. The *objective rationality* approach conceives of all human behavior as the result of utility-maximizing decision making by socially atomized individuals. Neither approach produces satisfactory accounts in many instances of concrete political action. Microsocial behaviors and macrosocial political institutions frequently perform in ways unanticipated by the normative conformity and objective rationality conceptions of action. Both approaches would benefit enormously from incorporating principles of the structural perspective advocated in this book. The dominant paradigms need not be rejected in toto, but their theoretical maturation requires them to be embedded in contexts constituted of social relations among actors (Granovetter, 1985). Thus, a sophisticated understanding of political action requires blending cultural, rational, and structural constraints in complex specifications for given substantive problems. The structural perspective should be seen as an enriching, rather than a competing, paradigm.

The following subsections lay out the basic assumptions and theoretical arguments for the normative conformity and objective rationality paradigms. They also present brief observations about the insights that social structural relations can bring to bear on these explanations. Detailed examinations of particular substantive issues must await subsequent chapters that address different aspects of political behavior.

Normative conformity

A norm can be defined as a "prescribed guide for conduct or action which is generally complied with by the members of a society" (Ullman-Margalit, 1977: 12). Any theory of social phenomena that emphasizes the primacy of *norms* or *values* as explanatory concepts is a quintessential sociological approach, in terms of Brian Barry's (1978) devastating critique of democratic governance theories. Concepts such as solidarity, civic culture (Almond and Verba, 1963), political subsystem (Easton, 1965), stable democracy, pattern variables (Lipset, 1964), legitimacy, influence, and integration (Parsons, 1969) ultimately assume that human action results from efforts to conform one's behavior to previously established standards.

The Parsonsian solution to the Hobbesian problem of social disorder lies in a social system that is integrated around a common set of core values, not by coercive institutions or through the self-interests of individual actors. That is, people typically conform their behaviors to these obligatory standards because they have internalized them as right and proper requirements, not because they fear punishment for their violation or because they expect important personal gains. The coordination of means and ends of action exhibits "sentiment attributable to one or more actors that something is an end in itself" (Parsons, 1937: 75). The internalization of normative patterns of the common culture and individuals' conformity to these patterns, with their ambivalent psychological reactions to strain, were subsequently formulated as an explicit theory of human motivation by Parsons and Shils (1951). As Warner (1978: 1321, fn. 5) pointed out, Parsons later included in his definition of the normative the criteria of "moral obligation" and the taking of an end in itself of socially oriented (and socially imposed) definitions of the desirable. The concept of moral obligations to conform to shared values is, of course, a seminal element in the writing of Emile Durkheim, one of Parsons' major influences.

People acquire norms through social learning, imitation, and pressures for conformity and against deviation. The essence of normative conformity perspectives on political action is the childhood socialization of basic value-orientation patterns and normative standards and their continuing reinforcement with positive and negative sanctions throughout adulthood. People frequently verbalize among themselves the norms concerning the behaviors they expect others to follow. Norms concerning fair and equitable treatment guide people's interactions in many social situations (Schwartz, 1977). The hypothesis that group norms induce conforming behavior is central to most versions of role theory, although programmatic research on the causes of nonconformity is difficult to find (Biddle, 1986: 80).

In contrast to the rigid utilitarian tradition that Parsons abandoned (he began academic life as an economist; see Camic [1987]), his social action theory conceived of behavior as primarily, but not solely, guided by norms. Enforced by formal and informal sanctions, a social system's normative prescriptions and proscriptions for behavior are internalized jointly among the system's actors. Although internalized shared symbolic directives ("oughts") are invisible in real terms, they are in fact more consequential for social behaviors directed toward desirable end states than are the more visible external material conditions. Thus, social action for Parsons cannot be reduced to a deterministic reflex of material conditions as it is, for example, in some Marxist or behavioral psychology theories. Like rational actor models, the normative actor model defines behavior as purposive rather than determinative. The main difference is that the rational actor model portrays interests (individually oriented conceptions of desired states) rather than norms (socially oriented conceptions of desired acts) as the central element in decision making.

At the analytic level, a normative actor experiences nonmaterial constraints upon her behavior. By internalizing social norms, actors interpenetrate one another in the sharing of symbolic beliefs. Unfortunately, some critics interpreted Parsons as proffering an overly socialized view of human action (e.g., Menzies, 1977). Allegedly, normative internalization allows for no autonomous, voluntaristic choices because supraindividual constraints fully determine those actions that superficially seem to be freely chosen. This interpretation of Parsonsian action theory is a caricature, as made clear in Alexander's (1978) essay on the formal and substantive voluntaristic sources of Parsons' theory. By synthesizing the individualist and collectivist traditions of social theory, Parsons sought to preserve individual autonomy vis-à-vis the material elements of the decision situation. Hence, social action must be seen as *both* instrumental and normative, with the former preserving its deterministic quality and the latter its voluntary nature. Apparently, Parsons used both individualist and collectivist paradigms to assert that action is constrained at the analytic level, while preserving, at the level of concrete individuals, freedom to pursue interests as persons come to define those interests. If this interpretation of Parsonsian action theory is accurate, the apparent theoretical incompatibility of a purposive rational actor model and a deterministic normative actor model is false.

From the structural perspective, a major shortcoming of the normative conformity approach is its failure to situate the normative processes in concrete entities and ongoing relationships among social actors. Political theorists must show how norms are created, maintained, modified, or destroyed as a consequence of the operation of other fundamental social forces: learning, social exchange, coercion and repression, competition, reciprocity, ideology, persuasion, rational calculation. How, for example, did old-time party machines obtain votes from the urban wards? Certainly not because of some vague process of voter adherence to political values. It was a sweaty, sprawling cacophony of smoke-filled rooms, brokered deals, torch-lit rallies, turkey and coal-bucket welfare distributions, contract-letting and ticket-fixing, and graveyard ballot-stuffing (see Chapter 5). The normative approach tends to emphasize consensus at the expense of very real divisions of interest and overt conflict. Norms and values are problematic attainments whose explanation requires attention to the social forces that promote disagreement as well as those that encourage acceptance.

The structural analyses of influence and domination networks can reveal how socialization and sanctioning processes actually operate to produce normative orientations in situated contexts where political actions take place. Structural relations can capture the dynamics among purposive political actors who are constrained to accept, reject, and innovate new norms of behavior. Without the concrete evidence of structurally situated roles, normative conformity arguments are doomed to be a misleading depiction of social action as oversocialized behavior. By taking structural relations into account, explanations for many kinds of political action can specify the explicit mechanisms for generating conformity and deviance. Thus, a structural approach has the simultaneous advantage of giving concrete shape to the normative conformity perspective, while exposing its limitations.

Objective rationality

The concept of objective, or substantive, rationality refers to choice behavior under constraints arising from external situations that can be "adjudged objectively to be optimally adapted to the situation" (Simon, 1985: 294). Objective rationality explanations of human behavior have been prominent at least since 1776 in classical economics and more recently in political science (Downs, 1957; Harsanyi, 1969, 1977; Ordeshook, 1986) and sociology, especially through exchange theory (Heath, 1976; Heckathorn, 1984, 1985). Enthusiastic proponents of objective rationality tend to see it underlying all forms of human action from fertility to crime:

> The economic approach is clearly not restricted to material goods and wants, nor even to the market sector. . . . Indeed, I have come to the position that the economic approach is a comprehensive one that is applicable to all human behavior, be it behavior involving money prices or imputed shadow prices, repeated or infrequent decisions, large or minor decisions, emotional or mechanical ends, rich or poor persons, men or women, adults or children, brilliant or stupid persons, patients or therapists, businessmen or politicians, teachers or students (Becker, 1976: 6, 8).

One might wonder if a theory able to explain everything is so tautological that it cannot specify the necessary conditions for its own refutation. Be that as it may, the rational actor models of economics, game theory, and social exchange theory are among the simplest and most elegant accounts of individual decision making. They have been applied to virtually all forms of political behavior, from voting to party competition, to interest group interactions, to bureaucracies, legislatures, and international relations. Their pervasiveness necessitates taking the objective rationality approach seriously in proposing the structural approach as an alternative theoretical stance.

Objective rationality explanations rest on a set of assumptions about social actors in decision making or choice situations. Most objective rationality theorists assume that:

1. A social actor holds a stable and consistent set of preferences over a

set of alternatives (i.e., a transitive ordering of alternatives exists for an actor). Human behavior is purposeful, that is, actors have objectives (interests, goals, ends) toward whose achievement their actions are directed. Rationality makes no assumptions about the origin of those objectives, but simply takes them as subjective givens that arise from values, socialization, or vague "tastes" (Riker and Ordeshook, 1973: 12). Duesenberry's (1960: 233) quip is apt: "Economics is all about how people make choices; sociology is all about how they don't have any choices to make."

2. Self-interest is *not* an essential element in rational actor models, although it is often thought to be (e.g., Harsanyi, 1969: 518). An actor's subjective utilities may reflect self-centered goals or altruistic objectives. A person can still act rationally even if the valued outcome is not a personal gain. For example, a parent may contribute to a conservation club to preserve wilderness lands for her unborn grandchildren's enjoyment (Mitchell, 1979; Godwin and Mitchell, 1982). In the extreme form, rational action might be undertaken to maximize the utilities of complete strangers; such altruistic individuals are often called saints or patriots.

3. An actor always chooses the alternative that has the highest utility. In other words, decision making consists of utility-maximizing behavior. Gains in utility from a decision are benefits while losses of utility are costs. Hence, objective rationality explanations are sometimes called cost-benefit models of decision making.

4. When a decision situation involves uncertainty about the connection between a choice and its outcome, an actor performs a calculation that allows her to choose the alternative with the highest *expected* utility. Typically, the subjective utility of each alternative is weighted by the actor's subjective probability estimate that the outcome will occur if she chooses that alternative. For example, if an actor faces two alternative actions (A_1 and A_2), whose outcomes (O_1 and O_2) have distinct utilities and probabilities (P_1 and P_2), then the subjective expected utilities of these two actions can be expressed as two equations:

$$E(A_1) = P_1(O_1)U(O_1) + P_1(O_2)U(O_2)$$
$$E(A_2) = P_2(O_1)U(O_1) + P_2(O_2)U(O_2)$$

where $E(A_i)$ is the utility expected from taking action i and $P_i(O_j)$ is the probability that by choosing the action i the outcome j will result. $U(O_j)$ is the utility of outcome j for the actor. (The two probabilities within each equation must sum to one, for example, when the outcome is passage or failure of a piece of legislation.) After the sophisticated rational actor makes all calculations, she chooses that action (A_1 or A_2) with the highest expected value.

Uncertainty pervades real-life situations, where ambiguous connections exist between actions taken and outcomes created. Many of the outcomes sought by political actors are public policies, that is, changes in the state of affairs in the larger society. Yet, the processes by which a society produces public policy decisions from aggregating its citizens' policy preferences is not as straightforward as in individual decisions about market transactions. The election of a candidate to a legislature is merely an initial step in the effort to enact laws that bind the society to a collective choice. Other public officials who seek opposing policy outcomes complicate matters. A politician's legislative promises will not lead with certainty to a policy result having known utility. Instead, voters must calculate their expected values for alternative choices (giving campaign contributions, voting, staying home) by weighting each possible outcome by the subjective probability that a given action will produce that valued outcome. For example, a blue-collar voter may hope for a protective tariff against Japanese auto imports by supporting a candidate who promises to enact such a bill. His decision to support a candidate then hinges on his subjective calculations about which voting choice would yield the highest chance of the bill's passage.

5. Actors are presumed to have perfect information about the alternatives available and about the intentions and likely reactions of other actors in the decision situation. The rationality paradigm is most often criticized for requiring the heroic assumption that persons possess complete knowledge about, and ability to compute and compare, the consequences of each alternative. One rebuttal to the human mind's limited knowledge and computing power is to argue, not that persons *actually* make such calculations, but that their choices merely show that they act *as if* such decision making were taking place (Friedman, 1953: see Moe [1979] for counterarguments). Other theorists deny that perfect information is essential for rational behavior (Moe, 1980: 16–19). Rather, people can act on limited and distorted knowledge about the options open to them. The "satisficing" or "procedural bounded rationality" version developed by March and Simon (1958; see also Simon, 1983, 1985) builds on experimental evidence from cognitive psychology (Kahneman, Slovic, and Tversky, 1982). Human organisms are just too limited in their information-processing capacities to behave as the objective rationality theorists presume:

> The models of problem solving describe a person who is limited
> in computational capacity, and who searches very selectively
> through large realms of possibilities in order to discover what
> alternatives of action are available, and what the consequences
> of each of these alternatives are. The search is incomplete,
> often inadequate, based on uncertain information and partial
> ignorance, and usually terminated with the discovery of
> satisfactory, not optimal, courses of action (Simon, 1985: 295).

6. Additional assumptions, particularly for economic transaction decisions, include homogeneity and infinite divisibility of commodities, perfectly competitive markets, and market equilibrium. Most objective rationality theorists depict decision-making units (people or firms) as independent of other actors. Even markets for goods and services do not require actors to interact directly with one another "through pressure, emulation, personal competition, or similar influences" (Leibenstein, 1978: 20).

In its less extreme versions, the rational actor model does not allow *every* action to be considered rational choice, simply by asserting that a decision is always the choice of the highest utility among all alternatives. Such an assumption would reduce the theory of rational action to a tautology that is untestable because the requisite conditions can never be approximated in the real world, or even in controlled experiments using human subjects (see Olson, 1965: 160, fn. 91). The essence of any rational choice model is that people choose among alternatives after assessing the probable gains and losses in well-being (their own and others') from a set of alternative actions. When an actor makes a decision without carrying out such calculations, the choice cannot be considered rational under the concept used here.

From the structural perspective, unrealistic assumptions about human thought processes are not the central problem with objective rationality explanations. The basic difficulty lies in the utilitarian tradition's conception of atomized, undersocialized human decision making (Granovetter, 1985: 483). Social actors are abstracted out of complex social contexts and depicted as pursuing narrow self-interests devoid of complex social connections to other system members. Even interactive game theories use highly simplified notions of contingent decision making, for example, in Prisoners' Dilemmas that reduce cooperative strategies to minimal joint cost-benefit calculi (Mueller, 1979: 14–15; see also Shubik, 1984; Ordeshook, 1986). Selecting a strategy of cooperation or resistance minimally requires players to assume that their opponents will perceive the situation and choose a response strategy in certain predictable ways. By hypothesis, objective rationality ignores the complex effects of social structure and social relationships on individuals' behaviors. But rational, purposive actions by real-world persons are obviously embedded in often complex networks of social relations that can be ignored only at the peril of incomplete and inaccurate explanations. Regarding the absence of social structure in conventional neoclassical economic analysis, Granovetter asserted:

> Standard economic analysis neglects the identity and past relations of individual transactors, but rational individuals know better, relying on their knowledge of these relations. They are

less interested in *general* reputations than in whether a
particular other may be expected to deal honestly with *them* –
mainly a function of whether they or their own contacts have
had satisfactory past dealings with the other (Granovetter,
1985: 491).

If histories of interpersonal trust relations are essential for maintaining
orderly economic markets, how critical must be such relations among
political actors whose negotiations involve more extended time frames and
nebulous numeraire!

The structural perspective corrects the tendency of rational actor models
to focus exclusively on the internal capacities of individual decision makers. The external context is brought into the analysis as influence and
domination power structures – opportunities for and constraints on the
flow of information and the exchange of resources. Thus, influence and
domination explicitly enter rational decision makers' calculi as they pursue
their individual and collective destinies. To illustrate, the strategy of a
manufacturing trade association seeking protectionist legislation can be
viewed as a strictly rational process involving cost-benefit calculations
about how much lobbying effort will produce a favorable congressional
vote. Even factoring in the countermoves by opponents still retains the
basic rational calculi. But a structural analyst would attend to the preceding
history of coalition-formation among interest groups in other legislative
fights, to the social and professional bonds among Washington representatives, to the legislator-constituent linkages and their implications for future
electoral contests, to the internal power configurations of federal bureaucracies, to grass-roots mobilization of social movements, and so on (see
Chapter 6). The structural model incorporates a far more complex set of
situated interactions that shape collective outcomes in ways unanticipated
and unintended by the rational plans of atomized social actors. Obviously,
structural analysis is more complex and perhaps much less tractable, compared to the simplistic purity of the rational actor model. But it is likely to
be more realistic and to render a more accurate explanation of the observed
behaviors.

The promised advantage of the structural approach lies in its ability to
unearth the buried assumptions of the rational approach. As Duesenberry's
aphorism implies, structuralism identifies the social roots of actors' values
and principles. Structural analysis can reveal how interpersonal networks
shape actors' perceptions of political objects, how mutual interactions
generate shared imputed meanings, how actors construe the probabilities
of choosing among alternative actions, and how subjective beliefs arise that
link personal actions to collective outcomes. Structural analysis is, again,
not so much an exclusive alternative to rational choice as it is an enriching
perspective that supplements, specifies, and extends the scope of that more

limited theory. In the following chapters, numerous substantive illustrations of this potential will be investigated.

Looking forward

This chapter, in conjunction with the Appendix, introduces basic concepts and principles of the structural perspective. It asserts their direct relevance to political power phenomena, particularly to influence and domination processes. The fundamental premise of structural analysis is that patterns of relations among social positions help to explain the behaviors of systems and their components. This perspective requires that a structural theorist embrace a genuine methodological individualism. That is, human action can be understood neither as a simple aggregation of psychological processes nor as a systemic holism emerging sui generis from lower-level processes (Haines, 1988). Rather, a comprehensive account of political belief and action requires a mutual interplay between social actors and social structures. The structural perspective offers a powerful dualism that links concrete microscale with macroscale phenomena in ways not possible with alternative theoretical paradigms.

The demonstration of the potential and the payoff of structural analysis may be found in the following chapters. Each chapter explores a different facet of political behavior, first considering predominant modes of explanation, then showing how the structural perspective can illuminate some of the key problems in that subfield. Agendas for future research projects from a network perspective are proposed. Chapter 2 examines individual voting decisions and participation in conventional political activities. In Chapter 3, social movements and revolutions are analyzed, with an emphasis on the recruitment of participants and interorganizational cooperation. Chapter 4 looks at power in and around organizations from a structural vantage. Local community power structures and national state elite networks are the topics of the next two chapters. Chapter 7 investigates research on the world system and dependency among nations. The final chapter speculates about the likely impacts of information technology innovations on networks in tomorrow's workplaces, political systems, and international relations. By the conclusion, readers should have acquired a comprehensive overview of structural political analysis and its potential contributions to understanding contemporary political life.

2 Voting and political participation

At the heart of politics in liberal democratic societies lies participation of ordinary citizens in selecting government officials and engaging in efforts to shape public policies. Two paradigms dispute the function of citizen involvement in creating and sustaining the democratic polity. Elite democratic theorists argue that the electorate's role is restricted to choosing leaders, who must then be left alone to govern without pressures from the populace (Schumpeter, 1943: Riker, 1982; Sartori, 1987: 108). Electoral majorities should control officials only through the threat of loss of office during periodic, contested elections. To permit popular access to day-to-day decisions of the government risks a mass society in which political elites are stampeded by the irrational whims of the crowd (Kornhauser, 1959; Halebsky, 1976). In contrast, populist theories of democracy require that the citizenry interact continually with officials about their public policy concerns (Pateman, 1970; Barber, 1984). Local participatory arenas – grass-roots parties, voluntary associations, industrial workplaces – provide institutions for aggregating popular preferences and practical opportunities for citizens to acquire democratic norms, skills, and experiences. These civic education functions of U.S. civil society have been remarked upon by political commentators since Tocqueville (1945: 115). Rather than threatening a delicate equilibrium, mass participation is seen as an indispensable ingredient for preserving democratic governance.

Both the elitist and the populist versions of democratic theory regard citizen involvement in political institutions as a significant problem. Most empirical assessments assume some model of individual decision making about voting and contacting of government officials. Some explanations emphasize primarily the social forces impinging upon the citizen, while others highlight the role of social psychological perceptions and beliefs. Very few consider how the interactions among citizens, parties, and officials shape the observed patterns of voting and participation. Yet neglecting these structural relational components of conventional political behaviors results in incomplete accounts. This chapter reviews the central

29

themes of various approaches to citizen participation in political institutions and shows how the explicit incorporation of network concepts could enrich our knowledge.

Voting behavior is the substantive focus of this chapter. Electoral choice can be conceptualized in terms of the two basic dimensions of political power discussed from the network perspective in Chapter 1. Voting exemplifies primarily influence relationships. Citizens are linked to one another through local ties of information exchange about parties, candidates, and issues. The resulting social comparison processes shape voters' views about the relative merits of the available electoral alternatives. Thus, measures of voters' embedment in microlevel communication networks are essential for explaining individuals' decisions to turn out on election day and to cast their ballots for particular candidates. The network approach to voting offers new insights into behaviors that are incompletely explained by the conventional approaches discussed below.

The Michigan model

For almost four decades, the Michigan model of election behaviors has dominated U.S. political science thinking and research about voting. A series of pioneering books and articles by the Survey Research Center (SRC) organized causal explanations of individual voting decisions and aggregate election patterns around social psychological factors (Campbell, Gurin, and Miller, 1954; Campbell, Converse, Miller, and Stokes, 1960, 1964). The Michigan paradigm eclipsed an earlier, sociologically oriented approach to voting developed at Columbia University's Bureau of Applied Social Research (Lazarsfeld, Berelson, and Gaudit, 1948; Berelson, Lazarsfeld, and McPhee, 1954). The premier position of the Michigan model among political scientists owed much to the SRC's control over the means of research. Their biennial surveys were eventually institutionalized in the continuing American National Election Surveys conducted under the auspices of its Center for Political Studies and overseen by the research community through a national board of scholars. The SRC's empirical measures were created within a conceptual framework that constrained the later empirical research community to work largely from its social psychological perspective.

The explanatory framework erected by Angus Campbell and his colleagues followed a temporal sequence of variables that caused an individual voter to decide for which party or candidate to cast a ballot. This so-called funnel of causality may be conveniently divided into long-term and short-term subsets (see Rusk, 1982). Long-term factors are the psychological identification of the voter (Republican, Democrat, or Independent) formed early in life and the strength of this party identity. Social locational factors such as class, education, and race are also long-term forces, but are less important in determining the vote. The short-term forces in the voter's psychological field are tied to a particular presidential or congressional campaign period and are more proximate causes of the partisan vote choice. The two major short-term forces are the voter's issue orientations or preferences and the appeal of candidate personality factors. The temporal order in which these four clusters of variables are allegedly formed gave rise to the standard Michigan causal sequence:

Social factors→Party identification→Issues and candidates→Vote

Thus, inner psychological forces originate in past experiences and interact with external environmental stimuli to produce modified attitudes, which in turn determine voting decision. Other forms of conventional electoral activity – campaigning on behalf of candidates, contacting public officials about personal and political matters (e.g., Verba and Nie, 1972) – may also fit into a parallel sequence of social background forces, attitudes, and actions.

Various analyses – ranging from simple cross-tabulations through complex simultaneous equation models – have tried to disentangle the relative causal importance of the social background, party preference, issue, and candidate variables in explaining the outcome of individual vote decisions in specific elections. A continuing theme over the decades has been the extent to which *issue voting* characterizes recent American elections (see, e.g., RePass, 1971; Nie and Rabjohn, 1979). Also providing material for innumerable books, theses, and journal articles were the alleged decline and/or realignment of party identification as the basis for a normal vote, and the heightened ideological polarization of the electorate under the impact of mass media campaigning, civil rights and antiwar movements, Watergate, and economic turmoil. The research literature supporting as well as criticizing the Michigan voting model is too voluminous to review in any detail. Rather than trying to summarize this legacy, two exemplars are discussed in the next section. These studies were chosen because they give a good feel for the core issues in recent electoral research. More important, each explicitly highlights significant limitations of the individual sample survey method for assessing electoral participation from a structural approach.

Empirical research exemplars

Fiorina (1981) attempted to represent how citizens form evaluations of the political parties and candidates. The Michigan concept of party identification was based on its high stability; only one-fifth of the sample respondents reported changing affiliations during their lifetimes (Campbell et al., 1960: 150; Knoke, 1976: 110–25). Party ID is analogous to a religious affiliation formed during infancy long before cognitive understanding of church dogma. In contrast to religious identities, Fiorina argued that party IDs are not as stable as the Michigan model would have us believe. Instead, they reflect a "running tally" on parties' past performances in office as well as voters' expectations about future performances. For example, the association of the Republican Party with the Great Depression in voters' minds may dispose many to reject Republican candidates as poor managers of the economy. But an economically successful Republican presidency, such as Reagan's better handling of inflation and recession than Carter, can substantially change voter evaluations of party ID: "As new evaluations form, an individual's identification may wax and wane" (Fiorina, 1981: 90). Thus, Fiorina questioned the stable social-psychological party identification of the Michigan model.

The key dynamic is the intervention of two types of retrospective evaluations, simple and mediated, that change a voter's political preferences. The former reflect direct experiences and impressions of political conditions. The latter are "summary judgments the formation of which is mediated either externally, by a citizen's choice of information sources and opinion leaders, or internally, by prior predispositions" (Fiorina, 1981: 80). Fiorina used SRC panel data to examine the usefulness of his voting theory. The SRC measures available for retrospective and future evaluations were predominantly fixed-choice attitude items toward political objects and events (e.g., pace of civil rights, anticipated inflation and unemployment, Ford's pardon of Nixon). Such evaluations were found to alter respondents' party identifications and to affect significantly their voting choices. In conclusion, Fiorina argued that his theory was a more realistic developmental model that explicitly represented voters' rational calculi better than did alternative models (p. 190).

The intriguing aspect of Fiorina's analysis lies not in his empirical findings, but in his inability from data limitations to take fully into account the social forces that shape retrospective policy evaluations. Cross-sectional and panel surveys assume that the most appropriate unit of analysis is the individual voter. A strong connection exists between the Western liberal concept that political participation is an individual citizenship right and the polling of individuals for public opinion research. Thus, to measure whether a popular majority supports the president's NATO troop reduction proposal, the evident procedure is to count noses. Consequently, survey samples are drawn using area probability techniques that select representative respondents in their places of residence, without regard to the ongoing social relationships they maintain in their households and their places of work, worship, and recreation. In effect, individuals are torn out of their social contexts and subjected to self-report interviews that generally ignore the meaningful social and political relationships in which their attitudes and actions are embedded. By ignoring these social relations, surveys threaten to reduce social science to "aggregate psychology" (Coleman, 1964: 88–9). Typical SRC questionnaires ask voters about personal characteristics (age, education, job), their opinions and beliefs (evaluation of the president, preference for economic policies), and their activities (turning out to vote, casting a ballot for Republicans or Democrats). Very little information is sought about the relationships respondents have with their spouses, children, parents, coworkers, or friends; in short, with their alters, the set of social actors with whom they have direct contact. Virtually no data are gathered about the respondent's perceptions of these alters' social characteristics or their subjective orientations. And, of course, no attempt is made to solicit such information directly from the alters themselves. The result is standard survey data that cannot address theoretical questions about the impact of voters' social and political networks in forming and carrying out their political thoughts and actions.

The quote above from Fiorina mentioned in passing how mediated retrospective evaluations could be formed through external information sources, especially opinion leaders (a concept from the Columbia voting tradition discussed below). Unfortunately, the SRC data did not allow him to assess directly the flow of factual and opinion information to the respondent from various external sources. Instead, all self-reported evaluations referred to the respondents' orientations as though they were self-contained and devoid of any connections to a web of group affiliations and influences. Hence, the estimated effects of past evaluations and future evaluations, as well as of the stability or lability of party ID, appeared to Fiorina to be a rational process occurring wholly within the individual. Any causal, persuasive, dispositional, or otherwise mutually interactive social comparison processes occurring between the voter and his or her alters were invisibly absorbed into the estimated net effects of the different personal variables on the vote decision.

Another voting study whose data also did not permit an adequate assessment of structural relations was Powell's (1986) comparison of U.S. voting turnout with eleven European democracies. His samples included measures of respondents' demographic and social psychological attitudes (party ID, political interest, and efficacy). Although the U.S. survey also asked how often the respondent discussed politics with others, Powell did not use this item in his equations to predict voting turnout. Because talking politics increases markedly with respondent education (Powell, 1986: 28), it may be hypothesized also to boost voting participation. That is, when a person communicates with others about an election, he or she is likely to be reinforced to turn out to vote. On the face of it, this simple indicator seems to measure important political relations. However, the item's simplicity belies potentially serious problems as an inexpensive network indicator. First, it asks only for a global judgment of political information exchange. It fails to capture quantitative variations among respondents in the number of discussion partners and the frequency of their interactions. It neglects the extent of political linkages among these alters. Second, the contents of these political discussions are unclear. As argued below, voting turnout could be depressed rather than increased by conflicting partisan messages. Thus, on the basis of both form and content, the simple ersatz measure of political discussion would probably be too crude to reveal the significance of political relations for voting turnout (see Burt [1987a] for a demonstration that global judgments of ego-network densities are highly unreliable).

The preceding examples suggest the range of microlevel electoral phenomena that grew out of the Michigan model of voting research. The heavy slant toward social psychological factors and the uprooting of the individual from his or her social contexts give a distorted view of how political orientations and actions come about. Even when the analysts are sensitive to the social systems within which political behaviors are embedded, they typically are frustrated by the inappropriate research designs and measures available in secondary data sets. Although the preceding examples could be multiplied numerous times, the situation has been sufficiently exposed to consider next some possible solutions. In thinking about how the structural perspective could be incorporated in political participation research, a look back to the pioneering efforts by the Columbia sociologists proves instructive.

The Columbia voting studies

The earliest academic surveys of individual voting in presidential elections were carried out by Paul Lazarsfeld and his colleagues in 1940 in Erie County, Ohio, and in 1948 in Elmira, New York (see Sheingold [1973] and Eulau [1980] for assessments). The decisive factors in individual vote decisions were the receipt of information and influence through interpersonal communication networks. Unlike the later Michigan approach, the Columbia model conceptualized perceptions of the political world primarily in network terms. Using a panel of 600 Erie County, Ohio, residents in the 1940 election, the researchers discovered that most people (88 percent) remained constant in their vote intentions from May to November (Lazarsfeld et al., 1948: 66). Contrary to prior images, the minority who changed parties were not thoughtful, conscientious voters. Social and political isolation apparently induced short-term flexibility and susceptibility to political persuasion, whereas social integration inoculated most voters against changing their intentions. An extreme version of a politically unanchored citizenry emerged in the theory of mass society, which stressed the vulnerability of socially malintegrated citizens to demagogic manipulation by unscrupulous political elites (Kornhauser, 1959; Halebsky, 1976).

The discovery that face-to-face contacts are centrally important in opinion formation was the Columbia researchers' major insight. A two-step flow from mass media messages to the individual voter is mediated by self-designated opinion leaders and group discussion (Lazarsfeld et al., 1948: 49–51, 151–2; also Katz and Lazarsfeld, 1955). The political homogeneity of social groups (religious, ethnic, class) is maintained through the "steady, personal influence of their more politically active fellow citizens" (Lazarsfeld et al., 1948: 149). An informal opinion leader "serves as a bridge over which formal media of communications extend their influence" (p. 152). The personal obligations, loyalties, affections, and trust that people have within their social networks exert powerful, persuasive influences that neither radio or newspapers can match. In the preface to the second edition of *The People's Choice*, Lazarsfeld and colleagues broadened the processes beyond leader-follower relations to include mutual interactions among group members which reinforce the "vague feelings" of the persons (Lazarsfeld et al., 1948: xxiii).

In the Elmira research reported by Berelson and colleagues (1954), the network metaphor was further extended in considering how union members' votes are influenced by their exposure to others in the work environment. The researchers measured an individual's connection to "whole networks of social relations that affect political behavior" (Berelson et al., 1954: 94) by collecting data on the voter's three best friends and three closest coworkers. These ego-centered networks are substantially "homogeneous and congenial" in their partisan composition, somewhat more so for friends than coworkers. Indeed, personal association "approaches a political monopoly" (p. 96) that follows social class lines and increases with age. However, where primary group environments are internally mixed, the "breakage effect" tends to favor voting for the Republican party, when such a vote is consistent with the larger political community (p. 100). That is, the benefit of the doubt is given to the party favored in the larger environment within which personal networks are embedded. The contents of political discussions among voters during campaigns are more likely to reinforce voting preferences than to evoke controversy or to convert persons to opposing viewpoints (p. 108). Finally, opinion-leading activity is diffused throughout all social strata, not concentrated in certain socioeconomic status (SES) or age categories (p. 110).

The Columbia studies implied that social network processes underlie the stability and volatility of people's voting intentions. However, the data to test such propositions came from survey respondents' self-reports about their sociopolitical interactions. To the extent that people's perceptions about the opinions held by their alters are deliberate or unintentional distortions of actual network structure and contents, the effects of ego networks on voting must remain inferential. Further, reliance on self-designation to identify opinion leaders risks measurement error that reduces the explanatory potential of the structural perspective (see Weimann [1982] for a critique and reemphasis on marginal actors as crucial nodes). Despite such limitations, the Columbia findings highlighted the importance of reinforced political cues in primary group communication (Sheingold, 1973: 714). Strong social attachments correlated with intense partisan commitments.

Without direct measures from all actors in personal networks, key hypotheses about the political impact of egocentric network structures cannot be rigorously tested. The critical problem lies in assessing the structural relations among the network alters. A survey respondent may lack reliable information about the exchanges of political information among her friends, coworkers, and kin. These linkages are critical paths through which influential information reaches or fails to reach a voter. For example, the flow of political communications and their consequences for voting decisions may be quite different for persons located in personal networks that are strongly or weakly connected to the larger society. Structurally isolated and structurally integrated voters may be mobilized for elections in quite distinct fashions by the same political messages. In current terminology, persons who are embedded in local communication cliques that are relatively disconnected from the larger network (i.e., strong ties are impacted) may be less likely to receive or to believe new political information than are persons whose interpersonal weak ties radiate outward in diffusely ramifying networks (Granovetter, 1973, 1982; Weimann, 1982). The more homogeneous and distrustful of outsiders are one's intimate social contacts, the less likely one is to be exposed to alternative political interpretations that might persuade one to change political orientation. Ego-network structures may be especially important during realigning elections, such as the 1932 to 1936 New Deal rise of the Democratic Party to majority status, when new information is acquired as a function of the social structures that constrain and facilitate its transmission (Sheingold, 1973: 718). Later sections of this chapter will consider more recent efforts to turn the Columbia model's promise into reality. The advancement of knowledge in voting research does not boil down to a zero-sum choice between the Michigan social psychological approach and the Columbia sociological approach. Rather, it lies in a judicious blending of relational with attitudinal elements into a comprehensive account of how voters' preferences are shaped through the interpersonal flow of political influences.

Spatial and rational actor models

An alternative approach to voting decisions began with publication of Anthony Downs' seminal *An Economic Theory of Democracy* (1957). This book set forth an elegant explanation of party-voter behaviors premised on neoclassical microeconomics principles of perfect competition. Downs assumed that political parties are analogous to firms facing consumers in a marketplace. Desiring to get elected to office, politicians are willing to promise the electorate whatever package of public policies will attract their votes. In a two-party system, both parties compete with one another for support from a common pool of voters. Their policy platforms thus tend to move toward the center of the electoral *issues space*. That is, by marketing themselves as sponsors of policies favored by the modal voters, parties avoid taking extreme policy positions. People follow their self-interests in deciding to vote for the parties and candidates that support issues closest to their own preferences. Therefore, an election will be won by the party that promises policies that most closely match the preferences of most voters. Because both parties desire to win elections, they move next to one another at the center of the electorate's policy preference distribution. In multiparty systems, winner-take-all electoral rules are more likely to produce such centrist parties than are proportional representation rules that allow specialist parties to carve out niches among minority segments of the electorate. Other perturbations of Downs's basic spatial model arise from variations in constitutional decision-making rules, such as agenda sequences for issue voting (see the variations in Arrow's paradox summarized by Ordeshook [1986: 65–71]).

The contrast between the spatial theory of voting and the Michigan model is instructive. In the Michigan model, an individual's vote is determined by a temporal sequence of social and psychological causal variables, not as a choice involving self-interest calculations. Party ID is a major predisposing factor that short-term issue and candidate forces may deflect only by a small degree. But the Michigan model has no explanation for the competing candidates' behaviors. In contrast, spatial approaches view candidates as active agents in modifying both their own and voters' behaviors (Enelow and Hinich, 1984: 2). Voters are assumed to recognize their self-interests and to choose the candidates or parties most favorably evaluated on the basis of this self-interest. In other words, voters are rational actors and candidates respond rationally by designing policy packages to attract enough support to win elections. Theoretical analysis consists of defining the relevant policy and candidate evaluation spaces and representing both voters and parties within this space.

A key assumption is that the candidates' and parties' actions appeal directly to voters' interests in an effort to attract their electoral support.

Although most spatial analysis is theoretically abstract, scattered empirical evidence suggests that, even in this modern era of electronic campaigning, interpersonal contacts remain a potent mode of party mobilization. A 1956 survey of Wayne County, Detroit, Michigan, found that, after excluding nonvoters, almost half the voters were contacted in some way by the party organization (Eldersveld, 1964: 535). However, barely half of these contacts involved personal canvasses at the respondents' homes. The consequences of such direct party exposure were substantial: raised political interest, strengthened party identification, increased vote turnout, straight-ticket balloting, and among Democrats, more favorable attitudes toward working for the party (pp. 536–7). Personal contact also made the Democrats more ambivalent about their party, as shown in delayed time to reach a vote decision. Other studies of party-voter interaction generally reached similar conclusions (e.g., Clarke, Price, Stewart, and Krause, 1978; Schlesinger, 1984). Measures of party contact tend to emphasize simple dichotomies or frequency measures. Surveys have never examined how receptivity to party appeals might vary with the structure of voters' personal political discussion networks.

The rational actor assumptions in Downs' spatial voting model have been applied to other areas of political behavior, such as interest groups, legislatures, and bureaucracies (e.g., Olson, 1965; Mayhew, 1974; Niskanen, 1975). Much of this work involved highly sophisticated mathematical models premised on simplified assumptions of individual and collective decision making as utility-maximizing processes (see Chapter 1). Often the proposed models required such stringent assumptions about observation and measurement of key variables that tests against data could not be conducted, even had the theorists been interested in assessing their empirical validity (e.g., Harsanyi, 1977; Shepsle, 1978; Gant and Davis, 1984; Shubik, 1984). Unfortunately, many rational choice theorists seem more content to refine the nuances of their elegant models than to assess their usefulness for explaining real world political phenomena.

Game theory offers perhaps the best opportunity to integrate rational political theory with the structural approach. The essence of game theory is the interdependence of choice – that individuals' decisions depend on the actions taken by others. For example, Palfrey and Rosenthal (1985) applied a variation of the Prisoners' Dilemma game to the analysis of turnout. If everyone else votes, then one voter's contribution is small and it is rational not to vote; but if everyone else abstains, then one voter can have a huge impact and it therefore pays to vote. Thus the equilibrium choice involves a complex game that is contingent upon a person's perceptions about what the other actors in the electoral system are likely to do (see also Ledyard, 1984). This game's theoretic orientation parallels the structural presumption that an actor's network configurations have important perceptual consequences. Different egocentric networks convey information about the state of the larger political system and other actors' intentions. In discussing impending political events with one's intimates, subjective impressions of probable event outcomes are formed, for example, the closeness of an electoral contest or a candidate's likely policy actions if elected to office. One's relations with other electoral system members enable one to make social comparisons and to exercise mutual and asymmetric influences through these connections. Where structural analysis and game theory part company is the latter's reduction of human decision making to simple utility calculi (Ordeshook, 1986: xii). Although necessary to render game models mathematically tractable, the assumption that all political phenomena reflect contingent individual choices is too simplistic to be credible as a serious explanation of most aspects of social behavior. This extreme stance crops up from time to time in sociology (e.g., Homans, 1964), but generally has made little headway outside of neoclassical economics and portions of political science.

The judicious use of game theory in the structural approach to politics must recognize that social phenomena emerge that are neither aggregates of nor reducible to individual rational choice processes. Complex microsocial and macrosocial networks constrain and facilitate people's perceptions, attitudes, and actions in ways inexplicable by a rational utility-maximizing calculus. The metatheoretical stance that underlies the structural perspective – methodological individualism – asserts that an adequate explanation of social behavior can be accomplished neither through psychological reductionism nor structural holism. Rather, to explain a social system's behavior as well as the behavior of its constituent parts, attention must be paid to the reciprocal effects of both individual actors and the larger structures within which they are embedded (Haines, 1988). Game theory in its present state of development appears to treat both macrostructures and microstructures as given conditions. For example, the effects of simple majority voting rules assume actors who have single-peaked preferences for the alternatives (e.g., Riker and Ordeshook, 1973: 100–9). The elegance of game theory explanations is purchased at the price of unrealism. The network approach to voting and political participation offers a way to merge the key insight of game theory – that political choices are interdependent – with a fundamental principle of structural analysis – that interactions among actors generate the conditions under which individual and collective actions are shaped. The following sections consider some substantive problems where such syntheses might be sought.

Structural relations in micronetworks

This section applies the structural perspective to individual political participation. First, some basic principles are presented for conceptualizing egonetwork phenomena. Then four problems are examined in some detail: political socialization in the family; cross-pressures and voting turnout; the political context effects of local residence communities; and the voting choices in political discussion networks. Past work that bears on these problems is reviewed and suggestions are made for future research that could improve our understanding by explicit use of network principles.

Egonetworks

Following the terminological conventions of the Appendix, an individual's egocentric network can be depicted graphically as a labeled point connected to other points by directed or undirected lines. The points represent actors and the lines stand for a specified type of relationship between the actors. The pattern of present and absent ties reveals the structure of the ego actor's network with its alters. For example, the diagrams in Figure 2.1 show the reciprocal political communication connections between an ego and three alters. Note that all alters have direct ties to ego, but only some of the possible links occur among the alters. Such ego-centered graphs are sometimes called "first order zones" (Boissevain, 1974: 25), or "stars." Missing from the diagrams is the "second order zone" that shows the alters' connections to additional actors who lack direct ties to the ego under consideration. Undoubtedly, ego-centered diagrams that might be drawn for actors *A, B,* or *C* would reveal configurations different from ego's personal net. For example, in part 1 of Fig. 2.1, actor C would include ego in its first-order zone, while *A*'s first-order zone would exclude C.

Parts 2 and 3 represent polar *forms* of egocentric networks. In part 2, none of ego's alters are connected to one another. That is, path distances between pairs *A* through *C* each have length 2, that is, *A* and *C* are connected by one intermediary. (This is true even if a pair of alters were

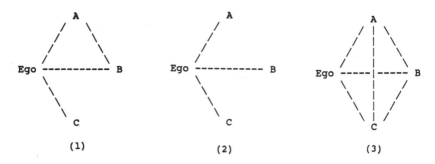

Figure 2.1 Three hypothetical egonetworks.

directly tied to another actor who is not directly tied to ego.) Any interaction among the alters requries ego to act as a go-between. Thus, failure
by ego to transmit information could disrupt the flow of communication
between alters. Part 3 describes a situation of completely saturated direct
connections; every alter is tied by direct paths. Here, ego cannot serve as
the exclusive mediator of transactions among pairs of its alters. Assuming
that capacity to control the flow of information or resources is a measure
of network power (i.e., an ego lies on a pathway between other actors),
then ego has great power in part 2, less power in part 1, and least power
in part 3. Although the picture is more complicated if the alters' alters are
considered, the basic principle remains that the formal structure of a
micronetwork reflects an actor's access to socially valued information and
resource transactions and hence reflects the power he or she enjoys in social
interactions. (See Freeman [1977, 1979] and Knoke and Burt [1983] for
quantitative measures of actor power – centrality and prestige prominence
scores – in micronetworks.)

   The egocentric network form is not the only aspect relevant to political
phenomena. Different *contents* may characterize relations among actors,
each type of content exhibiting a distinct pattern of interaction. In other
words, *multiplex* or multistranded relations (Boissevain, 1974: 30; Knoke
and Kuklinski, 1982: 15) may give rise to content-specific structural relations that must be kept separate in any substantive analysis. For example,
suppose that the hypothetical networks in Figure 2.1 represent a small
print shop in which ego is a union steward and *A, B,* and *C* are rank-and-file
union members. Network 1 might be affective friendship ties among the
workers, Network 2 the distribution of union campaign advice from the
steward to the printers, and Network 3 the informal discussion of the
pending union election issues and candidates. The concatenation of these
three network contents could help an analyst to understand how the shop
steward persuades the printers to cast their ballots for the union slate. (See
Lipset, Trow, and Coleman [1956: 176–86] for evidence that on-the-job
relationships affect union voting choices.) Thus, detailed knowledge of
both form and content is essential in any structural understanding of
micronets and their effects on political attitudes and behaviors. Not only
the pattern of ties but their frequency of activation and the nature of the
messages and resources exchanged must be included to explain individuals'
perceptions, preferences, and beliefs.

   One way to integrate conventional election studies with the structural
approach is to apply Harrison White's concepts of catness and netness.
There are categories of individuals who share some characteristic, such as
an occupation or a religious affiliation. There are also networks of people
linked by interpersonal relations. The probability that people will act
collectively or respond similarly to political stimuli varies with the degree
to which they form a *catnet,* "a set of individuals comprising both a

category and a network" (Tilly, 1978: 63). Most election surveys routinely measure only respondents' social and demographic categories – gender, race, age, income, ethnicity, class – to be used either as control variables or as substantive predictors of political orientations and actions. For example, Wolfinger and Rosenstone's (1980) explanation of voting turnout and Knoke's (1976) analysis of party identification relied primarily on covariations with such face sheet data. The proportions of variation explained (multiple R^2) by such factors tend to be disappointingly small, largely because sociodemographic categories by themselves yield only crude distinctions about the underlying social networks within which people are embedded.

Social categories do not measure genuine groups, but merely statistical aggregates. All blacks share a racial identity and some common socioeconomic experiences. All accountants enjoy a middle-class occupational prestige. But at the microlevel of personal interactions, individual blacks and accountants are typically embedded in quite diverse social networks. These small-scale interactions can be expected to produce different political consequences. To rely only on survey respondents' categories to explain their political orientations results in incomplete and inaccurate explanations. Understanding can be improved by bringing these social networks explicitly into account. For example, Finifter's (1974) study of blue-collar auto workers disclosed that the Republican Party supporters maintained their atypical identifications within the predominantly Democratic environment by forming exclusive friendship groups with other workers sharing their deviant preferences. Similarly, Burstein (1976) found that Israeli voting choices were better predicted by a direct connection to someone very active in party politics than by the voter's social background categories.

The catnet concept argues for a merger of social attributes with micronetworks to uncover the detailed processes by which a respondent's sociodemographic characteristics affect his or her political orientations and behaviors. People are embedded in ongoing networks that vary in social composition and convey different political contents. The forms and contents of respondents' interactions with their network alters shape their views of the larger political world and their orientation toward it. The frequency and intensity of their egonetwork interactions, the strength of loyalty and deference to network members, the extent to which contacts serve as reference points in organizing political opinions – all help to explain the convergence or deviation of people's voting and political participation from the norms of their micronetworks. For example, apart from their group interests, blacks and working-class people tend to be more Democratic and less politically efficacious than whites and middle-class people because of the latter groups' involvement in small, homogeneous networks where such political orientations are predominant, valued, and reinforced. When survey researchers ignore these catnets and measure only actors' categories, the results are the weak class and race correlations with political items observed in election surveys. If analysts would begin to measure directly the political content of respondents' egonetworks, they would better explain the gross cleavage patterns. They would very likely discover that deviants from expected patterns (Republican blacks, liberal bankers) are sustained by micronets that contain alters holding similar views.

Some modest efforts have already begun making inroads into the attribute approach to voting and political participation studies. The following subsections describe the most significant network findings and their implications for a genuine structural analysis of electoral phenomena.

Political socialization

Conventional models of voting behavior emphasize the intergenerational transmission of political orientations, especially party identification. The parental family is seen as a principal agent of childhood and adolescent socialization. Offspring learn their parents' values, beliefs, and attitudes in a variety of social and cultural domains (Glass, Bengtson, and Dunham, 1986: 685). Familial interactions generate intense, emotional identifications with many social groups – religious, racial, ethnic, gender, class, political – that persist well into adulthood (Campbell, 1969). The consequence is the high intergenerational agreement of many social attributes, particularly party identification, observed in cross-sectional surveys where respondents are asked to recall their parents' party affiliations (Campbell et al., 1960: 149; Jennings and Niemi, 1974, 1981; Goldberg, 1969; Knoke, 1976: 93–109).

The most widely offered explanation for this congruence is imitative transmission from parents to children (Tedin, 1980; Rosenberg, 1985). Strong parent-child emotional bonds generate a predisposition by offspring to accept their parents' political orientations, without full cognitive understanding or a consistency of personal preferences with the party's policies (Hess and Torney, 1967: 21). Alternatively, child-parent attitude resemblances may arise through occupying equivalent social status positions, or even by grown children reciprocally influencing their elderly parents (Glass et al., 1986). More recent research indicates that the intergenerational linkage is not invariant. In a 1965-to-1974 panel study of a high school cohort, dramatic declines occurred in the parent-child correlations on party identification and presidential preferences (Jennings and Niemi, 1981: 100). The waning of parental influence would be more understandable if the researchers had included measures of social networks into which the students had subsequently entered. Their college, friendship, marriage, work, and recreational interactions undoubtedly exposed many young adults to new norms and values that tugged their political orientations in directions different from the parents' preferences. Without such micronetwork data, the authors could only speculate that declining interaction with parents lay behind the diminished intergenerational co-variation (p. 112).

A study using data from three generations also found evidence that the forces generating parent-child similarities in gender, religious, and political attitudes varied over time. Direct parental influence over their offspring declined, but the children's influences on their parents strengthened steadily after early adulthood (Glass et al., 1986: 696). Although these relations appeared robust, the mechanisms by which reciprocal cross-generation influences occurred remain obscure. Kinspeople constitute most Americans' egocentric networks for discussing personal matters; almost one-third of such networks consist only of people having some family relation to ego (Marsden, 1987). This discovery strongly implies that reciprocal socialization between parents and children continues throughout individuals' lifetimes. Before a clearer picture can emerge, researchers must include measures of parent-child interaction frequency, indirect linkages through other kin and friends, and the explicit political content of these influence networks.

Cross-pressures and status inconsistency

A long tradition in political sociology relates multiple dimensions of social differentiation to individual political behavior. The Columbia voting analysts posited that many social categories, such as class and religion, exert causal pressures on the political choices of category members. For example, businessmen are pressured to vote Republican and union members to vote Democratic. The interesting phenomenon is the situation of a person who simultaneously occupies social positions that exert contradictory cues or cross-pressures on their political orientations. Thus, a Catholic businessman in 1960 confronted competing environmental tendencies from his religious and occupational affiliations in deciding between Richard Nixon and John Kennedy for president. With a foot equally in each social camp, the cross-pressured voter moves to a position midway between the choices. Lazarsfeld and colleagues (1948: 56) argued that the more evenly balanced are the cross-pressures, the longer such voters waited to make up their minds. Panel data from Erie County suggested that such individuals prolonged their final vote decision "because they were waiting for events to resolve the conflicting pressures" (p. 61). Campaign activities or family persuasion might tip the balance for the indecisive person to one side or the other. The Elmira study also found unstable vote intentions among persons in cross-pressured social strata (Berelson et al., 1954: 129–32). Because these people were members of distinct social groups that have about equally strong preference distributions, they have nearly equal chances of receiving social support for either preference (p. 131). Their dilemma is expressed by a fluctuating and prolonged vote decision.

The cross-pressure hypothesis is methodologically equivalent to the concept of status inconsistency that enjoys periodic vogues in political sociology (Lenski, 1954; Blalock, 1967; Segal, 1969; Knoke, 1973), although each hypothesis predicts different voting patterns from combinations of causal variables. Persons experiencing the effects of exceptionally disparate social categories – such as low-paid professionals, black physicians, and lawyers with farm-laborer fathers – are presumably exposed to a variety of contradictory cues about appropriate social and political attitudes and behaviors. The basic theoretical expectation is that stresses created by such status disequilibria are resolved by resorting to extreme actions – psychophysically by symptoms of mental distress and politically by supporting exceptionally liberal or conservative policies. This hypothesis was translated into sophisticated statistical models that predicted a significant interaction (nonadditive) effect of a person's multiple social statuses on the dependent variable of substantive interest (see Blalock, 1967; Hope, 1975). Unfortunately for the cross-pressure and status inconsistency hypotheses, rigorous tests with survey data almost universally found that only an additive process occurred. That is, people's behaviors were an average of the social forces in each of their status categories. For example, upwardly mobile people from blue-collar to white-collar occupations exhibit a political party preference halfway between their Democratic origins and their Republican destinations (Knoke, 1973; see Horan [1971] for a failure to find nonadditive cross-pressure effects on voting turnout in the Elmira data). As a result of this body of negative evidence (Jackson and Curtis, 1972; Davis, 1982), empirical interest in the political effects of multidimensional status contradictions has waned in recent years.

This eclipse was premature. It foreclosed subsequent developments that could incorporate micronetworks into the cross-pressure and status inconsistency hypotheses. The earlier studies used survey data that only measured individuals' social categories, such as income, occupation, race, religion, and ethnicity. The actual interactions involving cross-pressured and inconsistent persons with other social actors were never directly incorporated into the analyses. Yet, such microlevel processes lie at the theoretical heart of the alleged status disequilibrating processes. Without detailed knowledge of the political forces to which people are exposed, an exclusive focus on status categories seems certain to wipe out the subtle pulls of social interaction. Once again, both elements of people's catnets are essential. To illustrate how the contradictory situation may operate, consider two groups of extremely upwardly mobile individuals. Assume that they have risen to high-level corporate executive positions from families that were unskilled, unionized, and traditional Democrats. Suppose that half of these Horatio Algers completely sever their ties with the childhood origins and associate only with the haut monde. The other half find their new social circumstances discomforting and they actively maintain their friendships and kin ties to the old neighborhood. Although both groups exhibit identical origin-destination statuses, an analyst would be hard pressed to assert with a straight face that both groups are exposed to the same sociopolitical forces and that they will react the same way politically. The social strivers probably overemulate the reactionary politics of the superrich. The nostalgic group probably continues to express the liberal nostrums of their humble beginnings. The resulting average for the entire set is an intermediate political orientation that disguises the divergent pulls of the egocentric networks within which both groups of the upwardly mobile are enmeshed. This speculative example also highlights the importance of the causal order: Do changes in personal network composition induce changes in attitudes and behaviors, or are network contacts reshaped after a person modifies his or her political views? Without microlevel data to supplement the status-category variables, a proper examination cannot be conducted of the mechanisms through which cross-pressures and status inconsistencies are experienced politically in individuals' lives.

Contextual effects

One of the oldest empirical traditions in political science is the analysis of voting returns for areal units such as precincts, wards, counties, and states (e.g., Key, 1949). With the invention of individual survey sampling and the discovery that relations among aggregated variables did not always hold at the individual level, contextual analysis emerged as a substantive and methodological inquiry. The social and political environments of voters' residential communities are assumed to affect their political orientations through various intervening processes (Sprague, 1982). Individuals are embedded within a given context that structures their social interactions, constrains information exchanges, and determines their political responses. Community contexts can deflect individual political choices in directions toward or away from the typical patterns of the immediate social environment. Thus, in 1968 southern whites whose counties were heavily black were much more likely to vote for the antiintegrationist candidate, George Wallace (Wright, 1976; Knoke and Kyriazis, 1977). Blue-collar workers are more likely to vote for Republican candidates if they live in white-collar neighborhoods where Republicanism is the normative tendency (Segal and Meyer, 1969). Political participation, especially voting turnout, is greater among lower-status persons who reside in low-status districts and among higher-status persons living in high-status districts (Huckfeldt, 1979; Giles and Dantico, 1982). Residential contexts may interact with individuals' objective and subjective class positions to produce complex voting patterns not predictable from the additive effects of each of these factors (Butler and Stokes, 1974: 130–2). Although not all analysts have found robust social contexts effects after controlling for individual characteristics (e.g., Kelley and McAllister, 1985), researchers' fascination with contextual phenomena persists.

Contextual analysts traditionally have combined only two types of data: individual attributes and social unit composition. An improved understanding of contextual mechanisms could result from bringing in a third level – the individual voter's egocentric network. These micronets may serve as filters that connect individuals to the larger neighborhood and community social structures. Apart from perceptions acquired directly from mass media, most voters do not directly experience their precinct, ward, and districts as total political phenomena. Rather, through neighboring relations, friendships, and work groups, local residents are exposed to selective portions of their immediate political context. Their egocentric connections communicate varied political messages. Thus, even neighbors residing on the same block and having identical social characteristics may exhibit quite divergent political orientations. Unless these individuals' microcontexts are explicitly incorporated into contextual analyses, researchers will continue to make erroneous inferences about the impact of contextual influences on voter choices.

A graphic example of this approach was Huckfeldt's (1984) reanalyses of Laumann's data on friendship choices of Detroit white men. He reasoned that social behaviors are a complex product of individual preferences that are constrained by social interactions. In turn, opportunities for interaction are structured by the social composition of a person's local environment. The blue-collar and white-collar composition of a neighborhood shapes the formation of friendships by residents of one social class with members of another class. The larger the supply of a particular class of neighborhood residents, the higher the probability that a person will have a friend from that class, regardless of his own class location. But, demand for types of friends is also relevant; some people prefer to associate only with members of their own class. If a local context does not offer enough opportunities for in-group affiliation, a minority must seek its friends elsewhere (Blau, 1977). The political consequences of contextual mechanisms uncovered by Huckfelt were complex. Democratic party identification increased as a function of the neighborhood's working-class composition for all respondents except those working-class persons who subjectively identified themselves as workers. These class-conscious workers remained strongly Democratic regardless of the neighborhood context. Huckfeldt (1984: 414) speculated that social contexts may create their effects via both intimate networks and more frequent routine encounters among residents.

Neighborhood supply affects voters' abilities to choose discussion partners holding similar or opposing political preferences. In a study of the 1984 presidential election in South Bend, Indiana, Huckfeldt and Sprague (1988) found a pronounced tendency of respondents to misperceive the voting choices of their alters in the direction of the respondents' own biases. Thus, a voter disposed to support Reagan was likely to see her political intimates as pro-Reagan, even when their true preferences were for Mondale. However, such distortions were more difficult to sustain if the neighborhood context was overwhelmingly contrary to ego's preference. Misperceptions are increasingly hard to sustain when the evidence from even casual contacts is strongly consistent. Political minorities may turn inward, interacting only with others of their persuasion in an effort to avoid a flood of disagreeable partisan information. But their efforts were doomed to failure because the supply of information is determined by the political coloration of the surrounding social structures. High levels of resistance toward selecting discussion partners with opposing preferences cannot insulate the neighborhood minorities from exposure to majority preferences (p. 15). The next step for researchers should be to show how a respondent's vote choice is jointly constrained by the personal discussion network and the neighborhood context.

Voting choices

The network approach to voting behavior must incorporate the effects of both form and content of egocentric relationships upon an actor's vote decision. The form of a network is the number of alters to whom an ego is directly connected and the strengths of their political ties to ego and among one another. Ties may be dense and intense or sparse and infrequently activated. In his study of Detroit white men, Laumann (1973: 123) found that the more closely knit (densely interlocked) were the ties among ego's three best friends, the greater the political party homogeneity of the network. Radial networks (in which ego's friends did not know one another) tended to be less politically and socially homogeneous and to be more tolerant of political extremism (p. 127). Once again we see support for the fundamental network proposition that strong, impacted ties foster uniform political orientations, while ramifying connections expose people to diverse opinions, attitudes, and beliefs.

The content of a network consists of exchanges of political information that may influence ego's perceptions of political choices and their consequences. These communication contents may include the traditional Michigan trinity – party, issue, and candidate preferences – and other relevant persuasions, such as appeals to group loyalties or personal obligations. The content of political discussions can range from highly partisan and homogeneous information to quite diffuse and unfocused information.

Two basic propositions about the effect of ego nets on voting choices reflect both form and content dimensions: (1) Ego's decision is more influenced by alters to which it is strongly tied than by alters with which it has weak links and (2) the more consistent the partisan information received from alters, the more disposed ego is to vote for that party's candidate.

These speculations are illustrated by three hypothetical micronets in Figure 2.2, each of which contains an ego (*E*) and four alters (*A*). The subscripts show the partisan orientations of the actor, either Democratic (D) or Republican (R). A double line indicates a strong tie (e.g., frequent political discussions) and a single line a weak interaction between a pair of actors. The three diagrams display diverse balances of partisan influences in ego's local environment. Because we know that most people's confiding networks consist of kinspeople, we might think of alters as mainly spouses, parents, siblings, and children. Hence, political heterogeneity is most likely to occur through intermarriage across party lines. Part 1 of Figure 2.2 shows a dense clique in which all of ego's alters share her Democratic bias. She is thus intensely bombarded by consistent messages that reinforce her inclination to vote for the Democratic party. In part 2, the alters come in both partisan persuasions, but ego's strongest ties convey Democratic cues. Presumably, ego is still influenced to a Democratic vote, but not so strongly. But in part 3, the balance of partisan forces has clearly shifted toward the Republican alters (possibly by marriage to a Republican man), and the chances that ego will defect from her traditional support are now presumably much greater. Although the implications of these configurations appear obvious, the process would be more complicated if multiple network relations were considered. For example, suppose that each alter had inconsistent views on the issues and candidates of an election and that each opinion was communicated to ego with varying intensity.

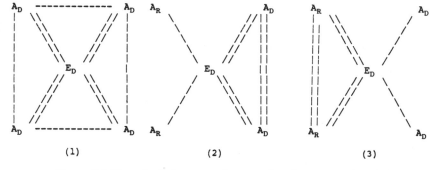

Figure 2.2 Hypothetical egocentric networks of varying political form and content.

Data from the 1987 General Social Survey (GSS) allow a modest examination of the relationship between respondents' political discussion networks and the voting decisions (Knoke, 1990b). The GSS is an annual cross-sectional survey of 1,500 American adults that collects data on a wide variety of social attitudes and behaviors. In 1987, a special module on political participation operationalized respondents' ego networks using an enumeration procedure developed in the 1985 GSS (see Burt [1986, 1987a] and Marsden [1987] for details and findings from that project). Each respondent was asked:

> From time to time, most people discuss *important matters* with other people. Looking back over the last six months – who are the *people* with whom you discussed matters important to you? Just tell me their first names or initials.

Because of time limitations, only three names were recorded. The GSS measured four aspects of network form and content. Respondents were asked whether they felt especially close to each alter named; the alters' various role relations with ego (spouse, child, coworker, friend, neighbor, etc.); the party preference of each alter (restricted to Democrat, Republican, Independent, and Other); and the frequency with which ego and alter talk about political matters (a six-point scale from never to almost daily). Although time constraints prevented asking respondents about the nature of the ties among the three pairs of alters, the 1985 survey had found that less than 15 percent of the first three alters were "total strangers" to one another. In the absence of other data, the assumption must be made that all alters had nearly equal close relations with one another.

Table 2.1 displays several descriptive statistics about respondents' egocentric discussion networks. Almost 95 percent of the respondents included at least one alter in their discussion networks, but more than one-third had fewer than three alters. A large majority said that they felt close to each alter, primarily because most of those named were friends and/or relatives. Neighbors, coworkers, and group members were infrequently mentioned (note that the categories used were not mutually exclusive). Respondents reported party identifications for 70 to 80 percent of their alters. They claimed to talk about politics at least monthly or more often with about 40 percent of their alters.

An index of the respondent's perceived partisan environment was constructed by subtracting the number of Republican alters from the number of Democratic alters. Independents, Others, and Don't Know responses were treated as having no partisan valence. Respondents reporting no alters were also treated as having politically neutral environments. The partisan environment index ranges from consistently Republican through neutral to consistently Democratic content. Thus, a three-alter network comprised of

Table 2.1 *Characteristics of ego political networks*

Variable	Alter mentioned(%)		
	First	Second	Third
Respondents mentioned no alters[a]	4.5	18.8	37.8
Respondents feel close to alter	72.8	65.4	60.1
Relation to ego[b]			
Friend	70.5	73.4	75.5
Family members[c]	67.7	52.8	47.0
Advisor	37.7	37.5	31.2
Coworker	15.0	19.0	18.7
Group member[d]	15.7	15.7	14.9
Neighbor	8.6	12.8	13.2
Other	2.9	1.5	2.2
Party Identification			
Democrat	36.9	36.3	33.6
Republican	24.2	22.8	23.0
Independent	16.6	10.5	9.4
Other	2.1	2.6	3.3
Don't know	20.3	27.8	30.6
Total	100.0	100.0	100.0
Talk politics			
6. Almost daily	14.6	6.4	6.7
5. At least weekly	9.4	17.8	15.1
4. At least monthly	15.5	26.4	25.2
3. At least yearly	22.0	19.9	23.4
2. Less than yearly	22.2	10.7	10.2
1. Never	14.6	18.9	19.3
Total	100.0	100.0	100.0
Number of respondents	1,738	1,481	1,138

[a] Excluded from rest of table statistics.
[b] Percentages do not total to 100.0% due to overlapping categories.
[c] Spouse, parent, sibling, child, other family.
[d] "Member of a group to which you belong."
Missing data: No information from 18 respondents.
Source: Knoke (1990b).

all Republicans was scored −3; a three-alter network of all Democrats +3; and a network having one Democrat, one Republican, and an Independent was 0. Persons whose ego nets have only one or two alters obviously may not have environment scores as extremely partisan as persons with larger homogeneous networks. But the former are also exposed to fewer sources of consistent partisan information.

The effects of ego network form and content on national political attitudes and behaviors were assessed by multiple classification analysis (MCA). This method is a version of analysis of covariance in which some of the independent variables are categoric and others are continuous. MCA estimates the effects of categoric variables as deviations from the sample mean of the dependent variable, unlike dummy variable regression whose coefficients are deviations from an omitted category (see Andrews, Morgan, and Sonquist, 1967, and Kerlinger and Pedhazer, 1973: 105–9, for more detail). Hence, MCA coefficients readily reveal whether a particular category increases or decreases the value of a dependent variable. MCA also permits tests for whether the categoric variables interact, that is, whether variables jointly or separately affect the dependent measure.

The three categoric measures used in each MCA pertain to the form and content of ego networks: political environment (seven categories from all-Republican to all-Democrat); closeness to alters (four categories from close to none to close to three alters); and frequency of talking about politics (four categories from low to high). Interactions between each pair of categoric variables were specified, but not the three-way effect. The ten covariates included in each MCA were respondent's party identification, race, age, region, education, income, occupation, and three religious classifications (Catholic, Jewish, none-other; Protestant was omitted as a reference category). To conserve space, only the effects of categoric variables are reported.

Table 2.2 applies the MCA to seven measures of political participation. Political interest is a four-point item from not interested to very interested in "politics and national affairs." Turnout and voting in 1984 are dichotomous measures of whether the respondent voted, and, if so, whether he or she voted for Reagan. The persuading others item asks, "During elections, do you ever try to show people why they should vote for one of the parties or candidates?" Answers were recorded in four categories from "never" to "often." Political work asks, "Have you done (other) work for the parties or candidates in most elections?" Responses were four categories from never to most elections. Finally, giving money to parties or candidates and attending political rallies in the past three or four years both are recorded as dichotomous (yes-no) responses.

The results reveal consistent, substantial effects of both partisan environments and frequency of political discussions, but not of closeness to one's alters, possibly because the level of intimacy varies so little across this set of alters. Persons who frequently discussed politics with their alters are much more likely to participate in the various activities than those who seldom talk about politics. Political discussions have significant effects on all measures except voting for Reagan. The effects of partisan environment are also fairly robust. Persons surrounded entirely by Republicans tend to be the most active on all seven measures. Those in less extremely Republican or neutral environments are frequently the least involved, while persons in moderately Democratic egonets are about as active as those in extremely Democratic circles. The absence of significant closeness effects for all except the political interest measure suggests that this aspect of ego-net form is irrelevant to political participation. What seems to count most is the partisan content and the frequency with which political information flows through the network, but not the emotional bonds among

Table 2.2. *Multiple classification analyses of political activities by ego networks: deviations from dependent variable means*[a]

Categoric variables	Dependent variables						
	Political interest	Turnout 1984	Reagan vote	Persuade to vote	Other work	Gave money	Attend rally
Partisan environment							
3 Republican	.26	.08	.09	.28	.33	.14	.13
2 Republicans	.07	.09	.08	−.12	−.10	−.03	−.03
1 Republican	−.07	−.02	.00	−.15	.07	.00	−.01
0 Neutral	−.08	−.06	.05	−.09	−.10	−.04	−.04
1 Democrat	.05	.05	−.06	.07	−.03	.01	.02
2 Democrats	.02	−.01	−.03	.11	.07	.05	.03
3 Democrats	.01	.03	−.07	.09	.03	−.01	.04
$(F; df = 6)$	3.05^c	4.05^d	2.61^b	3.65^d	5.20^d	2.91^c	3.28^d
Talk Politics							
Lowest	−.37	−.08	.02	−.34	−.09	−.06	−.23
Medium Low	−.06	−.04	.04	−.20	−.14	−.04	−.06
Medium High	.05	.04	.00	.10	.00	.03	.13
Highest	.30	.06	−.03	.32	.16	.05	.13
$(F; df = 3)$	48.18^d	8.34^d	1.27	34.15^d	12.57^d	6.14^d	18.43^d
Close to alters							
None Close	−.07	−.04	.05	−.07	−.03	.01	−.01
1 Close	.11	.00	−.03	.09	.02	−.02	.00
2 Close	−.05	.03	.00	−.05	.04	.00	.02
3 Close	−.02	.01	−.01	−.01	−.02	.02	.00
$(F; df = 3)$	3.55^b	1.31	1.39	1.65	0.57	0.81	0.43
Interactions (F-ratio)							
Environment X Talk	.62	.91	1.17	1.81^b	1.77^b	1.31	1.10
Environment X Close	1.30	.85	1.25	2.28^b	1.45	1.15	1.54
Talk X Close	.33	1.06	1.03	1.32	2.81^c	.60	1.66
R^2adj	$.220^d$	$.211^d$	$.420^d$	$.140^c$	$.112^c$	$.139^c$	$.112^c$
Number of respondents	1,598	1,501	1,048	1,595	1,598	1,598	1,595

[a] Covariates included in equations: party identification, race, religion, region, education, income, occupation, and age.
[b] $p < .05$.
[c] $p < .01$.
[d] $p < .001$.
Source: Knoke (1990b).

network members.

Significant interactions among the categoric variables occurred only for persuasion and other political work. In particular, persuasion increased within combinations of closely tied Republican environments and not-close Democratic environments. The other three interaction patterns are not clearly interpretable. Thus, for the most part, the three dimensions of ego networks tend to affect political attitudes and behaviors in additive rather than interactive fashion. The important result is that form and content affect people's political attitudes and behaviors, even after controlling for their own party preferences and social characteristics.

These results challenge our conventional understanding of how citizens come to receive and to act on political information. The dominant academic paradigm was built around national election surveys that stripped individual respondents out of their social contexts. They depicted atomized actors floating unanchored in a homogenized stream of national mass media stimuli, their perceptions unfiltered by constraining and validating personal relationships. Impressions of parties, candidates, and policy issues impinged on voters' consciousness without discernible mechanisms to interpret their meaning for the citizens' hopes and fears. Even using the superficial network measures available in the 1987 GSS, we see robust evidence that ego-centered structural relations are critical to shaping Americans' political attitudes and behaviors. The more frequently that people discuss political matters with their intimates, the greater their interest and participation in national campaigns and voting. The partisan composition of their microenvironments strongly influences ideologies, policy preferences, voting choices, and other forms of participation, even after controlling for the respondents' social locations and party identifications. However, closeness counts only in horseshoes and dancing, not in political networks. Given these cross-sectional data, we cannot assess whether the robust network effects represent causal impacts or the consequences of respondents selecting discussion partners holding compatible partisan views.

Reliability of respondent reports

The GSS findings are based solely on respondents' perceptions of their alters' party preferences. These perceptions are undoubtedly distorted to some unknown degree, resulting in biased findings about alters' relations with ego (Bernard, Killworth, and Sailer, 1981). Lacking direct measures of every alters' partisanship, we cannot determine whether the critical variable is ego's beliefs or alters' actual preferences. Even if egos erred in their reports, they may be revealing a cognitive network whose impact upon their own orientations is as significant as the objective relationship. As W. I. Thomas averred, a subjective definition of the situation may be as real in its consequences as the objective situation (Thomas and Znaniecki, 1918–20; also Krackhardt and Porter, 1985).

Some evidence about the unreliability of perceptual reports came from three community surveys of egocentric networks that also collected data on these characteristics directly from samples of alters named by respondents as one of their three best friends (Laumann, 1973; Pappi and Wolf, 1985; Huckfeldt and Sprague, 1987). In Detroit and Juelich, West Germany, ego's and alters' reports of one another's party identifications had substantially lower agreement with their actual preferences than did other visible social characteristics such as age, religion, occupation, and education. The intraclass correlations of party preferences were only .49 and .50 in Germany and America, respectively, in contrast to correlations in the .75 to .98 range for the other attributes. One-third of the Germans and one-seventh of the Americans were unable to report accurately their best friend's party. In Detroit, the men tended to disregard political independence of their friends and to report a party more similar to their own. Democrats were especially likely to perceive their Republican friends to be Democrats, possibly because of the respondents' lower education levels (Laumann, 1973: 31). Homophily, the tendency to choose friends who are similar to oneself, apparently is based less on political than on other social features, hence, the lower visibility of party identification and its systematic distortion in egos' reports about their alters. Huckfeldt and Sprague's (1987) survey of 1,500 South Bend residents collected both respondents' perceptions of the presidential vote choices of "those people you talked with most about events of the past election year [1984]" and direct reports from 500 of the alters. Ego's perceptions tended to be distorted in the direction of ego's own choice for president. Although ego correctly perceived alter's vote choice in more than 90 percent of the dyads where both partners voted the same, accuracy fell off to two-thirds among Reagan supporters and barely half of Mondale supporters whose alters voted for a different candidate. The granting of Robert Burns's wish, "Oh wad some power the giftie gie us / To see oursels as others see us!" might open many an eye.

These methodological analyses raised a caution flag about easy reliance on survey respondents' reports of their networks' characteristics. Much more research must be carried out on the consequences of using unreliable measures in analyzing structural processes. In particular, are the cognitive perceptions or the factual conditions more important in explaining the impact of local environments on voters' choices? How distorting are differences in the reliabilities of ego reports about alters' party, issue, candidate and other factors? Answers to these questions require painstaking and costly collection of data directly from alters who are named by egos as key members of their micronets. Only when such data become routinely available will the limits of self-reported network data become clear.

Looking forward

Most recent studies of citizen political participation concentrate on the national level – voting for the president and Congress, supporting or opposing issues of national importance. Yet if former House Speaker Tip O'Neil is correct, all politics are local politics. Candidates and citizens alike see the electoral process as a self-interested pursuit of mutual advantages through the aggregation of grass-roots support. What matters most to citizens is how distant political decisions will affect their personal lives. They cast their votes not to select policies, but to choose representatives who they believe (or hope) will make policies that favorably affect their communities and daily lives. Savvy politicians respond by tailoring appeals to their constituents' concerns and fears, as communicated to them through localized influence networks. In our age of homogenized national mass media messages, citizens' personal networks increasingly serve to filter the meaning of political images projected on the national screen. Contrary to the usual assertion that national political forces have eliminated local political variation, personal social relations have become more crucial than ever for comprehending a bewildering daily intrusion of signals about war, peace, economic reordering, famine, ecological collapse, crime waves, and displaced morality. Micronetworks anchor individual perspectives within a larger social context. They provide ordinary citizens with trusted interpreters who validate personal beliefs and reinforce divergent opinions. Rather than a passive, atomized mass, the contemporary political culture has created a genuine public, a rich, lumpy stew simmering over tens of millions of local fires.

The 1987 GSS was severely limited for exploring various facets of ego nets. The three political dimensions measured do not begin to exhaust the possible range of significant influences on citizens' decisions. We must probe deeper into details of the structural forms and political contents flowing through personal communication channels. How important are direct and indirect linkages among alters; substantive information versus emotional overtones; discussing the merits and flaws of candidates, parties, and issues? By asking respondents to name only those people with whom they "discussed important matters," do we omit important political informants from their networks? Which better explains the impact of microenvironments on citizens' actions: the respondent's cognitive perceptions of alters or the actual political preferences of alters? How can we disentangle causality from selectivity effects in network formation and impact? Only longitudinal data gathered directly from alters can satisfactorily address these questions. If we hope to understand how people become involved in politics, we cannot continue to ignore the networks of interpersonal relations within which they are embedded. What is now required is a resurrection of the agenda abandoned decades ago with the eclipse of the Columbia approach. The methodological tools for building a new political sociology paradigm are now available for this difficult and exciting task. Only lacking is the will to begin.

3   *Social movements*

with Nancy Wisely

Springtime 1989 brought reports of numerous collective actions from around the world. Following a decade of underground struggle, the trade union Solidarity swept almost all the parliamentary seats from Poland's bankrupt Communist Party in the first free elections since the end of World War II. In Beijing's Tiananmen Square, tanks crushed students and workers who were peacefully demanding democratic freedoms and an end to corruption in China's Communist Party. In West Germany, masked rioters injured hundreds of police in Berlin's squatter district, while rallies of resurgent right-wing political parties increasingly erupted in bloody fights with leftist hecklers. In Israel's occupied territories, the *intifada* entered its second year, the rock-throwing Arab youths buoyed by the declaration of Palestinian independence and the United States' agreement to talk with the Palestine Liberation Organization. Abortion foes and advocates in the United States stepped up their mass marches, clinic sit-ins, and political agitation, galvanized by the Supreme Court's restrictions on women's freedom of choice.

As these highly visible collective actions attest, social movements take a diversity of forms and seek a variety of objectives. What they share are coordinated efforts by people holding a common interest in social change who resort to nonconventional political means to reach their goals. Whenever such collective efforts fall outside the framework of institutional political systems, we define them as social movements. More formally, all social movements with political goals seem to involve at least four elements:

1. Socially disruptive actions targeted against public authorities and their symbols – ranging from peaceful public assemblies to civil disobedience and illegal violence – that transgress conventional norms of participation in electoral and pressure group politics.
2. Primarily purposive tactics and strategies, rather than emotional and expressive outbursts, that seek to shift power and policies from the status quo to new arrangements.

57

3. An emphasis on social organization that stresses a high degree of group activity rather than elite leadership.
4. Social movement organizations that are distinct from the movement's mass base in an aggrieved populace, several of which may complete as well as cooperate with one another.

It is important to realize that social movements should not be seen as qualitatively different phenomena from political behavior in more institutionalized arenas, such as voting and political participation discussed in Chapter 2. Rather, movements are the main vehicles for excluded people to gain access to and influence within an established political system. Only in rare instances do organized efforts aim to overthrow a political system, displacing one set of authorities with another. Such revolutionary upheavals appear to some analysts to involve qualitatively different processes than social movements that seek incorporation into the polity. However, because many revolutions grow out of initially disorderly protests, we see them as one end on a continuum of movement actions.

Although highly visible violent confrontations often capture worldwide media attention, social movement activities are typically more elaborate systems of interaction among participants and targets. Movement boundaries are porous, with individuals and organizations coalescing and dissipating in fluid rhythms that some observers liken to waves or cycles of protest (Truman, 1971; Tarrow, 1983, 1988: 433–5; Freeman, 1983; Foss and Larkin, 1986). Short periods of intense protest activity in some societal subsystem challenge the established institutions and power structures. New protest techniques are invented and diffuse across national territories and international borders. Following either success or repression, the movement collapses and a long period of stable power relationships ensues. Eventually, new social, economic, cultural, and political strains build up and new opportunities emerge for disadvantaged groups, latent movements revitalize or new ones crystallize, and the cycle of stability-disruption-protest continues. The history of illegal and legal abortion in the United States is a paradigmatic case, with pro-life and pro-choice movements copying one another's strategies and tactics to influence legislatures and court decisions (Luker, 1984).

The complex patterns in this dynamic dance are the focus of research by social movement analysts. At the macrolevel, what structural conditions lead to initial unrest and the outbreak of challenge? How do call and response between protestors and authorities unfold in successful or failed bids to change the situation? At the microlevel, which individuals can be mobilized to participate in movement actions? How are they organized socially for most effective involvement? Which information and resource exchange relations prove most suitable under various conditions for coordinating movement participants? What connections among individual, organizational, and systemic structures link them in comprehensive collective actions? What impact does a movement have upon its participants during collective activity and subsequently? What social forces result in repression, entry into the polity, or revolutionary transformation of the polity and society? Do social movements produce ephemeral or lasting transformations in the political life of nations?

In this chapter we review extant theories of social movement behavior with an eye to the relevance of social network explanations. First, we consider older approaches that emphasized atomized individual psychological and rational decision processes, and uncover their shortcomings as accurate accounts of movement dynamics. Then, we inspect contemporary theories of resource mobilization and political processes, showing how structural elements play an important role. We examine recent research on movement recruitment patterns and interorganizational relations that finds network ties to be critical factors in forging effective fighting forces. Finally, we speculate on how future social movement research can benefit by explicitly incorporating social network concepts at both microlevels and macrolevels of analysis.

Strain and stress psychology

Psychological explanations dominated the field of collective behaviors for half a century and still retain considerable allegiance. The most simplistic versions depicted participation in mass movements as an irrational emotional outburst by the discontented and the deprived, the anxious and the alienated (LeBon, 1896; Fromm, 1941; Adorno, Frenkel-Brunswick, Levinson, and Nevitt, 1950; Hoffer, 1951). Individuals experience intolerable psychological stresses in their daily lives, and their joining in mob actions is a safety valve that lets off much steam, but accomplishes little in the way of solving their problems. The collective behavior approach of Herbert Blumer (1951) sought to encompass a wide range of social activity from fads, cults, and crowds to panics, riots, lynchings, strikes, and revolutions. Many of these entities consist of aggregated individuals, not coordinated groups; that is, they are collected but not genuine collectivities. Consequently, Blumer's inclusive definition interpreted collective behaviors as emotional and irrational *reactions* to various social changes, disruptions, and strains in a social system. Purpose and intention by participants is in general absent; spontaneity reigns. Social movements are simply one of many types of noninstitutionalized collective behaviors, and their explanation requires concepts and principles different from those that produce conventional normative behaviors. Proponents of the collective behavior approach generally did not specify the sources of structural strain that produce the triggering individual stresses, although industrialization, urbanization, and sudden unemployment were commonly mentioned. Any rapid disruption of a social order induces psychological stress in some people and, thus, is likely to provoke a collective response (Smelser, 1963). When discontented individuals find themselves interacting with others in a spontaneous assembly, a behavioral norm may emerge that motivates the gathering to act in unison (Turner and Killian, 1972; Opp, 1988a). Note that structurally induced stress is the sufficient condition for collective action to occur. No mechanism is specified for bringing individual predispositions into alignment and coordinating their collective efforts to alleviate their stresses.

Other classical social movement theories explicitly traced the origin of psychological stress to macrostructural conditions. Status inconsistency (Geschwender, 1967), relative deprivation (Gurr, 1970), and rising expectations (Davies, 1969) theories all hypothesized that social movements would erupt when long periods of economic development were followed by short, sharp economic declines. Rapidly deteriorating conditions open a gap between people's expectations and the actual satisfaction of their needs. So do failures of present development to keep up the pace of past improvements. The resulting individual psychological frustration provokes aggressive group actions against the authorities and other perceived sources of injustice, including scapegoats such as foreigners and racial or religious minorities. Again, the translation of personal hardships into collective actions is largely unmediated by the structural relationships among people experiencing this common grievance. Indeed, mass society theory (Kornhauser, 1959) asserted that the key factor is an *absence* of local primary groups and secondary associations to integrate individuals into the normative constraints of the larger society. When social conditions approximate a "mass society" – where populations and elites can emotionally incite one another to extreme actions – unconstrained social and political movements erupt and may eventually be captured by totalitarian extremists (Kornhauser, 1959: 84). Because social bonds are weakened, people lose their grips on their social identities and they abandon conventional norms that govern self-regulated behaviors. Lacking a strong stratum of intermediate groups, individuals relate directly to the larger society and to the state only through inclusive nationwide structures. This situation approximates Simmel's (1955) concentric circles that expose the individual to total domination from the highest level. The prototype was, of course, the Nazi regime's capture of the politically and socially disorganized Weimar mass society (Allen, 1965). In contrast, strong and diverse secondary associations induce "multiple proximate concerns" (Kornhauser, 1959: 76) that diffuse the potential for massification. Extensive, ramified social networks may crosscut one another and produce a complex social mosaic of unique personal identities. Individuation is a structural condition that may inoculate people against political extremism. But formal associations can also provide their members with the structural vehicles that are essential to press their political demands on the authorities. This paradoxical capacity of intermediate groups simultaneously to aggregate and to diffuse collective energies renders any simple assertion about their effects difficult.

Unfortunately for the classical theories of social movements, research evidence began contradicting their basic propositions. At the macrolevel, time series data on hardship and collective violence from France (Snyder and Tilly, 1972), the fluctuating success and failure of historical American social movement organizations (Goldstone, 1980), and the evaporation of collective action from the prosperous 1960s to the stagnant 1970s (Jenkins, 1983: 534) all pointed to a tenuous connection between economic strains and collective actions. Contrary to the mass society model, data from the Weimar regime (Oberschall, 1973), urban riots in the United States (Paige, 1971), poor people's movements (Piven and Cloward, 1977), the southern black civil rights movement (McAdam, 1982, 1986; Morris, 1984), the women's movement (Freeman, 1983; Katzenstein and Mueller, 1987), and Three Mile Island protests (Walsh and Warland, 1983) consistently found that, rather than marginal and anomic persons, collective actions generally attract participants of higher socioeconomic status who are more integrated and better connected to societal institutions than are the nonparticipants. The truly deprived lack the necessary skills and resources to participate effectively in any variety of politics, conventional or extremist. Alienation, frustration, perceived and actual deprivation frequently cause passive withdrawal and personal turmoil. The empirical fact is that occasionally the poor or the unemployed revolt, but most often they do not. In other words, nonconventional political activity parallels conventional electoral and pressure group activity in involving more central rather than more peripheral citizens. These findings soon forced social movement analysts to reconsider whether the conventional-nonconventional distinction really warranted radically distinct theoretical explanations.

The classical psychological theories suffered from a simplistic vision of a direct, linear stimulus-response connection between social strains, psychological stresses, and social protests. When strain and stress occur, collective action automatically follows. The theories' failure to propose mechanisms for this causal process, or to explain the various conditions under which these relationships occur, prompted searches for better theories. Although theory construction continues in the social psychological tradition (Klandermans, 1984; Killian, 1984; Lofland, 1985), the dominant perspective resides elsewhere. The chief contenders at present are rational choice models and resource mobilization approaches.

Rationality of collective action

Both the power and insufficiency of rational choice models come into sharp focus when applied to social movements. For over two decades, the most prominent exemplar has been Mancur Olson's classic *The Logic of Collective Action* (1965). Because this economic approach has had such a seductive fascination for social scientists, its promise and pitfalls must be examined at length. The core of Olson's argument is that public goods are inadequate for motivating individuals' contributions to collective actions. In Samuelson's classic definition, public goods "are enjoyed in common in the sense that each individual's consumption of such a good leads to no subtraction from any other individual's consumption of that good" (Samuelson, 1954: 387). And, "they must be available to everyone if they are available to anyone" (Olson, 1965: 14). Most social movements try to persuade the government to produce public goods – such as civil rights, environmental protection, nuclear disarmament, and economic reforms – from whose enjoyment nonmembers cannot be excluded. Mass demonstrations, protests, strikes, boycotts, and sit-ins are basic collective action strategies designed to secure these public goods goals. In contrast, private goods are consumed individually. Their methods of production allow a collectivity to restrict these benefits to persons possessing property rights, that is, membership standing (Riker and Ordeshook, 1973: 245). Typical examples include an organization's newsletters and magazines, information services, group travel and insurance programs, workshops and social activities, and recognition awards.

For social movements that offer public goods as their sole incentive to potential participants, both the imperceptible effect and free-rider problems enter into a rational actor's calculations that participation's benefits are not worth the costs (Olson, 1965). First, when a person's share of a collective good is small, especially in a large membership group, the amount of resources he or she should contribute will also be minuscule (Olson, 1965: 64–5). Second, because everyone shares in any public good that is produced by collective action, an actor should maximize her or his benefits by not contributing. But, if all members use the same calculus, all will withhold contributions. Therefore, suboptimal amounts of the collective good will be produced (i.e., none) whenever nonexcludable public goods are the only benefits created by participation (Olson, 1965: 27–9).

Olson's solution to these twin dilemmas was to posit the necessity for a group to offer selective utilitarian incentives (private goods) to supplement the public goods and thereby to attract sufficient contributions for their production (1965: 50–1). Because noncontributors can be prevented from enjoying these desired selective goods, those who desire them must now be willing to pay for the costs of producing the benefits. Under this so-called by-product theory of collective action, the private goods incentives become the main motivator of individual participation (Olson, 1965: 132–5). Subsequent to Olson, various theoretical refinements of his collective action model were proposed: imperfect information, the selective inducement aspect of collective goods, and entrepreneurial emphasis on nonmaterial benefits (Moe, 1980: 18, 142–4; Jenkins, 1983); elaboration of the property space of utilitarian incentives (Zald and Jacobs, 1978); the differential side effects of positive and negative incentives for collective action (Oliver, 1980); the importance of leadership in fostering decision-maximizing behavior (Leibenstein, 1978); and the primacy of collective bads and the costs to the individual of not contributing to collective actions (Mitchell, 1979). But all modifications preserved the basic Olsonian notion that rational actors contribute to collective action only when the benefits to be gained are fundamentally private rather than public in nature.

Many theorists were more concerned with qualifying the choice process than with conceptualizing alternative participatory motives. But adherence to strictly utilitarian cost-benefit calculations may unduly limit the scope of relevant social movements. At one point Olson argued, "Logically, the theory can cover all types of lobbies," including such noneconomic groups as those with "social, political, religious, or philanthropic objectives" (1965: 159). Then he exempted philanthropic and religious lobbies (p. 160), as well as lost-cause groups consisting of persons with "a low degree of rationality" (p. 161), and mass social movements whose adherents are "psychologically disturbed" (p. 162). Olson appeared to recognize that motivations in addition to utility-maximization may lead some persons to engage in collective actions. Rather than subsuming these motives under selective incentives through a tortured logic and thereby making his theory "no longer capable of empirical refutation" (Olson, 1965: 160, fn. 91), he preferred instead to restrict severely the types of collectivities to which his by-product theory applies.

Several theoretical schemes have suggested other bases of member motives and incentives that cannot be reduced to utilitarian cost-benefit calculi: the instrumental-expressive dichotomy (Gordon and Babchuk, 1959); Clark and Wilson's (1961) famous material-purposive-solidary incentive typology; Etzioni's (1975) utilitarian-normative-coercive bases of organizational compliance; the importance of solidarity and moral principles (Fireman and Gamson, 1979); and Knoke and Wright-Isak's (1982; Knoke, 1990a) rational choice, normative conformity, and affective bonding motivations. These typologies share a recognition that people vary enormously in their preferences for and responses to a diversity of incentives offered by social movements. Participants' motives range from solving workplace and family problems to changing public policies affecting the lives of people in distant lands. Adherence to equity norms, standards of fairness, altruism, emotional ties to persons and groups – all may play some part in individual decisions to act collectively. Reducing such complexity to simple utilitarian calculi of net benefits minus costs distorts psychological reality and ignores movements' capacities to tailor their inducements to fit the diversity of members' interests. Efforts to test Olson's model and its alternatives have frequently discovered that a variety of motives are important, as the following paragraphs report.

The empirical literature on incentives, primarily in social movement and occupational associations, is a steady accumulation of findings that refute the Olsonian emphasis on selective goods as essential for collective action. Wilson's (1973) case studies supported his contention that political associations, such as Americans for Democratic Action and the NAACP, rely on purposive incentives (emphasizing public norms and values) as well as utilitarian incentives (private material rewards) to attract and hold members. In Tillock and Morrison's (1979) survey of Zero Population Growth members, the virtual absence of private goods meant that most participants were attracted by the association's political and public education activities from whose benefits noncontributors could not be excluded. Moe (1980), analyzing members of five large economic associations that engaged in legislative lobbying, found that their extensive packages of economic services were highly valued by members, but that many joined and remained for political (i.e., public good) reasons.

Godwin and Mitchell (1982) fitted six decision models to data from persons living in an Oregon coastal commission's jurisdiction and to data from members of five national environmental groups. They found that utilitarian models explained nonelectoral participation, but needed to be extended to include nonexclusionary norms of fairness and taking into account others' happiness. Marwell and Ames' field experiments with small groups of high school students also showed the importance of equity norms in overcoming free-rider tendencies (Marwell and Ames, 1979: 1359). After the 1979 nuclear power plant accident at Three Mile Island, most area residents took a free ride on community activists' efforts to halt the restart of the undamaged reactor (Walsh and Warland, 1983). But among people having the same level of discontent with the emergency, activism was greatest by those persons with strong preaccident solidarity and ideological beliefs. Oliver (1984) discovered that people active in their Detroit neighborhood associations were more pessimistic than token members about their neighbors' willingness to make contributions. Thus, in small organizations, where individual contributions *do* make noticeable differences, the community pessimists allow others to take a free ride on their efforts. Hansen's (1985) time series analysis of membership changes in three national interest groups indicated a strong response to the ebb and flow of public political rather than selective benefits. Research on participation in rebellious collective actions in New York and Hamburg, West Germany, rejected private incentives in favor of so-called soft incentives (public goods) as the major explanatory variables (Muller and Opp, 1986; Opp, 1986, 1988a, b).

A recent set of theoretical and simulation studies of collective action by Pamela Oliver and Gerald Marwell (1988; Oliver, Marwell, and Teixeira, 1985) examined the effects of such factors as group size, interdependence, and heterogeneity on organizing a group for collective action. The problem was to generate a critical mass of interested and resourceful individuals who coordinate their actions against targets of their grievances. The computer simulation findings for varied network structures suggested that heterogeneous groups with more centralized networks are better able to mobilize resources from potential participants through its members' personal organizer networks (i.e., other people whom an individual could directly organize). This organizer-centered effect strengthens with greater information about the potential contribution sizes of others in the group. Personal network size at the individual level translates to group-level importance of centralization. Sheer size of personal networks, not the strength or weakness of ties, dwarfed all other factors' contributions to successful or failed mobilization (Marwell, Oliver, and Prahl, 1988). Because their simulations make simplifying assumptions (e.g., rational individual decision making, perfect information, costs proportional to the number to be organized), the relevance of the theory for real social movements is still unclear.

Finally, Knoke's (1988) analyses of thirty-five professional, recreational, and women's associations in the United States found that selective material inducements had little effect on commitment to and participation in these groups. However, social-recreational benefits (a selective good) and group-oriented normative values (a public good) each had robust effects on increasing members' contributions of time, money, and effort on behalf of the organization. It is important to note that a measure of interpersonal relations – the amount of communication between members and leaders – produced substantial increases in member involvement. The more frequently that members discussed organizational matters with leaders and among themselves, the more they contributed resources, participated in collective actions, and identified themselves with the organization. In associations with political goals, a combination of high communication and strong lobbying (public good) incentives significantly boosted efforts by members to try to influence public officials (see also Knoke and Wood, 1981; Knoke, 1981b, 1989a).

In conclusion, the evidence above suggests that people are motivated to become involved in social movements through their interests in a diversity of public as well as private incentives. The pure utility-maximizing egocentric actor of Olson's model does not fare well in the real world. In conceptualizing human motivation as monocausal and in assuming that individuals make choices in isolation from social influences, Olson's rational men and women fail to act collectively as real people do. His image of an isolated individual choosing to affiliate with a group is at odds with the typical emergence of a movement from established groups. Thus, movements need not offer selective incentives to attract new adherents so much as penalize old members with the loss of member benefits for non-participation.

Equity norms, interpersonal attachments, and political goals figure significantly in many participants' decisions to participate in social movements. In particular, their interests in public goods may be especially potent for movements that try to influence public authorities. Because the goals sought are not personal but public (nonexclusionary) in nature, the primary inducement necessarily is an appeal to a public good rather than to selective benefits. In contrast, for groups that can supply their collective objectives primarily within a closed social system (e.g., a stamp collector's club), public goods seem far less relevant to engaging members' involvements. Hence, the political goals of social movements seem to be a major factor in explaining people's responsiveness to incentives; public goods motivate people who hold major political goals, whereas selective utilitarian inducements are more powerful for involving members of apolitical organizations. Many empirical analyses failed to specify fully the process by which interpersonal ties among movement supporters promote perceptions of and interests in public goods, reinforce normative rather than utilitarian preferences, and enable coordinated actions to take place. The alternative resource mobilization theories have been far more successful than rational actor models in bringing these elements to the fore.

Mobilizing movement resources

An explosion of social movements in the 1960s – civil rights, antiwar, feminist, homosexual, Native American – caught social scientists with their theories down. Psychological and rational actor explanations proved inadequate at both the individual and macrohistorical levels of analysis (Gurr, 1970; Hibbs, 1973; Tarrow, 1988). A detailed reconstruction of a century of civil strife in France, Germany, and Italy highlighted the central significance of shared group identities transmitted through communication networks (Tilly, Tilly, and Tilly, 1975). These collective political actions were primarily power struggles in the building of nation states. Previously excluded populations – peasants, industrial workers, ethnic groups – purposively tried to realize their interests by pooling resources and applying them against the government. These contenders or challengers (Gamson, 1975) sought to enter the national policy, rather than to break away or overthrow it. Their objectives were to become full-fledged polity members, enjoying the recognition of other members and exercising the political rights of low-cost access to government officials and policymakers.

The key factor in the success or failure of a challenging movement was the capacity of a latent population to organize in pursuit of its own interests. For example, artisans experiencing economic hardship during industrialization could be mobilized for joint action only when they strongly identified themselves as a group with distinctive interests and when they possessed extensive, absorbing interpersonal networks able to sustain their opposition. Thus, Marx's notion of a revolutionary *Klasse für sich* required both that proletarians become aware of their common interests in opposition to the bourgeoisie and that they gain access to means for communicating these grievances and planning common strategies (e.g., railways, telegraphs, newspapers, political parties; on the structural inability of the French peasantry to act as a class, see Marx 1852 [1978: 608]). Individuals in a latent group who lack these catnet characteristics (see Chapter 2) are unlikely to relinquish control over resources (money, bodies, arms, or votes) to an organized cadre able to direct a coordinated challenging movement.

From these initial insights a new analysis of social movements began to take root, a perspective that came to be called resource mobilization. Theoretical refinements began to fill in details of a structural model in which interpersonal networks and formal organizations occupied center stage (see Oberschall, 1973: 28; Gamson, 1975; McCarthy and Zald, 1977; Tilly, 1978; Fireman and Gamson, 1979; McAdam, 1982; Jenkins, 1983). Grievances alone could not explain the eruption of insurgency, since dissatisfactions are ubiquitous but uncorrelated with social movements' rises and falls. Instead, the key task became to understand how organized groups acquire collective control over resources needed for challenging the authorities and how these resources are applied to affect social and political changes. A *resource* is anything that permits one social actor to control, provide, or apply a sanction to another: money, facilities, labor, and legitimacy (McCarthy and Zald, 1977: 1220), group size, discretionary time, organizing experience, legal skills, even violence. Mobilization is the process by which such resources become available to a social movement. The crucial concerns are the quantities of resources available to an aggrieved population, the conditions under which supporters will provide them to the movement, the degree to which a movement's formal organizations enjoy autonomy over resource disposal, and how the resources controlled by the opposing government and countermovements affect a movement's success or failure. The theory necessarily spans individual, organizational, and systemic levels of analysis. Our purpose in this chapter is not to recapitulate the approach in detail, but to examine how network concepts and measures are coming to play an increasingly significant role in the analysis of social movement dynamics at all levels.

Earlier collective behavior theories' exaggeration of self-interest calculations obscured two important variables that allow movements to detach
resources from individuals: principle and solidarity (Fireman and Gamson,
1979). People are often motivated to contribute by nonutilitarian values,
principles of altruism, and sacrifice for a greater good. When people see
their fates bound up with those of other group members with whom they
strongly identify, they are not likely to base their decisions to participate
on mere utilitarian cost/benefit calculations. Among the important factors
promoting solidary ties are friendship, kinship, and joint organizational
membership (Fireman and Gamson, 1979: 22). Both variables are implicit
in the concept of cognitive liberation as a necessary precondition for
resource mobilization (McAdam, 1982: 34, 48–51). Potential supporters
are encouraged to join an insurgent movement when they receive a set of
cognitive cues that the status quo is increasingly vulnerable and responsive
to challenge. Buoyed up by the possibility of a breakthrough to the polity,
group supporters are energized to pull together and join in challenging
actions. This collective redefinition of a situation from hopeless to one
where change is possible occurs most readily where supporters are already
integrated into established social networks in a minority community –
neighborhoods, churches, unions, workplaces, voluntary associations, primary groups. These naturally occurring solidary structures permit rapid
communication of information about social and political opportunities and
obstacles. Further, because collective identities and interests are already
socially constructed to some degree within these nonmovement social foci
(Feld, 1981), an insurgency can more easily attach these loyalties to the
movement itself. Rather than arduously building new commitments from
scratch, activists can persuade potential supporters that the movement
organization offers a natural expression of their current solidary sentiments. Thus, resources can be most readily extracted from people who are
central to and involved in, rather than marginal to and alienated from,
community networks.

The resource mobilization perspective differs from earlier collective
behavior theories in assigning to interpersonal networks a basic role in
mobilizing participation. A high valuation of public goods, the emotional
bite of solidary bonds, and the robustness of normative principles are each
strengthened by personal micronets both external to a social movement
organization and within the movement. As the intensity of this reinforcement from one's network alters increases, the importance of nonmaterial
inducements also increases. A recently proposed integration of social psychological principles with resource mobilization theory also placed network elements in its core motivational explanation of participation (Klandermans, 1984). Mobilization campaigns succeed if a person believes that
her or his participation can help to produce the public good. People's
willingness to become involved increases when they anticipate that many

others will join in a collective action, thus increasing the subjective odds of successful results. And this perception increases where the significant alters in an ego's network express their support and desire to participate. Hence, contrary to Olson, collective action aimed at public goods *can* rationally motivate social movement participation, if individuals' networks reinforce perceptions and beliefs that many others will act together. (See Granovetter's [1978] theoretical discussion of threshold models of collective behavior for an attempt to explain how individual conformity to group action may be contingent on perception of others' choices.)

In breathing new life into social movement theory, the resource mobilization perspective focused researchers' attention on the details of participant recruitment and the dynamics of collective action. Some intriguing studies have begun to demonstrate the superiority of a structural approach over the social psychological and rational choice explanations.

Recruiting new members

Earlier explanations of why some people join a particular organization and others do not emphasized individuals' attitudinal dispositions. Thus, alienation, authoritarianism, relative deprivation, and similar constructs were invoked as motives operating without regard to constraining or facilitating contexts (see Jenkins, 1983). In the conceptual revolution propagated by resource mobilization, such dispositional susceptibilities are necessary but not sufficient. More recent recruitment explanations stress structural availability, a variation on the differential association hypothesis popularized by criminologists two generations ago. Recruitment to any social activity requires a preceding contact with a recruiting agent, more often a social intimate than an impersonal actor. People who are linked by preexisting social ties and information exchange relations to centrally located persons in activist networks are more likely to be exposed to a preponderance of social influences (peer pressures) that create or reinforce their predispositions to become involved in movement activities. Through their solidary networks, potential recruits encounter an excess of favorable messages and solidary benefits relative to countervailing experiences. Such well-integrated people are much more likely than peripherally attached individuals to accept and to adhere to the movement's norms about resource contributions, commitments to group goals, and the importance of participating in collective actions. Even a simple request by another person to participate can boost involvement substantially among persons already holding favorable attitudes, as shown by Eckberg's (1988) analysis of physicians signing an antiabortion ad (although Luker [1984: 149] found only one-fifth of California prolife activists were recruited by friends; the others were ideological self-recruits).

The widely observed principle of *social homophily* assures that people know and interact with others most like themselves in social attributes (age, education, race, etc.), attitude and beliefs, and routine activities (Rogers and Bhowmik, 1971; Verbrugge, 1977; McPherson and Smith-Lovin, 1987; Marsden, 1987). Hence, the most readily available potential recruits are network alters who are highly similar to a social movement's current members and consequently have strong social and emotional ties. As a result of this like-attracts-like principle, social movement organizations tend over time to develop increasingly homogeneous memberships that are relatively isolated from the surrounding social system. Movements carve out fairly narrow niches in a population, drawing their sustaining resources from specialized social regions (McPherson, 1983). Rapid resource depletion can follow. Information tends to recirculate among those who already possess it, and new ideas have difficulty taking root. To break out of these confines, social movements must rely on those members who have or can develop social contacts with broader ranges. They must recruit new participants from larger pools by exploiting their members' weak ties, which ramify outward, rather than by drawing on members' strong ties, which spiral inward to impacted networks. The expansion principle appears to be "lead me to green pastures."

Movements enmeshed in structurally insulated and impacted communities are likely to flounder and wither. For example, an ethnic social movement whose community is segregated from the larger society may experience great difficulty in expanding its membership beyond the ethnic boundaries. A labor movement may be unable to forge class solidarities when the micronetworks of an industry's workers are constrained within familial, occupational, or racial segments. Although a movement's initial expansion may be rapid, as available interpersonal bonds are drawn upon to recruit new members, it reaches saturation at the point where solidary ties are too weak or nonexistent. Thus, social movement temporal recruitment patterns should bear a striking resemblance to the general S-curve dynamics of innovation diffusion (Coleman, Katz, and Menzel, 1966). On a time graph, an initial period of slow growth is followed by a sudden and rapidly rising tide of participation and a subsequent leveling off as new recruits cannot be found. A classic example of how weak ties foster the rapid spread of collective action occurred when the thousand students participating in the 1964 Mississippi Freedom Summer project returned that fall to their campuses. They were able to draw on their interpersonal connections both within and between campuses to foster a large and loosely knit congeries of campus antiwar movements (McAdam, 1987).

The structural availability principle was especially clear in research on conversion to religious social movements (Lofland, 1985; Snow, Zurcher, Jr., and Eckland-Olson, 1980; Stark and Bainbridge, 1980). Preexisting and emergent intimate networks both fed and nurtured these movements.

Religious sects as ideologically divergent as the Moonies, Mormons, and Nichiren Shoshu Buddhists found most of their new adherents among the relatives, friends, and acquaintances of current members. These recruiters deliberately withheld disorienting discussions of beliefs and ideologies until the new member was thoroughly encapsulated socially within the religious community (Lofland, 1985): "Rather than being drawn to the group because of its ideology, people were drawn to the ideology because of their ties to the group" (Stark and Bainbridge, 1980: 1378–79). So powerful was the perceived influence of networks that severing all ties to external contacts was a common tactic to protect and insulate cult members against exposure to conflicting ideas. By eliminating linkages that might expose its members to countervailing viewpoints, the religious group sought to dominate the individual totally; a cult's power derives from its ability to sanction the thoughts and deeds of members who lack recourse to alternative social supports. At the extreme, cult domination may lead to devastating outcomes such as the mass murder-suicides at Jonestown and the credit-card scam of Lyndon LaRouche's political movement. The relevance of such recruitment processes for less totalistic social movements remains to be determined.

Interpersonal networks may prove very helpful for understanding how movement participants develop common beliefs that facilitate collective action. Initial recruits may bring ideas and perceptions at some variance with the movement's ideology. Unless they can be socialized to adopt the movement's perspective on affairs, new recruits are likely to drop out or at least to withhold their resources. At worst, bitter and destructive factional fights may erupt over the meaning, purpose, goals, and tactics of the movement, imperiling its viability. The history of revolutionary movements is replete with such fractures. To enable action toward collective goals, movement members must ultimately align their frames of reference to a common standard. *Frame alignment* is "the linkage of individual and SMO [social movement organization] interpretive orientations, such that some set of individual interests, values, and beliefs and SMO activities, goals, and ideology are congruent and complementary" (Snow, Rochford, Jr., Worden, and Benford, 1986: 464). Mutual understandings about costs and benefits, the reactions of significant social others, and the probability of an action's success or failure in producing the desired public good filter through each individual's interpretive framework. For coordinated actions to occur, some consistency must be reached among potential participants about these elements. Snow and his colleagues suggested four frame alignment processes – bridging, amplification, extension, and transformation – that enable individuals to integrate their beliefs with those of a social movement. Obscured in their presentation is how interpersonal ties foster or impede development of shared injustice frameworks that compel collective action. Movement leaders are a primary source of interest and value perspectives, but encounters among rank-and-file participants would also seem critical for sustaining any common set of meanings. Presumably, the old hands persuade the greenhorns to accept their way of thinking and acting and sanction those who do not comply. The stronger the personal, emotional bonds between new and old members, the more likely successful frame alignment will occur. For example, White's (1989) discussion of how supporters of the Irish Republican Army came to favor violent opposition in reaction to increased British repression contains several hints that this delegitimation was a mix of emotional, political, and rational cognitive processes sustained in small kin and friendship circles. However, such processes have not been observed in sufficient detail to determine the precise effects that personal networks play in creating the common social psychological orientations necessary to sustain collective action.

Research on both the Dutch antinuclear movement and the American civil rights movement underscored the centrality of network connections for micromobilization. Klandermans and Oegema (1987) analyzed participants in the Netherlands' enormous 1983 antinuclear demonstration (one-half million marchers or one in twenty-five of the nation's inhabitants; an equivalent figure in the United States would be 10 million!). By separating the mobilization process into four steps, they found that participation involved a sequence of decisions. Large numbers of potential recruits dropped out at each stage. Further discrediting the rational choice model, they showed that only a minority of participants firmly believed the demonstration would halt the Dutch government's deployment of cruise missiles. Those persons who actually attended the rally were likely to be better educated, seeming to reflect their greater awareness and sensitivity to economic and political conditions. Instead, the evidence revealed that the better-educated rally participants were disproportionately represented because of their formal and informal affinity ties, primarily to small radical parties, *and* because they were reached by mobilization efforts of antinuke activists. The broader population of sympathizers lacked these interpersonal ties and could not be mobilized despite their favorable attitudinal predispositions. These findings are consistent with earlier work by McPhail and Miller (1973) showing that the assembly process at an unscheduled basketball rally depended heavily on word of mouth to inform supporters of the time and place of the gathering (see also Aveni, 1977; McPhail and Wohlstein, 1986). Mobilization processes necessarily rely on interpersonal networks to increase the probability that supporters will be informed of collective actions, but networks are not sufficient to guarantee successful mobilization. Mass mobilization efforts also require communicating information to potential supporters to persuade them of the potential payoff from participation. This dynamic process works through political influence rather than dominance, as discussed in Chapter 1.

Using archival documents written mostly by white college students who applied to join the Mississippi Freedom Summer voter registration project in 1964, McAdam (1986) found that two critical factors explaining participation were the number of organizations and the number of other participants to which an individual was tied. Who went and who withdrew from this high-risk activity (three students were murdered by the Ku Klux Klan and others were beaten) was not explained by applicants' attitudes, as expressed in essays written by a pool of more than 1,000 applicants across the nation. But when the documents were coded for membership in campus activist organizations and personal ties to other applicants, both variables strongly predicted the candidates' subsequent involvements. When decomposed, the most predictive factors were strong ties to another participant or to a known activist (the applicant was likely to go to the South) or a strong tie to another withdrawn applicant (increasing the applicant's chances of withdrawing). Social ties seemed to induce involvement through both positive and negative influence processes. A decision to go to Mississippi would find support from other participants, whereas a decision to withdraw would result in a loss of face. People without ties experienced neither support nor ostracism and thus found it easier to drop out.

To further decompose this late phase in the mobilization process, Fernandez and McAdam (1988, 1989) and McAdam and Fernandez (1990) examined interpersonal networks among the Mississippi Freedom Summer applicants at the Universities of California (forty students) and Wisconsin (twenty-three students). They analyzed matrices of applicants' overlapping group memberships that were formed by counting the number of campus organizations in which each pair of students had a common membership. These simple shared memberships could not account for the decision to go or drop out, after controlling for personal attributes such as age, family income, and past activism. The crucial factor was the individual's structural location within the campus multiorganizational field, as measured by the person's prominence scores. That is, an individual's prominence in a network is a function of the centrality of the other persons to whom one is connected (Bonacich, 1972; Knoke and Burt, 1983). Network prominence was highly significant in predicting the Wisconsin students' mobilization, but was not significant in the multivariate equation for the Berkeley activists. The researchers argued that an important contextual effect had occurred. The network density among Berkeley activists (.145) was much higher than that among Wisconsin students (.083). Coupled with a long tradition of radical activity in the California community and its virtual absence in Madison, structural position was less critical to integrating the Berkeley network. Even people in peripheral positions had access to information and were subjected to compelling social influence. But for the less tightly knit Wisconsin network, occupying a structurally prominent position served as a compensatory mobilizing process.

Inside movement organizations

If evidence is scant about the importance of networks for recruiting social movement participants, data on the role of network processes within movement organizations are even harder to come by. Some of these concerns are dealt with in Chapter 4, which mainly considers work organizations. But, SMOs have unique features that warrant special attention here. In natural systems approaches, organizational structures reflect unplanned and spontaneous processes that enhance organizational success and survival. Social movement organizations do not face the technical efficiency constraints or the market mechanisms of control encountered by production organizations. They are freer to adopt shared, institutionalized structures that reflect prevailing social norms about what movement organizations should look like and how they should operate (Pfeffer, 1982: 244–6). Structures for communications, decision making, and administration all reflect the distribution of power among organization participants. Centralization of decision making concerns the way that an organization reaches binding decisions to allocate its collective resources to various goals. These objectives may be dictated by one powerful actor, be negotiated within a dominant coalition, or be decided consensually among all participants (Scott, 1987: 272–7). These different governance patterns within an SMO are alternative conceptions about the importance of member control and collective goals.

Jo Freeman's analysis of the resource mobilization efforts within the feminist movement exemplified the problems. She pointed to the dilemma of using scarce resources for maintaining the organization or seeking the movement's equity goals: "[A] centralized movement devotes minimal resources to group maintenance needs, focusing them instead on goal attainment," whereas a "decentralized movement on the other hand, is compelled to devote major resources to group maintenance" (Freeman, 1979: 183). Centralized movements can often better attain short-range institutional change goals, but at the cost of organizational survival. Decentralized movements can achieve person-oriented attitude changes "through recruitment and conversion in which organizational survival is a dominant concern" (Freeman, 1979: 183). The older branch of women's liberation (such organizations as the National Organization for Women and the Women's Equity Action League) tended toward centralization, whereas the younger branch rejected national structure, hierarchy, and division of labor. Freeman argued that although organizational structures were not specifically created to accomplish goals, once in place they constrained the strategic alternatives open to movement organizations.

Almost universally, SMOs purport to be participatory democracies whose constitutions enshrine the priority of member preferences in collective decision making. In practice, oligarchy seems the likelier fate for many mass membership organizations with long lives (Michels, 1949), although instances of genuine member control do occur (e.g., the League of Women Voters: Tannenbaum, 1968; a crisis center: Mansbridge, 1980). Organizational size, member apathy, and absence of formal mechanisms to reinforce participation (e.g., local chapter meetings, referenda, open communication channels) can conspire to restrict the scope of member decision participation. The more that power is concentrated in a few hands, the less reliably can an SMO depend on its mass membership to supply essential resources. Widespread member involvement in collective decision making promotes commitment and attachment to an organization, which in turn increases the collectivity's ability to obtain members' personal resources for collective use (see Knoke and Wood, 1981: 70–90; and Knoke, 1981b, 1988, 1989a, for evidence from associations). However, SMOs with more centralized decision-making processes may be judged as trustworthy and accountable by potential external constituents and sponsors, such as foundations and government agencies (Meyer and Rowan, 1977; see also Chapter 4).

Bureaucracy and centralization are well known to covary positively for work organizations; larger corporations are more differentiated but less bureaucratized and centralized in decision making than smaller ones, contrary to the Weberian model (Scott, 1987: 243–5). In large corporations, economies of scale reduce bureaucratic administration, decentralization increases to prevent overwhelming of top administrators, and standardization promotes routine decision making. Whether this relationship holds in SMOs is not clear. Gamson's (1975) study of fifty-three historical U.S. SMOs found bureaucracy and centralization to be unrelated (p. 94), though both structural dimensions were positively related to organizational success in winning acceptance and new advantages from the polity. Both dimensions appeared to interact with factionalism, such that bureaucratic groups were better able to overcome the debilitating effects of internal dissidence, while the combination of centralization with bureaucracy produced the most successful outcomes. Whether bureaucracy and centralization interact to affect resource management decisions in contemporary associations has not been determined.

Jane Mansbridge, analyzing the failure to pass the Equal Rights Amendment despite substantial feminist movement efforts, passionately advocated movement organizational arrangements that promote accurate information and dialogue: "On the organizational level, more democracy usually means better information" (Mansbridge, 1986: 192–3). She argued that such open structures as flat hierarchies, rotating offices, team projects, incentives to communicate outside usual channels, and brainstorming sessions where minorities are encouraged to speak were all essential to clarify group goals and build consensual norms: "Because individuals cannot usually come to understand what they really want without the different options and perspectives provided by discussion, they need organizations" (p. 193). She seemed to imply that extensive internal and external communication networks were indispensable for maintaining a collective memory about the lessons of experience and for avoiding the arrogance of insular ideological purity that cuts off SMOs from useful alliances with sympathizers who might support, but not be totally committed to, the organization's views.

One study of movement activism used network data gathered for Mansbridge's study of the Women's Center, part of the younger branch of the women's movement. Of the forty-three women who regularly participated in group projects, those who occupied prominent positions within an informal social contact network were far more likely to participate in the center's activities, after taking account of their personal family and job constraints, than were the socially peripheral women (Fernandez and Rowe, 1988). Indeed, social contagion seemed to occur, with women adjusting their participation levels to correspond to the activism of other women to whom they were socially linked. The implication of this microlevel study is obvious; to understand why certain people participate in social movement organizations, one must take into account their availability through interpersonal relationships. Of course, network selectivity on the basis of activism rather than a causal effect of networks is a plausible alternative explanation. However, ideological predispositions seem insufficient in the absence of structural connections that permit persuasion, contagion, and other influence inducements to ensue. The people most susceptible to mobilization are those whose preexisting or emergent social and communication exchange networks connect them to other prominent activists. The price paid for prominence is exposure to the call to the ramparts.

Linkages among organizations

The microlevel networks among movement participants are paralleled at the macrolevel by the interorganizational linkages among SMOs and their sponsors. Curtis and Zurcher (1973) identified a two-tiered "multi-organizational field," which at the organization level was "established by joint activities, staff, boards of directors, target clientele, resources, etc." (p. 53), and at the individual level by networks constructed from members' multiple affiliations. These intertwined phenomena reflect the dualism of persons and collectivities that is observable in any diagram or matrix mapping people's multiple memberships in organizations (McPherson, 1982; Breiger, 1974; Fernandez and McAdam, 1989). Thus, if A is a set of actors and O is a set of organizations (or events), the $[A \times O]$ set of relations can be postmultiplied by its transpose to generate an actor-to-actor network of shared memberships $[A \times A]$ such as those investigated in the previous section.

Alternatively, the [O × A] set can be postmultiplied by its transpose to create an organization-by-organization network [O × O] whose elements are the number of common members. Similar mapping could depict inter-organizational resource exchanges, sanctions, and other transactions. Depending on one's theoretical and research objectives, either of these actor-organization networks might be emphasized to the exclusion of the other, but with the full knowledge that flipping the perspective by 90 degrees will yield a different insight into the structural relations of persons and organizations. For many purposes of understanding collective outcomes in a social movement, the interorganizational network structure may prove the more useful perspective.

The success or failure of a social movement in reaching its goals of social and political change hinges only partly on its ability to mobilize resources. Movements typically consist of several organizational entities, SMOs that may simultaneously cooperate and compete with one another for resources, leadership, and influence over tactics and strategy (McCarthy and Zald, 1973). The Big Four of the black civil rights movement are perhaps the best-known examples: the National Association for the Advancement of Colored People (NAACP), Student Nonviolent Coordinating Committee, Congress of Racial Equality, and Southern Christian Leadership Conference. These organizations "jockeyed with one another for influence over the movement, as well as the increased shares of publicity and money generated by protest activity" (McAdam, 1982: 154; also Aveni, 1978). SMOs also confront institutions with varied interests in maintaining the status quo. Some polity members may be sympathetic supporters willing to lend resources and legitimacy to a struggling SMO, for example, a union that supports a farm workers boycott (Jenkins and Perrow, 1977). But, many groups that benefit from contemporary power arrangements do not want their privileged situations disturbed. The supportive and opposing groups – especially counter-movements (Lo, 1982) and the state's military, police, judicial, legislative, and executive institutions – comprise the *opportunity structure* that a social movement faces at a given historical moment (Tilly, 1978: 55; Kitschelt, 1986). Opportunity factors include the degree of openness of the political system, the stability of political alignments, the presence of allies and support groups, divisions within elites and their tolerance for protest, and the policy-making capacity of the government (Tarrow, 1988: 429). Analyzing the structure of interactions among SMOs and between SMOs and the polity members is critical to any comprehensive understanding of a movement's rise and fall. As with internal dynamics, the network of power relations between these organizations must come under increasingly rigorous theoretical and empirical scrutiny.

Resource mobilization theorists have disputed about an obvious basic dilemma: Because the deprived groups seeking to enter the polity have major disadvantages, they are unlikely to have sufficient resources; but how can they adequately assemble resources to launch and sustain a successful movement? At present two solutions have been proposed, the elite patronage-professional organizer model (McCarthy and Zald, 1973, 1977) and the political process model (McAdam, 1982; Jenkins and Eckert, 1986), representing contrasting views about the importance of external elites and indigenous resources. The patronage-organizer model draws from entrepreneurial theories in assuming that the political elites outside the aggrieved group is composed of willing and eager contributors to challenging movements. Although a mass base of the deprived is essential for occasional demonstrations and protests, sustained mass commitment is difficult and large memberships are expensive to maintain. Because social movements by definition represent the disadvantaged, few of their constituents have financial resources or adequate leadership skills. A social movement can improve its efficiency by reducing costs and centralizing decision making.

Both goals are accomplished when the movement organization is primarily run by a cadre of skilled and dedicated professional activists (Mansbridge, 1986, 188–248). Forging ties to wealthy elites and affluent middle-class sympathizers is also essential. These actors are an external conscience constituency of nonmembers who sympathize with the plight of the excluded population (McCarthy and Zald, 1977). Coopting institutional resources from foundations, churches, universities, government agencies, and the mass media provides the SMO with much of the money, skills, and legitimacy it needs. An effective social movement thus involves complex network linkages among professional SMO leaders and their external elite sponsors. The indigenous mass base is small or nonexistent and unnecessary to conduct the SMO's business. Because the key transactions involve exchanging money and leadership resources, the social structure of the professional organizer model consists of dominance relations. The unequal resource holdings of movements and their sponsors can raise troubling problems of resource dependency and control over the direction of movement activity. Dare an SMO challenge the hand that feeds it?

Reacting against the professional organizer model, which he considered inadequate, Doug McAdam proposed a political process model. Although societal resources are concentrated in a few hands, the possessors of wealth and power are fundamentally conservative. They have vested interests in preserving the status quo. Given that most elites are unwilling to underwrite movements for social change, the excluded groups are forced to generate their own resources for collective action. From his detailed study of the southern black civil rights insurgency, McAdam (1982, 1987) concluded that by the mid-1950s this minority community had developed sufficient leadership, organizational skills, mass base, and communication networks to undertake a sustained challenge to Jim Crow segregation. Virtually all of these resources were supplied indigenously. Both personal and interorganizational networks were key structural elements in making the resources available for collective protest. For example, the accelerating diffusion across the South of the lunch counter sit-in innovation in February and March 1960 occurred only in communities where a configuration of black urban churches, black colleges, and NAACP chapters had previously created a densely integrated network of leaders and masses that could be mobilized rapidly. Mobilization of entire church congregations took place overnight to provide sit-in volunteers, hold vigils, transport demonstrators, and raise bail (McAdam, 1982: 129; see Morris [1981, 1984] for extensive details about what he called "local movement centers"). Contrary to predictions from the professional organizer model, outside financial support poured into black SMO coffers following the movement-initiated activity, rather than the reverse (McAdam, 1982: 124, Jenkins and Eckert, 1986). Thus, the political process model gave a more accurate account of insurgent movement dynamics by attending to structural relations within a social movement. These recent analyses of the civil rights era, the women's movement, and protest in poor Latin American communities (Eckstein, 1988) emphasized that social movement theorists and researchers must include intra- and interorganizational networks in their explanations of the rise and subsequent fall of insurgent activities.

The block recruitment phenomenon, where an entire preexisting organization such as a church or voluntary association joins a movement en masse, emphasizes the networks of relationships among leaders of different SMOs (Oberschall, 1973: 125; Wilson and Orum, 1976). Movement leaders typically exhibit differing levels of involvement. Whereas most participants are only peripherally involved, there is always a small, committed core – the cadre – who make decisions and whose lives revolve around the movement. These key players are the nodes that link organizations and individuals within a movement and/or they may provide connections between one entire social movement and another, for example, between the antiwar and civil rights movements. The interorganizational network may vary contextually. For example, Rosenthal and colleagues' (1985) examination of the highly overlapped organizational memberships among nineteenth-century women's social club and reform organization leaders in New York state revealed more strongly bounded clusters within national leadership networks than within local community networks. Given the greater local scarcity of resources, especially of members, local organizations could not enjoy the rivalry and ideological distinctiveness preserved by the national organizations. Hence, the local context was a small, dense network, while the national network was more differentiated.

Impressive evidence for the impact of block recruitment appeared in Killian's (1984) account of the civil rights movement in Tallahassee, Florida. Although he favored a spontaneity interpretation, Killian gave impressive evidence for an intensive SMO network structure. One movement leader was concomitantly an official at Florida A & M University and president of the local black ministers alliance. A second leader was a member of the alliance and also president of the local NAACP. At that time, the university had a student chapter of the NAACP. A fourth organization similar to a black rotary club also existed. The NAACP, alliance, and the civic club eventually merged into a single organization that assumed direction of the local civil rights movement from that point on. While Killian cited the lack of formal organization prior to the merger, we emphasize the network connections within and between these organizations through both leaders and members. Perhaps most crucial was the tie to the university, since the student body provided the mass base that was called out for demonstrations. This infrastructure in a local multiorganizational field clearly enabled rapid mass mobilization under crisis circumstances.

The primary resource that poor southern blacks could mobilize was their willingness to disrupt business as usual in central city shopping districts. However, their ultimate success was contingent on the movement's interactions with southern white opponents and an initially neutral national government. Where local and state white authorities and countermovement agitators overreacted by beating and jailing the protestors, as in Birmingham and Selma, Alabama, they created more movement supporters and forced the federal authorities to intervene on the side of the challengers (Hubbard, 1968; Garrow, 1978). But where savvy mayors and police chiefs used legal tactics against the demonstrators and thus forestalled federal help, the black insurgencies fizzled, as in Albany, Georgia, and Danville, Virginia (Barkan, 1984; McAdam, 1982: 177). Similarly, the women's movement's effort to pass the Equal Rights Amendment failed under the increasingly sophisticated assaults of its business opponents and the movement's own ineptness at forging alliances with middle-of-the-road conservative legislators (Mansbridge, 1986: 149–64).

The political process perspective highlights the relative magnitudes of domination and influence resources that opposing sides bring to bear on social movements' demands for recognition and access to the polity. When the balance of moral, political, and financial resources lies with a movement's opponents, repression succeeds. A movement triumphs by combining resources extracted from its indigenous population with the political resources of external allies, especially the state's institutions, to tip the scales in the movement's favor. A central element of every social movement analysis must be to uncover the structural relations among social movement organizations, supporters, opponents, and authorities. Most critical are the preexisting and emergent networks through which these organizations' domination resources and influence communications are pooled, exchanged, and coordinated in struggles to win or resist political change. Until theorists and researchers bring these interorganizational relations explicitly into view, their accounts of movement dynamics are certain to remain premature. Nowhere is the call for inclusion of network principles more urgent than in the analysis of revolutionary upheavals.

Revolutionary movements

Revolutions are rapid, violent displacements of one set of power holders with another (Tilly, 1978: 191; Gamson, 1975: 41). The handful of paradigmatic revolutions in the modern era (France, Russia, China) each involved dramatic, large-scale popular uprisings, violent defeats of the ancien régime, and the capture of state power by wielders of new ideologies. A successful revolution is distinguishable from a palace coup or putsch by the changes in social class structure that accompany the political transformation of the society (Skocpol, 1979a: 4). The contrast in outcomes between reformative social movements and transformative revolutions raises the question of whether a single theoretical explanation can suffice for both phenomena. Some theorists sought the common causes of diverse collective political violence, with revolution as just one of several possible outcomes (Goldstone, 1980). Others, for example Moore (1966) and Tilly (1978: 189–222; 1985), implied that the proximate causes of mass rebellions and their successful revolutionary outcomes require unique constellations of social and military-political forces that differ qualitatively from challenging social movements merely demanding access to the polity. Resolution of this controversy is not possible in this book, but we will briefly assess the usefulness of structural approaches for analyzing revolutionary movements.

Two types of violent revolutionary actions seem especially amenable to structural analysis: (1) protracted rural rebellions, as in China, Cuba, Vietnam, and Nicaragua and (2) urban insurrections, such as 1917 Petrograd, Algiers, Teheran, and Manila. In both cases, insurgents confront the dual tasks of legitimating their opposition to the government among an aggrieved population of potential supporters and of neutralizing or winning over some portion of the regime's military forces (Russell, 1974). The key to a successful outcome lies in the insurgents' social and political connections with the populace and the armed forces.

When rebels are recruited from the indigenous rural population and maintain strong familial and ethnic ties to those local communities, they can more readily spread their message of alternative sovereignty. Mao's metaphor of Red Chinese guerrillas swimming like fish in the sea of the people made a virtue out of the necessity for rebels to organize their military units on a decentralized basis in constant direct contact with the peasantry (Kim, 1969). The insular, cohesive villages of rural South Vietnam were ideally suited to constructing a vast, complex network of Viet Minh cells that sustained a low-grade revolutionary struggle through decades until the conventional war showdown between the North Vietnamese army and the U.S.-backed ARVN settled the conflict (FitzGerald, 1972; Popkin, 1979). In contrast to these indigenous rebellions, Che Guevara's effort to export Cuban revolutionary fervor to Bolivia's highlands went down in ignominious defeat in the face of the peasantry's isolation and suspicion of outlanders (Debray, 1975; Daniels, 1968). Students of revolution have long pointed to the patterns of agrarian economic and social class relations as preconditions for a society's revolutionary upheaval (e.g., Moore, 1966; Paige, 1975). The precise course and outcome of an uprising depend on how well guerrillas integrate their cadres into the indigenous populace, in turn a function of how such impersonal forces as international commercialization of agriculture, international wars and depressions, and government repression affect the local network ties among villagers.

Urban insurrections, with their colorful barricades and daring assaults on government buildings, have continually captured the romantic imaginations of writers, filmmakers, and scholars. The twin revolutions of Petrograd and February and October 1917 certainly provide the most extensively documented case. The rapid rise of Bolshevik support (from fewer than 2,000 to more than 30,000 party members in four months; Rabinowitz, 1976: xxviii) and Lenin's cold-blooded plot against the hapless Provisional Government served as textbook for many subsequent would-be imitators. Anyone who reads detailed accounts of the numerous committees, meetings, strikes, marches, rallies, and riots of that confused period, whether by partisans like Trotsky (1957) or patient scholars like Schapiro (1984) and Rabinowitch (1976), must come away impressed by the Bolsheviks' exhaustive grass-roots networking that went into the preparation for the final uprising (Rabinowitch, 1976: 216). Party agitators concentrated on infiltrating and propagandizing neighborhood, factory, and garrison soviets (councils). They played on growing popular discontent with the liberal regime set up in the wake of the overthrown monarchy. To be sure, their prospects were immeasurably aided by the hardships from three years of war and the incompetence of the crisis-ridden Kerensky government in responding to popular grievances over land and peace. But the party of Lenin was the only social organization to have a clear vision of how to exploit these conditions to seize power that could transform a corrupt and faltering society. The top priority was neutralizing, then winning over, the support of the city's military guards. The war's early decimation of the army's professional officer corps brought numerous replacements from lower social classes who sympathized with their peasant troops' desires for land reform and to avoid being shipped to the front (Schapiro, 1984: 91). A presumptively spontaneous garrison mutiny by demoralized soldiers and hot-headed party cadres ("July Days"), quickly put down by loyalist troops, underscored the inability of grievances alone to spark a revolution. Much hard organizing effort was required to recoup, then to extend the Bolsheviks' position as vanguard of the revolution. By October, the Bolshevik Central Committee and the Petrograd Soviet's Military Revolutionary Committee were able to provide the essential coordinating capacity to direct a successful seizure of Petrograd, which nevertheless still required considerable improvisation as events unfolded (Schapiro, 1984: 132; Trotsky, 1957: 276–301, Vol. II). The tenuousness of the Bolshevik political networks in the countryside assured that the final triumph would be a long, drawn-out, and bloody affair, ultimately settled by resort to military might under Trotsky's brilliant direction.

Several contemporary instances of urban mass insurrections differ from the Bolshevik model in the mobilization of collective action by coalitions of regime opponents, rather than the conspiratorial uprising controlled by a single party. The 1979 overthrow of the Shah of Iran was accomplished by joint efforts of Islamic fundamentalists and aggrieved middle-class secularists. This marriage of convenience between mosque and bazaar shortly foundered on the incompatible ideological frameworks for reconstituting the post-Shah polity (Bakhash, 1984; Milani, 1988). In the Philippines, the 1986 people power coalition that brought down the rapacious Marcos kleptocracy combined elements from the church, students, middle class, and the military (Johnson, 1987) as well as the eventual withdrawal of support by the Reagan administration. At the decisive showdown, thousands of unarmed Filipinos responded to a call by Cardinal Jaime Sin (with the backing of the Vatican) to interpose their bodies between 200 rebel troops holed up in Camp Crame and a column of loyalist marine tanks. A helicopter squadron, ordered to rocket the base, instead landed inside the compound and their crews embraced the rebel leaders. The ouster of Marcos marked the high point of opposition unity; within months, President Aquino's government was itself under constant threat of military coup. The untold events behind Beijing's Tiananmen Square in the spring of 1989 may some day be revealed as the last gasp of a morally degenerate Communist Party gerontocracy. Despite extensive world media coverage of the peaceful occupation, the striking students and workers failed to forge essential alliances with the peasantry, emergent urban bourgeoisie, and People's Liberation Army factions that might have shielded them from the brutal massacre. Whether subsequent arrests and executions of the democracy movement leaders can successfully thwart incipient networks for a bloodier rebellion, only time will reveal.

Enough circumstantial evidence exists in primary and secondary accounts to support the general proposition that structural relationships among insurgents, supporters, the government, and the military are critical to the development and outcome of revolutionary struggles. What is now needed are careful comparative studies of successful and failed rebellions that determine which network factors are critical in swinging victory to the insurgents' or the regimes' side. We suspect that the same features that dispose

participation in high-risk social reform movements will also dispose recruitment to revolutionary actions: close personal ties to other movement
participants, communication channels disproportionately carrying challenging messages, formal organizations that coordinate resources and personnel. What may differentiate the two processes is not their mobilization
and collective action processes, but whether the government is responsive
to legitimate demands for redress of grievances or seeks instead to crush its
opposition. That reaction itself depends on the interorganizational networks of influence and domination within which the government is embedded.

Looking forward

Sufficient evidence appears in the scattered sources cited above to conclude
that social networks are fundamental features of every social movement.
Much hard work lies ahead to bring the structural perspective into the
mainstream of social movement analysis. Work should proceed at both the
microlevel (individual participant) and macrolevel (inter-organizational),
with the most fruitful efforts attempting to bridge both units of analysis and
to track their growth and decay over time. Conceptualizing a movement's
boundaries is critical, because mapping the linkages among actors requires
clearly delineated nodes. Boundary identification is highly problematic,
because joining a social change movement usually does not require taking
out a membership card. Their boundaries are porous and fuzzy, as numerous persons and organizations move into and out of contention over time.
Most often, analysts expediently apply a behavioral criterion; a person
belongs to a movement when he or she participates in some significant
portion of its activities. Although it superficially solves the membership
question, it sidesteps thorny issues of how participants view themselves and
their actions in relation to others, both inside and outside the movement.
More theoretical effort must be devoted to unraveling this tangled skein of
subjective self-identities, behavioral involvement, and interpersonal bonding that pulls people into high-risk collective actions for public goods goals.
Researchers may recover some useful network data from archival documents. But they must increasingly gather new relational information directly from contemporary movement participants, sympathizers, and opponents. This effort requires much ingenuity and persistence in gaining the
trust and cooperation of movement activists, who often see academic
researchers as distractions, if not outright hostile intruders. But few sub-
stitutes for direct observation and in-depth interviews are available for
obtaining the necessary information about structural relationships and
their subjective meaning.

4   *Organizational power*

with Naomi J. Kaufman

During the 1980s, corporate America endured another of its periodic merger manias. Billion-dollar companies snatched up multimillion-dollar firms, and were bought out in turn by still larger corporations. Some famous household names changed ownership and their operations were broken apart to pay off mountains of debt. Concentration within several industries increased substantially. A junk bond salesman became one of the nation's richest men, but was indicted for trading on insider information. Despite a historic stock market crash in 1987, the following year saw the biggest leveraged buyout of all time; RJR Nabisco, recently formed by merging a tobacco giant with a food conglomerate, became the target of a takeover bid by its president. The board of directors angrily rejected his initial bid as undervalued and sought outside offers. After frantic weeks of stock auctions by four groups, the board turned control of the company over to a Wall Street leveraged-buyout specialist for $25 billion in cash and securities. "Oreos will still be in children's lunch boxes," promised the winner (*Time*, December 12, 1988: 56). But with RJR Nabisco's stock price doubling in just six weeks, analysts predicted that as much as one-quarter of the firm would have to be sold to pay off its debt.

The RJR Nabisco fight dramatically depicted the interweaving of political and economic power in modern organizations; the internal clash of opposing strategies, the massive amounts of resources, the alliances formed among organizations, the fates of thousands of employees and shareholders hanging in the balance. Most people are involved with a variety of contemporary organizations. Often unaware of how organizations affect them, people would be astonished to realize how extensively organizations pervade almost every minute of their lives, from the radio station whose tunes wake them in the morning to the pharmaceutical company whose tablets put them to sleep at night. How much control does the city government have over the garbage and toxic waste we toss out? Can our banks turn information about our accounts over to credit agencies? Has the factory depersonalized the workplace by auditing our productivity with its computer monitors? What consequences will the grade school's tests have on our children's chances to get into college? Are we controlling organizations or are they controlling us? Although organizations are not organisms – they do not have a brain or a heart in the biological sense – they are commonly described as though they were unitary living entities. They make decisions, set and accomplish goals, require inputs of resources and disposal of outputs, sometimes express civic responsibility, and occasionally act in a benevolent philanthropic manner. In truth, they frequently outlive the individuals who work for or come into contact with them. Given the proliferation of organizations in modern societies and their unequal resources to people, researchers must be concerned with all aspects of their power.

Defining formal organizations

Weber provided one of the earliest definitions of formal organizations. He concluded that a corporate organization is a type of social relationship having an administrative staff engaged continuously in purposeful activity of a specific kind. A more recent definition of a formal organization is a goal-directed, boundary-maintaining activity system (Aldrich, 1979:4). The emphasis on the organizational boundary distinguishes actors and activities that are considered inside from those that are outside but can possibly affect the entire organization (Aldrich, 1979: 221; Aldrich and Marsden, 1988: 362). Boundaries maintained by organizational authorities or the participants themselves are more or less based on the type of organization. Total institutions, such as prisons, asylums, convents, and military units, enforce clearly defined activities that cut off most of their members from outside contacts. These organizations rigorously specify individuals' expected roles, and the authorities enforce conformity to the collective norms by coercive means (Etzioni, 1975: 12–13). Less rigid organizations, such as volunteer groups, maintain only informal boundaries; for example, the Red Cross counts as a member anyone who has ever donated blood. These porous boundaries are defined mainly by the members themselves, and the leaders have little power over them (Knoke, 1989a). Members of a given organization can, and frequently do, participate in several other organizations at the same time, increasing the fuzziness about where one organization ends and another begins. Boundaries are constantly being transformed as memberships grow, contract, and diversify.

Empirical boundaries are drawn somewhat ambiguously, but they are not arbitrary because differences occur among the processes internal to the organization and those that occur externally. Therefore, the distinction between intra- and interorganizational relations remains useful in structuring an analytical discussion. *Intraorganizational* relationships involve structures inside an organization's boundary. Researchers on intraorganizational elements seek to understand how internal structures and processes arise and change. Employee career mobility within a firm, managerial decision making, and the influence of unions and boards of directors on corporate strategy are a few of the relevant lines of inquiry. *Interorganizational* relationships take place between entire organizations. This aspect of organizations has focused on the transfer of information, obtaining resources, mimetic processes, and the effect of interlocking directorates on organizational strategy. Most organizational researchers view the individual organization as an *open* system rather than as a *closed* system unaffected by elements outside its boundaries (Thompson, 1967; Scott, 1988). The environment is thus viewed as a critical determinant of organizational structure and process because each organization is simultaneously dependent on and interdependent with other organizations.

Although the study of intra- and interorganizational relations has been artificially segregated for too long, theorists are slowly realizing the necessity of combining these complementary approaches (Fombrun, 1986). A more complete understanding of organizational processes will unfold by linking the two. Given the historical development of organizational theory, for the purposes of explaining power in and between organizations we find it analytically useful to treat intra- and interorganizational processes separately. In order to appreciate better organizational power from a structural perspective, we first consider the alternative approaches of objective rationality and normative conformity.

The objective rationality approach

Objective rationality derives formal implications for organizations' market pricing and outputs, resource allocations, market shares and profit-maximizing behaviors within an economic system (Moe, 1984). The economic framework situates firm interactions in a perfectly competitive market where exchanges take place between buyers and sellers based on negotiated contracts. The ideal market operates on the assumptions that preferences are known in advance of transactions and rational choice behavior prevails among all involved parties. But when uncertainty grows or predicting future outcomes becomes difficult, a hierarchical organization form develops to overcome the failure of the market. Hierarchies are more efficient than maintaining production processes that involve costly transactions. If pure market competition is assumed, there are costs involved in gathering information about prices as well as costs for setting up contracts (Williamson, 1975, 1981).

The concept of contracting is the key to principal-agent theory (Alchian and Demsetz, 1972; Jensen and Meckling, 1976). An agency relationship is defined as a contract under which one or more persons (the principal(s)) engage another person (the agent) to perform some service on their behalf that involves delegating some decision-making authority to the agent. Jensen and Meckling (1976) state that agency costs include structuring, monitoring, and bonding a set of contracts among agents with conflicting interests. Agency costs also include the value of output lost because the costs of full enforcement of contracts exceed the benefits. Internalizing these transactions reduces the costs of monitoring contract fulfillment (Moe, 1975). The developing authority structure is obeyed by organization members who voluntarily enter into its employ in the pursuit of greater personal gains.

Rational choice theory ignores many key concepts of other social sciences: formal structure, social context, worker psychology, bounded rationality, adaptive search, and goal conflict. Objective rationality depicts solitary actors making optimal choices as a function of given environments. The explanation for the development of hierarchical form highlights the internal structure of an organization, but empirical applications have been very limiting. Power, so crucial to political and sociological approaches to organizations, is virtually absent from the economic framework. The rationality perspective needs to be embedded in a context of multiple players (principals and agents), the role of interorganizational competition and cooperation, the diversity of individual participants' goals, and the existence of constraints on choice. Two organizational theories that have their foundation in the rational approach, but also include concepts of power, are strategic contingency and resource dependence.

The basic premise underlying strategic contingency theory (Lawrence and Lorsch, 1967; Galbraith, 1977; Child, 1977) is that an organization's external environments – its sources for production inputs, its markets for goods and services outputs, union and governmental regulations – pose uncertainties about the enterprise's survival and prosperity. These uncertainties affect the types of work activities that organizations can perform. Because environments vary across the different subunits of a firm, each unit tries to redesign its intraorganizational configurations to adapt to its specific external conditions. Those subunits that prove most successful in dealing with the organization's most critical contingencies will acquire greater domination over the company's resources and greater influence over its policies (Salancik and Pfeffer, 1977: 5). Thus, if consumer product lawsuits are a threat, the legal department's advice can alter production and marketing strategies. If production line breakdowns clog the loading dock, maintenance engineers gain power to dictate production schedules. If government regulations become burdensome, the legislative affairs office's impact on decisions increases. Control over essential information is a major source of influence for research and development, marketing, and computer subunits. The more critical an activity to an organization and the greater its scarcity, the more powerful become the persons and positions who can satisfy the demand. Thus, unequal domination and influence occur across departments because of differential abilities to cope with the most uncertain organizational contingencies arising in environments (Hickson, Hinings, Lee, Schneck, and Pennings, 1971; Hinings, Hickson, Pennings, and Schneck, 1974; Lachman, 1989).

Closely related to strategic contingency theory, the resource dependence approach begins with the commonplace observations that organizations cannot produce for themselves all the inputs necessary to sustain collective life: money, credit, zoning and tax exemptions, management and labor personnel, information, mass media audiences, and so forth. To acquire essential resources, they must interact with other organizations that control the valued commodities. Hence, all organizations depend on their environments for scarce resources (Pfeffer and Salancik, 1978: 258; Aldrich and Pfeffer, 1976; Pfeffer, 1982: 192–207). The theory emphasizes interorganizational relations as a basis of power:

> The resource dependence perspective posits that organizations attempt to avoid becoming dependent on others and seek to make others dependent upon them, and that the behavior of leaders and administrators is strongly influenced by the attention they pay to interorganizational dependence. (Aldrich, 1979: 119)

Thus, specialized boundary-spanning roles, such as marketing and purchasing agents and governmental affairs specialists, are created to mediate organizations' dependencies (Aldrich and Herker, 1977; Reingen, 1988). An organization may decide to bring its most problematic activities inside its boundaries, rather than remain vulnerable to environmental whims (Williamson, 1975, 1981). Make or buy decisions cannot be reduced to simple cost-benefit calculations, but must take into account the uncertainty and susceptibility to disruption of an organization's relations with its suppliers. The terms on which other organizations are willing to provide essential resources may be disadvantageous. The more scarce and critical a resource, the more power flows to actors who can supply the resource to those who need it. Thus, domination is a basic form of political power shaping resource transactions among organizations. To avoid dependence and constraints, organizations attempt to manipulate the flow of information about themselves and their activities, for example, their financial condition, the availability of alternative exchange partners, or the legitimacy of their claims for support (Pfeffer and Salancik, 1978: 261). Hence, the influence form of power also occurs within resource dependence relations. Analyses of interorganizational relations must take into account both domination through unequal resource transactions and influence efforts that manipulate persuasive information to preserve autonomy of action.

The normative approach

In contrast to the rational perspective, the normative viewpoint is more sensitive to conditions of uncertainty to the point of excluding efficiency criteria altogether. The rationality of people and groups is decidedly bounded, whereas conditions of uncertainty and complexity are common occurrences rather than exceptions. Institutionalization, a prominent normative theory of organizational behavior, embraces diverse sets of principles (Scott, 1988). Most institutionalists are concerned with the ways that meaning and values become instilled over time to promote the stability of an organization's structures. Meyer and Rowan's (1977: 341) definition captures this conception of shared social reality: "Institutionalization involves the processes by which social processes, obligations, or actualities come to take on a rule-like status in social thought and action." Zucker (1977: 728) concurred, adding that the social-fact quality of institutions is embedded in the formal structures of organizations. In contrast to strategic contingency and resource dependence approaches, these institutional perspectives argue that formal structures and processes are largely unrelated to any goal-attainment purposes. Organizations operate in certain ways not because these are the most efficient ways to produce desired results, but because of deeply socialized beliefs held by their participants that such procedures are the only legitimate ways to behave. Organizations may acquire certain structural features "not by rational decision or design but because they are taken for granted as 'the way these things are done'" (Scott, 1988: 505). Organizational conformity to an institutional order ("isomorphism," DiMaggio and Powell, 1983) is promoted through widely shared belief systems that prescribe adherence to particular "myths and ceremonies" (Meyer and Rowan, 1977). The multiple institutional environments of modern society reward organizations for their conformity to these norms by increasing the resources, prestige, legitimacy, and autonomy that flow to an organization from its various audiences (Scott and Meyer, 1983). Thus, power within and between organizations reflects institutionalized cultural beliefs that particular procedures – most notably those resembling hierarchical, bureaucratic configurations – are appropriate and necessary to accomplish given ends.

Both the rational choice and the normative conformity approaches point to particular elements within and outside organizations as critical to shaping the distribution of domination and influence. Strategic contingency and resource dependence theories argue that power is concentrated in those subunits that cope successfully with threatening environmental problems. The institutional approach locates the source of power in collective ideas about legitimate ways to express societal values. Strategic contingency emphasizes environmental effects on intraorganizational relationships, whereas the other two theories concentrate on interorganizational fields.

None of these approaches explicitly consider networks of intra- and interorganizational relations. But they all have something to say about the formal structures of organizational power, and so our attention turns there next.

Formal structures of intraorganizational relations

The formal structure of an organization is typically presented in an organization chart that shows the set of horizontally and vertically differentiated positions and the expected pattern of connections. This is an idealized and ideological image of the enterprise (Lincoln, 1982: 8). Nevertheless, analyses of formal structures have consumed a tremendous amount of research effort (e.g., Blau and Schoenherr, 1971; Hickson et al., 1971). As intentional designs for accomplishing an organization's work, formal structures offer a convenient jumping-off point for considering how the actual patterns of positional interactions deviate from the plan. Figure 4.1 illustrates the hierarchical structure of a department store with eighty-one people working in six departments and three other sections (Schofield and Alt, 1983). The vertical lines represent ties of immediate supervision between individuals or work units. Below we will see how a different image emerges when informal communication ties are considered.

The traditional Weberian bureaucracy follows the military's hierarchical principle of unitary authority; each position is linked to others in a vertical chain of command ("imperatively coordinated association," Dahrendorf, 1959: 138). The contents flowing through the linkages are simultaneously information (instructions going down and compliance reports going up) and control (rewards and penalties distributed from top to bottom to sanction performances). Each superior directly supervises a limited number of subordinates (his or her span of control), but every subordinate has exactly one clearly identified superior to whom he or she is responsible. The horizontal divisions show how various tasks are grouped according either to functions performed for the organizations or to markets within which the firm operates.

A traditional bureaucratic hierarchy is designed to reduce internal complexity, avoid conflicting commands, and concentrate control in the hands of the organizational elite. But these objectives grow problematic as increased organization size, product diversification, technological innovation, production task complexity, and environmental contingencies complicate the gathering of information and the coordinating of work. Some discretion to act autonomously must be delegated to lower positions, with day-to-day decisions made locally rather than centrally (Jennergren, 1981; Mintzberg, 1979: 275). Integration mechanisms correspondingly must increase to compensate for growing differentiations and decentralization in

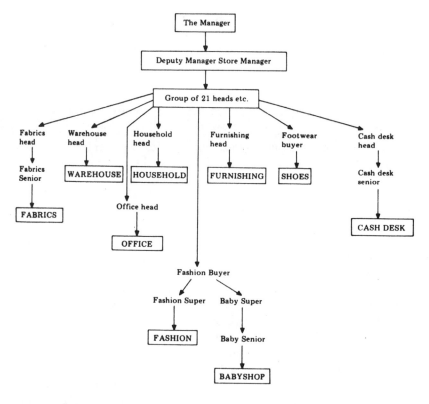

Figure 4.1 Hierarchical authority structure in a department store
Source: Schofield and Alt (1983).

large bureaucracies. An alternative is to sacrifice the unitary principle and reorganize the firm along other designs, such as a matrix form with functionally cross-cutting authority lines (e.g., Davis and Lawrence, 1977; Mintzberg, 1979: 168–75; Scott, 1987: 221–23; Sayles, 1976; Friedell, 1967).

The formal arrangement of positions has limited value for understanding what really goes on inside an organization. In the course of their daily struggles to perform their jobs, employees discover that the people who control resources and information necessary to their tasks are often unconnected to them by the organization chart mandate. Vital data, critical materials, and definitive authority may be located in remote positions. The only way to obtain these essential ingredients is for employees to construct direct or indirect social and political relations with their possessors. Thus, alongside the formal structure grows up a more complicated informal system of communication and resource exchanges. The combination of formal and informal structures constitutes the real power networks within the organization.

Informal communication structures

In the half century since the Western Electric researches, organization theorists have known that formal structures cannot tell the entire story about intraorganizational behavior (Roethlisberger and Dickson, 1939). Formal channels of communication frequently are ineffective or inefficient in getting things done, so parallel informal structures are inevitable (Rogers and Agarwala-Rogers, 1976: 100–1). These emergent systems of activity crosscut formal lines of authority and communication, creating new structural relationships that account for decisions, outputs, failures, and transformations that cannot be explained solely by reference to formal designs. Explicit control over information and communication channels provides superiors with knowledge that enables them to influence the organization (Michels, 1949; Hage, 1974). However, the devolution of task authority to lower-level participants (decentralization) provides them with some influence through their control over the upward flow of information (Mechanic, 1962). The informal communication relations continually generate and modify the distribution of legitimate authority among persons and groups inside organizations (Fombrun, 1986). In intraorganizational power relationships, the end result is that individuals cannot rely solely on their assigned formal roles, but must integrate as well into the informal structures (Kanter, 1977: 254–8). The most powerful actors are the incumbents simultaneously holding key positions within both webs of formal and informal relations to other organization participants.

An especially graphic example of how informal communication rearranges the formal hierarchical structure of an organization was Norman Schofield and James Alt's (1983) analysis of eighty-one people working in a department store. They subjected a matrix of informal communication rates among these workers to a clique analysis, resulting in the clusterings shown in Figure 4.2. In contrast to the neat bureaucratic structure shown in Figure 4.1 above, the store's informal clique structure is more fragmented and more complex. The fashion department is divided into various divisions by types of clothing and has many dyadic cliques reflecting the small size of these divisions. The authors speculated that this greater complexity might arise from a mixing of random psychosocial relations (affection and cognition) with formal organizational relations (hierarchical authority and formal communication) in the employees' informal communication ties.

Observing the impact of new information technologies on organiza-

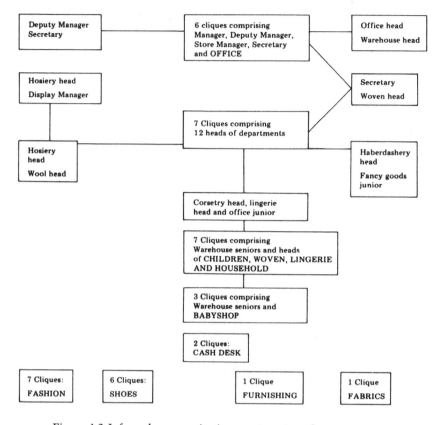

Figure 4.2 Informal communication structure in a department store
Source: Schofield and Alt (1983).

tional activity, Gareth Morgan commented that the very concept of a unified system is being replaced by a network perspective on organizations:

> The idea of a discrete organization with identifiable boundaries...is breaking down...Organizations are becoming more amorphous networks of interdependent organizations where no element is in firm control. Even though such a network may have a focal organization...the focal organization is as dependent as the organizations in the network. Interdependence is the key. Gone is the old-fashioned notion of hierarchy in which one member (for example, the focal organization) directs the activities of other members. In comes the notion of a network that must be managed as a system of interdependent stakeholders. (Morgan, 1988: 129)

His concept of network interdependence is applicable to intra- as well as interorganizational analyses. Investment banks are perhaps the prototypical network organization – ambiguous authority lines that are complex, flexible, and constantly reorganized as customers and issuers demand new products and services (Eccles and Crane, 1987). Within such protean systems, power increasingly derives from the capacity to manage relationships rather than to manage persons. Perhaps the best way to approach the informal structuring of organizations as networks of relationships among positions is through the analysis of communication patterns (Hage, 1974; Rogers and Agarwala-Rogers, 1976; Rogers and Kincaid, 1981; Tichy, Tushman, and Fombrun, 1979, 1980; Tichy, 1981). These networks serve simultaneously as information exchange and social control devices. The contents flowing through communication channels "can be reduced...to what people say (1) about themselves, their performance, and their problems, (2) about others and their problems, (3) about organizational practices and policies, and (4) about what needs to be done and how it can be done" (Katz and Kahn, 1978: 446). What is obscure in this scheme is that only some of the information pertains to work-related activities, whereas a portion is more personal in nature. As we see below, social and friendship ties may be an important component of informal relationships within organizations.

If power indeed derives from social actors' abilities to resolve an organization's work-related uncertainties, then occupying a central position within an intraorganizational communication network should strongly predict actor power (Pfeffer, 1981: 130). But the relationships turn out to be complicated. The early laboratory experiments on communication among subjects assigned to wheels, circles, stars, chains and other simulated arrangements found their effects to vary according to the types of tasks given to the subjects (summarized in Guetzkow, 1965; Rogers and Agarwala-Rogers, 1976: 118–23). When problems were simple and clear, a hierarchical structure offered the most efficient solution. But when tasks were complex and ambiguous, decentralized structures were more useful by permitting freer interaction that corrected errors, synthesized different viewpoints, and provided the socioemotional security that encouraged everyone to propose solutions (Blau and Scott, 1962: 116–28; Tushman, 1979; see Chapter 2 for similar observations about social movement organizations). In fact, a curvilinear effect might occur, with decentralized structures most suitable to situations requiring little information processing and hierarchies most suitable to intermediate levels of information processing. But when extraordinary amounts of data must be processed and numerous participants' actions coordinated, decentralization may again prove the only effective means of coping with saturation and overload (Scott, 1987: 153–4).

The generalization of small-group experimental findings to real-world organizations is tenuous, because so many other variables besides communication structures remain uncontrolled. Permission to study employees is often difficult to obtain from work organizations. Still, a few analyses of intraorganizational communication networks have been conducted, and their findings indicate the potential for this approach to reveal new dimensions of behavior. Lincoln and Miller (1979) found that primary ties (friendship) among employees in five organizations were more strongly structured by race and gender than were instrumental communication ties (work contacts). Subsequent to the data collection, half the employees of one private research company left to start a new enterprise. These defectors were clearly identifiable in the smallest-space clustering analysis of path distances in the work-contact network. Krackhardt and Porter (1985) also uncovered social network effects of high employee turnover. In a longitudinal study of a fast-food restaurant, those stayers who felt closer to their employee friends who quit work became *more satisfied* with their jobs, because the remaining employees were no longer bombarded with constant negative accounts from their departed friends. In a detailed analysis of a children's psychiatric hospital organized as a matrixlike structure, Blau and Alba (1982) showed that an individual's centrality within a work network was unrelated to self-attributed power, but the centrality of the clinical units within the organizationwide communication network did empower employees:

> [The] contextual analysis reveals the overwhelming importance of communication patterns among units and between staff and youngsters. Whatever a person's position or occupation, the more his or her unit is implicated in hospital-wide networks and involved in the mundane tasks of care and socialization of youngsters, the greater will be the person's influence. This, we assume, reinforces the process whereby emergent networks integrate a structurally complex system. (Blau and Alba, 1982: 377)

Similar significant effects of task communication on participant involvement in their organizations were uncovered in studies of research and development organizations (Fombrun, 1983; Tushman, 1979) and in voluntary associations (Knoke, 1981b; 1988). Their findings suggest that a person's location in central and prominent positions within the informal communication network increases performance effectiveness, morale, and productivity. In short, influence over organizational activities for collective or personal goals is a direct function of the structure of information exchanges between positions within the organization.

Perhaps the most intriguing examination of informal communication effects was Daniel Brass's (1984) research on nonsupervisory employees of a newspaper company. Through questionnaires, he obtained multiple network data on the communication, friendship, and workflow linkages among workers at the work group, department, and organization level as well as their ties to the dominant coalition (operationalized as the four people receiving the most nominations in the communication and friendship nets). Using centrality measures for each of these networks based on direct access to others and on control of information channels (*betweenness*), Brass related the employee's network positions to their supervisors' ratings of the employee's reputation for influence within the organization. Friendship networks were of little importance, but the task communication networks proved to be major factors in acquiring subsequent intraorganizational influence. Employee promotions to the supervisory level over the next three years, clearly a major reward for job performance, were also strongly predicted by occupying a controlling location in communication networks at all levels of the organization, even after taking into account criticality in the workflow network. Separate comparisons of employees in the technical core (e.g., printing) and in boundary-spanning jobs (e.g., classified advertising) showed that "contacts beyond the proximal workgroup and workflow were significantly related to influence for the technical core personnel, but not for the boundary spanners" (Brass, 1984: 534). The longitudinal design of his study helps to disentangle some of the problem of causality and selectivity, but more needs to be learned about how employees use their access to information to enhance their internal career prospects.

Details about information contents and the persuasion process are missing in the crude contact-frequency measures used by most network studies. Microlevel ethnographies of organizational communication are urgently needed to flesh out the picture. For example, Donnellen and colleagues (1986) speculated about how communication can allow collective action to occur despite different interpretations that individuals place on their actions. A collective decision to enter a new market, launch a new product, join a strike, or challenge the organizational establishment involves coordinated activity by numerous actors who do not necessarily share the same meaning about what they are doing. Various communication mechanisms may be deployed – logical arguments, metaphors, emotional manipulation, linguistic indirection – to define a social situation with sufficient ambiguity that diverse motivations can be effectively accommodated. The function of communication networks in promoting intraorganizational coalitions and bargaining is a research topic promising great theoretical and empirical advances.

A related question is the correspondence between the actual interaction patterns and the images of the network that people carry around in their minds. The information transmitted through intracorporate channels is used by the receivers for sense making and meaning construction. Presumably, the subjective pictures of intraorganizational networks that people build and use in their daily activities depend to some degree on which objective positions they occupy within that network. That is, there are different views from different pews. Although formal structural explanations are not incomplete by themselves, the subjective views seem to be grounded in them. Tracing how people's symbolic maps or sociocognitive networks (Bougon, Eick, and Binkhorst, 1977; Dunn and Ginsberg, 1986; Krackhardt, 1987) vary as a function of network structure will require the painstaking integration of individual psychological data with interpersonal social relations to uncover both the individual and the collective frames of reference that employees use in their daily work activities. Conceivably, the geometric mushrooming of these data, even in a small organization, would require the numerical crunching power of a supercomputer. A fascinating project would be to trace over time how the communication of perception and preferences among participants changes their comprehension of the organization's power structure and their own performance capabilities.

Social exchange in networks

Communication patterns are clearly critical for explaining the distribution of intraorganizational influence among participants. But power also originates in the domination of some positions over others by virtue of the control and use of organizational resources to reward and punish participants' actions. Understanding the domination process requires investigating structural relations of resource exchanges among actors. Fortunately, some excellent theory construction is already beginning to meld social exchange principles and network concepts. Richard Emerson and Karen Cook (Emerson, 1972, 1976; Cook, 1982) began with an initial focus on dyadic exchange relations, then shifted to their embeddedness in larger systems of exchange. Their theory was intended to bridge the gap between the microlevel of individuals and dyads and the macrolevel of collectivities such as neighborhoods, associations, and organizations. Emerson's (1962) basic power/dependence principle asserts that, for a pair of actors, the relative power of each is determined by the dependence of one actor on valued resources controlled by the other. For example, a patient places greater value on a physician's expert services than does the doctor on the patient's fee. In the Emersonian theory, power is inverse to dependence; that is, the party with the least interest in exchanging has the upper hand and is better able to dictate the terms of the exchange. Unequal dependencies in such unit exchange relations result in an imbalanced exchange ratio that gives a power advantage to the less-dependent member in that relation. Hence, the physician enjoys greater power than the patient in their exchange relationship. Not only is the patient likely to follow the doctor's instructions, but the doctor enjoys the potential for extracting additional benefits: belief in his medical infallibility, esteem within the community prestige system, even deference to his opinions on extramedical matters. Or consider the greater access and control over corporate assets and earnings enjoyed by top company executives relative to the other participants. Management has greater legal rights to commit these resources to alternative programs and policies of their choosing. Protected by legal barriers and golden financial parachutes, the executives are less dependent on the company's employees, unions, customers, creditors, and stockholders than are these groups on the top leadership for their paychecks, dues, services, bills payable, and dividends. Hence, we should not be surprised that top corporate managers' monopoly of knowledge about ongoing operations gives them impunity to influence and dominate the enterprise, even to run it into the ground while the less powerful constituencies watch helplessly. The leaders' control over information exchanges further enhances their ability to conceal what they are doing in the resource exchange network.

The four logical mechanisms for restoring power balance in an exchange relationship include withdrawal by the less-powerful actor from the relation; increasing the value of the exchange for the more-powerful actor; increasing the number of alternative exchange partners available to the less-powerful actor; and coalition formation that reduces the more-powerful actor's alternatives (Emerson, 1972: 67–8; see also Blau, 1964: 118–19). Of special theoretical interest are the latter two structural changes that may occur in exchange networks involving three or more actors. By turning to alternative sources, social actors can increase their power vis-à-vis other individuals. However, the availability of alternatives may be constrained by the existing structure of the exchange network within which each actor is embedded. Power through social exchange is not simply a matter of how many direct ties an actor has to others, but also how the patterns of indirect ties enables an actor to acquire resources from other network positions. Hence, social exchange theory's relevance to organizational power research lies in its attention both to the forms and contents of exchange relations and to the coalitions formed by exchanges of side payments among the partners. By emphasizing the transmission of material benefits, this approach falls clearly into the domination conceptualization of power.

Emerson and Cook's theory seeks to predict the distribution of actors' power from the structural characteristics of exchange networks. A network consists of sets of dyadic relations linked together such that exchanges in one location have predictable consequences for exchanges in another location. Their theory emphasizes two types of *connections* between pairs of relations: (1) positive connections, in which an exchange between actors *A* and *B* facilitates the exchange between actors *B* and *C* and (2) negative connections, where the *A–B* exchange diminishes or prohibits the *B–C* exchange (Emerson, 1972: 70–1; Yamagishi, Gillmore, Cook, 1988: 834–6). Mixed connections, perhaps the most common empirical types, combine both elements. For example, an auto producer's relation with a dealer is positively connected to that dealer's relation with his customers, since the supply of cars permits their sale. But the Pentagon's relations with Grumman and Lockheed are negatively connected, because a contract for a fighter plane that is given to one firm prevents its letting to the second. Positive connections foster cooperation while negative connections characterize competition for scarce resources (see also Burt, 1987b, for similar notions of cohesion and emulation). This contingent nature of connected exchange relations is critical to the Emerson-Cook theory. Not just any set of dyadic exchanges will do (Cook, 1982: 181). That is, the flow of resources between one pair of actors is conditional on resources flowing between the second dyad. To the extent that this condition prevails, power-dependence principles yield testable predictions about the distribution of power among network actors.

Network structures – the size, shape, and types of connections – are major determinants of the power that actors can attain through their control over and exchange of resources. Using computer-controlled experimental and simulation methods, Emerson, Cook and colleagues conducted several laboratory studies to verify the effects of both positively and negatively connected small (five to ten actors) exchange networks on the acquisition of resources by actors occupying different positions (see Cook and Emerson, 1978; Cook, Emerson, Gillmore, and Yamagishi, 1983; Yamagishi et al., 1988; also Cook, 1982). The basic measures were the amounts of profit from repeated exchanges of small amounts of money that were divided among the participants through negotiation. In general, actor power was found to be a joint result of network position (how distant an actor was from resourceful actors in an exchange chain) and positional control of resources, following the patterns predicted by power-dependence reasoning. It is important to note that the outcome distributions did not correlate with measures of position centrality, but depended crucially on the total configuration of dependencies within the network.

The successes of the Emerson-Cook research program and those of other network power analysts (Markovsky, Willer, and Patton, 1988; Molm, 1985, 1989) convey some clear implications for understanding organizational power. Much of the dynamics of resource flows within formal organizations is a consequence of the informal systems of bargaining and negotiating that arise between individuals within units or between units as social actors within organizations. Who dominates whom in scarce resource allocation decisions, which coalitions form and how side payments are distributed, and the power accruing to the players can be examined as effects of intraorganizational exchange networks. Unfortunately, the pure positively and negatively connected networks of the laboratory do not exist in the real world of business enterprise. Further, gaining permission to observe detailed corporate interactions is difficult for academic researchers, who are more interested in verifying their theories than in applying the principles to help business operate more smoothly. To date, rigorous field tests of the social exchange paradigm have not been conducted. Nevertheless, its concepts may eventually prove useful in illuminating the complex interactions among organizational participants, as discussed in the following sections.

Networks as career resources

The importance of informal structures is particularly clear from studies of personal networks as social resources for job searches and subsequent career mobility within organizations (Granovetter, 1974; Lin, Ensel, and Vaughn, 1981; Marsden and Hurlbert, 1988; De Graaf and Flap, 1988). The usefulness of combining analyses of formal and informal structures inside organizations is revealed in studies of advancement opportunities of individuals based on their gender and racial statuses.

Historically, research on gender and race demonstrated disadvantaged employment and promotion rates of women and minorities relative to their white male counterparts. Empirical studies that controlled for differences in age, education, and work experience found that race and gender remained significant factors in firm hiring decisions. Women and blacks were restricted from entering many occupations. Current gender and race disadvantages occur less from overt discrimination than from subtle processes that transform investments in educational credentials and authority experiences into career progress (Miller, Lincoln, and Olson, 1981; Bielby and Baron, 1986; Beller, 1982, Lewis, 1986). Recent societal pressures and specific affirmative action laws have contributed to increased participation by women and minorities in the workplace. However, this legal-rational attempt to create a more equal work status has not been completely successful, as women and blacks remain underrepresented in top positions within organizations. Wolf and Fligstein (1979) showed that employer policies and practices contribute to the unequal access to and possession of authority in the workplace. Although formal channels of power are provided, they are a necessary but not sufficient ingredient for status gains. Other dynamic factors must exist that the rational explanation cannot fully identify. Thus, although organizations comply with employment opportunity guidelines, women and minorities are still struggling to achieve equal status. Network analysis promises to illuminate the dark corners of institutional sexism and racism within large corporations.

The small numbers of women and minorities who have penetrated the upper rungs of the corporate ladder still face restrictions (glass ceiling) on full occupational equality. Judith Long Laws (1975) introduced the concept of the *token*, a person occupying a marginal position within an organization. She asserted that although a woman may be promoted to a position of higher authority in an organization, she is not necessarily accorded full acceptance and equality among her male peers. Rosabeth Moss Kanter (1977) expanded and formalized the token concept, pointing to structural constraints inherent in corporate management positions. Her definition of the token included anyone, not only a woman, who faces blocked opportunities and lack of meaningful organizational power. Such situations are likely to occur for anyone in a social group where she or he exhibits rare and salient characteristics – a woman among men, a foreigner among natives, a black among whites, a technician among professionals. Kanter suggested that minority persons' disadvantaged positions in an other-dominated organization would improve if their numbers were substantially increased, thus eliminating their token status.

Subsequent tests of Kanter's hypothesis (Fairhurst and Snavely, 1983; Molm, 1986; Zimmer, 1988) indicated that although sheer numbers played a part, more relevant explanations for women's persistent subordinate status exist. The effects of tokenism may be amplified by an individual's limited access to informal influence, making attainment of positional power even more difficult (Fairhurst and Snavely, 1983). From a more structural vantage point, such organizational characteristics as size, subunit size, task structure, and hierarchical structure may limit women's abilities to get and use influence (Martin, 1985). Informal power derived from differential network contacts outside an organization, for example in professional associations, should be considered as well (Waters, 1989). Thus, tokens who occupy equivalent formal positions to majority members may, in fact, have much more limited access to resources necessary for influencing others.

Pfeffer (1981) argued that regardless of the source of power, the ability of an individual to exercise persuasion skills has an effect on power acquisition. Fairhurst and Snavely expand on this point: "Individuals can acquire power if they can 1) affect the assumptions, basic values, or objectives on which decisions are based, 2) control the alternatives to be considered or 3) influence the information generated about the alternatives" (1983). The cultural effects of sexism have been found to affect women's behavior in organizations and the relationships between men and women, especially in newly integrated organizations (Offerman and Schrier, 1985; Wiley and Eskilson, 1982, 1983; Zimmer, 1988). Kanter pointed out that women are especially likely to be left out of the informal socializing, mentoring, joking and schmoozing relations that are critical to building interpersonal trust that leads to advancement to jobs with greater authority and power to get things done (1977: 206–42).

Personal contacts are resources of information and influence that people can mobilize to act as direct or indirect go-betweens to help advance their employment prospects. *Social capital,* in the form of egocentric information and helping ties, can mediate between educational credentials and occupational status and income achievement. The higher the status of one's network contacts, the greater the chances for career advancement. Persons unable to tap into well-connected networks have comparative disadvantages in a system where whom you know is essential to success. To add to this body of research, network analysts can contribute insights into how structures of informal communication limit women's and minorities' access to critical information and experiences essential for career development. *Old-boy networks* still flourish in business, government, and academic organizations, giving differential advantages to the protégés of established executives, bureaucrats, and professors in the scramble for preferred positions that are chained into the most desirable career ladders. Recent national efforts by a few senior women to construct deliberate mentoring networks for their younger female colleagues testify to the popular awareness of *networking* as a strategy for occupational mobility. How successful such conscious efforts to create informal influence relations will be in overcoming deep-seated systemic biases depends on whether such components can be linked into mainstream sources of information or become isolated and detached circles of impacted communication.

Power processes: bargaining and coalitions

Identifying structural relations is important for understanding the sources of organizational power, but such descriptions do not illuminate the process of power acquisition. Many studies of intraorganizational networks are static and deterministic. They also ignore the fact that each person brings to his or her organizational role unique capabilities that could affect an assumed equilibrium among positional power relations. A subunit leader's knowledge of power distributions or political skills in presenting a subunit's case to superiors is likely to affect the power of the subunit (Pettigrew, 1973). For example, Rosabeth Kanter described how an effective middle manager in an industrial corporation could use his connections to more powerful actors in the organization to acquire critical resources that empower the members of his work team. His "ability to get for the group" enhances the leader's credibility with both higher management and his subordinates, ultimately improving morale, productivity, and the manager's own career opportunities (Kanter, 1977: 168). Such informal structures have been described, but details of the political processes by which alliances are formed and leadership roles developed have not yet been specified (McElroy and Shrader, 1986).

We emphasized above that informal structures inevitably intertwine with the formal structures. One explanatory mechanism is a continual knitting together of employees by social ties. Friendships alone may not yield power, but their access to information or resources may be a prerequisite to building influence and domination. A natural extension of research on friendships and acquaintanceships is an analysis of how informal communication fosters socio-emotional attachments among positions differing in rank or function (Lincoln and Miller, 1979). By looking deeper into the instrumental relationships that promote cooperation and coordination among members, network theorists may uncover the dynamics of power acquisition and its exercise.

Every organization can also be conceptualized as coalitions of individuals and groups (Cyert and March, 1963: 27; Weiss, 1981). Its human components include workers, managers, stockholders, suppliers and customers. Because each interest group pursues its divergent preferences, the conflicting expectations and demands on scarce organizational resources may threaten the firm's continued existence. For example, shareholders desire larger profits, unions want higher wages, and managers seek increased market shares. Within a given stratum, interests may diverge; thus, the research, production, marketing, and sales coalitions each strive after separate and often contradictory agendas. Although these actors may try to impose their interests on the organization as a whole, typically none by itself can impose its will unimpeded. Instead, to be able to influence corporate strategy, subsets of actors holding similar preferences must form alliances and bargain among themselves and with other interest groups over the distribution of collective resources (Abell, 1975; Pettigrew, 1975). Negotiations can take place within a coalition about how much benefit each member will receive as payoff for its collaboration – money, status, authority, control over organizational policies. Similarly, the coalition can negotiate with the other organizational interest groups, conceding payoffs (*side payments*) for their cooperation (Scott, 1987: 270). For example, management may offer to improve plant conditions for workers in return for their acceptance of technical innovations that help boost productivity, with the increased profits to be split by stockholders and management. The result of a bargain struck among intraorganizational interest groups becomes the strategic choice or operating goal of the entire organization (Hickson, Butler, Cray, Mallory, and Wilson, 1986).

The coalition that succeeds in controlling an organization's course of action is that organization's *dominant coalition* (Thompson, 1967; Zald, 1969; Pennings and Goodman, 1977: 152). This coalition marshals sufficient resources to determine the internal structural form of the enterprise, its relationships with organizations in the environment, and the types of performance standards that will be rewarded. Clearly, the dominant coalition constitutes the power core of an enterprise's political economy. Of course, "Goals change as new participants enter or old participants leave the coalition" (Cyert and March, 1963: 115), which is simply to say that power is always a process, never an outcome. If we want to understand how an enterprise distributes its earnings, why it enters a new market, or when it disintegrates in rancorous conflict, then we must pay close attention to coalitional struggles for domination over the collective fate.

Under normal circumstances, a dominant coalition's power is not very visible. The enterprise operates according to established routines that are accepted as legitimate by the organization's members. Business as usual is the order of the day; what structures are in place tend to stay in place. Decision making under conditions of normal doubt and uncertainty resembles a garbage-can mixture of unclear problems, murky goals, and confused solutions (March and Olsen, 1976; Padgett, 1980). Ever-present latent conflicts are submerged while management tries to carry out its mediating and coordinating activities. But, in times of crisis – typically triggered by disruptions in the external political-economic environment, such as declining sales or increased government regulation – the lines of conflict are clarified and challengers to the dominant coalition emerge into the open. Claimants to power include outside parties, previously excluded internal groups, and even dissident factions within the dominant coalition itself.

Whether taking the form of a coup d'etat, insurgency, or mass movement (Zald and Berger, 1978), struggles over control of corporate strategy rearrange the alliances among intraorganizational interest groups. Choosing a company president and board of directors are often the occasions that symbolically signal the outcome of a power struggle among managers, boards, stockholders, and participants (Zald, 1969; Pfeffer, 1981: 254–66, 320–22; Mizruchi, 1983). So are struggles over the introduction of new production technologies, especially electronic data processing systems (Whisler, 1970; Pettigrew, 1973; Porter and Millar, 1985). During the twentieth century, large firms saw the successive rise to power of manufacturing entrepreneurs, sales and marketing personnel, and finance executives (Fligstein, 1987). Control within organizations changed as a result of how both environmental and internal structural contingencies affected various actors' abilities to define and implement corporate strategy. Thus, financial officers were better able to exploit the multidivisional form, product-related and conglomerate strategies, and merger manias of the contemporary era (Fligstein, 1987: 56). Consolidation of control by one coalition indicates successful mobilization of resources internal and external to the organization, with the victors implementing their concept of appropriate corporate strategy.

Coalition processes depend on several factors whose contributions are not well understood. Bacharach and Lawler (1980, 1981) found at least

five major theories of authority structure and coalition activity, but many
of the predictions were unsupported in empirical studies of small artificial
groups. Rooted in game theory and small group social psychology, coalition analysts emphasize the conditions under which actors jointly pool
their resources to pursue a common goal and the consequent distribution
among them of the benefits (payoffs) received when the goal is obtained
(Hinkley, 1981: 37–47; for formal definitions of varying complexity see
Caplow, 1956; Riker, 1962: 255–6; Gamson, 1964; Kelley, 1968;
Browne, 1973: 13–14; De Swaan, 1973: 30). Whether treating purely
imaginary situations or examining small group experiments, parliamentary, and cabinet governance behaviors, coalition analysts typically assume
that actors are rationally motivated to maximize their gains from a joint
action. A usual assumption is that rational actors have complete information about how joint decisions determine outcomes and about the utilities
assigned by every player to the outcomes. Actors may be motivated to seek
greater power relative to others in their coalition (control over actors), or
they may prefer to maximize the coalition's chances of winning (control
over outcomes). Regardless of these motives, collective action occurs only
when two or more actors each calculate that they can do better together
than by acting alone. But the rational actor model is inadequate to represent actor decision making, because real persons cannot obtain all the
necessary information, process it in real time, and accurately calculate the
probabilities for every potential outcome.

   Coalition theory and research seek to uncover the significant individual
and structural factors that predict which coalitions are most likely to be
assembled. Empirical work statistically compares predicted coalitions to
those actually formed (see Groennings, Kelley, and Leiserson, 1970, and
Holler, 1984, for collections of research articles). Given several potential
partners initially holding unequal resources, none of whom can dominate
the situation alone, coalition theorists ask who joins with whom; who
wins; who loses; how large is the winning coalition; what division of spoils
occurs; and how durable is the coalition over repeated trials? Choice of
partners is usually seen as a negotiated outcome that primarily depends on
the players' initial resources (power, votes, tokens) and, perhaps, their
ideological preferences for payoffs (De Swaan, 1973: 8–9). Thus, Riker's
(1962) famous minimum-size hypothesis predicted that only those coalitions will form that are winning and that pool the smallest total resources
necessary to win. Leiserson's (1965) minimal-range theory argued that
actors try to form coalitions with partners who are most ideologically
similar, thereby minimizing the attitudinal diversity of the group. Although
impressive empirical studies have been undertaken for numerous coalition
theories, critics have noted persistent indeterminacies between predicted
and observed coalitions, particularly when applied to historical data (e.g.,
Zinnes, 1970; van Winden, 1984; Pridham, 1986).

Informal communication networks are critical to the formation of coalitions, because the exchange of information among potential allies is a prerequisite to negotiated agreements (Pfeffer, 1981: 166). Lack of knowledge about the perceptions and preferences of other organizational participants is a major barrier to coordinated action on policy decisions. And informal communication offers the opportunity to coopt potential opponents to support one's views, a quintessential political influence process. Bacharach and Lawler (1980: 203–9) suggested several propositions relating intraorganizational networks to coalition power. As organizations become internally more structurally complex (both vertically and horizontally differentiated), network complexity also increases and any single coalition of interest groups is less likely to prevail on all strategic decisions. Similarly, as decentralization promotes work autonomy, thereby increasing role uncertainty among organizational personnel, a dominant coalition becomes increasingly hard to sustain. Finally, external environment heterogeneity and complexity also reduce coalition viability by giving rise to competing demands that fragment monolithic structures. As plausible as each of these hypotheses seem, no solid empirical evidence has yet been presented to support or refute them.

Most analyses of intraorganizational networks tend to ignore the environmental contexts within which formal and informal structures arise. Because data on structural relations among participants are usually collected by case studies of a handful of organizations, sufficient variation in external contingencies is absent, rendering impossible a meaningful account of environmental effects on intraorganizational structures. Despite the lack of well-designed cross-level studies, substantial research has accumulated on networks among organizations taken as entire units. To appreciate fully how radical a departure is this approach from conventional economic analyses of organizational behavior, we must first contrast the standard markets-and-hierarchies perspective.

Neither markets nor hierarchies

In neoclassical economic theory, exchanges take place between rational calculative actors in a market, an anonymous, atomized setting where prices and quantities are set by a competitive bidding process. An invisible hand coordinates supply and demand. Social connections among the actors are absent; indeed, the assumption is that exchanges are unlikely to be repeated in the future. Reputation, trust, reliability, and other interpersonal relations play no part in efficient transaction behaviors. Even when problematic economic activities are brought inside the boundaries of hierarchically integrated firms (Williamson, 1975, 1981), transaction-cost theory treats intrafirm exchanges in conventional exchange terms. A vertically coordinated administrative staff replaces the decentralized market, with management fiat arranging efficient transactions. Yet, as Mark Granovetter so convincingly demonstrated, evidence is rife that "business relations spill over into sociability and vice versa" (Granovetter, 1985: 495). Conflict, dispute resolution, transfer cost-accounting and auditing, and corporate control all point to the embeddedness of economic actors in concrete networks of social relations, shared understandings, and political negotiations. Economic actors enter contracts with others known from past experience to deal honestly and dependably, at all levels within and across firms. Even seemingly technical cost-based accounting rules for internal pricing are subject to intensive political influences (p. 500). In sum, power relations cannot be neglected in seeking explanations for firm economic behavior.

Walter Powell (1989) argued that network forms of resource allocation are especially likely to evolve where resources are variable, exchange values are difficult to measure, and environmental conditions are uncertain. Settings that increasingly exhibit network characteristics include traditional crafts (construction, publishing, films and recordings), regional economies and industrial districts (e.g., Italy's Emilia-Romagna; see Lazerson, 1988), and high technology fields. Although some of these innovative arrangements among firms may actually increase transaction costs above those in markets and hierarchies, their benefits are greater in reduced uncertainty, increased trustworthiness, faster access to technical know-how and economic information, and responsiveness to changing market conditions. Powell's claims about interorganizational networks are based on their ability to disseminate and interpret new information with greater speed and reliability than markets. Because communication linkages are essential for generating new meanings and innovations, the influence relations comprise the quintessential form of interorganizational power in these networks.

Granovetter's and Powell's theoretical reconstructions of the social roots of economic behavior paved the way for bringing power relations into interorganizational economic analysis. As sympathizers of the network perspective, they saw communication relations as a fundamental element for explaining both influence and domination among firms operating under market exchanges. The next section interprets recent empirical efforts from a network perspective.

Interorganizational networks

Both the rational choice and normative conformity perspectives on organizational behavior address central issues in interorganizational networks.

Economistic arguments emphasize calculative market transactions among a set of organizations seeking scarce inputs of money and material resources and outlets for their products (Williamson, 1975, 1981; Pfeffer, 1987). In pursuit of survival, growth, and profits, organizations engage in antagonistic, competitive, and cooperative interactions with one another, and these relations collectively identify a multiorganizational field or sector (Curtis and Zurcher, 1973; Laumann, Galaskiewicz, and Marsden, 1978). Within this field, organizations continually jockey to gain advantages in resource transactions, seeking to reduce uncertainty and avoid becoming overly dependent on their suppliers and customers (Benson, 1975; Cook, 1977). In other words, organizations seek to dominate the network of stable exchange relations by controlling those resources critical to others, thereby setting the terms of trade. They try to engage in exchanges that involve the least cost to themselves in loss of autonomy and power (Cook, 1977: 78). The imperatives of profit maximization compel organizations to construct dyadic exchange relations with their suppliers and customers. Interorganizational network structures are initially unintended consequences of purposive organizations' self-interested actions. But once a stable configuration emerges within a sector, this network is a fact of social life that all organizations must take into account. Accretions of law, tradition, and ideology as well as norms of reciprocity underpin the system and strongly constrain individual organizations' abilities to alter their positions in the network.

Most stable interorganizational networks contain a central core of organizations that dominate the flow of resources (Knoke and Rogers, 1979). These core actors display relatively dense mutual exchange ties, but they develop less frequent and more asymmetric ties to the peripheral organizations. Thus, exchange relations tend to form a hierarchical structure, resembling an intraorganizational authority structure: "A combination of network centrality and the exchange value of resources controlled defines the position of an organization in the status hierarchy which emerges as a consequence of the restricted exchange process" (Laumann et al., 1978: 471). Prestige and power accrue to organizations that occupy structural positions commanding resources that are in demand throughout the sector (Burt, 1977b). Unequal rates of exchange between center and periphery allow the core to maintain its domination, a generic process also observed in such diverse political systems as community politics and patron-client relations (Chapter 5) and international relations (Chapter 7). Organizations that send one type of resource tend not to receive the same type of resource from others. That is, reciprocity is made in different kinds of goods. For example, a state legislature sets the budget allocations of a vocational college, which uses some of these funds to purchase a computer laboratory from a local firm. The school then trains students to use the machines so they can be productively employed in the state's economy, eventually paying taxes that a future legislature will allocate.

The normative, or institutional, approach to interorganizational relations shares with rational choice explanations the notion that interactions occur primarily among members of a field or sector, comprising "those organizations that, in the aggregate, constitute a recognized area of institutional life: key suppliers, resource and product consumers, regulatory agencies, and other organizations that produce similar services or products" (DiMaggio and Powell, 1983: 148). The contents of their interactions are not only physical resources, but also political legitimacy and normative approval (Galaskiewicz, 1985). Coercive governmental regulation, pressures from professional associations, and imitation of other organizations' behaviors are significant constraints that institutionalize the normative climate for the organizations in a sector. Institutional theorists debate whether networks offer the best approach to studying these institutional complexes. Meyer and Rowan (1977: 341) asserted that an institutional environment is *not* reducible to the "effects generated by the networks of social behavior and relationships which compose and surround a given organization." But Zucker (1987: 454) argued that interorganizational ties in general can contribute to institutionalization by pressuring organizations to become increasingly similar, because making changes in any one element of a network is difficult without altering other interconnected elements.

Communication networks certainly play an important role in the institutionalization of new elements. These channels convey the collective wisdom about the best way to conduct task and governance activities. The information flowing between organizations includes technical knowledge and normative imperatives. Successes and failures – what's hot and what's not – are transmitted, received, and evaluated for implementation or avoidance. Mass media can be important components of these networks, but so are interorganizational and interpersonal relations based on common regulatory ties, professional association contacts, and social and business interactions. Understanding how institutionalization is facilitated or impeded requires a detailed investigation of the structure and operation of interorganizational communication networks. Both administrative and technological innovations diffuse through institutional networks, and some of these innovations subsequently become institutionalized. The speed with which a new machine or a new managerial practice diffuses and the probability of its retention vary directly with its effects on enhancing an organization's reputation and survival chances (Knoke, 1982; Tolbert and Zucker, 1983; Zucker, 1986). Earlier adopters are more likely to be network stars (i.e., prominent actors with links to many other prominent organizations). Their central position in a communication network exposes them more quickly to new ideas and to evaluations of significant others. Thus, they are more susceptible to identify and adopt innovative concepts and procedures that will enhance their reputation as leaders within the institutional environment (see Rogers and Shoemaker, 1971). In contrast, late adopters occupy the more marginal positions in communication networks and are prone to uncritical imitation of what they view as rational behavior by network leaders. The strength or weakness of ties among organizations can also affect the acceptance of an institutional thought structure or ideology about appropriate intervention methods (Warren, Rose, and Bergunder, 1974; Nelson, 1986).

A large number of interorganizational network studies have been conducted over the past two decades, many inspired by the development of block-modeling and hierarchical clustering methodologies. Extended reviews and critiques of these projects appear in Chapters 5 and 6, which deal with municipal and national political policy networks, respectively. Space is available here to discuss briefly the empirical findings in two types of institutional sectors: human services and the national corporate economy.

Human service networks

People-processing organizations are predominantly governmental and nonprofit enterprises that deliver medical, educational, penological, welfare, mental health, and similar services to individual clients and patients. Many of their relationships are mandated by legal statutes governing their operations (Raelin, 1980; Milner, 1980: 119–20; Halpert, 1982: 67–8; Morrissey, Tausig, and Lindsey, 1985), but other structural ties arise informally from combinations of funding and client-referral transactions. Agencies that occupy prominent positions at the center of multiple resource exchange and institutional ties with other powerful community organizations seem to fare better in acquiring the resources they seek. Central actors are more often sought as coalition partners and hence can dictate the terms of their participation. The influence attributed to them by the rest of the network might also reflect how aggressively these top organizations seek to gain a central position within service networks (Pfeffer and Leong, 1977; Provan, Beyer, and Krytbosch, 1980; Whetten and Aldrich, 1979; Hanf, Hjern, and Yorter, 1978; Boje and Whetten, 1981).

In one of the most detailed comparative analyses of human service systems, Fennell and colleagues (1987) examined three types of networks among cancer hospitals, satellite hospitals, clinics, and physicians in cities in six regions. These networks were patient transfers, shared facilities, and staff privileges. Each service region's resource environments (availability, dispersion, and homogeneity of the health delivery system and patient population) were examined in relation to three dimensions of network structure (density, internal viability, and complexity) as measured by archival documents and questionnaires to the chief executives of the organizations. When the matrices representing the three exchange networks were jointly block modeled, six inclusion lattices of diverse complexity emerged, reflecting differences in the strength of an overall integration within the network (see Boorman and White, 1976). Despite the small number of communities, substantial correlations occurred between the environment and network structures; environmental homogeneity (hospital similarities in size and facility mix) was associated with denser, less complex and less viable networks, while resource dispersion (ratio of specialists to general practitioners) covaried positively with network density and viability:

> Differentiation within the network (possibly in terms of status, as well as size and facility mix) may lead to complexity in dominance patterns and the development of spheres of influence (linkage blocks) within networks. Further, heterogeneity is strongly tied to a preponderance of internal linkage, again suggesting the importance of either functional divisions of labor, or status hierarchies, in the structuration of local fields. (Fennel, Ross, and Warnecke, 1987: 336)

The authors concluded that their findings consistently supported neither resource dependence nor institutional theories, but that a synthesis of market and nonmarket principles is necessary. Their project showed how a structural approach to interorganizational behavior could illuminate gaps in organizational theories that future theory construction must address.

A limitation in most previous network studies of human services systems is their reliance on a single informant in each organization to report on a diverse set of agency activities. Future studies must use multiple informants within each organization, spanning the hierarchy from boards and chief staff officers to front-line care givers, to provide detailed interview and questionnaire data on their information exchanges. By measuring intraorganizational variation in both perceptions and behavioral interactions, analysts will discover which agents report consistent and reliable data on which aspects of interorganizational relations. By disaggregating networks into several interaction dimensions (e.g., funding flows, client referrals, professional contacts, formal agreements, mandated ties, informal discussions, etc.), they could pinpoint those features most conducive to system integration, stability, and change. Finally, by comparing differences among research sites and relating changing network structures over time to program adoption rates, organizational influence reputations, client service utilization and treatment impact, and other effectiveness indicators, researchers could assess the contributions that each element makes to human service delivery.

Cooptation and hegemony in intercorporate ties

Large corporations – Fortune 500 firms – comprise the core production and distribution units of capitalist economies. The network of relations among these organizations must be taken into account by every nation state in formulating its economic policies. Interorganizational relations – joint ventures, mergers and acquisitions, interlocking boards of directors – have been variously interpreted as indicating three types of economic behavior: as control of one corporation by another; as a reflection of economic interest cohesion; and as efforts to overcome the uncertainties of market resource dependence (Mizruchi, 1982: 34–5). Many analysts of directorate interlocks view this strategy as cooptation, bringing potentially troublesome elements into the top decision structure (e.g., Pfeffer and Salancik, 1978). For example, a firm with declining profits invites a major bank to take a seat on the board in order to assure the firm's access to needed capital. Other interpretations stress that the acceptance of an offered seat may reflect the invitee's needs to monitor and control the actions of its economically dependent firms. Only a few interlock researchers have addressed the overtly political aspects of interlocks, such as coordinated corporate efforts to influence governmental policies and campaign contributions (see Chapters 6 and 8). Nevertheless, these board interlock studies have direct relevance for structural politics because they reveal the significant economic constraints within which the nation state must operate.

A directorate interlock occurs when two corporations share a member of their boards of directors. An official of one firm may sit on the board of another firm, or a person who is not a corporation officer may sit simultaneously on two or more boards. Because more than 60 percent of large, publicly held corporations have more than half their board members from outside (Waldo, 1985: 6), overlapping directorates occur frequently in the United States and in other capitalist economies. Publicly available data about board members and organizations allow numerous researchers to undertake structural analyses of the nation's largest corporations and banks by treating a common board member as a direct tie between organizations. The literature is too vast to cite here, but see summaries in Fennema and Schijf (1978), and recent results by Mizruchi (1982), Stokman, Ziegler, and Scott, (1985), Bearden and Mintz (1987), and Richardson (1987). Many of these studies identified subgroups, or cliques created by direct or indirect ties. Despite a variety of analytic methods, a consistent finding was that the major New York and regional banks and investment firms are the most heavily interlocked and central corporations in the U.S. national network (Mariolis, 1975; Mizruchi, 1982).

For decades, researchers have sought the elusive meanings of corporate interlock networks, especially industrial-financial ties. Some argued that directors' seats are filled to serve corporations' or banks' economic purposes to gain some control over the most economically problematic uncertainties in these organizations' environments. Thus, industrial firms allegedly use directorate ties as cooptive devices to avoid constraints on their profits (Burt, 1982, 1983). Other researchers, focusing on the reconstitution of accidentally broken directorate ties, emphasized how some firms, particularly banks, try to infiltrate other firms' policymaking bodies in order to safeguard their interests (Palmer, 1983; Palmer, Friedland, and Singh, 1986). Mizruchi and Stearns (1988), in an event history analysis, uncovered evidence for both cooptation and infiltration processes, with the magnitude of effects possibly depending on the stage of the business cycle. Because the data for interlock analyses are largely objective measures of ties, firm characteristics, and macroeconomic conditions, determining the actual use to which interlocks are put is still largely circumstantial. A new generation of network studies is urgently needed, in which researchers would painstakingly gather information about the subjective meanings, environmental perceptions, and interpersonal interactions that go on among corporate directors as they meet behind closed doors to decide major policy matters. Only when we are able to reconstruct the details of interfirm decision making can we hope to provide more than inferential insights into the impact of the corporate interlock network on firm behavior.

The political functions of the corporate interlock network are likewise largely inferential. For Mintz and Schwartz (1985), the fundamental dynamic of U.S. capitalism is hegemonic control of firms by financial institutions. Hegemony occurs when unilateral decisions by one organization limit the options from which a second organization may choose. The banking industry's decisions to extend or withhold credit from various economic sectors wield enormous power to redirect their customers' activities. For example, in the late 1970s banks and insurance companies were unwilling to lend U.S. automakers adequate capital to invest in new plants to make smaller cars. The banks' decision forced the auto companies to abandon their new parts-manufacturing subsidiaries and return to outside contracting. Smaller firms thus entered and competed in the auto parts industry (Mintz and Schwartz, 1985: 42). Economic decisions by corporations are conditioned by their continual needs for scarce capital. In directing investment flows through loan decisions, the large money market commercial banks regularly exercise hegemonic leverage without directly intervening in the discretionary decision of corporate boardrooms.

Only financial institutions can plan policies that compel coordination among other economic sectors (Mintz and Schwartz, 1985: 126). Large investments create a community of fate that links lenders to borrowers. Suppliers of capital need to protect their investments by continually monitoring and evaluating their borrowers' activities. Thus, the flow of capital shapes the interlocking directorate network to the advantage of banks' interests. Risky, unpredictable joint ventures compel financial and industrial companies to share directors as reliable sources of information because "they rely on personal trust and individual integrity to a much greater degree than a business transaction" (p. 183). Commercial banks and major insurance companies located in New York occupy the stable core of a constantly changing board interlock network. The centrality of industrial corporations rises and falls with their status as major recipients of investment capital. The outcome is a loosely coordinated economy dominated by no more than fifteen major banks:

> Collective decision making within the business world directs capital flows that commit the resources of the country as a whole to projects selected by financial institutions. This form of corporate coordination is, in our opinion, the primary decision making apparatus in American society. (Mintz and Schwartz, 1985: 252)

Policies set in bank boardrooms reverberate through the entire society, constraining public choices without involving the government. For Mintz and Schwartz, financial hegemony over capital flows is the skeleton beneath the skin of business-government relations. Hegemonic domination is the enduring context within which major corporations seek unity to pursue favorable government policies. In proper Marxist terminology, the economic foundation constrains the political superstructure.

Looking forward

Despite some promising beginnings, the structural analysis of intra- and interorganizational power still has a long way to go. Knowledge of domination and influence processes is essential to understanding why various changes occur in business, government, and nonprofit sectors. Some topics that call for more theoretically grounded network studies include:

1. Management power and tenure (Allen, 1981; Yates, 1985). Current explanations are predominantly functional accounts that emphasize size and organizational performance. They largely disregard the origins of managers' power in the unequal distribution of expertise and resources within the organization, and the dynamic aspects of conflict management.
2. Consequences of top leadership succession for organizational performance (Allen and Panian, 1984). We know too few details about the internal power struggles in large organizations, although

the implication is that managerial succession matters because it reveals the changing internal power structure.

3. Effects of ownership and management performance on tenure (Salancik and Pfeffer, 1980). Although good organizational performance allegedly prolongs executive tenure, the intervention of owners, board directors, and other interest groups remains to be examined.

4. Access to and control over communications and resources. Several researchers have demonstrated differential control within organizations, but we still know too little about how such structural inequalities arise and are maintained for the advantage of some participants.

5. Incorporation of network monitoring and performance evaluation technologies in management practices (Lee, Moeller, and Digman, 1982). With the advent of new computerized work systems (see Chapter 8), networking principles will be moving out of the academy and onto the shop and office floors. Employee adaptation and resistance to these supervisory intrusions will be a fascinating chapter in the history of work.

6. Strategic or top decision making (Hickson et al., 1986). What impact do internal coalitions and alliances with external interests have on how major corporate decisions are reached? Can political cleavages explain the success or failure of implementation?

7. Differential power attainment within organizations across gender and race. The research on women as tokens should be broadened to consider other minorities and to change focus from descriptive to more explanatory accounts. Research is needed on emerging mentoring practices, formal support groups, and networking activities geared to helping women and minorities establish contacts and fulfill career goals.

8. Dynamics of interorganizational systems. How do the resource and information flow environments of an organizational sector shape the structural contingencies of its member organizations and their relative capacities to dominate and influence collective actions?

9. Linkages between intra- and interorganizational network phenomena. How do constraints and opportunities at one level affect structural relations at the other, for example, can employee morale and performance be increased by forging more multiplex relations between firms and community service organizations?

Much of the research to date has focused on describing existing organizational power arrangements at a given moment. In effect, they merely depict the *results* of ongoing political processes. The dynamic aspects are treated as a black box. The structural relations among actors and the distribution of power are correlated, but we do not know how arrangements arose or how they will be transformed. A structural approach that links personal, organizational, and systematic components over time will go a long way toward explaining organizational power in all its manifestations.

5   Community power structures

During the past half century, research on community power structures increasingly embraced the structural perspective. The earliest case studies of small towns and cities tried to find people and groups that wielded disproportionate power over public decisions. Who controlled spending on schools, sewers, parks, sports arenas, and other public works? Who decided zoning regulations, pollution controls, and urban renewal programs? What determined private investments in homes, businesses, new plants, and employment? Several studies revealed wealthy local business elites at the core of leadership cliques that dominated municipal politics to the exclusion of the larger populace. Pluralists challenged this monolithic image, arguing that power was broadly dispersed among many competing political groups that resolved controversies by negotiation, accommodation, and compromise. Unfortunately, the initial structural insights were soon obscured by a sterile debate over reputational and decisional methodologies alleged to produce foregone conclusions about power distributions. By 1970, political scientists had largely abandoned community power research (Ricci, 1980: 462; but see Bulmer [1985] who argues that neighborhood research is being revived with a network emphasis).

The early structural analyses of community power were further eclipsed by a diffusion of multivariate methods from status attainment research to the ecological analysis of urban phenomena. Using data on entire cities as units of analysis, researchers tried to explain taxing, spending, and municipal policies as linear functions of such variables as formal government, urban populations, growth rate, racial composition, poverty, city age, and absentee-owned corporations. These high-level aggregations ignored significant interactions among different political factions struggling to shape collective resource allocations. In particular, power as relationships of domination and influence among community elites was impossible to measure with such data.

Fortunately, political sociologists soon revitalized the microanalysis of community power structures, examining structural relations among contending municipal elites. Combining reputational and decisional methods,

119

these comparative case studies dissected the internal network arrangements among the most powerful community actors. Their approaches emphasized how personal and interorganizational resource exchanges resulted in collective actions to influence the outcome of local political controversies. Taken together, these recent studies pointed to the necessity for a structural explanation of municipal politics. Community power research is a logical extension of the intraorganizational network analyses considered in Chapter 4. Collective decision making among a plurality of interested organizations parallels similar processes among the individuals who occupy positions within a formal organization. In both cases, participants seek to form coalitions with other like-minded actors to pool resources, and influence or dominate the outcome of decisions to be made by the authoritative actors. The formal analogy between the intraorganizational dynamic described in Chapter 4 and the interorganizational processes described in this chapter is so tight that ultimately an integrated model must be synthesized across these two levels of analysis. However, that creative revelation is not yet at hand.

Although most community power research concentrated on elite decision makers, the relationship between city government leaders and the larger community population remained an important component. Competitive electoral systems require that public officials aggregate sufficient votes to win office. Historically, many U.S. cities created political machines that brokered citizens' demands for personal services and public goods in exchange for their electoral support. Such patron-client systems are still much in evidence throughout the developing world. This chapter examines both the elite power structures and their clientele interfaces and suggests further steps for the community power structure research agenda.

Power elite or plural system?

Floyd Hunter (1953) set the initial terms for a debate over the lost world of municipal government with a sociometric analysis of leadership in Atlanta, Georgia. His data collection technique, subsequently labeled the reputational method, resurrected Lincoln Steffens' muckraking approach:

> Say, kid, who is "it" around here?...What I mean is, who's running the shebang? Who knows what's what and – who decides? (Steffens, 1931: 403)

Hunter asked a panel of community informants to rank order ten people from four sectors (civic, government, business, and status-society) who were the most influential persons "from the point of view of ability to lead others" (Hunter, 1953: 265). Thus, Hunter's concept of power appeared primarily to involve influence through interpersonal persuasion, rather than domination by exchanges of material sanctions. During interviews with twenty-seven of the forty nominees, Hunter asked them to choose ten people from the list who would be acceptable to nearly everyone on an unspecified hypothetical community project. Hunter drew three socio-grams (pp. 68–71) showing mutual choices within this top-leaders group. An internal stratification appeared: the twelve upper-limits people (chosen most often as potential project leaders) tended to confine their choices among themselves, while the fifteen lower-limits group picked their pre-ferred top leaders mostly from the upper set (p. 74). Additional structural relations among the leaders – working on the same committees, joint corporate directorships, common social club memberships – confirmed the power elite's internal cleavage and their separation from both underlings and the general populace. Hunter concluded, "Over and over, the same persons were named as influential and consequently able to 'move things' in [Atlanta]" (p. 73). Most of these elites were businessmen, although political eminence, society prestige, and wealth were not primary criteria for admission to the upper ranks: "within the policy-forming groups, the economic interests are dominant" (p. 82).

Hunter depicted the overall community power structure as multiple pyramids rather than a single unified hierarchy (p. 62). Each large business enterprise comprised the nucleus of a power clique or crowd whose members "tend to act together, and they depend on men below them to serve as intermediaries in relation to the general community" (p. 79). The various cliques were connected through their top leaders who "would 'clear with each other' informally on many matters" (p. 79). Municipal govern-ment departments also consulted and cleared with these top civic leaders (p. 102). The Atlanta power elite typically exerted its control through a "fluid committee structure" staffed by public relations men and civic asso-ciation secretaries who filled committees set up to carry out specific com-munity projects (p. 90). These professionals, "likened to a keyboard over which the top structure personnel play," did not make policy but were in charge of implementing decisions made by the top leaders (p. 94).

Hunter did not systematically examine the Atlanta elite's relations to actual decision-making events. Rather, he gave narrative accounts of events such as tax changes, industrial relocation, housing, traffic control, and race relations. Because he failed to track the elite's participation in important community events, Hunter could not demonstrate rigorously that the power elite always prevailed in the outcome of collective decisions. Rather, he inferred their prominence from reputational accounts and from their possession of large economic resources, not from systematic observation of their efforts to control community decisions. As Polsby pointed out, the anecdotal events reported by Hunter on which the power leaders met with relative success were either trivial or of concern only to businessmen. Issues where the elite was internally split or that activated other community actors were not adequately analyzed (Polsby, 1980: 54). Nor did Hunter suggest how structural relations among the top leaders and their subordinates might shape the elite's involvement in collective decisions. Thus, the promising insight that a community's political power structure resides in its leadership networks was not pursued thoroughly enough in Hunter's research.

Hunter's impact on a generation of community power researchers was enormous, both for those who followed his lead (e.g., Form and D'Antonio, 1959; Presthus, 1964; Miller, 1970, 1975; Ratcliff, 1980a; Trounstine and Christensen, 1982) and for his critics. In numerous communities, positional and reputational approaches typically uncovered an upper economic class constituting an integrated power elite that controlled the community's political and economic life. Political and civic leaders were subordinate to this elite's policy preferences. And the power elite served its own class interests whenever they conflicted with the interests of other community groups and classes. Impervious to influence from outside, the local power elite was clearly an antidemocratic structure lurking behind the nominally democratic facade of the municipal polity.

Robert Dahl disputed this dominating elite structure in conceptual papers (1957, 1958) and his classic monograph on power in New Haven, Connecticut (1961). The crux of his attack was that examining only people's reputations led to erroneous conclusions about how power was actually used in community decisions (see also Wolfinger, 1960). The investigation of collective decisions is essential to disclose whose interests ultimately prevail in community affairs. Such analyses require fine-grained inspection of concrete political controversies and community leaders' involvements in their resolution. Dahl selected three policy arenas that affected large segments of New Haven (downtown urban renewal, public education appointments and construction, and political party nominations) and that necessitated formal authorization by local government officials. He investigated each decision with public documents, participant observation, and personal interviews. The data revealed not a single economic elite deciding every outcome, but a diverse and shifting plurality of major players. This political stratum was a relatively open group without well-defined class interests (p. 91). It had "many lines of cleavage," symbolized by affiliations with the two major political parties and their numerous factions and rival coalitions (p. 92). Yet communication ties within the stratum were "rapid and extensive," helping to sustain a shared set of political values and goals that kept conflict from becoming rancorous and destructive (p. 91).

The pluralistic power structure uncovered by Dahl in New Haven was strikingly at odds with the monolithic economic power elite in Hunter's Atlanta. To the extent that a New Haven elite existed, it was political rather than economic or social in origin. Power did not accumulate across a range of issues, but was dispersed because inequalities of such resources as money, credit, jobs, expertise, authority, and social position were not concentrated. Although the structural aspect was not clearly developed in Dahl's analysis, the political leadership appeared to act more as a broker between groups with conflicting interests than as an aloof directorate passing down decisions to subordinates.

Numerous case studies of community power structures were carried out during the 1950s and 1960s (Clark [1973: 29] counted 166). Summarizing this wealth of raw data, several theorists proposed classification schemes to systematize the variations among them. For example, Rossi (1960) distinguished pyramidal, caucus rule, polylith, and amorphous forms. Miller's (1970: 15–16) five types included three unified pyramidal structures, a ring or cone model, and segmented power pyramids. Clark (1968: 37–9) contrasted monolithic and polylithic forms with mass participation and pluralistic models. Pyramids or monolithic elite structures involve small numbers of actors who are active in every policy decision. Pluralistic or polylithic elites involve many actors who are active only in specialized decisions (although each specialized arena may itself consist of a pyramidal structure). These typologies shared the assumption that the important features of a power structure are the number of powerful decision makers and the number of policy event arenas in which they participate.

By varying the formal linkages among actors and events, complex structural patterns could be specified whose appearance in particular communities became the object of scientific explanation. Such typologies implicitly recognized that communities may differ: Atlanta's power structure might not resemble New Haven's power structure. Most important, they emphasized three significant types of structural relations for the study of community power:

> Actor-actor relations. Stable patterns of resource exchanges among actors, especially of information about community affairs, allow them to monitor their environments for opportunities and threats. Interactor links make possible the formation of coalitions to engage in mutually advantageous collective actions.
>
> Actor-event relations. Community politics is a continuous stream of contested events whose outcomes hinge on which actors become involved because they believe their interests to be at stake. Generalists participate in a wide range of events, whereas specialists care about only a few.
>
> Event-event relations. The differential involvements of actors in events link together a population of events by the degree to which they have common or dissimilar audiences. Events are tightly connected if they attract an invariant set of actors or disjointed if they provoke continuing turnover among participants.

These manifold interdependencies among actors and events reflect the structural duality of persons and groups inherent in network analysis (Breiger, 1974). A structural connection among actors through events can also be examined as a structural relation among events through actors (see Chapter 3). This protean capacity to analyze community power structures using alternative frames of reference holds out promise for a richer, more nuanced rendering than a simple elite-pluralist dichotomy.

The debate between elite and pluralist versions of community power structure was never satisfactorily resolved. Disagreements about patterns of policymaking soon degenerated into an acrimonious and barren quarrel over appropriate methodologies for studying community power (see Ricci, 1971; major contributions included Agger, 1956; Danzger, 1964; Wolfinger, 1971; Frey, 1971). Using the cumulated case studies as data, some analysts discovered that centralized or pyramidal structures seemed to be uncovered when a researcher (frequently a sociologist) relied on reputational methods, but decentralized or factionalized structures were often found when analysts (usually political scientists) followed the decision approach (Walton, 1966; Gilbert, 1968; Aiken, 1970). The possibility of reaching firm substantive conclusions and advancing theoretical understanding seemed increasingly remote.

In posing the question as a mutually exclusive choice between either reputations or decisions, researchers erroneously assume that complex processes can be captured by a singular approach. Reputational methods might uncover important actors lurking behind the scenery, but they also confuse latent power resources with actual influence in collective decisions. Similarly, decision methods may identify significant players in overt collective actions, but fail to learn how issues are prevented from coming to a decision in the first place (Bacharach and Baratz, 1962) or even from gaining a place on the community's political agenda (Lukes, 1974). A more judicious stance must conceptualize community power structures as variable configurations over time and place, amenable to study only through a plurality of methods capable of assessing diverse dimensions of community power. From the ashes of the initial debate, an alternative political ecology paradigm emerged that, while falling short of a genuinely structural approach, at least prepared the ground for its eventual full flowering.

The ecology of policy outputs

The Johnson administration's ill-fated War on Poverty created an urgent federal concern with communities, populations, and policy impacts. Scholarly research shifted from intensive case studies to large-scale comparative investigations, taking advantage of large secondary data sets on community characteristics, high-speed computers, and quantitative multivariate data analytic methods (e.g., Aiken and Alford, 1970). The community power field was redefined to explain public policy outputs as a function of aggregate community characteristics. In the human ecology paradigm, entire communities rather than individual people are the units of analysis. Dominance within a community division of labor attaches to key functions that mediate the flow of sustenance resources. Power is conceived as an attribute of the political system as a whole, a latent capacity to mobilize resources for application to community social problems (Hawley, 1963). A community's power structure was often treated as a scalar variable intervening between community attributes (such as occupational and racial composition) and the policy outcome variables of interest (e.g., Lineberry and Fowler, 1967; Rosenthal and Crain, 1966). Unfortunately, the high level of data aggregation prevented direct assessment of how interest group interactions with political leaders and bureaucratic agencies produced these policy decisions.

The importance of municipal organization networks was implied by Turk's (1977) study of 130 cities' involvement in federal antipoverty programs such as Model Cities. He argued that a community's success depended on the capacity of local organizations to forge links with national political centers. But Turk's measure of a city's interorganizational network was simply to count the number of headquarters of national voluntary associations located in that city. His highly aggregated data did not directly measure structural complexities, such as network density or the content of linkages between municipal and national organizations. Instead, the scalar variables appearing in his linear equations concealed the underlying political interactions that created the policy outputs observed at the macrolevel. In its inability to capture the fine detail of policy networks, Turk's work closely resembled most other ecological approaches to community power (e.g., Liebert, 1974; Grimes et al., 1976; Lyon and Bonjean, 1981; Hunter and Staggenborg, 1988).

One comparative urban project managed partially to break the barrier to structural analysis in a highly aggregated data set. The National Opinion Research Center's Permanent Community Sample (PCS; Rossi and Crain, 1968) interviewed eleven elite informants in fifty-one cities, including the mayor, newspaper editor, chamber of commerce head, urban renewal director, and health commissioner. Identical ersatz decisional method questions were posed about community group involvement in four issues: urban renewal, antipoverty programs, air pollution, mayoral elections. Thus, the PCS combined the Hunter tradition of asking about reputed power and the Dahl approach of investigating actual decisions. Clark (1968) used these data to calculate a decentralization index score for each city. The larger the number of elite participants and the less similar the cluster of actors from one issue area to the next, the greater the city's decentralization. Clark's general finding was that the greater the differentiation between municipal elites, the more decentralized the decision-making structure, leading to less coordination between sectors and lower levels of city outputs (Clark, 1968: 582; see also Clark and Ferguson, 1984: 326).

The PCS data were noteworthy for using multiple informants for many cities to identify the joint presence of community leaders on specific events. However, it fell short of a genuine comparative network analysis in its inability to reveal which political transactions occurred among these elites in their struggles over event outcomes. No evidence was presented about how these or other actors communicated their interests or exchanged political resources to influence or dominate the collective decisions. Fortunately, networks of community action were finally being taken seriously by political sociologists.

Networks of community power

The large-scale comparative urban analyses described above uncovered gross relationships between city characteristics and public policy outputs. As a general rule, heterogeneous, differentiated, and decentralized cities were more likely to make policy decisions responsive to citizen needs and demands. Missing from these studies were details of how the internal structural configurations among a city's political actors facilitated or impeded its collective decision making. The intervening political interactions could not be examined with the typically highly aggregated measures available for large numbers of cities, even when informant surveys were used. Several political sociologists began to refocus their theoretical interests on the internal structure of relationships among community leaders, eventually coming to reconceptualize the basis of community power as interorganizational networks. These networks are the essential mechanism through which scattered political resources are assembled and applied to affect the outcomes of community controversies. Taking advantage of rapidly developing methodologies for collecting and analyzing entire networks, the new community power studies took major strides toward a genuine structural perspective.

The new community power studies tried to answer two questions: (1) How do interorganizational structures of communication and resource exchange mobilize actors to participate in collective actions? (2) Which interests prevail, and under what conditions, in making binding decisions about community events? The application of network methods to these questions produced new insights into domination and influence processes in local communities.

Perhaps the earliest glimmering of a serious network treatment of community power as an organizational phenomenon was Freeman and colleagues' (1960) study of Syracuse, New York. They found that the reputational leaders were primarily heads of formal organizations extensively active in community affairs (see also Freeman, 1968). A fuller recognition that interorganizational networks constituted the foundations of a community's power structure appeared in Robert Perrucci and Marc Pilisuk's (1970) study of West Lafayette, Indiana. They explicitly assumed that community power was held not by individuals but in institutional contexts. Using a variety of sources, Perrucci and Pilisuk identified 434 organizations in the community of 50,000 residents. Only twenty-six persons held executive positions in four or more community organizations. These twenty-six top interorganizational leaders (IOL) were compared to a matched sample of single-organizational leaders (OL) randomly sampled from the population holding three or fewer top positions.

As expected, the interorganizational leaders were more likely to be identified as influential members of the community across one actual and two hypothetical community events. Their general reputations for power were also significantly higher than the organizational specialists. A unified network of interorganizational ties, constructed by the multiple executive positions held by the IOLs, created a community power resource that could be activated whenever a major policy decision arose. Each person occupying overlapping positions was an interorganizational link who allowed resources to be mobilized and coordinated among organizations. Hence, drawing on the duality of people and groups, the researchers were interested in how organizations were connected through their common executive members. Perrucci and Pilisuk's contribution lay in acknowledging the primacy of the total network over the individual participants. Empirically, a resource network was defined as a direct or two-step path linking three or more interoganizational leaders to two or more organizations. In West Lafayette, six community organizations were linked through eleven common interorganizational leaders, including eight of the ten most highly reputed IOLs. This core consisted of two banks, two educational institutions, a hospital, and a voluntary association. This subset of leaders had an exceptionally high level of value agreement (homophily) and strong social ties among themselves. Perrucci and Pilisuk interpreted this core as a *ruling elite* within the community power structure – members of a common resource network who were interchangeable (i.e., structurally equivalent) in the roles they played in community decisions. It is important to note that the key social structure was the resource network itself, not the individual participants. (p. 1056).

Notable as Perrucci and Pilisuk's advance was, it failed to specify the contents of a resource network and to show that exchanges of resources or information actually took place between the organizations. It was most significant that they omitted to analyze actual instances of community decisions in which the network was mobilized to affect the outcomes. Without a demonstration that this core group won its fights, the designation of ruling elite seemed premature. Despite these limitations, their study was an important advance toward developing a genuinely structural analysis of community power. By attending to the pattern of ties among people who connected organizations, they shifted focus away from the reputations and attributes of individuals to the total interorganizational configuration.

Alternative views of community power structures depend on which of the duality components is emphasized (Galaskiewicz, 1989):

1. Organizations serve as arenas in which persons with shared interests meet to coordinate their common strategies. A community power structure is a device through which personal and family interests can be realized.
2. People serve as linkages between organizations by virtue of their joint memberships. A community power structure is the pattern of information and resource exchanges that enable sets of organizations to aggregate sufficient power to realize their unique and common interests.

The principal-agent duality is starkly posed by these alternative conceptualizations. Do individual elites (upper class, managerial) manipulate organizational resources to further their own interests? Or do organizations have imperatives that compel them to pursue their interests and agendas in community affairs? That is, are the leaders of community organizations acting as agents of the organizations' interests? The matter is difficult to resolve by empirical analysis, because these questions take meaning within the theoretical stance adopted by the analyst. Still, the structural perspective allows the issues to be clearly framed.

Networks of community affairs

Edward O. Laumann, Franz Urban Pappi, and their colleagues undertook four community studies in West Germany and the United States during the 1970s and 1980s that demonstrated the full potency of network analysis theories and methods for producing startling insights into collective action. They examined the power structures of three midsize cities – twice in Altneustadt, West Germany (Juelich, population 20,000), and once each in Towertown (DeKalb, Illinois, 32,000) and River City (Aurora, Illinois, 80,000). They began by identifying, from official records and informant nominations, the actors with the highest authority in each community's organizations. The two German studies examined both elite individuals and organizations, while the two U.S. studies concentrated on formal community organizations (Laumann and Pappi, 1973, 1976: 271; Laumann, Marsden, and Galaskiewicz, 1977; Galaskiewicz, 1979b: 167; Kappelhoff and Pappi, 1987; Kappelhoff, 1989). Their results transformed the face of community power studies from descriptive case studies to quantitative comparative research that dissected the inner workings of elite decision-making systems in ways undreamt by aggregate secondary data analysts. Because these studies represent the state of the art in community power research, a detailed examination is warranted.

Resource exchanges

Over time, modern industrial societies move from functionally diffuse to functionally differentiated structures. This trend is manifested by an increasing specialization among a society's units and an accompanying need to turn physical resources, goods, and human services into disposable facilities. The Laumann-Pappi program was theoretically based on Talcott Parsons' functional subsystems (AGIL) framework, an approach that is currently out of favor among sociologists. In this framework, the analysis of community power structures requires inclusion of the highest authority positions in organizations and institutions whose primary functional responsibilities are *adaptive* (business firms, banks), *goal-attainment* (government, judicial), *integrative* (voluntary associations, labor unions, political parties), and *latent pattern maintenance* (education, religion, health, culture). Different generalized media are exchanged within and between these organizations (Parsons, 1963, 1974). These media, or resources, are money (adaptive), influence (integrative), political power (goal-attainment), and value-commitments (pattern maintenance).

This differentiated subsystem framework guided the construction of lists of target organizations to be investigated in each community. During interviews with actors, these lists of community elite persons and organizations were presented. The respondents were asked to indicate multiple types of information and resource exchange relationships they had with the other elites. In Altneustadt, the elite individuals reported their personal business-professional, social, and community affairs discussion partners. In Towertown and River City, the organizations' agents revealed the other organizations with which they exchanged money, information, and moral support. From these reports, the researchers reconstructed the complete set of exchanges linking elite individuals or organizations within each of the three exchange networks. Given the relatively small sizes of these elite populations (from fifty-one to one hundred and forty-eight actors), binary matrices representing the entire set of dyadic exchanges could be quantitatively analyzed to reveal the whole network structure. Respondents were also asked about their organizations' specific interests and involvements in important community decisions.

The central findings of these studies are readily summarized. People and organizations that were more central in community resource-exchange networks were: (1) seen by other community actors as more influential in community affairs; (2) more likely to become active in community controversies; and (3) more likely to achieve their desired outcomes for these events (Galaskiewicz, 1989). Basically, actors were central if they had connections to many other actors in a given resource exchange relationship. Positional centrality gave persons and organizations access to resources that could be converted to influence over the outcome of political controversies. Thus, the structural relations among community actors had to be taken into account to understand fully how a community power structure operated.

Network centrality and influence reputation

Using cohesion measures of actor proximity (path distances; see Appendix), Laumann and Pappi (1976) analyzed the sociometric choices of the fifty-one Altneustadt elites. Separate analyses were made of the business-professional, community affairs discussion, and social relations networks. For example, in the social relations network, each respondent was instructed to name the three people with whom he was most likely to meet socially. This entire set of dyadic choices was pooled into a single square (51 × 51) matrix and subjected to a strong components analysis. A strong component is a network subgroup in which every actor can directly or indirectly reach one another (Knoke and Kuklinski, 1982: 57). Thus, subsets of actors were identified who were mutually reachable by directed paths of three or fewer steps. A clear cleavage occurred among the fifty-one Altneustadt community influentials. Three cliques were centered primarily around the Christian Democratic Union (CDU, twenty-six members) and the German Socialist Party (SPD, seven members), and a three-man county business clique, with the remaining people scattered as social isolates or specialized interest groups (p. 104). Figure 5.1 shows a version of this graph, with the internal structures of the three cliques condensed to a single point. Note that several of the social isolates and coalitions served as bridges between the SPD and CDU cliques. The CDU clique members received but did not reciprocate choices to the isolates or the two other cliques.

Each of the three Altneustadt path distance networks was subjected to smallest space analysis, a version of multidimensional scaling. This technique calculates and plots, in two or more dimensions, the positions of actors close to or distant from one another (Kruskal and Wish, 1978; Laumann and Pappi, 1976: 133–44). Figure 5.2 displays the community affairs discussion spatial representation (the symbols next to each actor's

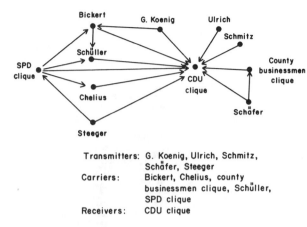

Transmitters: G. Koenig, Ulrich, Schmitz,
Schäfer, Steeger
Carriers: Bickert, Chelius, county
businessmen clique, Schüller,
SPD clique
Receivers: CDU clique

Figure 5.1 Condensed digraph of elite informal social relations in
Altneustadt. Source: Laumann and Pappi, 1976: 105.

position also designate his influence rank and main resource holdings).
This graph reveals two principles of elite social structure in Altneustadt:

Integrative centrality. Actors playing key integrative or coordinating roles in a given structure tend to be located in the central
region of a spatial representation of that structure, whereas
actors located increasingly in the periphery have less functional
importance in performing integrative activities.

Sector differentiation. The space is divided into relatively homogeneous regions radiating from the center, and each region is
occupied by actors from the same functional subsystems who
are likely to share values, attitudes, and interests. Actors in a
given sector are potential coalition partners on community
issues.

In Figure 5.2 the center of the community affairs discussion space was
occupied by top-ranking community influentials who held authority positions in the city government and incumbents of the largest economic and
financial units (Laumann and Pappi, 1976: 142). Small businessmen, religious, education, and scientific research center personnel were relegated to
peripheral zones, in clearly demarcated sectors at some distance from one
another. The county leaders, whose political concerns diverged from the
city leaders, were located in the periphery. Similarly, spatial patterns occurred for the Altneustadt social relations and business-professional networks (see secondary analyses by Breiger, 1979; Breiger and Pattison,
1978; Burt, 1976, 1977b; Gould, 1989).

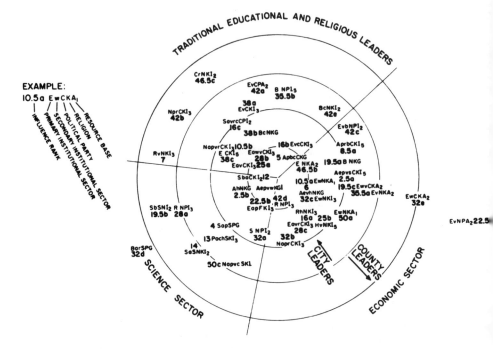

Figure 5.2 Community affairs discussion network in Altneustadt, smallest space analysis. Source: Laumann and Pappi, 1976: 141.

Galaskiewicz (1979a, b) found comparable patterns in his spatial analyses of the Towertown data. Using data distance measures, he calculated the seventy-three core organizations' positions in the money, support, and information exchange networks. As in Altneustadt, the central positions were occupied by actors engaged in general community problem solving, including the mayor, city manager, and city council, mass media, Chamber of Commerce, and United Way (Galaskiewicz, 1979b: 75). Specialized sectors radiated out from the center, differentiating into social service, economic development, religious, and labor organizations. Galaskiewicz discerned sector-specific control agents – such as the medical society in the health services sector or the service clubs in the industries sector – that might perform the coordinating functions within each of these domains (p. 78).

An actor's position in resource exchange networks is strongly related to his or her influence reputation among system peers. Influence reputation reflects a latent capacity to affect the outcome of events in which an actor has an interest or stake (Knoke, 1983: 1068). An amalgam of past and expected behaviors, influence reputation is proportional to an actor's credibility in convincing others about the trustworthiness of his or her information and intended actions. The higher the perceived influence, the greater others' awareness of an actor's autonomy in pursuing his or her objectives. Most measures of influence reputation, beginning with Hunter, simply ask informants to rank or rate their perceptions of the other elites' capacities to achieve their goals within the system. Laumann and Pappi (1976: 142) found that elite members' proximities to the center of each exchange network were significantly correlated with reputed influence (social = .17; community affairs = .30; business-professional = .40). Similarly, the rank order of organizations' influence correlated .42 with closeness to the center of a space defined by shared elite memberships (p. 178). In Towertown, reputed influence correlated with scales measuring resources sent to and received from exchange partners (money = .41 sent and .53 received; moral support = .33 and .55; information = .43 and .51; Galaskiewicz, 1979a: 144). In Knoke and Wood's (1981: 180) study of social influence associations in Indianapolis, a structural equivalence analysis (block model) of exchanges in money, support, and information exchange networks found a .71 correlation between network position and influence reputation. The total number of resource exchange ties received by associations from public-sector and private-sector sponsoring organizations also correlated .68 with reputed influence (Knoke, 1983: 1078). Knoke gave a resource-dependence interpretation of these findings:

> By cultivating diversified ties to large numbers of community organizations capable of supplying sustaining resources, an association's leaders can lessen the group's dependence on a single source. By spreading its needs for valued resources of money, information, and moral support among many organization sponsors, an association can better retain substantial autonomy and power to pursue its collective social influence objectives. (Knoke, 1983: 1067)

Not only are actors central to a network perceived as influential by their peers, but their more numerous connections to other actors offer them potential access to the resources controlled by these actors. Thus, centrality in resource networks itself becomes a resource that community actors may use in pursuing their ends.

The degree of agreement among community leaders about influence reputations may reveal whether a stable local power structure even exists. Bolland's (1985) examination of thirteen data sets collected in six cities found that perceived leadership stability was positively correlated with each network's structural integration. That is, agreement among informants about who were the local movers and shakers increased with network density, heterophily (occupational diversity), and proximity. Although familiarity often breeds contempt in social circles, in urban communities familiarity may be essential for the emergence of a dependable political structure. How much such local elite stability contributes to the resolution of community conflicts remains to be determined.

Activation in community controversies

The early community studies did not systematically explain how elite structural relations affect collective decisions. Laumann, Pappi, and their colleagues found evidence that actor participation in controversial events was a function of resource exchange network structure. People or organizations with interests in a given event outcome would mobilize others' resources by getting them involved in that issue. In turn, these actors would pull in other actors with whom they had communication or exchange relations (Galaskiewicz, 1989). Actors' preferences for event outcomes and their network relations jointly define the oppositional structure of a community elite. Figure 5.3 suggests some of possible oppositional structures for a single hypothetical event. Actors are labeled by capital letters. Actors A, B, and C share a preferred outcome for the event (e.g., pro), and actors X, Y, and Z all take the opposing position (e.g., con). Actors located near to one another in the space maintain direct or short-distance indirect relations; those far apart have either lengthy, indirect relations or no relations at all. In the centrally administered model, all actors are closely connected, allowing for face-to-face adjudication of the controversy. In the polarized model, the opposing sides are separated by a great distance, with no intermediaries to dampen their rancorous conflict (Coleman, 1957). In the bargaining model, however, representatives of the opposing coalitions are in close proximity, acting as negotiating agents for resolving the disagreement. Finally, the polycentric structure implies the existence of multiple bases of interest accommodation without a coordinating center.

These four diagrams represent ideal-typical cleavages among actors for a single event. The models can easily be extended to encompass multiple events. Each point now stands for a different *collective actor,* a subset of actors in close communication who share preferences for a specific event outcome (see Laumann and Marsden, 1979; Knoke and Burleigh, 1989). For example, all organizations that favor building a garbage-burning plant and that communicate directly or indirectly through two or fewer intermediaries can be designated the proincinerator collective actor. Typically, a given event produces two collective actors comprising the potential opposing coalitions. A second event generally creates a somewhat different pair of collective actors, each of whom may include some of the same people or organizations involved in the first event's collective actors. (Actors taking no position on an event can be ignored.) The more members that the collective actors for two events have in common, the nearer they will be located in a graphic representation of the collective actor social

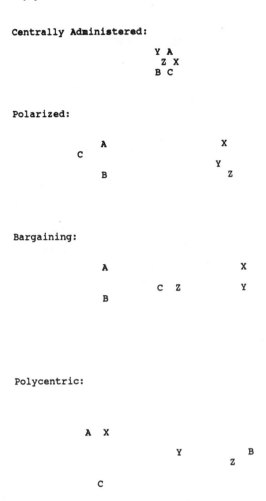

Figure 5.3 Hypothetical oppositional models.

space. For example, in the polycentric diagram of Figure 5.3, collective actors B and Z are close because a large proportion of the same organizations take the pro position on event B and the con position on event Z. In contrast, collective actors Z and C are far apart because they have few common members. Thus, the oppositional network structures in a set of community controversies may be characterized at several levels, from a single event to an entire population of events. This flexibility allows a researcher to identify recurrent and unique configurations when investigating numerous community controversies. Chapter 6 considers collective actors at the national level.

In Altneustadt, Laumann and Pappi (1976: 163–81) examined three actual and two hypothetical controversies. The Towertown and River City studies both investigated five actual events (Marsden and Laumann, 1977; Laumann et al., 1977; Galaskiewicz, 1979a). For example, in Towertown, construction of a new airport, building a new health services center, and imposing a curfew after a violent student demonstration evoked both support and opposition from various community organizations. Each elite actor's positions on every event (for, against, or neutral) were obtained during the interviews. Not surprisingly, the actors holding similar positions tended to be located close to one another in the resource exchange networks. Opponents clustered in one region, proponents in another portion of the space. Although the fault lines separating antagonists might shift from event to event, the contours still followed the network structure. In Altneustadt, for example, conflicts over a pop festival and over building a confessional school divided the Catholic and religious traditionalists from the scientific research center, whereas a city annexation controversy united all city factions against the county political leadership (Laumann and Pappi, 1976: 171). These differing coalitions across events indicated the absence of any sharply defined oppositional structure within the community that organized every conflict in an invariant polarized pattern. It is important to note that no evidence was uncovered that an overarching economic-class-based cleavage recurred across every controversy. Hunter's image of dominating business crowds did not appear. Collective actor analyses for both Altneustadt and Towertown found the German cleavage to resemble a combination of centrally administered and polarized groups, whereas the U.S. system was a multidimensional cleavage (circle or rim) structure with no central coordinating center (Laumann and Marsden, 1979).

For the ten controversies in Towertown and River City, communication linkages between active organizations with the same event preferences appeared with greater than chance frequency on every event (Laumann et al., 1977: 611). But contacts between active opponents were also over-represented in seven of the ten events (although only one differed statistically from chance). This pattern implied stronger support for a bargaining than for a polarized oppositional model. Thus, opposing participants in controversial community events did not avoid communicating with one another. They may even have sought out their opponents to discuss mutual concerns and to reach an agreement on solutions. Galaskiewicz's (1979a: 91–127) detailed microanalyses of activation on the five Towertown events did not bear directly on the cleavage structure. But he showed that central location in the three resource exchange networks significantly boosted an organization's event involvements, even controlling for various organizational attributes. In sum, community actors' ties to other elites were directly related to their likely participation in events for which they held preferred outcomes. The conclusion that interorganizational network ties promote participation in community decision making is inescapable. The community power studies failed to investigate details of collaborative action among members of the collective actors, a topic explored in Chapter 6.

Outcomes of events

The outcomes of community controversies are also related to the structure of ties among actors having common interests in a collective decision. Winning or losing a policy decision depends on whether opposing sides can draw on their network connections to mobilize and coordinate greater quantities of political resources to support their side of an issue controversy. These direct relations require a minimum level of trust among like-minded actors that is essential for cooperation in fighting together to achieve victory. In Altneustadt, the correct winning side on all five events could be predicted by simply picking the side whose elite supporters had the higher average influence reputation (Laumann and Pappi, 1976: 99). But as emphasized several times above, influence reputation is only a convenient proxy for more complex structural relations among actors. Indeed, the perception that an actor influences a community substantially derives from that actor's location toward the center of multiple networks of resource exchange. Thus, to predict event outcomes by just adding up the quantity of reputed influence is to obscure the complex underlying processes by which various types of resources are cumulated and deployed to produce collective decisions. Some promising initial steps toward disaggregating these components were made in the community power studies.

Galaskiewicz (1979a: 140–1) proposed simple but elegant measures of interorganizational resource inflows and outflows. First, each Towertown organization could tap resources from its support system. Similar to Knoke's (1983) concept of sponsorship, an organization receiving numerous money, information, and moral support contacts has potentially greater access to the resources of those partners than does an organization with fewer such connections. Second, an organization's resource dependents – the organizations to which it sends money, information, and support – are also potential sources of resources that could be obtained by calling in debts. Galaskiewicz calculated six indices that measured the total amount of money an organization might mobilize through its support and dependency networks. These inflow and outflow linkages significantly explained both an organization's influence reputation and its success in affecting four Towertown community events, independent of the organization's funds and personnel and its purpose:

> [A]ctors on whom wealthier organizations depended for money, information, and support tended to be seen as more influential in community affairs while organizations that had the moral

support of wealthier actors tended to be more successful in various issues. Particularly in the more expressive issues [e.g., the student curfew], linkages of moral support may have been very important in mobilizing the resources of other actors. (Galaskiewicz, 1979b: 151)

A parallel effort to explain collective community decision making was Marsden and Laumann's (1977) application of a collective action model developed by James S. Coleman (1973) to the Towertown event data. Because this model is examined more closely in Chapter 6 in the context of national policymaking, its details will not be presented here.

Theses on community power

The community power studies discussed above lead to several important conclusions about the structural foundations of such collective action systems:

- The principal political actors in local communities are organizations, not individuals. As communities increase in size and complexity, organizational imperatives surpass family and class interests as the principal structuring dimension of community domination and influence.
- A major problem for all organizations is reduction of resource dependency. Actors try to use their interorganizational relations to acquire necessary inputs and dispose of outputs, while avoiding control by other organizations. Structural autonomy (low resource dependence) within networks enables an organization to pursue its goals with fewer constraints.
- The most important feature of a community power structure is its multiple networks of interorganizational information and resource exchanges. Organizations' locations within networks of communication, support, and money exchange affect their abilities to achieve both organizational and collective objectives.
- An organization's ability to get the resources essential for its political purposes is increased by its access through multiple networks to other resourceful organizations.
- An organization's influence reputation varies with its centrality in communication and resource exchange networks. Influence reputation reflects others' perceptions of an organization's past and future capacity to persuade other community actors to support its interests.
- Formation of coalitions on a specific community event is helped by ties of sponsorship and obligation through interorganizational

networks. Organizations having common interests and short communication linkages form alliances that can more easily undertake
coordinated action to achieve a collective outcome.
- Activation on community events and success or failure in community controversies involves exchanges of control over resources
and coordinating actions through restricted interorganizational
networks.
- Most community power structures are decentralized bargaining
systems, rather than hierarchical orders controlled by a central
economic elite.

The evidence supporting these propositions comes from a handful of
community studies that examined networks among actors and events. The
warrant to generalize to a wide range of communities is limited. Still, these
sophisticated applications of network methods remain among the best
examples of the structural perspective's potential to explain the internal
differentiation of community elites and the dynamics of collective action.

Political patronage organizations

Most community power research that uses a structural perspective concentrates on actor-event connections within the top leadership. With the
notable exception of a community resident survey conducted by Laumann
and Pappi (1976: 217–53) and a neighborhood power study by Crenson
(1978), little attention has been paid to the network connections linking
elites and community citizens. One potential avenue is the analysis of urban
political machines and patron-client relations. Research on such systems
typically finds that machines' power derives mainly from elaborate domination networks. Leaders provide followers with valued personal goods,
jobs, and other services. In return, their supporters' votes enable the leaders
to gain offices whose public resources are then exploited for the leaders'
personal gains and to further entrench themselves with their supporters.
Thus, one electoral faction dominates the municipal polity by excluding
others from enjoying the spoils of victory. Pure patronage systems may also
involve access to personal influence networks, if the experience of one of
the United States' classic urban machines is any guide.

The Chicago Democratic machine

Undoubtedly the most intensely scrutinized American urban machine was
the Chicago regular Democratic organization. Its rise to domination began
with the New Deal and reached its apex in the six-term reign of "Hizzoner"
Mayor Richard J. Daley (1955–76). The machine's essence was a shifting

coalition of fiefdoms controlled by the fifty ward committeeman (Rakove, 1975: 106–31). Most of Chicago's 30,000 patronage jobs distributed by the Cook County central party committee were funneled through these ward bosses, who enjoyed absolute discretion over appointment and dismissal. Their power was perpetuated only so long as a committeemen and his precinct captains continued to deliver their ward's expected vote totals to the party. To secure the vote, precinct captains serviced the concrete needs of their local constiuents. They built up ties of loyalty by providing food, coal, Christmas baskets, rent money, legal advice, and by brokering citizens' relations with local, state, and federal bureaucracies (Gosnell, 1937: 71; Forthal, 1948). Thus, the classic machine exchanged modest material resources for the basic coin of local politics – votes. Because the Democratic politicians under Daley often perpetuated for decades their control over regulation and law enforcement, they could gain further material benefits through graft and the corruption of local businesses and organized crime (Gosnell, 1937: 191–3; Guterbock, 1980: 39).

The Chicago machine was often depicted as thriving in poor, socially disorganized neighborhoods of newly settled immigrants, who lacked connections to alternative power centers. A more sophisticated view, emerging from the ethnographic tradition of Chicago social research, recognized that strong community attachments could also integrate voters into the machine:

> Living in one area for a long time and developing social ties to
> people and groups in the area will enhance the citizen's chances
> for contact with the local party by integrating him or her into
> the local network of communication....Community attachment
> also increases the probability that a party agent will solicit a
> request from the citizen....Thus, community attachment
> involves enhanced access to the local communication networks
> which facilitate both contacts initiated by citizens and those
> initiated by party agents. (Guterbock, 1980: 118–19)

As a more residentially stable, educated, and economically comfortable electorate evolved, the basis for the Chicago machine's power shifted. Rather than dominating through material exchanges, the party leaders learned to influence the normative sentiments of the city's diverse class, race, ethnic, and territorial segments. Because it labored under electoral rules that required majorities, the machine had to appeal to aggregative rather than divisive concerns. By accessing communication networks among the numerous primary groups in the neighborhoods, precinct captains could appeal to voters' symbolic virtues and passions, such as their fear of crime and social disorder, as well as to their material interests.

Kornblum's (1974) participant observations of South Chicago's polyglot

Tenth Ward provided an especially cogent account of how a blue-collar community – splintered along territorial, age, occupational, and ethnic cleavage lines – was continually reintegrated around socially constructed common identities. Outside the steel mill unions, the Democratic organization was the only communal institution able to bridge the long-standing solidary segments of Croatians, Slovenes, Serbs, Poles, Italians, and Mexicans. Ward committeemen and precinct captains strove to aggregate votes by appealing to experiences shared by these communities' primary groups. Especially for adult males, intimate ties crystallized around the taverns dotting the old neighborhoods (Kornblum, 1974: 68–87). These cliques formed the nuclei of party activists, as well as linkages for building winning coalitions during campaigns. As newer generations and ethnic groups ecologically succeeded the earlier ones (most notably the Mexicans replacing the Slavs during the 1960s), precinct leadership underwent a parallel transformation. This succession depended on negotiating new primary groups that broke down social barriers in the ethnic neighborhoods (p. 32). Most of South Chicago's party adherents rejected the classic material rewards as tools for forging electoral victories. Instead, their political allegiances grew from networks based on ethnic solidarity, personal loyalties, and the pursuit of local respectability (p. 201). These alliances stitched together a new constituency from the mosaic of little local worlds, creating a more unified working-class culture. Although the Daley machine fractured in the 1980s after the mayor's death into a bitter struggle between white ethnic and black communities, its long success at bridging these latent divisions testifies to the resilient strength of primary group networks.

Patron-client systems

The spirit of patronage politics continues to thrive in the more personalistic polities of developing nations. Patron-client systems are especially pervasive in Mediterranean, Asian, and Latin American cultures with heavily collectivist conceptions of social organization, such as Confucian or Catholic ethics (Weingrod, 1968; Richardson, 1974; Graziano, 1975; Carlos and Anderson, 1981; Eisenstadt and Roniger, 1984). Indeed, two neighboring South Tyrol villages conducted their civic lives along starkly divergent lines reflecting their historically distinct ethnic cultures. The German-speaking St. Felixers were integrated to the political order outside the community through hierarchical formal and voluntary associations. The Italian-speaking Trettners relied on flexible social networks of kinship ties and personalized connections that were antagonistic to the state (Cole and Wolf, 1974: 259–88). The latter pattern is typical of traditional localized patron-client systems where patrons are interested in keeping governmental agencies away from their established power domains. In modernizing forms of clientelistic networks, patrons attempt to link local power domains with supralocal institutions, often blurring the distinction between particularistic allegiances and bureaucratic administration (Eisenstadt and Roniger, 1984: 243–5).

The personal entourages and cliques surrounding a patron form networks modeled after the extended patriarchal clans and families of these societies. Indeed, kinship settings seem to be the bedrock on which all patron-client systems are erected. Clientelistic relationships are constructed on the basis of social exchange (see Chapter 4), reinforced by trust and feelings of ascriptive solidarity (Luhmann, 1979; Eisenstadt and Roniger, 1984: 19–42). The extension of kin intimacy to a larger circle of friends and acquaintances allows a social order of unconditional mutual obligations to emerge that could not be sustained only by exchanging economic and power resources. Thus, patron-client systems combine strong emotional, particularistic ties with simultaneous but unequal exchanges of different types of resources (Eisenstadt and Roniger, 1984: 48). Clients exchange personal loyalty, deference, and awe for the protection, understanding, and material benefits provided by their patrons (Pye, 1985: 48). Boissevain's detailed studies of Maltese and Sicilian ego-centered networks highlighted the basic domination aspect of these relationships. An entrepreneur builds his personal enterprise by manipulating one of two types of resources: those that he directly controls (land, jobs, scholarship funds), and his strategic contacts with others who control such resources or have access to such persons (Boissevain, 1974: 147). People who dispense resources directly are patrons, whereas brokers are specialized actors who manipulate others' resources for their own profit. Brokers operate not through domination by resource exchanges, but by influence through their key locations in communication networks. A closer look at the brokerage process is taken in the next section.

Patron-client relations create vertical status hierarchies that link higher with lower strata in a society (Trouwborst, 1973: 112). The request for protection, a gift, or assistance from a patron reveals a subordinate's inferior position. Prestige and deference accrue to a superior whenever he grants something of value to an inferior (Blau, 1964: 131). Universal norms of reciprocity, distributive justice, and equity obligate the recipient of a favor to attempt to restore the balance. But given their unequal resource holdings, clients can almost never repay their debts. They remain forever entangled in the patron's web of paternalistic authority, returning favors for new favors without clearing accounts. The Chinese power game, *renqing*, a variation on the reciprocity norm with affective as well as material aspects, is an especially potent structural exchange rule (Hwang, 1987: 946). Because *renqing* is impossible to calculate objectively, such obligations can never be repaid, even when some new reciprocal exchange occurs. Both patron and client are ensnared into a continual ritual of orderly exchanges that constructs a political system to which all must conform and from which none may withdraw without great loss of face. The complexity of such power relations led one astute observer to comment that it is unclear "whether it is the few patrons or the many clients who are manipulating the relationships" (Pye, 1985: 118).

Dyadic power relations between clients and patrons ramify endlessly into larger political networks, as patrons themselves become clients of even more powerful patrons. The resultant political system is noncompetitive and intolerant of dissent that threatens its stability. Contention is stifled in deference to orderly exchanges, conformist values, and deferential paternalism – in short, the authoritarian style of governance so prevalent in developing countries from South Korea to the Philippines to Burundi. These local entourages form the microlevel foundations for the coherent national power structures examined in Chapter 6. Behind the seemingly rationalized bureaucratic pyramids lurk numerous clientelist groupings that carry on the genuine politics of patronage (Broadbent, 1985).

Mexico's polity illustrates how a nationwide system of local patronage networks integrates rural and urban communities into the more inclusive, coercively structured national government (Carlos and Anderson, 1981). These interpersonal ties cut across formal parties, bureaus, and regions. Organized either by an officeholder or a nonofficial broker, the networks are primary constituencies (*clientelas*) from which demands are generated and to which services are delivered. A political leader's base in a local constituency is a power resource that he uses to negotiate with high-level state authorities. Bargaining is limited to exchanges of the state's material rewards for political obedience and passivity by the leader's constituents. Often, several levels of intermediaries must be traversed before the person controlling the desired resources is reached (p. 175). Note that the basic power relation in this system is domination through resource exchanges between self-interested sets of actors in the national polity. Marginal Mexican groups, such as Indian villages and urban slums, lack leaders with access to the power networks that would connect these constituencies with the resource wielders. The urban power elites comprise a horizontal network at the very top of each region's power structure. Their ability to impede or support any lower-level demands also rests on internal communication and influence networks (p. 180). The entire Mexican state is little more than a public codification of the political brokerage system that has evolved since the 1910 revolution. It functioned sufficiently well to assure Mexico's stability for many decades as a one-party state. How this system was transformed by the 1980s financial crunch is a project urgently awaiting investigation, particularly since the opposition parties are now beginning to win subnational elections. Although network analyses of such clientelist systems are still in the early stages, additional theoretical advances can be made by formal consideration of the brokerage role.

Brokerage as network mediation

As should be clear from the preceding discussion, brokerage activity is a basic network function in both political machines and patron-client systems. Brokers act as go-betweens who put interested actors in touch with one another so that they can strike a deal. A brokerage relation involves at least three actors, in which the intermediary smooths the transactions between other actors who lack access to or trust in one another (Marsden, 1982: 202). In communication networks where access is restricted (i.e., not every actor has direct ties to all others), certain actors will occupy more central positions (in Freeman's [1977] betweenness sense of lying on channels that pass information between pairs). A broker gains power from the perception among interested parties that the broker can arrange resource transactions that are not otherwise likely to take place. As the number of indirect ties between actors decreases, power accruing to any one broker rises.

Brokers wheel and deal primarily within communication networks, hence they are concerned with influence rather than domination forms of power. In a stock market, a broker acquires information on demand, supply, and price from potential buyers and sellers. The broker's own benefit is a profit that comes from a commission charged as a share of the sales price. Similarly, in political information networks, brokers are distinguishable from patrons because they do not commit their own resources to the negotiations. Rather, pure political brokers are fixers or "inside dopesters" (Riesman, 1961) who arrange for exchanges of other people's resources. To make the process worthwhile, the political broker must also receive some sort of commission, whether a money fee (as in former White House aides who set up consulting businesses that implicitly promise their customers access to the Oval Office) or a qualitative benefit such as personal status or prestige.

A logical typology of brokerage roles among three actors can be constructed by taking account of actors' catnets (see Chapter 2). Following Gould and Fernandez (1989), Figure 5.4 presents five ideal-typical brokerage relations. They are distinguished by the circles that show actors belonging to the same or different category. As a substantive example, consider a legislature consisting of several party blocs. Suppose a member of one party wants to approach someone in a rival party about forming a short-term coalition to pass a bill. If the two partisans have no direct positive tie, an intermediary must be sought to make introductions, vouch for trustworthiness, soothe past misgivings, and so forth. Such a broker can be a member of the same party or a different party from the initiator. The meaning of the transaction can be quite different depending on these shared party memberships. In the liaison role (a) the broker is a third-party

(a) Liaison

(b) Representative

(c) Gatekeeper

(d) Itinerant Broker

(e) Coordinator

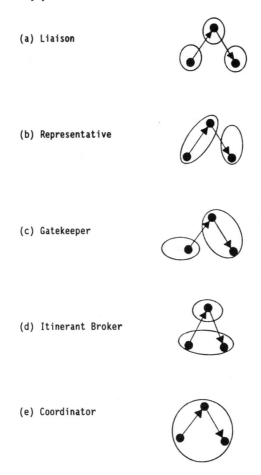

Figure 5.4 Ideal types of brokerage roles. Source: Gould and Fernandez (1989).

member, who presumably has no partisan stake in the outcome of the negotiated deal except to see that it goes through and he gets his cut. Movie and book agents are well-known economic examples for brokerage for short-term projects (Faulkner and Anderson, 1987). A representative role (b) is created whenever one party delegates one of their own members to negotiate with outsiders. Party leaders such as the Speaker of the House and the minority leader in the U.S. Congress are formally institutionalized examples. This role contrasts with the gatekeeper (c), who can decide whether and under what conditions to grant an outsider access to his party's members. Gatekeepers often occupy relatively low-status yet powerful positions, for example, secretaries and receptionists who shield their bosses from frivolous requests. The two remaining types of mediation involve within-group communications that are mediated by an itinerant or cosmopolitan broker (d) or a coordinator (e). The main distinction is whether the broker is also a member of the intraparty group whose transactions he arranges.

Although any given brokerage relation may fall into one of these five categories, individual actors may perform several functions simultaneously. The extent to which certain brokerage types appear singly or in combination is an empirical question. The only data bearing on the matter is Gould and Fernandez's (1989) application of the brokerage definitions to a measure of centrality based on betweenness. This measure basically counted the shortest paths (either direct ties or through a single intermediary) between pairs of actors in a communication network. Data about interorganizational political communications in a medium-size city were used to classify organizations into the for-profit, government, or voluntary sector. Application of the betweenness measure revealed distinct multiple and specialized brokerage roles. For instance, labor unions tended to act only as coordinators within their own sector, but the newspaper facilitated communication between sectors as well as within subgroups to which it did not belong. Future research on brokerage relations must move beyond this descriptive application to show how differentiated brokerage roles affect the operation of political systems. For example, the relative inability noted above of Mexican poor and minority groups to gain resources from the state might be traceable to brokers who lack liaison or cosmopolitan connections. The rigorous theoretical language now available for the analysis of brokerage relations should lead to a new empirical understanding of the phenomenon.

Looking forward

Structural analyses of community power systems are very expensive undertakings. To collect complete network information on the most important political actors in even a small city may require several months' effort and tens of thousands of dollars. Extensive interviews with all major political participants and detailed archival reconstructions of community controversies are crucial ingredients that require painstaking efforts by a small team of researchers. The hard work of developing such projects means that few studies are launched and wisdom cumulates slowly. Yet no feasible alternative exists, if a deeper understanding of community processes leading to collective decisions is to be gained. Further advances depend on a strategy where later community projects replicate the network procedures and measures used in earlier studies. The more consistently are theoretical and methodological components applied across research sites, the more solid are the conclusions that can be reached about local community power structures. The tentative knowledge derived from a handful of cities can be strengthened by extending network analysis to a wider range of settings. Either initial discoveries about power structure will be confirmed or factors creating differences among communities will be identified. In either event, the systematic replication strategy permits an accumulation of knowledge through comparing networks of community power across an increasingly broader range of social conditions.

One important extension is to analyze ethnically diverse communities. Racially, religiously, and linguistically divided cities have seldom been the object of network analysis. Determining how ethnic political elites forge the connections that bridge these subpopulation cleavages would be a major contribution. How have American communities avoided the open communal warfare plaguing other pluralistic societies such as Lebanon, Northern Ireland, South Africa, and other nations embroiled in violent separatist conflicts? The bargaining, negotiating, and compromising necessary to reach stable, mutually beneficial accommodations among these groups are obvious network processes. The historical U.S. urban political machines operated one structure for dampening conflicts by spreading electoral spoils among its diverse supporters. But what institutional structures carry on the machine's functions in this modern era of welfare institutions and telegenic campaigns? How do the micronetworks of individual voters described in Chapter 2 interface with the decision networks of community leaders in ways that avoid both massification and elite insularity? What impact do changes in ethnic groups' demographic and socioeconomic fortunes have upon their positions within community political networks? These questions can be answered only by detailed examinations of how interethnic networks are built, maintained, and used to produce collective decisions offering something for every group interest.

As mentioned at the beginning of this chapter, undoubtedly the most ambitious task awaiting students of community power networks is to integrate its structural principles with the internal study of organizational power. At the conceptual level, the processes by which participants in a single organization decide its collective policy preferences are formally equivalent to a set of organizations struggling to shape a community's collectively binding decisions. In the former case, the core actors are employees or members who form coalitions to influence their organization's positions. In the latter case, the core actors are those same organizations, now viewed as unitary actors who join into collective actors to pursue common policy interests. The most challenging theoretical question is how the resource constraints and internal power cleavages inside organizations affect their consequent abilities to play in the community power game and vice versa. The answer will require both sophisticated conceptualizations of cross-level mutual effects and ingenious methodological innovations to handle complex multilayered data.

Much important work remains ahead for structural analysts of community power. A concerted effort must be made to disentangle the familial, class, and organizational components of actors' participation in community events through their interorganizational relations. The importance of multiple types of networks has been alluded to, but the next undertaking must be to disaggregate further these material and communication exchange relations into discrete substantive contents. The evidence that political actors exchange resources and information in order to further their political interests is largely inferential. Systematic data remains to be gathered that would show explicit deals being struck across a series of community decisions. We still have only vague notions of how political trust enters into the equations: How do people and organizations generate sufficient confidence in one another's reliability to exchange mutual support over long spans of time? The volume of unresolved problems in community power research will keep network analysts busy for many years to come.

6   Elites in the nation state

The debates over community power structures also raged at the national level. Pluralist, elitist, and Marxist class theorists argued about the nature of the nation state and the extent to which a cohesive capitalist class dominated the decisions of government officials. Their initial objective was to identify the most powerful actors involved in state policies. Each conjectured about various mechanisms for creating unified collective actions by state managers, political parties, corporate organizations, interest groups, social movements, class segments, and other social formations. As with most approaches examined in this book, few researchers worked from an explicitly structural perspective. However, several recent studies used network methodologies to examine interactions among national policy elites. These analyses yielded new insights into the formation of coalitions and their ability to influence and dominate state policies. This chapter extends the discussion of interorganizational relations, begun in Chapter 4 and continued in Chapter 5, to consider policymaking networks in the nation state.

The state as an object of inquiry

Today, few scholars believe that the state is subject to "relatively clear-cut empirical identification and delineation" (Nordlinger, 1981). Conceptually, a state is a specialized institution of a society that exercises sovereignty, that is, the capacity to make and implement laws for a population (Eckstein and Gurr, 1975: 4). Although monopoly over the means of coercion in a territory is often cited as an essential feature (e.g., Weber, 1947: 156; Tilly, 1978: 52), the more fundamental principle is that a state enjoys legitimate authority in the eyes of its members (citizens or subjects). Indeed, one thrust of research on Western states is to analyze sovereignty as primarily a cultural project: "The issue essentially is the culturally determined location of the rational capacity to achieve progress and of the moral capacity to devote this project to improving human welfare" (Tho-

149

mas and Meyer, 1984: 471). In large measure, the Western state's legitimacy seems to have devolved from the hierarchic feudal community under the aegis of the church.

But states are more than abstract legal and cultural forms. They are also bureaucratized apparatuses structured as social organizations that enjoy a privileged relationship with the rest of society. States are not unitary enterprises, but complex organizational entities with diverse purposes. For example, Seidman (1980: 22) enumerated "executive departments, independent agencies, assorted commissions, boards, councils, authorities, wholly-owned corporations" and numerous other organizational forms. Miliband (1969: 49–53) described the modern state as composed of variegated executive, civil, military, and police bureaucracies. Similarly, Wright (1978: 210, n. 5) mentioned "a complex network of institutions, organizations, and social relationships." For Skocpol (1979a: 29), a proper state was "no mere arena in which socioeconomic struggles are fought out. It is, rather, a set of administrative, policing, and military organizations headed, and more or less well coordinated by, an executive authority." All these perspectives share a concern with rationalized formal organizations as the basic components of state structure. As these bureaucracies proliferate, understanding the structure of political bargaining relations among state organizations becomes critical to explaining state policymaking.

With penetration of the modern state's bureaucratic arms into the larger society, the boundaries between the state and nongovernmental organizations become increasingly blurred (McNeil, 1978; Alford and Friedland, 1985: 436). The state's statutes, regulations, and court rulings shape the environmental conditions of other social actors, especially economic producers and consumers. A rigid distinction between public and private sectors is difficult to maintain when resources, power, and legitimacy flow back and forth between policy actors in complex patterns that defy such simple classifications (Knoke, 1989a). In the corporatist polities of Western Europe, "interorganizational networks of interest representation which stabilize collective action are an important element of such institutional constraints" (Lehmbruch, 1984: 60). This intermix is captured in Laumann and Knoke's (1987: 380–7) concept of the *organizational state* as a congeries of associations, bureaus, and corporations that pursues policy outcomes favorable to their interests. The central concern of contemporary theoretical debates is the conditions under which various interests – class, industrial, status group – benefit from the unequal distribution of power among participants in the modern organizational state.

Nonnetwork approaches

This section offers an overview of five current approaches to state policy-making that seldom use structural concepts and methods. These approaches provide progressively more detailed accounts of state policy processes and increasingly point to the need for genuine structural analyses.

First, a thriving fiscal sociology of the capitalist state explores revenue and expenditure policies developed in unprecedented Keynesian intervention of governments into national economies after World War II. Of particular concern are the relative distributions of national income shares going to social classes (Hicks, Friedland, and Johnson, 1978; Devine, 1983, 1985), the responsiveness of social welfare programs to expanding population needs (Camerson, 1978; Wilensky, 1975; Hicks and Swank, 1984), urban decay and fiscal crises (Block, 1981), and the mutual impact of elections and macroeconomic policies (Tufte, 1978; Hibbs, 1976, 1981; Brown and Stein, 1982). Whether motivated by pluralist or Marxist conceptions of the state, these budget analysts share the assumption that fiscal policies resulted from the effects of exogenous economic forces (unemployment, inflation) and endogenous political factors (interest group demands, class struggles) on the state authorities. However, these underlying relationships are not directly accessible in the highly aggregated time series data analyzed with econometric methods. Researchers rely mainly on data collected by state agencies, such as parties' votes, corporations' profits, and unionized labor's enrollments. The microlevel interactions of budget mak-ers and constituents could only be inferred from structural parameters that estimated how such policy indicators were translated into fiscal decisions.

Second, public choice approaches to political behavior explain state policymaking as rationally motivated decisions by state managers, who manipulate budgets to maximize their utilities (Mueller, 1979; Abrams, 1980; Ordeshook, 1986). Cooperative games played according to various rules (i.e., constitutions) result in calculable outcomes that can be compared to actual policy actions of real world governmental institutions (Mayhew, 1974; Fiorina, 1977). Representative democracies operating under majority rule principles are subjected to pressures to expand the state provision of defense, welfare, and other public goods. A political party in control of the government rationally desires to maximize its probability of reelection (Downs, 1957; see Chapter 2). As monopoly producers of public goods, the incumbent politicians enact legislative and executive policies that seek to elicit or maintain electoral support, particularly by offering added benefits for those special interests that provide money and votes for the politicians' campaign (Breton, 1974). Further expansionary pressures come from the bureaucracies charged with producing or purchasing the policy outputs decided by the politicians. The vast public choice literature typically assumes an atomized actor who maximizes self-interest in institutions of interdependence and conflict. In some applications, game theory hints that cooperation may structure interactions among players. Coalition formation and vote trading (logrolling) necessitate agreements among two or more actors to coordinate their choices. Thus, communication of intent and interpersonal trust are implicitly involved in decisions to join minimal winning coalitions (Riker, 1962) or to vote for a piece of legislation contrary to one's preference in return for support on a future bill (Miller, 1977). But as noted in Chapter 2, game theorists do not explicitly include network concepts in their models, preferring instead to maximize their own theoretical utilities by examining formal properties of highly simplified situations whose approximations to reality are tenuous.

Third, most of the debate over the class nature of the state takes place on terrain staked out by Marxist theory. The polar positions are occupied by theorists who contend that the state is controlled by a ruling capitalist class and those who argue that state organs exercise considerable discretion in formulating and implementing policies. The instrumental view of the state takes its cue from Marx and Engels' famous assertion in the *Communist Manifesto* that "the executive of the modern state is but a committee for managing the common affairs of the whole bourgeoisie" (Tucker, 1978: 475). In its most vulgar form, instrumental analysis depicts monopoly capital directly controlling a unitary state (Weinstein, 1968; Miliband, 1969; Therborn, 1976). Either members of the capitalist class themselves staff positions in the state executive bureaucracies, or they subordinate state managers through strong ties of friendship and sponsorship. Capital's ability to dominate the state stems from its class consciousness and cohesion of action and from capital's overwhelming possession of economic, political, social, and ideological resources to reward its supporters and punish its opponents. Thus, the capitalist class is a ruling class; its interests are always favored by state policies regardless of opposition from the working class.

In contrast, the structural autonomy view argues that states cannot be reduced to the imperatives of class relations of production. The economic and political spheres are independent but interacting orders or regions of society. States originated in the multiple economic, political, and ideological practices of historic civil societies (Gramsci, 1971; Poulantzas, 1975). This formulation asserts that states possess limited capacity to act against the interests of any class or class faction, while remaining susceptible to their influence. A state acts to neutralize or displace economic and political contradictions to preserve the system without always favoring only the long-run interests of the capitalist class. At the same time, the state's autonomy makes it the object of class struggles, with both workers and capitalists trying to influence the policy decisions of state managers. Hence, a three-sided political process ensues whose outcomes are historically contingent on the interplay of political power.

Although Marxist and neo-Marxist class analyses of the state are often called structural because of their focus on relationships within a mode of production, they seldom explicitly examine networks of interaction among specific political actors. Typical empirical researches are historical case studies employing thick descriptions of actors' interests and actions to further their economic and political objectives. Recent exemplars in this vein included such diverse analyses as the creation of the U.S. social security system (Quadagno, 1987), French working-class formation (Aminzade, 1981), California transportation policies (Whitt, 1982), British welfare programs (Gough, 1979), St. Louis bank loan policies (Ratcliff, 1980a, b), New Deal welfare legislation (Skocpol, 1979b), and Nordic social democratic parties (Esping-Andersen, 1985). Useful as these studies were in revealing various internal facets of the state, they largely eschewed a rigorous network treatment of relations among state actors.

Fourth, a widely entertained alternative to the class model is the power elite approach, inspired by historical analyses of Mosca (1939), Michels (1949), and Pareto (1968), and elaborated by Mills (1956) and Higley, Field, and Groholt (1976). Elite theorists asserted that political resources are concentrated in the hands of persons occupying strategic positions in public and private bureaucracies (Field and Higley, 1980: 20). Unlike the class model, the interests pursued by power elites are more likely to reflect institutional and organizational imperatives than overtly capitalist class concerns. The power elites' consciousness and value cohesion resides in common social origins, collective socialization experiences, intimate social and professional interactions, and sequential career moves across institutional settings (Mills, 1956: 279–81; Hunter, 1959: 176; Dye, 1986: 160–83). Elite unity of purpose and action is often problematic, given the diversity of institutional interests. Some analysts perceived concerted action mainly on major issues (Mills, 1956: 276), whereas others saw a structure of many discrete power hierarchies confined to specialized policy domains (Keller, 1963; Rose, 1967).

A frequently proposed mechanism to overcome factional splits within the power elite is an extensive set of connections between institutional leaders generated by formally interlocking memberships on directing boards of corporations, banks, foundations, social clubs, and policy planning organizations (Mintz and Schwartz, 1981; Useem, 1979; Domhoff, 1967, 1978; Dye, 1978; Salzman and Domhoff, 1980). Such joint memberships provide elites with opportunities to interact regularly, to represent and communicate their institutions' interests, and to forge consensual mind-sets about policy direction for the state (Barton, 1975, 1985; Putnam, 1976; Field and Higley, 1980: 36–9).

> Its most crucial feature is a personal interaction network which gives governmental and nongovernmental elites relatively direct, unfettered access to each other and especially to those elite persons who occupy the most central public and private decision making positions. Possessing this access, each elite group can be reasonably certain that on salient policy questions or national issues it can make itself heard effectively. Elite factions and groups which are otherwise diverse and competing thus have a common interest in observing the informal rules by which the interaction structure operates and in upholding the institutions in which it is embedded. (Higley and Moore, 1981: 584)

The structural aspects of these networks are examined in greater detail below.

A fifth and final approach to state policymaking is the pluralist pressure group system. The U.S. federal structure of fragmented electoral districts and geographical decentralization encouraged the proliferation of interest groups. Beginning in the 1960s, a major advocacy explosion in Washington forced thousands of organizations to maintain a continuing presence in the capital, either by setting up their own headquarters or hiring legal counsel (Schlozman, 1984; Schlozman and Tierney, 1985; Knoke, 1986, 1990a). Citizen lobbies (so-called PIGs, or public interest groups) became especially active (Berry, 1977), often under the sponsorship of well-heeled patrons and foundations (Walker, 1983). Businesses countermobilized to promote corporate interests (Hayes, 1978; Gais, Peterson, Walker, 1984). Each distinct policy domain, from aerospace to uranium mining, allegedly formed a subgovernment (iron or cozy triangle) consisting of congressional subcommittee, federal bureaucracy, and interest group clientele that resisted the intrusion of a strong central authority (Ripley and Franklin, 1978; McFarland, 1983). Mass membership organizations – labor unions, political parties, trade associations, and professional societies – became increasingly disadvantaged relative to the dominant power of institutions, such as corporations and local governments, in cutting deals with the federal government (Hayes, 1983; Salisbury, 1984). In the more corporatist polities of some Western European nations, governmental authority devolved to a set of intermediary (peak) associations of employers and workers (Panitch, 1977; Schmitter, 1981; Lehmbruch, 1984). The state authorized and negotiated with these associations over policies affecting their members, for example, setting wages and prices, production and labor conditions, occupational qualification and training programs, and welfare provisions (Williamson, 1985: 78–9).

Political scientists who study agenda setting ask how policy issues arise in these systems and who participates in decision making (Cobb and Elder, 1972). In his close examination of twenty-three health and transportation issues during the Carter administration, Kingdon (1984) concluded that issues arose from multiple sources: bureaucrats, politicians, interest groups, media reports, academic institutes, public opinion. Instead of a comprehensive, rational search for alternative solutions to well-identified problems, a garbage can process occurred (Cohen, March, and Olsen, 1972). Which proposals reached the agenda and which policy outcomes were finally adopted resulted from a fortuitous and unpredictable mix of problems, policy proposals, and politics (Kingdon, 1984: 91). Despite its unpredictability, the agenda-setting process was not random. Policy actors were constrained by external conditions, budget priorities, previous policy decisions, group resources, national mood swings, and political entrepreneurship (pp. 216–17).

Among the important constraints not considered by Kingdon are how the network of relations among state policy actors shaped the flow of information about policy options. Heclo (1978) identified such a fluid *issue network*, which he argued was replacing the traditional iron triangles of policy control. Membership in these networks was constantly changing, as large numbers of actors "with quite varied degrees of mutual commitment or dependence on others in their environment" moved in and out of the policy debates (pp. 102–4). Rather than a tight-knit consensual grouping, an issue network loosely ties together contradictory tendencies in both narrowly technocratic skills and organizationally based policy interests. In other words, an issue network closely resembles a *social circle* – a set of directly or indirectly sociometrically linked actors who share common political or cultural interests, broadly conceived (Kadushin, 1968; Laumann and Marsden, 1979). These interests are not specific goals or policy outcome preferences, but general expressions of concern about central issues (e.g., foreign policy, welfare, or labor issues). Heclo asserted that issue networks break down the "neat distinction between governmental structure and environment" (p. 106). However, his evidence was anecdotal, rather than a systematic examination of influence and domination linkages among policy actors. Nevertheless, Heclo pointed to the need for an overtly structural approach to the state pressure group system. The remainder of this chapter considers some significant efforts to move state policy analysis in this direction.

Structural relations in the ruling core

In recent years, several national power structure researchers attempted to uncover the pattern of relations among business, government, and other elite social institutions (Domhofff, 1983; Useem, 1983; Dye, 1986). Their common procedures began by identifying, for various economic, political, and social sectors, both the most important organizations and the persons occupying the major executive positions in these organizations. Then, some type of network analysis was applied to the matrix of person-by-organization relations. Given the duality of persons and groups (Breiger, 1974), analysts might emphasize either the persons occupying central and peripheral positions in the network or subsets of organizations differentially connecting parts of the network. After mapping the relevant structural relations, power structure researchers typically argued that the core persons or organizations exercise greater domination or influence over state policies than either the peripheral actors or those completely excluded from the elite system. Because of their explicit use of network concepts and methodologies, these studies warrant close inspection of both procedures and substantive findings.

Through more than two decades, G. William Domhoff doggedly pursued the underlying power structure of society in the United States. In a series of increasingly detailed and sophisticated research reports, he mapped the complex and partially coordinated sets of institutions, organizations, and persons that he believed set the conditions for state policy-making (Domhoff, 1967, 1975, 1978, 1979, 1983). Domhoff's thesis was that "There is a social upper class in the United States that is a ruling class by virtue of its dominant role in the economy and government" (Domhoff, 1983: 1). By domination, he meant not total control, but the "ability to set the terms under which other groups and classes must operate" (p. 2). Because shaping policy conditions requires manipulation of resources, Domhoff's concept of domination is close to the one used in this book. He depicted the U.S. ruling class as a three-sector *power elite* composed of:

> *The upper social class.* The top half percent of wealth holders. It is a real social institution, achieving class consciousness and cohesion through private schools, universities, social clubs, debutante balls, and similar social organization.
>
> *The corporate community.* The owners and major stockholders of the largest corporations and financial institutions, along with the top-level executives of these organizations. Its most visible manifestation is the interlocking directorate system "that unites the corporate community and creates a dense and flexible communication network" (1983: 77).
>
> *The policy-planning network.* Nonpartisan organizations, foundations, and research institutes that bring together academic experts, businessmen, and political leaders to discuss general problems and propose policy solutions.

Domhoff's persistent empirical concern was to trace the personal and interorganizational connections among these three sectors. The structural relations thus uncovered formed the prerequisites for policy consensus and concerted action by the power elite.

Using secondary data sources such as *Social Registers, Who's Who*, government directories, corporation annual reports, and social club membership rosters, several researchers have identified the persons and organizations comprising the national power elite in the United States. The picture emerging from these empirical analyses is one of enormous resources controlled by a relatively small number of actors who are linked in networks of overlapping position holders. For example, in 1980 and 1981, Thomas R. Dye found that 5,778 persons occupied the 7,314 top positions in some 400 core organizations spanning a dozen institutional sectors, which collectively account for the majority of public and private financial assets of the United States (Dye, 1986: 12–13; similar data from 1970 and 1971 appeared in Dye, 1976). At least one-third of these positions were interlocked with one or more others through a single person, while 15 percent of all persons held more than one position (Dye, 1986: 13). Persons from upper-social-class origins were heavily overrepresented among top corporate leaders (chief executives and directors), a relationship well-documented in other studies (Zeitlin, 1978; Dye, 1986: 194; see also Dye, 1976: 151–2; Domhoff, 1983: 68; Domhoff, 1967: 53–5; but see Alba and Moore [1982] for broader class recruitment patterns).

Several studies traced leadership connections across institutional sectors, with some examining the business origins of presidential cabinet secretaries in historical and contemporary periods (Freitag, 1975; Mintz, 1975; Prewitt and McAllister, 1976; Useem, Hoops, and Moore, 1976; Burch, 1980). Using people as the units of analysis, Dye concluded that more specialization than convergence occurred across a dozen sectors (Dye, DeClerc, and Pickering, 1973; Dye and Pickering, 1974). Contrary to Mills' contention about the 1950s, he discovered that:

> There is very little overlap among people at the top of the corporate, governmental, and military sectors of society. To the extent that high government officials are interlocked at all, it is with civic and cultural and education institutions. It is *within* the corporate sector that interlocking is most prevalent. (Dye, 1986: 184)

This conclusion rested on concurrent position holding, so not surprisingly few persons simultaneously hold down full-time jobs in two or more sectors. But even when lifetime career moves across sector boundaries are examined, most government leaders gained their experience in governmental positions or the law and not in the corporate community. Although

40 percent of corporate leaders held at least one governmental post during their careers, only about one-quarter of top government elites had previously held corporate jobs (Dye, 1986: 169–71; see also Dye, 1976: 130 for similar findings based on earlier data).

In two studies using different network methods to trace intersectoral connections, Domhoff argued that much greater convergence occurred across sectors. The membership rosters of twenty elite social clubs and sixteen policy-planning organizations revealed that 12 percent of the 20,000 members belonged to two or more organizations (Bonacich and Domhoff, 1981). A latent structure analysis of these joint memberships uncovered three core clusters (a Washington-based group, an Eastern establishment, and a Western establishment) and four hybrid or bridging clusters. Organizations in the latter groups had higher centrality scores, implying that they linked the three regional subsets into a national elite system. People belonging to organizations in both the Eastern establishment and the Western establishment were especially important and powerful in the corporate community. Multiple-establishment actors were more likely to hold directorships in many large corporations than were people belonging to only one or neither regional establishment. Thus, a coalescence of wealth, expertise, and corporate control was apparent in the pattern of person-organization memberships.

In a second network analysis, Salzman and Domhoff (1980) used Dye's 1970-to-1971 data to reveal extensive interchanges of personnel between the corporate community, civic organizations, and the federal government executive branch during the Nixon administration. With organizations rather than persons as the foci, they concluded that Dye had underestimated the extent of sector integration. In particular, major legal firms and secondary positions in the corporate sector were a main source from which federal executive appointments were filled. Of 120 Nixon appointees, most had corporate or small business backgrounds, whereas only one-quarter came from strictly government careers. During the subsequent decade, a great majority of the federal appointees resumed or entered new careers in the corporate sector. Salzman and Domhoff (1980: 251) interpreted this revolving door phenomenon, well-known to journalists, as evidence that the state enjoys temporary autonomy. That is, business people who entered the government experience sufficient distance from the short-run interests of their firms that they transcend parochial concerns and act on behalf of the general interests of the corporate community. And their impending return to the corporate realm assured that they would act to promote long-run corporate interests.

A mechanism for capitalist class cohesion was proposed by Michael Useem in a series of articles and a book. He evoked a *classwide rationality principle* under which elite membership is "primarily determined by position in a set of interrelated networks transecting virtually all large corporations" (Useem, 1982: 202). These networks include personal acquaintance circles, corporation ownership webs, major business associations, and, "perhaps the most important element," interlocking directorates. An interlock exists when two corporations share a common board of directors member, either by an official from one firm sitting on another's board or by a person who is not an officer sitting simultaneously on two boards (see Chapter 4). For Useem, the directorate ties serve as more than the means for economic interchanges between company dyads. Instead, their primary purpose is to allow large corporations to scan their environment continuously, monitoring it for new developments in governmental policies, labor relations, markets, technological changes, and the like (p. 209). The centrality of banks in the directorate network stems from firms' critical needs for financial trend information (see also Chapter 4; Mintz and Schwartz, 1985). Thus, the inclusive but diffuse structural network created by interlocking directorates is mainly a communication network that serves to further the political influence of the corporate community.

An unplanned consequence of this structure is the emergence of a *dominant segment* (Useem, 1982) or *inner circle* (1983), consisting of a small elite who simultaneously hold multiple directorships in major corporations. This special segment can act as the politically conscious vanguard of the capitalist class. Because its members are exposed to the needs and circumstances of several economic sectors, the inner circle can transcend the parochial concerns of individual firms and speak for classwide interests. It "possesses both the cohesion and broader concerns necessary for it to serve as a vehicle for promotion of the interests of business in general" (Useem, 1982: 212). In particular, the inner circle elite is more likely to be involved in business associations, governmental advisory boards, and financial support of political parties and candidates. These business-to-government contacts enhance the business-scanning function, but not primarily for lobbying on behalf of the participants' main firms. Rather, they promote a broader vision of capitalism: "Special pleading...is discouraged by informal norms that prevail. 'A frank exchange of views' on broad economic policies of the moment, on the other hand, is expected" (Useem, 1982: 216). Presented with an integrated world view of public policies by this core segment, government is strongly compelled to defer to the interests of the capitalist class as a whole.

Useem presented empirical evidence consistent with his theory. Data from 1969 on 2,003 directors of the 797 largest corporations in the United States revealed that inner group members (defined as those holding four or more directorships) were more likely than other business directors to be directly involved in the governance of a range of private and public institutions. Specifically, compared to single directors, the inner group was more than three times as likely to serve on federal advisory boards and half again as likely to serve on state and local government boards (Useem, 1979:

562). Ratios ranged from 1.18 for charitable organizations to 2.44 for economic organizations (p. 561). For twelve major business policy associations (such as the Council on Foreign Relations and Committee for Economic Development), less than 1 percent of single directors were members, whereas 19 percent of multiple directors were members (p. 563). Inner group members are also overrepresented on the boards of trustees of private colleges and universities (Useem, 1981) and in raising funds for political parties and candidates (see Clawson, Neustadtl, and Bearden, 1986). Parallel differentials occurred within the inner circle of British multiple directors (Useem and McCormack, 1981; Useem, 1982: 213). Interviews with more than a hundred in the United States and Britain confirmed the existence of consciously held inner circle norms promoting the broader needs of big business and downplaying the special interests of individual firms (Useem, 1982, 1983).

Useem's analyses presented compelling evidence for the existence of a politically active segment of the corporate community. However, his data were not sufficient to demonstrate that this inner circle succeeded in promoting an elite policy consensus or in exerting either domination or influence over government policymaking. In fairness, he recognized the limits of his approach:

> [I]t also remains an open question whether the two overrepresented class segments [large industrial firms and multiple directors] are able actually to impose their views upon the outside institutions in whose governance they directly participate. Scattered evidence suggests that they can significantly influence institutional policies under certain, specific circumstances..., but direct verification of the impact of the business elite in these specific areas of outside governance is still needed. (Useem, 1980: 222–3)

The beginnings of such verification can be found in a series of recent projects that directly collected political communication network data from national elites.

Communication in issue networks

A comparative U.S. and Australian project used communication linkages among samples of institutional leaders to identify an overarching central circle that consensually integrated both nations' elites (Moore, 1979; Higley and Moore, 1981). The American Leadership Study, conducted in 1971 and 1972 by the Bureau of Applied Social Research (Barton, Denitch, Kadushin, Moore, Parsons, and Weiss, 1981) and a 1975 survey by the

Australian National University used almost identical sampling and measurement methods. The universe of elites was composed of the key organizations in ten institutional sectors: industrial firms; nonindustrial corporations; wealth holders; labor unions; political parties; voluntary associations; mass media; and the national legislature, executive, and civil service banks. From 50 to 60 top leaders were selected from each sector along with additional elites nominated by the respondents. Interviews were completed with 545 Americans and 370 Australians (response rates of 70 percent and 74 percent, respectively; see Higley and Moore, 1981: 585). Each elite person was asked to name one national issue on which he or she had attempted to influence policy or public opinion during the past year. Then each was asked to name people with whom the respondent talked about that issue (see pp. 595–6 for exact wording). From these data, the analysts constructed a communication network among the 941 Americans and 746 Australians mentioned as discussion partners. The density of actual to possible connections was very sparse, less than 1 percent in both countries (Alba and Moore, 1978: 180; Higley and Moore, 1981: 588).

The direction of structure in these two large communication networks drew from the social circle concept as developed by Kadushin (1968) and from methods formalized by Alba (1972, 1973). Circles are subsets of social actors with similar interests and concerns but differing formal affiliations and obligations. Their members are not all in direct contact with one another. Indeed, a circle is not clearly bounded, lacks definite leadership, and is relatively invisible to its members. Hence, a circle differs from a maximally connected clique by including some designated proportion of its membership that is reachable only through short chains of intermediaries. Alba's computer program, COMPLT, locates denser portions of a large graph by aggregating cliques of three or more actors whose members overlap sufficiently by an analyst-designated criterion (typically requiring that two of three clique members overlap before aggregation is allowed). The theoretical significance of social circle analysis for national elite research is that it "can constitute a mechanism for substantial communication and interaction among large numbers of persons who are located in otherwise disparate organizations and sectors" (Higley and Moore, 1981: 587). Of course, such circles may not exist, and a national structure instead may consist of numerous small cliques unable to communicate through bridging actors.

The U.S. and Australian analyses each uncovered one large central circle, having 227 U.S. members and 418 Australian members, and many small circles with fewer than 10 members. Structurally, the central circles consisted of many highly overlapped cliques. About two-thirds of the U.S. circle and 86 percent of the Australian circle members were mutually reachable by no more than a single intermediary (i.e., by two paths). Further, the central circle was closely tied to other elites through numerous links to the smaller circles and cliques. Yet despite this aggregation, the overall central circle densities remained relatively sparse; the U.S. density was less than 4 percent of possible ties (Alba and Moore, 1978: 182; the Australian circle's density was not reported). Because direct ties within the core were relatively rare (averaging fewer than nine direct links for the U.S. respondents), the central circles' distinctiveness came from a ramified network of indirect paths of few steps that would permit information to be transmitted with fewer intermediaries.

The U.S. and Australian national elites strikingly resembled one another because of the presence of a large core group of positional elites maintaining indirect communication ties of short length involving discussions over national policy issues. Both central circles drew members from all ten institutional sectors, but governmental and political elites were heavily overrepresented. The U.S. central circle contained a larger proportion of business elites, which the analysts attributed to the United States' larger and more diverse economy and to its more centralized federal government (Higley and Moore, 1981: 592). Central circle members, in contrast to noncircle elites, were the most influential members of their sectors, as indicated by service on federal advisory committees, testifying at legislative hearings, and serving on policy-planning organizations. But most central circle elites did not have significantly higher class origins or better connections to upper class social clubs and corporate directorship ties. Moore argued that these findings disproved the existence of a cohesive ruling class or power elite rooted in upper-class affiliations (Moore, 1979: 689). Nor did these data support the notion of numerous isolated, peripheral, and autonomous specialized elites, such as described by Keller (1963). The evidence was most consistent with the consensually integrated elite model developed by Field and Higley (1980). The extensive and inclusive communication linkages of the central circle permit government and nongovernmental elites relatively easy access to the most central public and private decision makers (Higley and Moore, 1981: 584). A comprehensive and tightly integrated structure of personal interaction connecting all institutional sector elites (with the notable exception of U.S. civil servants) was conducive to stable democratic political systems.

The leadership studies pointed to potential unity among the U.S. and Australian elites, but they failed to demonstrate that concerted action actually took place. Indeed, by emphasizing network form instead of content, the two study designs may have exaggerated the extent to which intersectoral elite connectivity occurred (Knoke, 1981a: 308). Each respondent was asked to nominate only a single national issue of importance and to provide names of discussion partners. Yet the communication matrix conflated these heterogeneous specific contents. Thus, discussion linkages involving defense policies were concatenated with those addressing women's rights, agriculture, space exploration, and many other issues. By failing to discriminate among the diverse contents about which elites interact, the Moore and Higley analyses overlooked the possibility that the huge central circles were merely analytic artifacts masking fragmented communication patterns, each confined within highly particularized institutional sectors. Fortunately, some recent comparative projects examined structural relations among elite organizations within narrow national policy domains.

Policy domain structures

Network principles and methods were featured prominently in analyses of the U.S. energy and health domain (Laumann and Knoke, 1987) and the U.S. and West German labor domains (Knoke, 1989; Knoke and Pappi, 1989). Parallel projects examined the Belgian defense policy domain (Manigart, 1986) and the social organization of the Washington representatives in agriculture, energy, health and labor (Salisbury, Heinz, Laumann, and Nelson, 1987; Nelson, Heinz, Laumann, and Salisbury, 1987; Laumann et al., 1985; Heinz, Laumann, Nelson, and Salisbury, 1988). Given the voluminous results of these large projects, only salient common features can be presented here, illustrated mainly by the U.S. labor policy structural relations.

Laumann and Knoke's concept of a policy domain resembled the Moore-Higley and Dye notions of institutional sectors (Knoke and Laumann, 1982). It is a subsystem whose organization members are identified "by specifying a substantively defined criterion of mutual relevance or common orientation...concerned with formulating, advocating, and selecting courses of action" to solve the domain's problems (p. 256). A domain's members consist only of those organizations whose interests and actions must be taken into account by other participants. Numerous national policy domains exist in modern states, and their core organizations may overlap to a greater or lesser degree. For example, the labor policy domain encompasses all issues dealing with the pricing, conditions, regulation, and provision of labor inputs to the economy. Hence, its core participants typically include labor unions, trade associations, business corporations, and governmental bureaucracies and legislative committees having primary authoritative responsibilities for these issues. But the domain may also involve various public interest groups such as civil rights, women's and senior citizens organizations with interests in employment discrimination against their constituencies. The labor policy domain may also draw the attention of health domain organizations (concerns about occupational safety) as well as members of the education policy domain (interests in vocational education and retraining programs). Thus, the boundaries between policy domains are somewhat fuzzy and porous, and a given political actors' membership in the core set depends both on the actors' own interests in domain issues and the capacity to make other actors take it into account when collective decisions are made. Ultimately, specification of policy domain membership is an empirical matter.

Policy domain analysis typically begins with multiple methods to delineate the core set of domain actors, events, and issues for a given period (Laumann and Knoke, 1987: 94–108). Researchers assume that the most significant policy organizations would leave public records of their efforts to influence domain policies. They cull lists of witnesses before congressional committees, newspaper accounts of domain activities, legislative lobbying registrations and amicus curiae participants in federal appellate court cases. They also ask for nominations from panels of academic and journalistic experts. Because a thousand or more organizations may surface, some criterion must reduce the numbers to a manageable core set. Typically, those organizations that reappear numerous times (at least five or six times across the various media) identify a hundred or so consequential movers and shakers. Next, personal interviews are conducted with a government affairs specialist or similar executive informant from each organization. With persistence, response rates can exceed 95 percent. The interviews ask about interorganizational communications, resource exchanges, and participation in various domain policymaking events during the period under study (typically a recent national administration). Informants are generally able to report whether their organizations had any particular interest in each event. For those events, they will also report their organization's position (for or against the proposal) and the types and levels of activity, including coalitions with other organizations. Thus, a complete sociopolitical map of the entire set of core organizations' involvements in domain policy events can be reconstructed. The cost of such data collection is generally much less than for a sample survey of the U.S. public.

At the heart of every policy domain analysis is the structure of its policy communication network. Laumann and Knoke argued that specialized communication linkages among consequential actors allow them to accomplish two critical purposes: (1) to monitor the ongoing stream of activities in their external environments for opportunities and threats to organizational interest and (2) to interpret this information for strategic interventions into events whose collective policy decisions are consequential for the organization (Laumann and Knoke, 1986: 87–88; 1987: 212–15)

> The monitoring function broadcasts information to as many targets as possible and receives information from as many as possible in an effort to dredge up as much factual information as possible. The interpretive function is more selective,

targeting those actors that may affect the success of an
organization's policy influence efforts with persuasive
information. (Laumann and Knoke, 1987: 215)

Communication networks are operationalized by presenting each organizational informant with a complete list of all domain core organizations
and asking him or her to check all with whom he or she exchanges information about domain policies. Communication matrices can thus be
constructed from the dyadic data, with each cell indicating the sending of
information from the row organization to the column organization. Because a communication relationship allows information to pass in both
directions, an appropriate measure of network density is the ratio of reciprocated direct ties between organizations to the total possible ties (Knoke
and Kuklinski, 1982: 45). The U.S. energy and health domains had densities of .30, whereas the U.S. labor domain's density was .385 and the
German labor domain density was .20. These results contrasted markedly
with the .038 density found by Moore (1979) in the American Leadership
Study that drew elites from a wide range of institutional sectors. Clearly,
organizations in a specific policy domain are substantially more connected
among themselves than they are to other domains. In all domain communication networks, every organization was mutually reachable by three or
fewer paths. No organization was isolated, and most required only two
intermediaries to pass a message to any other domain participant.

The binary communication matrix for the 117 organizations in the U.S.
labor policy domain was submitted to a hierarchical clustering program
(STRUCTURE; see Burt, 1987c). This routine aggregated the organizations according to their structural equivalence using a Euclidean distance
measure. That is, two organizations were joined in a cluster if they maintain
similar patterns of communication to the other 115 domain actors. Successively larger clusters were agglomerated according to the maximum distance of existing clusters (the so-called diameter method). This analysis
resulted in a reduction of the 117 organizations to 14 relatively homogeneous clusters, whose detailed memberships are not reported here. The
matrix of communication densities within and between these 14 blocks was
spatially analyzed using the ALSCAL program (Schiffman, Reynolds, and
Young, 1981), producing the two-dimensional solution in Figure 6.1.
Blocks of organizations that have high rates of communication are located
close to one another, whereas those that rarely exchange information are
further apart. Full details of the composition of the 14 positions cannot be
presented here, but some of the major organizations and the number of
organizations in each cluster are listed in the figure's key. The essential
structure is fairly easy to grasp by looking at distances from the spatial
center. Closest to the center of the communication space are the congres-

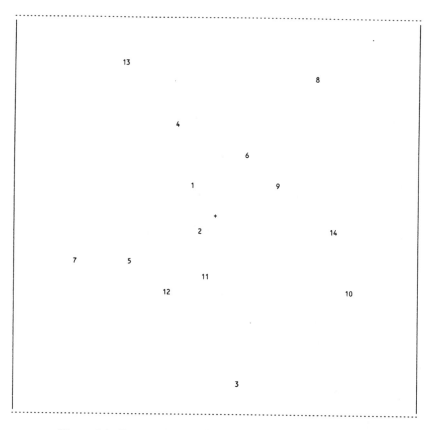

Figure 6.1. Communication distances among fourteen labor policy clusters.

1: Congressional Committees (4)	6: AFL, UAW, UMW (5)
	7: Business Assns. (26)
2: Labor Department, White House, EEOC (4)	8: Labor Unions (8)
	9: NAACP, ACLU, NFIB (10)
3: Justice Department, INS, Civil Rights Commission (3)	10: WEAL, LULAC, NUL (15)
	11: Public Employers (12)
	12: AMA, AHA, ANA (5)
4: OSHA, NIOSH (2)	13: Miscellaneous (15)
5: Chamber, NAM, BRT (3)	14: Miscellaneous (5)

sional committees (block 1) and the Labor Department-White House-EEOC (block 2). These core positions are clearly the major public authorities able to make binding policy decisions for the domain as a whole and hence are the target of numerous policy influence communications from the private sector organizations and the more specialized government agencies. At a farther remove from the center are five blocks of peak organizations: the Chamber of Commerce, National Association of Manufacturers, and Business Roundtable (block 5); the AFL-CIO and four of its major unions (block 6); a set of public employers such as cities, counties, and governors (block 11); a group of predominantly civil liberties interest groups (block 9); and a health associations block (block 12). At the farthest distances are the Justice Department and the remaining business, union, minority and women, and miscellaneous organizations. These latter blocks generally have much narrower, more specialized interests in labor domain issues and events. The locations of the 14 policy domain positions reveal a pervasive business-union cleavage within the U.S. labor policy domain; business and labor appear on opposite sides of the space, whereas the Congress and core administration agencies mediate their communications. Civil liberties and minority/women groups are closer to the labor union side of the space, whereas the public employers and health associations maintain stronger ties to the business community. Similar results occurred in both the U.S. energy and health domains, where the centers of their communication spaces were jointly occupied by the most influential congressional subcommittees and federal agencies and the peripheries by specialized claimant associations (Laumann and Knoke, 1987: 242–8).

Structural networks are important for understanding how policy domain organizations become involved in policy influence activities. Analyzing the energy and health domains, Laumann, Knoke, and Kim (1985) specified a causal model in which an organization's positions in communication and material resource exchange networks mediated between three antecedent factors (the organization's interests in issues, its external monitoring capacity, and its influence reputation) and the organization's policy event participation. Positions in both exchange networks were measured as prestige prominence scores, which take account of how direct relations connect an actor to many other prominent actors (Knoke and Burt, 1983). Event participant scores were measured by spatial dispersion among the eighty-odd policy domain events in which an organization actively tried to influence the outcome. The basic hypothesis was that organizations occupying prominent positions in the two exchange networks would participate in a wider range of domain policy events. The more central an organization's location in the two interorganizational exchange networks, the more likely the organization would be to interpret the information it received as calling for strategic interventions into policy events. This mobilization would occur apart from an organization's interests in issues affecting the events.

In both the energy and health domains, the three antecedent factors were positively and moderately intercorrelated (Laumann, Knoke, and Kim, 1985: 14–15). Issue interests and influence reputation each had significant effects on communication network position; organizations with broader policy interests and higher influence reputations were located in more prominent positions of the network (see also Chapter 5). But communication prominence was unrelated to resource exchange network prominence in either domain; clearly these were quite distinct structural relations. Most important, the domains differed markedly in the factors affecting policy event participation. Issue interest exerted a large direct effect in both domains, meaning that the broader an organization's issue concerns, the greater the number of events in which it is actively engaged:

> But, for energy organizations, issue interest is the only variable with a significant coefficient. The results support our expectations concerning the noninstitutionalized nature of the energy domain in the 1970s. In contrast, the health domain exhibits significant net relations from both measures of network location. (Laumann, Knoke, and Kim, 1985: 15)

Resources exchange prominence only slightly increased health policy event participation (path coefficient of .17), whereas prominence in communication substantially raised event participation (path coefficient of .44). This effect was as strong as that for health issue interests. The authors concluded that the greater importance of network position for event mobilization in health than in energy reflected the greater institutionalization of the latter domain: "In this context, institutionalization means that a domain has become a routinized, calculable, well-integrated system, with rules of legitimate policy participation well understood and accepted by all players" (Laumann, Knoke, and Kim, 1985: 16). Because policy information is less accessible in such domains, an advantageous network position allows an organization to reduce some of the higher costs of obtaining relevant data. By contrast, the turbulent, highly visible energy domain of the 1970s did not impose serious information impediments to policy involvement. Hence, privileged locations in the communication or resource exchange networks did not convey special advantages to mobilizing an organization's policy event participation. Simply having an interest in a policy issue was sufficient to stimulate involvement.

Another major consideration in policy domain analysis is the oppositional structure of domain events. A legislative, executive, or judicial controversy typically attracts opposing sets of organizations, each side seeking an outcome favorable to its interests. But these lines of consensus and cleavage between pro and con organizations generally do persist across numerous domain events (Laumann and Knoke, 1987: 311–42). Rather than the bipolar sets of opponents implied by class conflict or power elite theories, each event seems to attract unique opposing sets of organizations. Because every organization maintains a different portfolio of issue interests and also communicates with distinctive sets of organizations, very few of these groupings can be exactly reassembled as new events move toward a decision.

This highly fluid situation is illustrated by an analysis of collective actors (see Chapter 5) in the U.S. labor domain. Twenty-five congressional bills were sampled from the hundreds of congressional events from 1981 to 1987. Each organizational informant was asked what position his or her organization preferred for the outcome of the proposed legislation: for, against, neutral, or not interested. Although many organizations monitored the progress of every event without stating formal positions, for only two events did more than half the 117 members of the domain population take either the pro or con positions (the 1982 CETA-JTPA and 1987 parental-disability leave bills). For six events, fewer than two dozen participants took positions. The collective actor analysis begins by identifying for every event the sets of organizations in close communication who also take the same position on that event (see Laumann and Marsden, 1979; Knoke and Burleigh, 1989). For example, all 36 organizations in communication with one another who favored increasing the minimum wage comprised one collective actor. The 20 communicating organizations opposed to the wage hike comprised a second collective actor. On other policy events, the members of these two sets of organizations may take differing positions or remain inactive. In all, 46 collective actors having at least 3 member organizations formed around the 25 labor policy events (for 4 events only 1 collective actor was formed; for the other 21 events, both pro and con collective actors occurred).

Figure 6.2 shows the spatial organization of collective actors based on the degree to which their members overlap. This overlap measure is higher to the extent that the same organizations take the same position on a pair of events (see Laumann and Marsden, 1979). If identical pro and con groups occurred for every event, the diagram would consist of just two points at opposite ends of a line (see Figure 5.3 in Chapter 5). But, as some organizations joined and others left an event-specific collective actor, the changing composition would move their locations apart. The closer two collective actors appear in the space, the more similar their memberships, whereas those furthest apart have the fewest members in common. In Figure 6.2, enclosed lines have been drawn around sets of collective actors on opposite sides of each event. As with the issue interests above, no collective actors occupied the center of the space. Instead, a clean cleavage resulted; collective actors that favored business interests are located on the left and those that favor labor union interests are on the right. But these are not monolithic blocks. Considerable dispersion from extreme polarization occurred, particularly on the right side as various organizations joined and left the prolabor collective actors. The two points at which the opposition blocks came into closest contact are at the top (mining safety and ERISA pension events) and bottom (JTPA and vocational education), issues where some commonality between business, labor, and minority groups can be reached. But those events that involved labor-management issues and social policies had the fewest members in common, yielding collective actors at

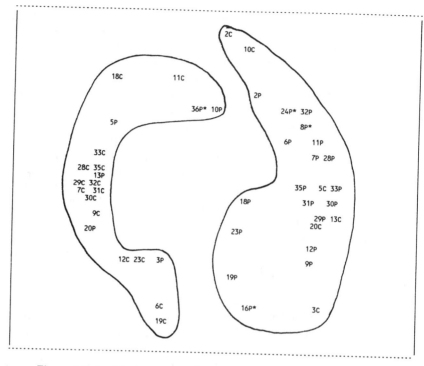

Figure 6.2. Legislative event collective actors in U.S. labor policy domain.

2:	Black lung benefits	19:	JTPA summer remedial education
3:	CETA and JTPA		
5:	Union pension fraud	20:	Teenage sub-minimum wage
6:	Public employee pensions		
7:	Automobile domestic content	23:	Immigration reform
*8:	ERISA benefits recovery	*24:	American Boxing Corporation
9:	American Conservation Corps	28:	Occupational risk assessment
10:	Mine safety cooperation	29:	Parental and disability leave
11:	ERISA pre-1974 benefits		
12:	Public Works Compensation	30:	Minimum wage increase
13:	Garment homework limits	31:	60-day plant closing
*16:	Vocational education renewal	32:	Bankruptcy benefits
		33:	Double-breasting
18:	ERISA pension spousal equity	35:	Polygraph ban
		*36:	PBGC premium increase

*No opposition on these events.   P = Pro; C = Con

maximum distances from one another. Figure 6.2 is stark evidence of the great gulf dividing much of the U.S. labor policy domain during the Reagan era.

Beyond collective actor analysis are the structural relations among action sets, "a group of organizations formed into temporary alliance for a limited purpose" (Aldrich 1979, p. 280; see also Boissevain 1974, pp. 170–205). An action set may have formalized agreements, an internal division of labor, behavioral norms vis-à-vis other organizations, and clearly defined principles for recruiting new members (Aldrich 1979, p. 281). Thus, action sets are short-term arrangements, most formed only for single-event collaborations and disbanding after success or failure. They are subsets of those members of a collective actor that work together to influence a specific public policy decision. Berry (1984, pp. 202–5) attributed the fragility of most interest groups' joint lobbying efforts to *organizational ego* – the desire of group leaders to claim credit to enhance their own organizations' reputations. He concluded that success was greatest if lobbying was an informal, low-key effort whose "membership comes from an issue network in which the lobbyists have experience working with each other," and was limited to one specific issue that the government was likely to implement (p. 205). Knoke and Pappi (1989) uncovered evidence in both the United States and Germany that most labor policy legislative events were fought by small opposing action sets. Preliminary results suggested a more polarized opposition structure between business and labor in the United States. At this writing, research is continuing on the role of action sets in determining the outcome of legislative struggles.

Exchange and policy outcomes

The final analyses of the national policy domain projects explored the effects of network relations on event outcomes. Attempts to explain event decisions as the result of exchanges among interested and resourceful actors have mostly involved simulated data (Coleman, 1973, 1977: Marsden, 1981, 1982, 1983). The essence of Coleman's approach considers how actors with interests in different events exchange resources that influence the event outcomes. Following from resource dependence principles, actors are more powerful and more likely to achieve their preferred outcomes if they possess resources that control events in which other actors have strong interests. For example, a mayor may control the city council votes needed by a social service bureaucracy that wants authorization to expand its program budget. In return for yielding this resource, the mayor will expect to receive control over resources of the bureaucracy that affect events in which the mayor has an interest, such as campaign help in the next election. The outcome of events depends on the intensity of interests in the various events and the controlling resources held by each actor. In a pure market situation, every pair of actors can directly exchange with one another. But in community elite systems, where mutual trust is required before such transactions take place, resources exchanges most likely occur only through well-established networks of direct and indirect connections. Brokerage relations may also be critical in bringing potential exchange partners together (see Chapter 5). The absence of any communication channel between actors signals a lack of information or access for making an exchange on one event that will be reciprocated during a later event.

Few applications of the Coleman exchange model have used data from real collective action situations. Michener, Cohen, and Sorenson (1977) examined exchanges of colored tokens within experimental small groups. Marsden and Laumann (1977) studied five events (including two hypothetical ones) in a small city in the United States. Using ten types of resources controlled by the community organizations (ranging from money and credit to influence with subgroups), they estimated the power of each actor and the probabilities of the outcome of each event. The correlation between actors' power predicted by the Coleman model and direct measures of their influence reputations was .90. In accord with the principle of integrative centrality, exchange power was highly correlated with centrality in networks of social relations ($r = .58$) and business-professional ties ($r = .61$). However, the Coleman model correctly predicted only three of the five event outcomes, a result the authors attributed to incorrect assumptions about the closed nature of the community system for all events (Marsden and Laumann, 1977: 223; see also Pappi and Kappelhoff, 1984; Pappi and Melbeck, 1984; Kappelhoff, 1989).

Using data from U.S. national energy and health domains, Laumann, Knoke, and Kim (1987: 343–73) applied a modified version of Coleman's exchange model to sixteen energy and health domain event outcomes. The details of this model are too complex to explicate here, but the findings are easily summarized. The resource deployment model depicted one domain organization as allocating valuable resources to another organization to achieve a favorable event outcome. The deployer delivers resources to a deployee or its agent to create the latter's dependence on the former (see Chapter 4 for basic exchange principles). This power dependence allows the deployer to ask the recipient to do something in the deployer's interest, such as support legislation favored by the deployer. The classic example is a trade association giving campaign money to a public official in implicit exchange for the official's vote on a bill favored by the association (see Chapter 8). If an actor has a monopoly over the supply of needed resources (i.e., substitute sources are unavailable), that actor is more powerful within the system. Thus, the more essential one actor's resources are for another, the greater the dependency in the exchange relation.

For their application, Laumann, Knoke, and Kim (1987) combined the candid confidential communication network with the money, staff, and facilities exchange network to identify the presumed equilibrium pattern of restricted exchanges among government and private sector organizations in the energy and health domains. They then selected eight controversial events in each domain that spanned the entire range of substantive issues. Finally, the organizations' policy interests were determined by their activity levels and outcome preferences on these events. According to the resource deployment model, organization j's power, P_j, was defined as:

$$P_j = C^*_{j1} P_1 + C^*_{j2} P_2 + \ldots + C^*_{ji} P_i + \ldots + C^*_{jm} P_m$$

where C^*_{ji} is organization j's resource exchange relationship with the ith organization. The C^*_{ji} are constrained to sum to 1.00 for organization i across the m organizations in the system to show the fraction of i's dependency on organization j. Power in the resource deployment model is estimated simultaneously for all organizations as a system of equations. Thus, this concept of power is a function of dependencies among organizations, as shown by their resource exchanges with other powerful organizations.

The resulting power estimates were strongly correlated with the independently measured reputed influence standings of the organizations ($r = .58$ and $.73$ in energy and health, respectively). The ability to deploy resources to create dependencies among other organizations thus covaried highly with peer attributions for domain influence. An organization's estimated impact on event outcomes varied from event to event, as expected from their expressed differential interest in the outcomes. Business corporations formed a major portion of consequential energy domain actors, but professional associations were the movers and shakers in the health domain. For each of the sixteen events analyzed, the model quite accurately predicted the collective outcome, failing in only one of the eight health events to designate correctly the actual result (Laumann, et al., 1987: 362–3; however, one of the eight energy events was erroneously reported as accurately predicted). In conclusion, the external checks indicated that the predictive efficacy of the resource deployment model were quite good. They yielded "valuable insights into the nature of influence processes and the interorganizational resource transactions in national policy domains" (p. 368), suggesting how dependency-creating resource exchanges enable some organizations to gain control over policy events of interest to them.

More recently, Stokman, van den Bos, and Wasseur (1989) proposed a general model of policymaking that integrates a preliminary stage of mutual interactor influence and a final stage of decision only by the actors entitled to vote on the binding decision (i.e., government authorities).

Applied to the U.S. energy domain data, they demonstrated that the positional power of various types of organizations depended especially both on their resources and their voting power, indicating that the distinction between governmental and nongovernmental actors is important to preserve. Another intriguing development is Peter Kappelhoff's (1989) development of power in exchange networks beyond the Marsden reformulation, taking into account clientelistic dependency (using Bonacich's [1987] measure of centrality) and barter exchange relations among actors. These analysts are continuing to develop the dynamic and predictive aspects of their models to the ultimate improvement of our understanding of elites in the nation state.

Looking forward

A solid foundation has been laid for structural understanding of national policy influence systems. The basic methods of data collection and analysis have been refined and replicated on several domains, resulting in substantively meaningful insights into their social organization and collective outcome processes. The relevance and limitations of simple exchange models for explaining legislative struggles have been shown. Cross-national research is now underway to compare the U.S., West German, and Japanese labor policy domains, which promises to expand knowledge about the importance of history and political culture in shaping distinctive policy regimes. There can be little doubt that networks of communication and resource exchanges are essential for this task. In liberal democracies, the lawmaking process requires bargaining, negotiation, compromise, and persuasion to resolve disputes in an incremental fashion that permits players to return to the game for the next round. Without effective channels through which interests are expressed, power resources are mobilized, and mutual support is exchanged, binding collective actions would prove difficult if not impossible. The recurrent relationships between authoritative public organizations and private-sector interest groups comprise stable power structures in a policy domain. These networks' operations are rules of the game that must be mastered by every participant who hopes to nudge public policy in directions favoring its interests. Social analysts can ignore the central role of these structural components only at the peril of reaching an inaccurate and unsatisfactory account of how elites and citizens jointly govern the modern organizational state.

7 *International relations*

with Jodi Burmeister-May

By the end of the 1980s, Third World nations owed more than $1.2 trillion to the banks and governments of the industrialized nations. Amassed in the wake of the 1970s oil shocks, many loans were squandered on ill-advised development schemes ranging from dams in Brazil to cattle ranches in Botswana. Interest payments on these foreign debts annually divert tens of billions of dollars in scarce capital resources away from productive development. The debt mountain generates stagnant economies, rampant inflation, food shortages, environmental destruction, and wage-price austerity controls. Both leftist insurgents and military mutinies threaten the stability of newly created democracies from Argentina to the Philippines. Mexican and Yugoslav workers shouting antigovernment slogans have stormed their countries' parliaments, demanding pay hikes. The United Nations Children's Fund warned that 18 million children might die of malnutrition by the end of the century. Faced with the prospect of huge losses and potential collapse of the domestic and international banking systems, the World Bank, International Monetary Fund, and Group of Seven major industrial creditors balk at forgiving or reducing the borrowing nations' debts. Yet they continue to carry bad debts on their books and to roll over new loans that add to the red ink. Postponing some payments is only grudgingly granted under threats of unilateral moratoria. This international game of chicken holds industrial and developing nations mutually hostage.

The intractable debt crisis is just the latest in a centuries-long history of troubled relations among the world's nations. The virtually instantaneous contact with people, organizations, and events in remote areas is a relatively recent phenomenon, dating from the mid-eighteenth century. Spatial and temporal distances have been collapsed, resulting in increased social, cultural, economic, and military proximity and accessibility. Indeed, a global system has emerged characterized by the increasing interdependence of daily routines in one part of the planet with those in other regions. Yet the practical conquest of time and space over the past five centuries has not been accompanied by corresponding political and economic equality. Great disparities have widened the gap between a handful of rich devel-

175

oped countries and the far more numerous and populous poor under-developed countries. Network analyses of the international system provide insightful perspectives on the power relations among countries. Much theory and research concentrates on the structures of domination, through which some nations exploit others economically and militarily. But, as we will suggest below, influence processes are coming to play an increasing role in shaping international behaviors.

Development: modernization or dependency?

Social theorists have long been concerned about national development and social change at the global level. Grounded in the nineteenth-century fascination with Darwinian concepts of evolution, early analysts concept-ualized social, political, and economic development as a series of discrete stages or societal types through which all societies must pass on their way to a universal type, which, not surprisingly, closely resembled the authors' own nations (e.g., Comte 1855; Spencer, 1910; Ward, 1906; Parsons, 1966). Although disagreeing about the institutional loci and causal mecha-nisms for societal change, those writings that are referred to as *moderniza-tion theory* shared a progressive vision of linear societal development. Whether using a dichotomous (traditional versus modern) or a trichoto-mous (primitive-intermediate-advanced) classification, all societies could be ranked along a unidimensional developmental continuum. A variety of empirical studies that emphasized different components of sociocultural evolutionary development constitute the main research using this perspec-tive (e.g., Rostow, 1960; Black, 1966; Organski, 1965). Implicit in the modernization approach was a quasi-religious belief that the introduction of Western values, capital, and technologies could ultimately civilize so-cieties that were termed as backward or undeveloped. Industrialization, with its corresponding increases in rationality, specialization, and institu-tional differentiation, was viewed as an essentially progressive force. Thus, industrial capitalism was upheld as the proper solution to backwardness and as the sole realistic path to national development.

The evolutionary theories of development, however, suffered serious inadequacies. First, they insisted on a unitary evolutionary path of develop-ment for which Western societies served as the only viable model. Con-sequently, development could occur only in contexts where pluralistic politics, tolerant attitudes, and liberal social values prevail. Second, these analysts considered societal change as ontogenetic (immanent or endog-enous to a nation). That is, the sources of modernization lie within the nation, emerging through a cumulative differentiation and integration among its subsystems (Parsons, 1971). Thus, development occurs in isolation from external influences, including economic exploitation and military domination by other societies. Third, the modernization perspective is fundamentally ahistorical, because it assumes that processes of change are themselves unchanging. Because the international context has no important impact, developmental dynamics remain identical for all nations. None of these assumptions seems plausible in light of recent research on detailed historical development processes (Nisbet, 1969).

The creation of an explicit alternative to modernization theory and similar evolutionary perspectives was initially elaborated by a group of Latin American economists associated with the United Nations Economic Commission for Latin America (ECLA), established in 1948. Fundamentally disappointed with the inadequacies of conventional theories of capitalist development, they sought a more adequate interpretation of Latin American and other less-developed nations' experiences (Dos Santos, 1970; Sunkel, 1972; Frank, 1967). In contrast to free-trade principles espoused by mainstream economists, these critics argued that Ricardo's theory of comparative economic advantage does not operate in the long-run favor of primary producers. This principle asserts that unrestricted exchange between nations is mutually advantageous if every country specializes in those goods that it produces most efficiently. Thus, an industrial nation should export manufactured goods and a nonindustrial nation should export raw materials and agricultural produce. Allegedly, each country's economy would prosper through free trade in those commodities in which each enjoys a comparative advantage. Instead, the Latin American critics argued, free trade benefits the industrial nations but retards the development of poor countries; a primary export economy is fundamentally vulnerable to shifts in the international economy. Autonomous domestic economies consequently failed to develop in poor nations because of prolonged unequal terms of trade with developed countries.

These writings provided the initial formulation of what is commonly referred to as *dependency theory*. Essentially, these theorists divide the international economy into two parts: a center (core) of industrialized countries and a periphery of underdeveloped countries. Common to analyses within the dependency paradigm is the assertion that capitalist development in one set of countries (i.e., the core or metropole) necessarily creates and sustains underdevelopment in another set of countries (i.e., the periphery or satellites) within a single-world capitalist system. In general, dependency theorists argue that international economic dependence produces the "development of underdevelopment" in peripheral countries of the world economy (Frank, 1967). A central assertion is that development and underdevelopment can be attributed neither to different stages of development nor to distinct economic structures. Rather, development and underdevelopment are simultaneous processes representing "the two faces of the historical evolution of the capitalist system" (Sunkel, 1972: 520). As

Frank elaborated:

> economic development and underdevelopment are relational
> and qualitative, in that each is actually different from, yet
> caused by its relations with, the other. Yet development and
> underdevelopment are the same in that they are the product of
> a single, but dialectically contradictory, economic structure and
> process of capitalism. . . . One and the same historical process
> of the expansion and development of capitalism throughout the
> world has simultaneously generated – and continues to generate
> – both economic development and structural
> underdevelopment. (Frank, 1967: 9)

> Yes, *development of underdevelopment* – because
> underdevelopment, as distinct perhaps from *un*development,
> did not pre-date economic development; nor did it spring up of
> itself; nor did it spring up all of a sudden. It developed right
> along with economic development – and it is still doing so.
> (Frank, 1967: 242)

Specifically, Frank argued:

> The metropolis expropriates economic surplus from its satellites
> and appropriates it for its own economic development. The
> satellites remain underdeveloped for lack of access to their own
> surplus and as a consequence of the same polarization and
> exploitative contradictions which the metropolis introduces and
> maintains in the satellite's domestic structure. (Frank, 1967: 9)

Dependence is "a situation in which the rate and direction of accumulation are externally conditioned" (Evans, 1979: 27). A dependent country is one whose development is "conditioned by the development and expansion of another economy" (Dos Santos, 1970: 231). Classically underdeveloped countries are those that have been historically integrated into the international economy through the specialized production of primary products for export and whose development is contingent upon the continued acceptance of its products in the core market. Many of these nations emerged from a colonial relation with a core country and persist as economic suppliers of raw materials and dumping grounds for finished products.

Dependency theorists asserted that the emergent economic structures of the periphery nations are distorted in such a way as to create obstacles to those nations' development (Dos Santos, 1970). Initial formulations by the ECLA theorists regarded unfavorable terms of trade in the periphery over time as a fundamental impediment to development. Focusing on relations of unequal exchange, they argued that prices tend to favor export of industrial goods from advanced countries over exports of primary agricultural or raw materials in peripheral economies. Osvaldo Sunkel, a Chilean economist with the ECLA, further argued that dependency is not merely an external condition, but that foreign influences must also be examined as internal effects. Focusing on multinational corporations (MNCs), Sunkel argued that penetration of local economies by these firms results in denationalization of capital, increased internal inequality, and external dependency (Sunkel, 1972). Further, Sunkel conceptualized the creation of doubly disadvantaged dichotomies: (1) an international division of countries between a set of developed, industrialized, central northern countries, and a set of underdeveloped, dependent, peripheral southern countries and (2) within each peripheral country, a division between an advanced/modern group of individuals and regions (i.e., those associated with the foreign-owned sectors) and backward/primitive groups and regions (i.e., the rest of the population). Extending his analysis to embrace both international and national levels of analysis, Sunkel viewed the state in peripheral nations as a subsystem component serving the international capitalist system (as noted by Chilcote, 1984: 29–30).

Frank argued that integration into the international economy through specialized externally oriented production of a few primary products for export results in the development of an infrastructure oriented toward ports of export. This orientation inhibits the creation of an internally linked national economy. The link between the metropolis and its satellites is reproduced internally between regions and between industrial centers and agricultural areas:

> Once a country or a people is converted into the satellite of an external capitalist metropolis, the exploitative metropolis-satellite structure quickly comes to organize and dominate the domestic economic, political, and social life of that people.
>
> Analogously, the regional, local, or sectoral metropolises of the satellite country find the limitations on their development multiplied by a capitalist structure which renders them dependent on a whole chain of metropolises above them. . . . Therefore, the capitalist satellite countries, regions, . . . are condemned to underdevelopment. (Frank, 1967: 10–11)

In contrast to the modernization approach, dependency theorists clearly proposed a new paradigm for explaining national development and underdevelopment. Arguing that underdevelopment can only be understood in terms of an historically grounded structuring of a single capitalist world system, dependency theorists drew attention to the reciprocal relations between core/metropolis and periphery/satellite economies. The development of underdevelopment is a consequence of integration into an increasingly unitary world system based on asymmetrical economic exchange relations that disproportionally benefit the core countries and distort growth patterns in the periphery. Furthermore, this international division of labor reinforces and perpetuates structural inequalities both between and within nations. Early *dependentistas* argued that the global expansion of capitalism results in stagnation and underdevelopment in the periphery. Consequently, mature capitalist development of the periphery is an impossible dream. Therefore, structural defects in peripheral economies are fundamentally consequences of their subordinate positions and roles within the capitalist world economy.

The theoretical rephrasing of questions about pathological development represented an important contribution in the debate over global development. However, with the late twentieth-century advent of industrial production processes within peripheral countries, the limitations of initial dependency theories soon became apparent. In their book, *Dependency and Development in Latin America* (1979, originally published in Spanish, 1971), Cardoso and Faletto proposed a more historically informed and dynamic conceptualization of international relations and peripheral development. Inspired by the early dependency formulations, they maintained that countries in the periphery can only be understood in terms of how they historically became integrated into the world economy. However, they further argued that to comprehend fully the underdevelment process, analysts must explicitly incorporate noneconomic factors (such as the structure of the state, internal class formation, role of the military, social movements, etc.) that modify development. Contrary to earlier formulations, Cardoso and Faletto argued that capitalist development within peripheral economies is possible. However, such development is distorted as a consequence of the interplay of internal and external economic, political, social, and geographical factors. Cardoso and Faletto emphasized not only external relations of dependence, but also the impact of international relations on domestic structures. They asserted that "the [international] system of domination reappears as an 'internal' force, through the social practices of local groups and classes that try to enforce foreign interests" (Cardoso and Faletto, 1979: xvi). And the "local socio-political process, as well as local economic organization, insofar as we are dealing with dependent societies, supposes and reproduces the general features of capitalism as it exists on a global scale" (p. xvii). Using an historical-structural approach, they emphasized "not just the structural conditioning of social life, but also the historical transformation of structures by conflict, social movements, and class struggles" (p. x). The diversification of the international dependency contexts permits a significant theoretical refinement of earlier dependency theories. Relating external and internal forces through the dialectical analysis of concrete situations of dependency, Cardoso and Faletto redirected structural dependency toward "explain[ing] the inter-relationships of classes and nation-states at the level of the international scene as well as at the level internal to each country" (p. xviii).

In their conceptualization of the "new dependency," Cardoso and Faletto used a broader definition of dependency than earlier writers who narrowly identified dependent relations as based on the export of raw materials and single-crop production for export. They argued that dependency conditions may also occur in economies where industrial production has been recently introduced, but where the dynamic mechanisms for its reproduction and expansion lie outside the local economy. For example, a consumer electronics assembly industry in a poor Asian nation requires capital inputs and market outputs in Japan and the West, because its production cannot be based on sales to its own populace. Therefore, a nation is dependent "when the accumulation and expansion of capital cannot find its essential dynamic component inside the system" (Cardoso and Faletto, 1979: xx).

In their analysis of industrializing peripheral nations, they identified a situation of "associated dependent development." This process is characterized by patterns of industrialization in peripheral economies based on the production of goods associated with mass consumption in core countries that remain luxury items for the dependent society. Peripheral industrialization sharply increases productivity within the internationalized sector based on modern technology, while production of basic goods for consumption by the masses remains based on traditional technologies and relations of production. The result is an internal "structural heterogeneity" in which those sectors of the peripheral economy identified with international capital (e.g., primarily MNCs) expand at the expense of traditional sectors (p. xxii). Associated dependent development concentrates wealth and concomitantly deepens income disparities within the dependent society. Unlike earlier dependency writings, Cardoso and Faletto's theoretical framework allowed for limited capital accumulation in the periphery. However, because development is fundamentally based on coordination with the international economy, relations of dependence persist among the peripheral countries.

The importance of understanding dialectical relations between international and domestic forces within specific historical contexts is evident in studies of national development in Brazil (Evans, 1979) and Taiwan (Gold, 1986). Responding to Cardoso and Faletto's call for more comprehensive analyses of social processes employing an historical-structural method, Evans examined how the dynamic relations between external and internal forces were expressed in the economic development of Brazil during the early 1970s. In elaborating his model of Brazilian development, Evans asserted that "dependent development" represents a special instance of dependency characterized by an association of international and local capital that enjoys the active support of the state (Evans, 1979: 32). He identified an emergent triple alliance, consisting of the national state, multinational corporations, and a segment of local capital that jointly provide the conditions for domestic industrialization. He concluded that collaboration among these distinct kinds of capital led to a successful strategy for accumulation and that none alone could have initiated Brazil's capitalist development. He asserted, however, that the interests of private capital, exerted primarily by the MNCs, played a dominant role in directing the processes. In his study of Taiwan's recent rapid economic growth, Gold (1986) similarly concluded that the same type of triple alliance was key in directing domestic development. However, in contrast with Evans' study, Gold depicted the state as playing a much more active role and dominating the Taiwan collaboration. Given distinct historical patterns of class relations, land tenure patterns, and stronger state capacity to assert a directive role in industrialization, Taiwan experienced a decidedly different form of dependent development within the international economy. These and other historical case studies of industrialization efforts are essential to fleshing out the detailed mechanisms by which foreign investments affect rates of economic growth.

The world-system perspective

The original *dependentistas* conceptualized a bipolar international division of labor in which surplus value is transferred from the dependent periphery to the dominant core. This dichotomy, however, was a relatively simplistic vision of global structural relations. Expanding on the classic dependency analyses, *world-system theory* asserted that the global economy consists of a complex but integrated network of economic, political, and cultural relations. This perspective was systematically formulated and refined in a series of seminal works by Immanuel Wallerstein (1974, 1980, 1982, 1988). World-system theory argued that a single, comprehensive capitalist global economy has been evolving since the sixteenth century, and that "its development has been the driving force of modern social change" (Hopkins and Wallerstein, 1982: 11). The world system is an exogenous global system that exists independently of its component national societies. It encompasses diverse structural processes, also transcending geopolitical boundaries, that fundamentally direct the global development of all countries within this planetary complex. Hopkins and Wallerstein asserted that this system is characterized by three interrelated structural processes: (1) a single, increasingly integrated global economy; (2) expanding multiple sovereign states; and (3) capital-labor relations based on an unequal global division of labor (Hopkins and Wallerstein, 1982: 11).

In the formation of this unified world-scale economy, labor processes are organized on a global basis, with capital in the form of profits accumulating in a more advanced and geographically shifting core, while physical production remains in a less-advanced periphery. Core societies are economically diversified, rich, and autonomous. Peripheral societies are economically specialized, weak, and subject to direct intervention and manipulation by the core. Core-periphery economic relations, in conjunction with parallel processes in international political-military relations, constitute the essential structural dynamic that drives developments in the world system. The global division of labor stems primarily from the unequal exchange of fundamental commodities:

> The division of labor in this exchange network was not only functional but also geographic, involving the exchange of relatively processed and differentiated goods for raw materials. The main structural feature of this world system came to be this division of labor between the emerging core areas producing manufactured goods and the emerging peripheral areas producing raw materials. The boundaries of the system were determined by the extent and intensity of economic production and exchange. (Chase-Dunn and Rubinson, 1977: 454)

Wallerstein (1982: 37) theorized that the developmental dynamics of capitalism were initially created by expanding networks of world trade and the collapse of world military empires (Spanish, Portuguese, Dutch, British, etc.), resulting in a global historical progression through a series of mini-systems to the contemporary world systems (see Chirot [1985, 1986] and Chirot and Hall [1982] for overviews of these historical sequences). Defining the capitalist mode of production as "production for sale in a market in which the object is to realize the maximum profit," Wallerstein (1974: 15) argued that a world economy has existed since the sixteenth century in Europe and parts of the Western hemisphere, when agricultural commodities began being produced for sale in nonlocal markets. The world system is based on a single division of labor that is producing for a world market:

> It is a "world" system, not because it encompasses the whole world, but because it is larger than any juridically-defined political unit. And it is a "world-*economy*" because the basic linkage between parts of the system is economic. (Wallerstein, 1974: 15)

Wallerstein (1982: 38–39) identified the commodification of labor as a distinguishing feature of capitalism but asserted, contrary to traditional Marxist analyses, that wage labor is merely one among several modes of labor recruitment and compensation.

It is important to note that Wallerstein included the socialist and communist countries in the world capitalist system. He reasoned that while the absence of private ownership of the means of production in some countries resulted in internal reallocations of consumption, these nations' enterprises still participate in and conform to the constraints of global capital markets. That is, even the socialized economies seek "increased efficiency of production in order to realize a maximum price on sales, thus achieving a more favorable allocation of the surplus of the world-economy" (Wallerstein, 1982: 49). Because the socialist countries are part of a dynamic network of economic trade relations with other countries within the world system, they are fundamentally integrated into the world division of labor and thus occupy a distinct position within the capitalist world system. Frank (1980: 178) concurred that socialist societies are integrated into the capitalist international division of labor, as evidenced by appreciable East-West trade and industrial cooperation.

Wallerstein further concluded that a world division of labor based on trade relations historically gave rise to regional economic specialization and to an international structure of unequally powerful nations. States are increasingly used to secure favorable terms of trade, including military threats and interventions. This tendency of politics to serve economic ends accelerated the unequal distribution of production and wealth within the global system:

> Once we get a difference in the strength of the state
> machineries, we get the operation of "unequal exchange,"
> which is enforced by strong states on weak ones, by core states
> on peripheral areas. Thus capitalism involves not only
> appropriation of the surplus value by an owner from a laborer,
> but an appropriation of the surplus of the whole
> world-economy by core areas. (Wallerstein, 1982: 40)

Thus, the capitalist world system increasingly polarized into a core of wealthy, technologically advanced countries and a periphery of poor countries from whom key primary goods and capital are extracted on unfavorable terms. Core countries enjoyed a position of global dominance as the result of their structural relations within the world economy. This structural hegemony – with its reinforcing multiplex linkages in political, military, and economic domains – sustained a continual accrual of new advantages by the core nations. Likewise, peripheral countries encountered structural constraints on their political economies that precluded any fundamental changes in their disadvantaged positions. Hence, uneven development was endemic within the capitalist world system.

Of particular theoretical significance in Wallerstein's framework was the inclusion of an important third structural position within the world economy – the "semiperiphery." Semiperipheral countries, such as Brazil, South Korea, and pre-Khomeini Iran, are situated between the core and periphery in terms of economic power. These societies are in the process of industrializing and diversifying their economies. Wallerstein surmised that the semiperiphery plays a critical role in the world system because "the existence of the third category means precisely that the upper stratum is not faced with the *unified* opposition of all the others because the *middle-stratum* is both exploited and exploiter" (Wallerstein, 1982: 43). They "deflect the anger and revolutionary activity of the peripheries" (Chirot and Hall, 1982: 85). In addition, the semiperiphery provides secure investment locations for core capital whenever core wages become inflated by well-organized labor movements. However, the semiperiphery serves less overtly economic or political functions than as a structural prerequisite for systemic stability: "When and if this ceases to be the case, the world-system disintegrates" (1982: 42). Finally, as Chirot and Hall noted (1982: 86), Wallerstein's thesis asserted that class, ethnic, and other internal structures of individual countries must be considered fundamentally as reflections of the international capitalist division of labor. Whereas internal relations are important in understanding the performance of individual countries within the international system, all countries are fundamentally and inescapably constrained by the transnational system.

Research issues

Both world-system and dependency theories became increasingly influential during the 1970s and 1980s. Indeed, the dependency paradigm was significantly incorporated into the theoretical orientations of social scientists well beyond the borders of Latin America. Dependency and world-system theories assert fundamentally similar views about structural relations in the international capitalist economy (e.g., that they are increasingly integrated, capitalist, and unequal) and the necessity for using historical-structural methods to analyze international dynamics. The common thesis of these paradigms is that a nation's occupancy of a particular structural position within the international system has important consequences for that nation's development. That is, a country's position in the global division of labor is regarded as a major constraint on its historical development or underdevelopment. However, neither dependency nor world-system approaches comprise rigorous formal theories with explicit hypotheses capable of empirical test. Instead, many researchers inspired by both perspectives tended to emphasize differential consequences of nations' positions in the international order for economic growth, foreign investment, MNC penetration, profits, income inequality, occupational distributions, school enrollments, political instability and violence, and other population indicators (see Evans and Timberlake, 1980; Bollen, 1983; Bornischier and Chase-Dunn, 1985; Timberlake and Williams, 1987; Chase-Dunn, 1988 for recent exemplary studies).

Substantial efforts were directed toward empirically specifying the primary dimensions of structural relations in the international system. Although comparative studies using quantitative measures are not the only way to investigate dependency and domination relations (indeed, perhaps not the most appropriate way; e.g., Frank, 1978), many researchers used aggregated, cross-national data to perform quantitative analyses that purportedly examined the adequacy of the theoretical formulations. These diverse studies may be conveniently grouped according to three primary emphases: (1) nature and size of the sample (for example, studies may be organized by geographic region, population, resources, etc.); (2) operationalization of the independent variable (e.g., external dependence may be operationalized in terms of trade, aid, foreign direct investment, etc.); and (3) the dependent variable (e.g., economic development, income distribution, quality of life, etc.). As is evident, quantitative analyses of various aspects of dependence and development incorporate a multiplicity of indicators. For example, measures of external dependence include exports, export concentration, commodity concentration, level of processing, terms of trade, investment, investment concentration, foreign aid, debt service, arms transfers, number of students abroad, etc. The assumption was that the higher a country ranks on these indicators, the greater its external dependence.

Given the inherently supranational scope of dependency and world-system theories, data availability and operationalization pose inherent difficulties in conducting macroquantitative studies of development. Further, although substantial evidence suggests structural impediments (i.e., dependency) that limit the development of the peripheral and semiperipheral nations, the dynamic breadth of these relations cannot be fully realized in large statistical analyses. The unique national configurations through which temporal processes of development/underdevelopment occur and are modified necessitate complementary case studies. Two primary modes of inquiry from the dependency and world-system perspectives are evident: studies focusing on the historical development of the world-system and studies examining the domestic effects of incumbency in a particular structural position within the world economy. Apart from critiques of Wallerstein's historical account of the rise of the world system (e.g., Brenner, 1977; Friedmann 1988; Denemark and Thomas, 1988), structural analysts have faulted him for failing to provide criteria that can be used to classify empirically each nation's precise location in the trichotomous structure. By default, many researchers of the contemporary world system deployed such continuous indicators as foreign investment penetration and trade concentration (e.g., Rubinson, 1976). But as noted above, such procedures fall short of fully incorporating the structural insights of dependency and world-system perspectives. Because some strides have been made in recent years to take structural concepts seriously, the remainder of this chapter considers empirical research that explicitly uses network concepts.

Measuring international transactions

Political scientists were among the first researchers to attempt quantitative data analyses of international behavior. The earliest studies measured each nation's position in the international system by its attributes along various linear dimensions, such as ratios of foreign to domestic trade or military spending levels (e.g., Rummel, 1963; Tanter, 1966). Using factor and regression analyses, these researchers interpreted patterns of covariation among the linear indicators as evidence of causal effects in international relations. But such aggregated attribute measures captured only the grossest levels of international activities. They failed to distinguish the differential inflow and outflow patterns of communication and commodity exchanges between nations that lie beneath the aggregate statistics (Hopkins, 1978). Two countries might have the same proportion of their gross national products (GNP) in foreign trade, but the first may trade a single key commodity with only a handful of partners while the second may trade many commodities among a diversified exchange network. This differential dependency on trading partners requires data analysis methods that preserve the structure of interactions among system members. A genuinely structural perspective must take into account details of the entire configuration of transaction flows among every pair of nations in the system. The international system of state relationships consists not of individual transactions between nations, but the total arrangement of all these transactions. As Haas (1964: 53) put it, "the system consists of the relationships among the *patterns* of trade, war, migration, and subversion."

Such patterns cannot be detected by summing across the rows and columns of a matrix that reports linkages among all pairs of nations. Rather, for the focus to remain on the system of interactions, positions in the system must be identified by the structural similarity of ties among the nations. To illustrate this concept of structural relations in an international system, consider the example in Table 7.1 based on total exports among twelve nations in 1980. These countries were deliberately chosen because they clearly formed four distinct trade blocks of three nations each. The top matrix reports the actual total dollars of 1980 exports and imports for

Table 7.1. Exports among twelve nations in 1980

Actual total exports (in $10 million)

	USA	JAP	UK	USR	EGR	CZE	BRA	MEX	ARG	LIB	NIG	SYR
United States	0	2156	1031	200	0	0	254	908	96	0	86	0
Japan	4328	0	494	282	0	0	74	58	31	36	57	0
United Kingdom	1266	120	0	67	0	0	24	24	0	41	121	0
Soviet Union	44	111	159	0	914	790	14	0	0	36	41	28
East Germany	0	0	25	890	0	170	12	0	0	1	13	69
Czechoslovakia	6	4	18	689	151	0	2	1	1	22	1	26
Brazil	652	166	71	86	16	13	0	17	65	0	20	0
Mexico	1225	146	86	0	4	3	64	0	4	0	0	0
Argentina	102	28	7	158	0	3	57	11	0	0	0	0
Libya	427	33	7	0	14	0	32	0	0	0	0	0
Nigeria	742	2	99	0	0	0	3	0	2	0	0	0
Syria	1	0	1	23	3	0	0	0	0	4	0	0

Block image ($900 million or more)

	UJ SAU APK	UEC SGZ RRE	BMA RER AXG	LNS IIY BGR
USA	011	100	1 11	000
JAP	101	100	000	000
UK	110	000	000	010

USR	011	011	000	000
EGR	000	101	000	000
CZE	000	110	000	000
BRA	110	000	000	000
MEX	110	000	000	000
ARG	100	100	000	000
LIB	100	000	000	000
NIG	101	000	000	000
SYR	000	000	000	000

Reduced block image

	WELO
WEST	1111
EAST	1100
LATIN	1100
OTHER	1000

all pairs of nations, to the nearest $10 million (United Nations, 1983). If one focused only on the row and column totals in this minisystem, certain pairs of nations would appear quite similar. For example, Mexico and Britain export comparable amounts, while Mexico's imports are the same magnitude as East Germany's and Czechoslovakia's. What is obscured by examining only the trade totals is where the commodities are coming from and going to.

An inspection that preserves the relational trade patterns reveals quite a different story. The second matrix in Table 7.1 is a binary block image of the dollar matrix, in which exports under $900 million have been replaced by zeros and exports above that value were replaced by 1's. Finally, the third matrix is further reduced to just the four trading blocks, with a 0 indicating that none of the nations exceeded the $900 million trade threshold with any other member of the block, and a number one where at least one nation sustained that level of exchange. The patterning of ties suggests that each block of nations occupied a distinct position in the international economy, as revealed by the 1s and 0s within and between blocks. The three Western block nations were completely interlocked with one another, and they maintained export and import ties to at least one nation in each of the other three blocks. The Eastern block nations also traded among themselves, but they imported and exported only with members of the Western and Latin American blocks. Neither the Latin American nor the Other block nations traded among themselves. Although members of both latter positions traded with the West, only the Latin nations exported to Eastern block nations. Thus, asymmetrical trade ties for the entire twelve-nation, four-block system clearly formed a hierarchical exchange pattern: the West at the top, the Others at the bottom, and the East and Latin blocks in the middle. This global arrangement could not be detected by measuring only aggregate trade levels in the margins of the data matrix. Only by attending to all the exchange information could the research uncover the system's structure.

In structural analyses, every nation is ideally conceived as one unit among many in several such networks of exchange relations. The substantive contents of some networks are primarily information flows, for example, the diplomatic messages exchanged between nations' foreign ministries. When hostile nations lack direct diplomatic ties to one another (e.g., the U.S. and Iran), vital back-channel information can usually be transmitted in both capitals through the embassies of a neutral third country (e.g., Switzerland). Joint membership in intergovernmental organizations (IGOs), such as the United Nations and the Organization of African Unity, serve a similar purpose of enabling nations to exchange information about their intentions and to coordinate collective action around common purposes. Other networks involve flows of material resources, particularly the exchange of trade goods and military hardware. Nations seek comparative economic advantages and collective security through their trade and military linkages with other nations. The global patterns of goods and arms shipments, military assistance treaties, and actual interventions (attacks, wars, incursions) constitute networks of domination processes. Each information and resource exchange network is likely to give rise to a unique structure, although all are strongly shaped by geographical proximity in the selection of allies and trading partners. Researchers may separately analyze each network or seek to uncover the total international structure by treating each network as one strand in a bundle of multiplex ties among nations.

Networks of the world system

Brams (1966) analyzed matrices representing three types of transaction flows between nations. He looked at diplomatic missions, total trade volumes, and joint memberships in IGOs among 119 countries in 1963 and 1964. The basic measure of pairwise relations was the deviation from a baseline model of expected origin-destination exchanges. This measure operationalized the relative salience that a nation's decision makers attached to another country's affairs. By performing separate hierarchical cluster analyses on the relations in each of the three matrices, Brams inductively generated transaction flow maps of the international system. Geographical proximity appeared to be the primary ordering principle, with regional neighbors appearing together. For example, on all three maps, the Latin American countries showed up in the same cluster. Historical colonial ties sometimes cut across geographic boundaries, as in Spain and Portugal's strong diplomatic connections to South America. Ideological affinity was most strongly evident in two distinct communist nation clusters in the shared IGO map. Brams concluded that trade flows were much more sensitive to disruptions than were institutionalized diplomatic and treaty relations. Hence, the dynamics of the international system appear in the formation and dissolution of economic exchanges over time.

Hierarchical clustering imposes a clear-cut pattern on relational data by requiring that every nation be located in one and only one cluster chain. But actual transactions among nations may consist of messy overlapping and disconnected linkages rather than neat vertical dependencies (Galtung, 1970). If import and export transactions are disaggregated to detailed product levels, the structure of exchanges may reveal cyclical patterns in which all nations are both sources and sinks of commodities. Cliques and cycles are as likely – if not more likely – to occur as simple hierarchies. Jeffrey Hart's (1974) didactic overview of graph theoretical methods described many of the possible configurations that could be detected. In his illustrative centrality analyses of asymmetric import ties among twenty-three Western hemisphere nations, he discovered a *hishinter* influence structure (*h*ierarchical *i*nfluence *s*tructures with *h*orizontal *inter*dependence) in 1958 and 1968. In other words, the United States, Canada, and Mexico formed a dominating clique with direct import influence over the Central American economies. Similarly, the United States dominated import relations with the South Americans. These simple examples seemed "to confirm Latin America's view of itself as the victim of a centralized and hierarchical trade structure" (Hart, 1974: 153). Cuba was able to free itself from dependency on the United States, but at the price of dependency on the Soviet Union. In another example of import network influence structure, using Organization of Economic Cooperation and Development [OECD] data (the major NATO nations and Japan), Hart found two cliques (European Economic Community [EEC] versus others) at a low trade threshold (1 percent of total imports). However, a more hierarchical structure emerged at a higher threshold (10 percent), with the United States-Canada-Britain at the top, Germany-France-Japan in the middle, and Italy-Belgium-Netherlands at the bottom. But the advanced industrial countries clearly formed a less hierarchical structure than that found in the Western hemisphere. A similar analysis by Breiger (1981) simultaneously examined four binary matrices of goods traded among twenty-four advanced industrial nations in 1972, using a computer algorithm for block models (CONCOR) developed by Boorman and White (1976). After adjusting the data for total import and export levels, he detected a strong center-periphery pattern. The United States-Canada-Japan and the five original EEC countries (Germany, Italy, France, Belgium, Netherlands) clusters occupied two segregated and competing trading positions, while the sixteen other nations occupied two peripheral positions. Thus, even within the alleged core of the world economic system, a considerably more differentiated, nuanced structure could be found.

The first empirical effort to model the entire world-system structure based on multiplex relational data was attempted by sociologists David Snyder and Edward Kick (1979). Combining Bram's diplomatic exchange data with binary matrices of exports, treaties, and military interventions in the 1960s, they simultaneously block modeled these four networks. Their analysis successively split the 118 nations into increasingly refined groupings according to their structural equivalence (see the Appendix). Nations within the same block more strongly resembled one another in their pattern of interventional, trade, diplomatic, and treaty ties with other countries than did nations belonging to different blocks. Based on a visual inspection of various partitions, Snyder and Kick concluded that a ten-block disaggregation strongly supported the core-semiperiphery-periphery image proposed in Wallerstein's world system theory. The core contained the capitalist nations of Western Europe and North America, Japan, Australia, and South Africa. Only one block was clearly a semiperiphery, inasmuch as its members had patterns of transactions characterizing the core, but to a lesser degree. It consisted of the Soviet Union and Eastern Europe, Cuba, Ireland, Cyprus, Kenya, Iran, Turkey, Iraq, Lebanon, Jordan, and Israel. Two other blocks that were also possibly semiperipheral contained some South American, South Asian, and East Asian nations. The six distinctly peripheral blocks were clearly constituted of all African and many Asian and South American countries.

The core nations maintained strong trade linkages to all other blocks in the system, while the periphery blocks were integrated into the world economy only through their trade ties to the core. The three semiperiphery groupings maintained extensive mutual trade links within and between themselves, but they were not connected directly to the six peripheral blocks. Thus, the trade structure resembled a hangers-on pattern, rather than a simple hierarchy (Snyder and Kick, 1979: 1115). The military-interventions pattern was consistent with the trade networks. Although the core nations often intervened to police the peripheral nations, the core itself was insulated from territorial attacks, just as Wallerstein described. The semiperiphery was also a frequent intervenor, but was itself the target of incursions, including attacks by the core (e.g., the Cuban missile crisis). Military relations among the other blocks were less clearly hierarchical. The core also clearly dominated the flow of information through the system in the form of diplomatic bonds between blocks. The treaty structure reflected almost entirely regionally based pacts.

Snyder and Kick's blockmodel analysis produced a structural snapshot of the world system at one point in time. To investigate the basic premise that position in the world system affected a country's economic well-being, Snyder and Kick resorted to conventional linear data analyses in which block position was treated as a predictor of growth. By dominating the international economy, the nations of the core block could set favorable terms of trade with all other blocks except the semiperiphery. Hence, the core should experience the greatest economic growth in the system. Because the semiperiphery's trade ties avoided domination by the core, these nations should have the next greatest growth. And the peripheral blocks, because of their dependency ties to the core and frequent military disruptions, could be expected to have the least successful growth rates. Per capita changes in gross national product from 1955 to 1970 for ninety nations were regressed on nine dummy variables representing their world-system positions (omitting the core block to avoid linear dependence). Controlling for initial GNP levels and other independent variables, such as school enrollment rates, significant negative effects were obtained in the direction predicted by world-system/dependency theory. Relative to the prosperous core, location in the periphery or semiperiphery cost these nations roughly $500 per capita over the fifteen-year span (Snyder and Kick, 1979: 1120). Respecification revealed, as expected, that nations that initiated more trade and diplomatic flows had higher economic growth. But, surprisingly, the growth effects of receiving military interventions were negligible, while nations that attacked others experienced substantial negative economic growth. The persistence of blockmodel effects after various statistical controls led the researchers to conclude that "the effects of structural position on the economic growth of nations from 1955 to 1970 are highly consistent with world-system/dependency formulations, although they do not differentiate between the economic costs of peripheral versus semiperipheral location" (Snyder and Kick, 1979: 1123). Although structural positions alone did not determine economic growth, they could not safely be ignored in any models. In effect, nations' positions in the world system seemed to constrain their development possibilities.

In subsequent articles, Kick (1980, 1983) broadened and deepened the structural inquiry into military intervention and internal war linkages. From 1960 to 1967, the formidable military power of the core states made them immune to attacks by other states (Kick, 1983). But the core often initiated incursions against peripheral and semiperipheral states, largely in support of governments in their former colonial areas (by France, Portugal, Belgium, and Britain) or in opposition to insurgencies involving communist forces (by the United States in Cuba, Vietnam, Angola, and other Third World nations). Peripheral countries were targets of interventions from other nations where internal wars had erupted. That is, rather than a conventional war of aggression in which one nation directly attacked a second, the typical external intervention was a covert response to a neighboring nation's rebellion or civil war, with an external nation either supporting or opposing its neighbor's rebels. Foreign interventions by the core into the semiperipheral countries were almost entirely in support of semiperipheral regimes' fights against insurgents, suggesting that these nations possessed adequate military power to deter unsupported incursions. Cuba and the USSR were the main semiperipheral sponsors of military interventions, usually supporting communist rebels and client states around the globe. In general, Kick's findings were consistent with the proposition from world-system/dependency theories that structural location in the international system affects the connections between internal war and external military interventions.

In an effort to project the future condition of the world system, Kick (1987) expanded and updated his interaction matrices for 130 nations in 1970 to 1975 to include eight types of transaction and joint membership relations: exports, bilateral economic aid and assistance treaties, transportation and communication treaties, sociocultural treaties, administrative and diplomatic treaties, political conflicts, armament transfers, and military conflicts. Lacking any theoretical guidance about the relative weights each network should have, Kick simply simultaneously block modeled all eight matrices. The result was eleven blocks, ranked in a roughly hierarchical four-tier structure of the world system, including: (1) a Western industrial core; (2) an Eastern socialist semicore; (3) two capitalist industrialized semicore blocks; and (4) four industrializing semiperipheral blocks plus three peripheral blocks of poorer, less-developed nations. Projecting 1960 to 1980 economic and social welfare indicator trends, Kick concluded that national wealth gaps were likely to widen between these four structural positions. Despite the decline in the United States' economic, political, and military hegemony within the core, and the expansion of anticapitalist movements outside the core, the dependency structure of the world system was too stable to imply its eventual replacement by a socialist world order in the foreseeable future. Current economic and political developments in East Europe and the Soviet Union seem to lend credence to this prognostication.

The most recent efforts to apply structural analysis methods to world-system/dependency concepts have followed Breiger's early lead by separating economic exchanges into more homogeneous matrices of commodity flows (Streiber, 1979; Nemeth and Smith, 1985; Schott, 1986; Smith and White, 1988). Drawing on the UN's *Commodity Trade Statistics* annual volumes, Smith and White obtained matrices on imports of fifty-five commodities (two-digit Standard International Trade Classifications) among sixty-three nations with populations over one million for 1965, 1970, and 1980. For each period, the fifty-five commodities were factor analyzed, resulting in five dimensions (Smith and Nemeth, 1988). These basic dimensions were: (1) high technology/heavy manufacture, (2) sophisticated extractive, (3) simple extractive, (4) low wage/light manufacture, and (5) food products and by-products. Next, they selected the three commodity matrices that most consistently had the highest loadings on each of the five factors. Then, for each year these fifteen trade import matrices, involving 3,906 ordered pairs (dyads) of nations per matrix, were subjected to a relational equivalence distance algorithm (REGE-D) (White and Reitz, 1983). This procedure iteratively identified global similarities in the more abstract pattern of trading positions in the multiple exchange networks, irrespective of specific partners. The relational distance coefficients were then rescaled and hierarchical clustering was used to identify boundaries between blocks of nations.

Two-dimensional spatial plots revealed great continuity in hierarchical global positions across the fifteen-year period. The horizontal dimension accounted for most of the variance in the relational distances: two periphery blocks at the left, two semiperiphery blocks in the middle, and a single core at the right. The international system experienced substantial upward mobility during this period. From 1965 to 1970, only four nations occupied the core: the United States, Canada, West Germany, and the United Kingdom. By 1980, six other European nations and Japan had graduated to core status, and Japan had passed Britain into fourth position.

Similar changes occurred between 1965 and 1980 among countries moving from the lower to upper semiperiphery (Brazil, South Korea, Yugoslavia, Greece, and Singapore); from upper periphery to lower semiperiphery (Ecuador, Libya, Morocco, and Tunisia); and from lower to upper periphery (Gabon, Cameroon, and Jordan). Only two nations, India and Pakistan, experienced declining positions (no data was available on Bangladesh). The authors interpreted their structural results as casting doubt on claims that the global economy is a zero-sum game, where gains by some countries are paid by losses to others. However, the absence of data from several dozen of the poorest nations makes that conclusion premature.

Examination of the exchange matrices for specific commodities within and between blocks revealed complex asymmetric trade patterns (Smith and White, 1988). For example, the ratio of exports to imports showed higher blocks to export heavy manufactures and certain industrialized extractive goods (gas, cereals) and to import raw materials and light manufactures from the lower blocks. The data supported world-system/dependency theoretical arguments about unequal exchange across a processing gradient that concentrates high-wage finished goods industries in the core and low-wage extractive industries in the periphery. All core countries had diversified economies. Entry into the core seemed to require high technology and heavy manufacturing. Specialized semiperiphery countries (like Ireland and New Zealand) seemed destined to remain there, while nations that exhibited some heavy and light manufacturing could move up. Specializing in food and materials extraction offered limited possibilities for peripheral countries to move up the hierarchy.

The trade and treaty structure

As a final illustration of structural analysis that jointly analyzes economic and politicomilitary networks, Figure 7.1 is a two-dimensional display of positions in the 1980 world system for sixty-two nations with at least $1 billion in total annual foreign trade (imports plus exports). Two binary matrices were created, one representing trade flows and the other joint treaty organization memberships. An asymmetrical 62 × 62 matrix was formed to show the import and export relations between pairs of nations. The entry in the ith row, jth column was 1 if the 1980 exports from nation i to nation j totaled at least $5 million; otherwise, the cell entry was 0. Using United Nations information about intergovernmental organizations, joint memberships in 30 military and economic treaties were tabulated (Table 7.2). This symmetrical matrix has a 1 in cells (i,j) and (j,i), if nations i and j both belong to at least 2 IGOs. The two matrices were stacked, then submitted to STRUCTURE (Version 3.0), specifying a hierarchical cluster-

Table 7.2. *Military and political treaties (1980)*

African Development Bank (AfDB)
Asian Development Bank (ADB)
Association of South East Asian Nations (ASEAN)
Australia, New Zealand, and United States (ANZUS)
Bank for International Settlements (BIS)
Columbo Plan for Cooperative Economic and Social Development in Asia and the Pacific
The Commonwealth
Communist Economic Community (COMECON)
Council of Arab Economic Unity (CAEU)
European Development Bank (EDB)
European Economic Community (EEC)
European Free Trade Association (EFTA)
Group of Ten
Islamic Conference
Islamic Development Bank (IDB)
Inter-American Development Bank (IADB)
Inter-Governmental Commission for Migration (ICM)
International Energy Agency (IEA)
International Investment Bank (IIB)
Latin American Economic System (SELA)
League of Arab States
North Atlantic Treaty Organization (NATO)
Organization of African Unity (OAU)
Organization of American States (OAS)
Organization for Economic Cooperation and Development (OECD)
South Asian Association for Regional Cooperation (SARC)
South Pacific Commission (SPC)
Warsaw Treaty Organization (WTO)
Western European Union (WEU)

ing of the Euclidean distances between pairs of nations. The matrix of distances was then submitted to ALSCAL (SPSSX version). The stress coefficient for two dimensions was .190.

Distances between nations were computed according to structural equivalence criteria, where a pair of countries is considered close if they maintain similar trade and treaty ties to all other nations in the system. Contiguity lines are drawn in Figure 7.1 around the eight blocks of nations that emerged from a joint hierarchical cluster analysis of the two matrices. Even at this high level of aggregation, geographic and ideological clusterings are clearly apparent. A core Western capitalist block, a second Western block, and a three-nation semiperiphery (Israel, Ireland, South Korea) appear on the left side of the diagram. At the top, all ten Latin American nations appeared tightly clustered. Nine Asian-Pacific nations, including Australia and New Zealand, are spread across the bottom. To the lower right are found a tightly interwoven Eastern communist block and sprawling clusters of Arab nations and residual countries (China, Iran, Hong Kong, South Africa, Saudi Arabia). Some evident distortions in the map arise from cultural affinities, for example New Zealand's and Australia's

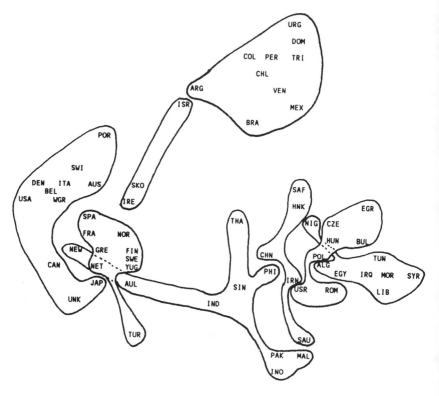

Figure 7.1. Spatial distances in a world system of trade and treaty relations.

1. **Western Block**

AUS Austria	BEL Belgium	CAN Canada
DEN Denmark	ITA Italy	JAP Japan
POR Portugal	SWI Switzerland	UNK United Kingdom
USA United States	WGR West Germany	

2. **Other Western nations**

FIN Finland	FRA France	GRE Greece
NET Netherlands	NOR Norway	SPA Spain
SWE Sweden	TUR Turkey	YUG Yugoslavia

3. **Semiperipheral nations**

IRE Ireland	ISR Israel	SKO South Korea

4. **Asian Block**

AUL Australia	IND India	INO Indonesia
MAL Malaysia	NEW New Zealand	PAK Pakistan
PHI Philippines	SIN Singapore	THA Thailand

5. **Latin American Block**

ARG Argentina	BRA Brazil	CHL Chile
COL Colombia	DOM Dominican Re-public	MEX Mexico
PER Peru	TRI Trinidad	URU Uruguay
VEN Venezuela		

Figure 7.1. *(cont.)*

6. Arab Block

ALG Algeria	EGY Egypt	LIB Libya
MOR Morocco	NIG Nigeria	SYR Syria
TUH Tunisia		

7. Eastern Block

BUL Bulgaria	CZE Czechoslovakia	EGR East Germany
HUN Hungary	POL Poland	ROM Romania
USR USSR		

8. Other Nations

CHN China	HNK Hong Kong	IRN Iran
SAF South Africa	SAU Saudi Arabia	

proximity to the United Kingdom despite their location in the Asian block. (Most African countries were omitted because they failed to achieve the necessary trade levels for inclusion.) Note the absence of any block occupying the center of the system.

Table 7.3 displays block images for both the trade and treaty matrices, where an entry of 1 indicates that the density of ties between blocks is above the mean for the world (means are .58 for trade and .30 for treaties). The two Western capitalist blocks clearly dominate world trade, accounting for twenty-two of the twenty-seven import-export ties. The Asian, Latin American, and Eastern communist nations trade with members of their own blocks, but have few ties to other nations outside the West. In the treaty matrix, ties are even more concentrated along regional geographic lines. Both Western blocks and the semiperipheral nations are integrated, as are the Latin American, Asian, Arab, and Eastern blocks. The only between-block treaty connections occur between the Western center nations and those in the Asian and Latin American blocks. The picture emerging from this rather gross analysis agrees with the general contours of tripositional and multipositional empirical classifications derived by other network analysts working in the world-system/dependency tradition. The fact that such groupings have recurred using a variety of nations, operationalizations, time periods, and substantive relations suggests that the theoretical tradition has much to commend itself.

Looking forward

Structural analyses have found significant support for world-system dependency hypotheses about the structure and dynamics of international relations. Network studies, which are intrinsically focused on relational aspects

Table 7.3. *Block images for trade and treaty relations*

	Trade ties								Treaty ties							
	1	2	3	4	5	6	7	8	1	2	3	4	5	6	7	8
1. Western block	1	1	1	1	0	1	0	1	1	1	1	1	1	0	0	0
2. Other Western nations	1	1	1	0	0	1	1	1	1	1	1	0	0	0	0	0
3. Semiperiphery nations	1	1	0	1	0	0	0	0	1	1	1	0	0	0	0	0
4. Asian block	1	0	0	1	1	0	0	1	1	0	0	1	0	0	0	0
5. Latin American block	1	0	0	0	0	0	0	0	1	0	0	0	1	0	0	0
6. Arab block	1	1	0	0	0	0	0	0	0	0	0	0	0	1	0	0
7. Eastern block	1	1	0	0	0	0	1	1	0	0	0	0	0	0	1	0
8. Other nations	1	1	0	1	0	0	0	0	0	0	0	0	0	0	0	0

of the global system, have identified conditions consistent with the dependency paradigm. Specifically, nations vary markedly in the extent and concentration of their external ties, leading to an identifiable global structural hierarchy across a variety of key interactions (e.g., commodity flows, military interventions, diplomatic exchanges, treaty arrangements). Using aggregate cross-national measures, these studies have revealed important social, economic, cultural, and political consequences of nations' structural positions in the interlocked world system. We now have a much better understanding of the basic roles that countries play within the international system and the major networks through which dependency processes seem to operate. Macrostructural analyses of national development, however, must not be accepted uncritically. Although studies that judiciously use highly aggregated structural data have yielded important insights into global structural characteristics and dependency processes, they cannot by themselves fully account for fundamentally important sociopolitical and economic processes within each country in the world system. This shortcoming is critical, because the complex webs of within-country relations – the interactions among elites and masses, parties and enterprises, bureaucracies and classes – may mediate much of each nation's connections to the world system. By thus far failing to look beyond the global abstractions of macrostructural relations, researchers have avoided the complex challenge and promise of the world-system/dependency paradigms.

Students of national development must coordinate global network analysis with a series of selective case comparisons. This two-pronged approach will enable historically contingent similarities and differences among comparable countries to provide contextually bound explanations of structural transformations in the world system. Aggregate cross-national structural analyses provide general evidence of important international associations, but they fail to specify intermediate and lower-level causal connections. To appreciate fully the manner in which structural position in the world system affects national development, analysts must also identify the mechanisms through which these large-scale relations operate. Although countries located in structurally equivalent positions in the world system share some common structural relationship's, the integration of each country into the international political economy is fundamentally mediated by specific circumstances of historical development (see Bradshaw [1988] for the example of Kenya). As Cardoso forcefully argued, analyses must incorporate the historical and dialectic nature of the interplay between the international and national levels.

A good example of how nested network applications can help to disentangle such complex effects occurs in Thomas Schott's (1987a, b, 1988) investigations of international influences in science, as reflected in flows of information among individuals residing in different nations. Using country-to-country citation indices to measure communities' contributions to scientific knowledge, he uncovered a robust center-periphery model with the United States, Great Britain, and West Germany as centers and six structurally equivalent regional subcultures. The factors having the strongest international science influences were aggregate collegial and educational ties (e.g., faculty and student exchanges), which were promoted by national geopolitical proximity, language commonalities, and cultural ties. Within two countries (Israel and Denmark), Schott found that information exchange between dyads of mathematicians was a function of expertise, experience, and extensive professional ties to colleagues, such as shared specializations, participation in research seminars, and university appointments. The common theme in both sets of analyses was the channeling of information flows through interpersonal interactions at both the individual and the international level. A promising research line would investigate how scientific relations in the world system subsequently affect national economic development and politicomilitary prominence.

Another urgent task for structural analysis is to combine several different units of analyses into a comprehensive account. All previous international network studies used nation states as the sole units for block modeling and spatial mapping, with regional clusters the most evident result. Yet the nation state is not the only significant actor on the scene. Many other important interactions occur among less-aggregated units that transcend national boundaries, such as multinational corporations, intergovernmental organizations, professional societies, labor unions, and even social movements (Friedmann, 1988: 308). The challenge for network researchers is to discover how simultaneously to include these diverse entities into multilayered, richly textured interpretations that capture the complex influence and domination processes in the global arena. New ways to incorporate individual, organizational, and system properties with meaningful temporal dimensions must be invented. Multiplex data configurations of state-by-enterprise-by-market-by-class relations will have to be designed and subjected to sophisticated disaggregation and reaggregation to reveal the deep structural mechanisms that make the world system go. The challenges are immense, but so too is the world we live in and so must be our efforts to improve our understanding.

8 *Toward a structural political economy*

The world and the nation are in the midst of fantastic and bewildering social, economic, and political changes. Structural analysis is indispensable for documenting and explaining these upheavals. The network perspective on power relations among social actors, traced in the preceding chapters, can contribute important insights at every level of analysis. Table 8.1 summarizes these basic components in a rough hierarchy from the individual to the international system of nation states. Without recapitulating the table in detail, we can appreciate the vast range of influence and domination relations that appear in many guises. As exchanges of informative communications, influence relations span the dyadic persuasions among friends to the cultural imperialism of modern science and business. Domination relations, based on positive and negative resource sanctions, likewise range from the gift giving and mutual supports that generate reciprocal obligations among persons to the coercive trade and military interventions of nations. Comprehending the complexities of these manifold power dynamics within any single type of social formation is fraught with the difficult tasks of conceptualization, measurement, and interpretation. Consequently, most network theorists and researchers still confine their efforts to the characteristic nodes and ties within one level of analysis. Yet the central challenge for the coming years will be to extend the structural approach to networks crossing multiple levels, showing how they simultaneously condition and constrain one another. For example, how are workers' primary group affiliations, embedded within formal work organizations, altered by the changes in interorganizational networks that result from intensified economic competition within the world economy? In what ways do these primary networks impede or promote the organizations' capacities to adapt to the new market realities? The recent quickening of interest in micro-macro linkages among sociologists (Hechter, 1983; Coleman, 1986), political scientists (Eulau, 1986), and organization researchers (March and Olsen, 1976) augurs well for the structural agenda. Much hard and thoughtful work remains before the solution is unlocked,

203

Table 8.1. *Microstructural to macrostructural relations*

Level of analysis (nodes)	Networks (ties)	Power relations	
		Influence	Domination
Individuals	Egocentric nets	Persuasion	Social supports
Groups	Kinship and primary bonds	Normative socialization	Clientelism
Movements and classes	Elites and followers, recruitment blocks	Ideological consciousness	Resource mobilization
Formal organizations	Work and authority, informal exchanges	Corporate culture	Dominant coalitions
Economies	Industrial transactions, directorate interlocks	Emulative competition	Autonomy and dependency
Polities	Collective actors, action sets	Policy communication	Regulation and collective decisions
Nation states	Trade relations, military alliances	Cultural penetration	War and exploitation

but the social world is a complex place that demands an equivalent complexity on the part of those who would understand it.

This concluding chapter aims to peer into the mists of the near future and to speculate about structural relations emerging from rearranged technological, social, and political components. These speculations could serve as an agenda for ambitious social researchers to apply and to extend principles of network analysis. Many of these research opportunities are noted below, but many more await discovery and investigation by creative network visionaries. Our proclivity for viewing the world through network lenses may be dismissed as the passion of enthusiasts, but it will suffice if it promotes new efforts to understand these nascent social phenomena.

The electronic information revolutions

The running theme linking these speculations is how communication ties within and among social formations are generating new social structures in three arenas: the workplace, the polity, and the international order. The forms and contents of information exchanges shape the capacity of individuals and groups to influence collective decisions. Increasingly, information exchanges are superseding material domination as the primary power relationships among social actors ranging from primary groups to nation states. Persuasion rather than coercive control is generally a more effective and durable way to get work done, to choose leaders, and to transform the global political economy. Although resource exchanges will always remain an essential component of any political system, the communication of cognitive and normative information increasingly directs how these material rewards and penalties are deployed to achieve various goals. Coercion by deprivation, force, threats, and manipulation is rendered ineffective when people and groups gain access through alternative channels to news, data, advice, and moral support that can show them how to resist and overcome opposition to their interests. Where formerly the seeds of revolution were sown by the mimeograph machine, today they are watered by the fax machine. Information in all its variegated manifestations is a unique resource whose value is undiminished through transmission (except for secrets, which suggests their value lies mainly in abetting coercive control). Rather, shared information permits its recipients to coordinate their efforts when it persuades them that a proposed action merits their attention and involvement. Because information can change perceptions of conditions and the potential consequences of altered behavior, information networks empower their participants far beyond the feeble capacities of brute force to maintain power. The fantastic new information technologies now routinely careening into one another are progressively reconstituting the ways that political power is amassed and allocated. If we want to anticipate the impending transformations of the national and international political economy, we should begin with an appreciation of the revolutions in electronic information exchanges.

Even the most casual observer must be impressed by the bewildering array of communication hardware inundating consumers, businesses, universities, the military, and government organizations: laptop word processors, smart typewriters, cordless telephones, fiber optics, teletext and videotext, minicam uplinks to geostationary satellites for narrowcast telecommunications, laserjet printers, universal remote controls, microcomputer networks. The less visible software products are even more impressive in their capacity to store, retrieve, manipulate, and transmit millions of data bytes instantaneously through real-time world-spanning information systems. Machines now coming onto the market can translate from one human or machine language to another with increasing accuracy, if not exactly poetic fidelity. Over the horizon are high-definition televisions, voice-interactive computers, self-taught artificial intelligences, and yet undreamt machines. Smaller, faster, and cheaper devices accelerate the obsolescence of machines and programs before their useful lives end. But these revolutions comprise more than mere technology. They are grafted onto planetary social systems consisting primarily of political regimes designed during premechanical agricultural modes of subsistence. Enormous populations are still illiterate in the preindustrial, let alone the postindustrial, information technologies. Within the advanced nations, differential access to the new technologies threatens to widen economic and political inequalities further among citizens (Gandy, 1982: 177–96). The painful adjustments and dislocations for these unplanned innovations will transform contemporary networks of economic and political power.

No portion of our shrinking world remains unpenetrated by these technological marvels, not even remote jungles and deserts. Electronic networks infiltrate the homes, factories, corporations, schools, hospitals, research institutes, libraries, newspapers, brokerage houses, armies, police stations, and amusement palaces of all cities and nations. Computerized conferencing capabilities exponentially expand the number of people with whom an individual can maintain active and close communications. *Electronic tribes* may emerge with distinctive linguistic, cultural, and economic relations (Hiltz and Turoff, 1978: 482–4). The huge on-line data files compiled about employees, suppliers, students, patients, clients, subscribers, customers, soldiers, prisoners, and patrons breathes new meaning into Francis Bacon's aphorism, "Knowledge is power." The KGB well understands that principle in restricting Soviet citizens' access to personal computers and keys to the Kremlin photocopying rooms. So do the Japanese financiers who electronically chase the world's monetary markets around the daily meridian, leveraging tiny differences in exchange rates and stock prices into huge fortunes. And so does the teenage hacker who breaks into his high school grade file and electronically rewrites his transcript.

Corporations and government agencies seek increasing control over the flow of unfavorable or embarrassing information about their activities, personnel, and products and services (Schiller, 1986; Downing, 1986). At the same time, they try to manipulate the release of positive images and to rally public opinion through swollen institutional advertising and public relations operations. Breaching the walls of secrecy becomes increasingly problematic for citizens, journalists, and watchdog organizations. The Pentagon's news blackout during the three-day invasion of Grenada, concealing substantial U.S. military incompetence, was perhaps the most blatant recent example (Halloran, 1984; Smith, 1988: 434–7). The democratic principle of a free press is difficult to sustain when national security is routinely invoked to restrict access to information and to cover up covert operations in the basement (Abrams, 1983; Smith, 1988: 79–80). Journalists resort to their networks of personal contacts with self-serving officials to obtain inside dope, leaks, and scoops. This twilight struggle between publicity and secrecy, between fact and propaganda (Herman, 1982), can only intensify with the flourishing of new information technologies. If the potential for abuse of power is magnified by the vast concentrated quantities of data, so is the possibility for inspection, detection, and correction.

The inherent power of large-scale communication networks potentially cuts both ways. Paradoxically, the very complexity of information systems that grant their designers unprecedented surveillance over their devices and contents also creates unprecedented opportunities for misuse and for expropriation by the opponents of an elite power. The amassed data stored in central locations become enticing targets for outsiders and insiders seeking to manipulate the information to their own ends. Elites' control over their data bases becomes increasingly vulnerable as entry ports proliferate and more savvy users probe the limits of system security. Many users are venal and self-serving industrial and military spies out to plunder an organization's information wealth (Heims, 1982). Computer crimes, which by definition could not exist a generation ago, now strain the law enforcement and judicial professions' capacity to define, detect, and punish. Perhaps only a fraction of electronic bank and credit fraud is discovered. Other users are merely malicious. Just recently a graduate-school computer hacker inserted a nondestructive virus into the 60,000 computers of the Defense Department's ARPANET system, clogging its key nodes. So far, the nation's electronic funds transfer, air traffic control, and electric power grid systems have not been compromised, but the potential for sabotage by disgruntled employees or terrorists grows daily.

As dangers to the security and integrity of computer information systems multiply exponentially, new methods for hardware protection and software encryption (vaccines) are being developed (Hsaio, Kerr, and Madnick, 1979; Hutt, Bosworth, and Hoyt, 1988). Power will gravitate to those organizational units charged with securing their data networks against intrusion, as it does to any functional unit that copes with an organization's most problematic contingencies. We can anticipate the emergence of entire new service industries devoted to combating electronic pirates. The density and complexity of interorganizational communication networks will multiply as these special services are integrated into information systems. Legal and governmental policies will be forced to adjust their premises to the new realities of the global electronic village.

The most explicitly political form of power-through-knowledge is composed of legitimate users who seek access to a data bank in order to challenge the authority of its original compilers. Courts and legislatures are steadily redefining the rights of individuals to access, evaluate, and alter data bank records kept by schools, credit bureaus, and government agencies (Marchand, 1980; Freedman, 1987). Class-action suits on behalf of consumers, employees, minorities, and other aggrieved populations rely heavily on the statistical interpretations of information in data banks originally compiled for other purposes. Organizational routines embedded in computer bits and bytes are revealed by reams of printout coaxed by clever lawyers and their programmers. Women passed over for promotion can document systematic corporate discrimination. Unions can tap company's financial records or accident files to build a case at the bargaining table. Environmentalists can examine government pollution records to bring suit against an industrial buccaneer or even against the government's own lax oversight agency. Stockholders may implicate their management for foolish corporate investment and production strategies. The political contents of information networks are fundamentally neutral; they may entrench one faction or empower another.

The faction that succeeds in wresting control of information resources away from others gains an upper hand in struggles for organizational power. Success is contingent on access to relevant information technologies and the capacity to interpret this information in meaningful ways that mobilize the collective energies of system participants. The answer to Humpty Dumpty's question – "Which is to be master?" – depends on the cleverness of social actors in making their data mean as many different things as they choose. Although the manifest contents of every communication system appear as cognitive elements (facts, raw data, technical jargon), its latent contents always carry normative implications for the system's very authority, legitimacy, and sovereignty. The skillful presentation of information to relevant audiences is the primary means by which authorities and challengers contend for control over large public and private enterprises. Without access to the means of communication, social actors are rendered impotent to influence the perceptions and beliefs of other people and organizations on which ultimate legitimation of political power structures rests. Consequently, the ongoing revolutions in information exchange technologies will set the limits within which tomorrow's political economy will be constructed (McQuail and Siune, 1986). Nowhere is this transformation more evident than in the U.S. workplace.

Transforming the workplace

The U.S. economy is reeling under the double whammy of diminishing productivity growth and increasing international competition. The information technology revolutions cited above are drastically changing the social structural relations within contemporary workplaces for workers and managers alike. To accommodate these changing economic realities, organizational forms and processes are rapidly evolving into unrecognizable structures. The social relations of production will be sorely tested in the ensuing struggles over corporate power and privilege. Structural analysis can reveal the dynamic transformations of workplace and interorganizational networks.

Only a hermit could escape noticing that the U.S. economy has been severely buffeted and battered over the past two decades. Its share of the world's economy declined from 35 percent in 1965 to 28 percent in 1985 (Johnson and Packer, 1987: 6). In just five years, the United States went from the largest creditor to the largest debtor nation in the world. Hourly earnings and real family income stagnated during the 1980s, while inequality increased (Levy, 1987). Personal savings rates in the United States fell to an all-time low and manufacturing profit rates were halved (Grayson and O'Dell, 1988: 8–10). The United States' earlier technological advantages in older industries such as textiles, steel, automobiles, consumer electronics, and shipbuilding drastically eroded. Its superiority in new technologies such as aerospace, computers, robotics, and biotechnologies came under increasing challenge from the European Community, Japan, and newly industrialized countries in Asia. Headline-grabbing scandals on Wall Street and a real-world Monopoly game in corporate mergers and leveraged buyouts masked an underlying deterioration of quality and reliability of U.S. goods and services. In sum, "The decline of American productivity growth over the past twenty years is clear and threatens the future standard of living of Americans and our ability to compete in the international marketplace" (Chisholm, 1984: 261).

Foremost among the macroeconomic forces transforming the U.S. economy is the long-term shift away from agriculture and heavy industry toward services entailing an increasingly high-technology component (Singelmann, 1978; Johnson and Packer, 1987; Rees, 1986; Markusen, Hall, and Glasmeier, 1986). A deindustrialization debate was triggered by a wave of plant closings and disinvestment in domestic manufacturing facilities that crested in the 1980s (see Bluestone and Harrison, 1982; Fieleke, 1988: 142–50). Manufacturing as a proportion of the U.S. economy has been steadily declining since the 1950s (Johnson and Packer, 1987: 20–9; Eckstein, Caton, Brinner, and Duprey, 1984: 6–20); in absolute numbers, manufacturing employment peaked in 1979 at around 19 million jobs. Since the recovery from the 1981-to-1982 recession, most new jobs have been created in such service sectors as government, health, education, and FIRE (finance, insurance, real estate). Many of these new jobs require higher cognitive skill levels – reading, following directions, using mathematics – than needed by workers in an earlier era. One study estimates that 60 percent of U.S. workers are now employed in creating, processing, or distributing information rather than physical goods (Feketekuty and Aronson, 1984). But many other service jobs remain low-skill, low-wage, and dead-end jobs in personal services, retailing, and fast-food restaurants. Productivity gains in all services are notoriously difficult to achieve, further constraining the rapid increases in the standard of living to which Americans had become accustomed. Compounding the sectoral shifts is a flood of women, youths, and minorities into the U.S. labor force (Klein and Hall, 1988). Some of these new workers bring inferior skills and experience, poor work orientations, and distracting family considerations that make them less productive than the traditional white male work force. With demographic trends forecasting a labor shortage in the coming decades, companies' abilities to find competent workers will be strained.

A second major trend paralleling and exacerbating the shift to services was the intertwining of the U.S. economy with those of the recovering European and Asian nations. The German and Japanese *Wirtschaftswunder* consisted of business-government corporatist collaborations that fostered increasingly competitive industries able to capture export markets from U.S. producers and eventually to penetrate the United States' domestic markets (Olson, 1982: 75–6; Harper, 1984). Jobs and profits shifted to off-shore sites where workers could be paid a fraction of U.S. wage rates. Unfavorable exchange rates for the dollar against the mark and yen in the mid-1980s, coupled with a squeeze on financial markets by colossal federal budget deficits as far as the eye could see, further aggravated U.S. producers' disadvantages vis-à-vis their foreign competitors. Strident calls for protection of domestic industries were only partially resisted by the Reagan administration's free enterprise philosophy, typically passing the high costs per job saved onto U.S. consumers in the form of higher prices and inflation (Thurow, 1985: 90–109; Fieleke, 1988: 29–66; Grayson and O'Dell, 1988: 250). As the balance of trade shifted into deep red ink, Americans began to face an unpleasant future of paying for their import splurge by a reduced standard of living, low growth, and high unemployment (Baumol and McLennan, 1985).

Perhaps the single statistic that best cuts to the heart of the U.S. economic dilemma is *productivity*. Productivity can be simply defined as the relationship between the economic inputs (amounts of labor, capital, and material) and the resulting outputs (goods and services produced) (Baumol and McLennan, 1985: 3; Rosen, 1984). Labor productivity, which is calculated at the national level as the value of output per worker or hour of work, is generally easier to estimate than total factor productivity (taking all inputs into account). It also roughly corresponds to a nation's per capita income, a conventional standard of living measure (Wolff, 1985: 30). While productivity clearly increased almost annually since 1965 in the advanced industrial capitalist nations (the United States, Japan, Germany, France, and Great Britain), it is even more obvious that the United States entered the postwar era far ahead of other industrial nations in total and per capita gross national or gross domestic product. The United States' slower productivity growth has steadily narrowed the gap. Continuation of the present trends could push the United States to seventh place in national gross domestic product/employee by the end of the century (see Grayson and O'Dell, 1988: 40–41; Leichter, 1984: 50). As a general prescription for raising U.S. productivity, former Labor Secretary Ray Marshall's (1986: 200) terse summary is hard to top: "Whatever the reasons for the slowdown, it is clear that productivity improvements will require investment in physical and human resources, improved management and industrial relations systems, and, most important, economic policies to promote more effective use of physical and human resources." Structural transformations and the opportunities they offer to network researchers are considered in the following five subsections.

Investments in capital and advanced technology

Foremost on almost everyone's list of causes of the productivity slowdown is U.S. firms' failure to invest as much as other industrial nations in capital formation (Baumol and McLennan, 1985: 5; Norsworthy and Malmquist, 1985; Thurow, 1985: 83–6, 207–8; Leichter, 1984). Despite a rising proportion of GNP invested in capital from 1977 to 1983, the capital-labor ratio actually fell because the labor force expanded even faster (Denison, 1979; Thurow, 1985: 84; Kendrick, 1980; Wolff, 1985: 34). New workers entering both the public and private sectors have used insufficient and obsolete equipment to perform their jobs. Relative to other industrial nations, the United States now saves far less and invests a far smaller share of its GNP, a condition difficult to remedy while the federal budget deficit competes for scarce savings. Major shifts in federal fiscal and monetary policies will be essential to alter the savings and investment behavior of people and firms to increase capital for a more competitive stance in the international political economy.

A similar situation occurs with both private and public outlays for the research and development (R&D) of new technologies. Although total U.S. R&D expenditures have fluctuated between 2 and 3 percent of the GNP (Wolff, 1985: 42–4; Thurow, 1985: 273–7), the rate is lower than those of competing industrial nations and is heavily concentrated in the less productive defense and space industries. Critically important are the low levels of industrial investments for speeding development of new products and new processes for making old products. To stay competitive, U.S. firms must retool by investing more heavily either in developing or adopting such innovations as information storage and retrieval, communications, advanced materials, superconductivity, and biotechnologies (Johnson and Packer, 1987: 32–7). Industries that produce these new technologies locate their new plants or retrofit their old ones based on accessibility to universities, skilled work forces, transportation, climate, and business service complexes (see Hicks, 1985; Rees, 1986; Markusen, Hall, and Glasmeier, 1986: 144–69). Firms using these innovations must forge closer network connections with producers to gain a competitive edge in the race to adopt the latest technology.

For network analysts, the critical research issue is how the relations among finance, production, and government regulatory organizations constrain the flow of capital investments in technological innovations. The long-standing U.S. aversion to anything that smacks of industrial planning (i.e., state socialism) could be profitably contrasted to the corporatist and cartelist strategies that have given Sweden and Japan the most robust, low-unemployment, market capitalist economies. Some of the necessary data are available in secondary sources showing sectoral flows of commodities and finances, corporate board interlocks, and government-business personnel interchanges. But structuralists must take seriously the need for original data collection to flesh out the subjective meanings and instrumental intentions of the participants: How are professional and social ties among corporation and bank agents deployed to constrain investment decisions? How do information exchanges within the boardroom influence the massive movements of material resources between industries, communities, and countries? How do cohesive and structurally equivalent positions in the economy translate into emulatory competition and collaboration, under the various politically mandated rules of the economic game? The network approach to capital formation offers the best chance to uncover the political foundations of macroeconomic behavior.

New production and marketing strategies

In the integrated global economy, markets become specialized and organizations find their former mass production behaviors are inappropriate. Corporate activities are increasingly driven by market demand. Surveillance and response times are drastically shortened. The diffusion of productivity enhancing innovations requires that increasingly fine-grained new products must be targeted at narrower and narrower market segments spanning broader geographic bases (Piore, 1987). Finding or creating these specialized market segments (niches) is a critical survival function that U.S. firms have been forced to develop. Product technologies are becoming increasingly sophisticated, differentiated, and developed in shorter life cycles (Thurow, 1985: 53–6; Pennings and Buitendam, 1987). Consequently, organizations that are heavily involved in these technologies must alter both their internal structures and their external interorganizational relations (Child, 1987; Tuttle, 1988). Some companies, most notably in the automobile industry, have resorted to joint ventures and mergers with foreign partners to preserve profitability (Olmer, 1986). In past decades, U.S. firms have steadily fallen behind Japanese and European firms in anticipating, developing, and marketing many products, most visibly in wide-bodied aircraft, fiber optics, VCRs, semiconductor chips, and high-definition TV. Poor quality control of assembly lines and postpurchase servicing continues to plague U.S. products, giving the "Made in America" label the bad odor formerly reserved for Japanese products. To become competitive again, U.S. organizations must improve their network capacities for monitoring their production, distribution, and marketing systems. More boundary-spanning personnel engaged in internal and external intelligence functions are essential to remain on top of a turbulent environment (Aldrich and Herker, 1977). Without the intimate collaboration of production and marketing departments, firms cannot develop the "dynamic flexibility required to launch and maintain a constantly shifting menu of innovative products" (Piore, 1986: 165).

When corporations and government agencies invent or adopt new production technologies, they must simultaneously cope with complex problems in reorganizing their workforces to make proper use of the equipment and procedures. Human-factors-engineering concerns play an enhanced role in workplace design. Programmable automation in factories (robotics; computerized numerical control [CNC]; computer-assisted design [CAD]) and computerization of clerical offices are accelerating and blurring the classic distinctions between white-collar and blue-collar workers (Office of Technology Assessment, 1984, 1985; Howard, 1985: 15–90). For example, when the printing industry became increasingly capital intensive, many editorial and advertising staff assumed a substantial portion of the work formerly done by craftsmen (Wallace and Kalleberg, 1982). As computers allow more workers to locate physically at far distances from one another and as home workplaces increase in number, monitoring worker productivity becomes more difficult for organizations (Feketekuty and Aronson, 1984).

A structural analysis of the firm is urgently needed to counterbalance the dominant rational actor explanation. Corporate and governmental managers must cope with numerous internal and external relations under severely limited budget constraints. How they make allocation decisions is presumably a function of their networks' forms and contents, but we presently have only sketchy notions of how communication and resource transactions shape firm behaviors. For example, how is the choice to make or buy an essential product component constrained by the firm's ties to potential suppliers and customers? What internal firm relations shape perceptions that current equipment and shop workforce can or cannot cope with new production requirements? Do employee recruitment networks put blinders on production innovations by drawing workers from a limited pool of training institutions of poor quality? Will the introduction of versatile networked production and monitoring equipment result in enhanced capacity to find and competitively enter new market niches? Opportunities abound for intense on-site scrutiny of both managerial and shop floor politics using participant observation methods of data collection. Given the shakeouts going on daily in U.S. industries, many firms would undoubtedly welcome all the help they could get.

Hiring and job training

Profound demographic shifts in the U.S. labor force portend major problems for developing a competitive economy. The pool of new workers (16/24-year-olds) is shrinking rapidly. The fastest growing occupations in the next decade will require higher than average levels of skill and education preparation (Johnson and Packer, 1987: 97–101). As with most economic transformations, these skill changes are driven by technological imperatives. But by all accounts, the preemployment education of Americans is vastly inferior to that of other nations in inculcating essential verbal and mathematical skills (Lerner, 1982; Fiske, 1984; Thurow, 1985). The basic and technical illiteracy of the coming labor force clashes with the growing reliance on computer-assisted production processes noted above. Minority groups are especially ill-equipped to present potential employers with the human capital that makes them attractive, productive prospects. During the recent period of a rapidly expanding labor force and high unemployment, U.S. firms had compensated for the poor quality of workers by selective hiring, or creaming, of new employees. Now, with the absorption of the baby boom generation into mid-career, this strategy is no longer viable. Employers will rely on interpersonal bonds to sustain their attachments to the organization (Granovetter, 1974; Lin et al., 1981): "In order to attract the employees they want, organizations may be forced to change the inducements that they offer starting employees" (Klein and Hall, 1988), as well as those available to current employees. A starting list begins with wages and pensions and adds medical and dental insurance, parental leave, child care and recreational facilities, vacations and sabbaticals, relocation programs, retirement counseling, and so forth. Climate and urban amenities become increasingly important in plant location decisions.

Rather than engaging in a costly bidding war for superior workers, organizations should resort to alternative skill-upgrading strategies to improve their workers' productivity (Choate, 1982). A review of government job training programs found that participants increased their earnings by $400 to $3,000 in the next year (Borus, 1980). To judge from company expenditures, firms have also found it cost-effective to provide remedial education for new employees and retraining for older employees. In some companies, unions and management are collaborating to upgrade employee skill levels. Carnevale and Goldstein (1987: 78–82) estimated that combined business and government in-house formal training totals $14 billion per year and out-house training perhaps another $10 to 20 billion annually. Informal on-the-job training may account for six times more employer expenditures, but its efficiency and distribution is unclear (Carnevale, 1987). However, "to date, no empirical surveys have succeeded in developing economy-wide estimates of the amount of employee training" (Carnevale and Goldstein, 1987: 35). This vacuum clearly invites research into the kinds of training programs that firms are providing and the types of on-the-job learning their workers are acquiring.

Network-oriented sociologists of work organizations can contribute new understandings of how workers' egocentric networks motivate or impede the hiring and training processes. Reliance on strong or weak ties for finding potential employees may differ according to industry, community, and business cycle conditions. Skilled professionals undoubtedly construct and use contact networks of radically different form and content than those available to semiskilled laborers. How people perceive and evaluate firms' inducements is shaped by the comparison levels of their alternatives, which are influenced by the information coming in from one's network. Structural analysts can begin to map the microlevel relationships that employees construct within the firm and maintain to the local community and show how these patterns are implicated in the success and failure of job-training efforts.

Industrial relations

Another bundle of causes of the U.S. productivity slowdown is located in the institutional configurations of labor-management relations. That the enrollment rate of workers in labor unions has shrunk to one-sixth of the workforce is well known. Equally salient are deteriorating industrial relations, signified by Reagan's 1981 firing of the striking air traffic controllers. A survey of plant managers in twenty-nine major corporations (McKersie and Klein, 1985) found them attributing the main obstacles to worker productivity to resistance to change (43 percent), absenteeism (37 percent), and work rules (seniority [30 percent], crew size [19 percent], subcontracting [20 percent]). Noticeably absent among these attributions were any self-critical recognition of flawed management procedures. Marshall suggested several approaches to enhanced productivity through restructured industrial relations:

> greater worker involvement in production decisions and in the development and introduction of technology; job security, which provides flexibility of internal labor utilization and strengthens employers' incentives to finance continuing human resource development programs as integral parts of the production process; flexible bonus-based compensation systems that combine basic wages, more egalitarian compensation systems, and bonuses based on company performances; consensus-based decision mechanisms that provide better information to all participants in the production process, greatly improving the quality of decisions; enterprise-based industrial relations systems which, along with bonuses and job security, cause workers to identify more with their companies and to be more concerned with quality and productivity. (Marshall, 1986: 194)

This list does not adequately reflect the deep-seated suspicion and hostility pervading current labor-management interactions on the shop floor and across the bargaining table. The unions' long struggle for acceptance, now tilting strongly against them, left a bitter legacy of antagonistic domination that cannot be rapidly transformed to mutually persuasive influence (Sabel, 1982; Harrison and Bluestone, 1988). But labor productivity boosts hinge on cooperation by workers willing to communicate their interests and knowledge of the work process to management on a collaborative basis. Forging a union-management partnership (Grayson and O'Dell, 1988: 225–36) in the interests of improved competitiveness is easier to propose than to implement. Whether firms' efforts to enhance their employees' quality of work life remain more than piecemeal fads and whether these efforts are paying off in increased productivity have not been the focus of systematic empirical studies.

Network researchers have a golden opportunity to integrate both theoretical and applied interests in studying contemporary industrial relations. Numerous natural experiments are taking place across the country as some daring firms seek to reconstitute their industrial relations on more cooperative grounds. An imaginative network study would contrast such firms with others in their industries that follow a confrontational union-management style. By measuring changes in form and content of worker-management relations as the new order is implemented, structural analysis could demonstrate whether firm productivity, worker satisfaction, and product quality actually improve. Gaining the trust and cooperation of all parties is essential for researchers to measure accurately the transformations stemming from new structural configurations. But as a disinterested party in the middle of the action, a network researcher occupies an advantageous position from which to make practical recommendations for securing a mutually beneficial result.

Organizational restructuring

A final prominent critical stream in the productivity literature focuses on executives' failure to better manage their organizations. Hayes and Abernathy's (1980) classic blast charged management with short time horizons detrimental to long term investment in technological payoffs. To avoid firings and hostile takeovers, managers strive to prop up current price/earnings ratios without regard to their firms' long-run prospects (Abernathy, Clark, and Kantrow, 1983). In the long run, contrary to Keynes, executives will have bailed out on golden parachutes while the firm goes under (Hirsch 1986). The result is management by fear and a me-first orientation detrimental to corporate viability (Deming, 1985). The stark contrast to Japan's group-oriented management style is revealing (Vogel, 1979; Ouchi, 1981; Pascale and Athos, 1981; Bronfenbrenner, 1985: 89–90; Lincoln and McBride, 1987). The creation and maintenance of personal long-term trust relations between firm managers compose the absolutely critical underpinnings of Japanese economic transactions. The notorious after-hours socializing that sustains formal business ties has led numerous Japanese managers to risk alcoholism and obesity on behalf of the firm.

The U.S. institutional environment for organizational restructuring consists of complex networks of information exchanges, at the executive level for corporate strategies and at the managerial level for production and distribution operations. These networks convey the collective wisdom about the best way to organize work organizations. The contents flowing through the channels include technical knowledge and normative imperatives. Successes and failures – what's hot and what's not – are transmitted, received, and evaluated for implementation or avoidance. Mass media (the *Wall Street Journal, Harvard Business Review*) are important components of these networks, but so are interorganizational and interpersonal relations based on common school ties, professional association contacts, and social and business interactions. Understanding how organizational restructuring is facilitated or impeded requires a detailed investigation of the structure and operation of high-level corporate communication networks.

U.S. firms may be beginning to restructure their management practices along lines different from conventional bureaucratic hierarchies. Computer-integrated manufacturing technologies make possible many alternative physical and social arrangements of machines, workers, and supervisors, reflected in the new management jargon: just-in-time, total quality control, group technology, manufacturing resource planning (Gunn, 1987: 23–61; Lubben, 1988). Piore's (1986) interviews with managers and engineers of some major U.S. corporations indicated conscious efforts to transform them into more flexible institutions. Piore's list of reform efforts could serve as the foundation for a more systematic study:

> They include the elimination of in-process inventories; the development of design teams which replace the traditional engineering hierarchy of product, process, and industrial engineering departments; new design procedures replacing sequential engineering, which moves down the old engineering hierarchy, with parallel engineering; systems of matrix management in which individual managers report to more than one boss in such ways as to force lateral communication along lower levels of the corporation as managers attempt to forestall conflicts among their several supervisors by anticipating problems and working out solutions in advance; and a whole series of new and/or restructured relationships with outside enterprises which range from venture capital divisions which foster entrepreneurial relationships (and which parallel the development internally which the business press has labelled "*in*trapreneurship") to new cooperative relationships with parts' producers in which the number of suppliers is reduced and a more permanent and intimate relationship is fostered with those that remain. (Piore, 1986: 162)

Profit sharing and worker participation in management (quality circles) are additional social structural reforms intended to enhance productivity. Just how widespread such changes are and how successful they become in creating more competitive firms remains to be assessed. The planning, representing, coordinating, and negotiating functions of managers are likely to increase in the future (Carroll, 1988), with concomitant pressures on organizational structures. The searches for enhanced organizational control and flexibility promote simultaneous tendencies toward greater centralization and decentralization. The resolution of these contradictions inevitably triggers political struggles between workers, managers, and owners in the context of the ongoing transformation of the world economy. Interdependencies between information technology and workplace structural relations will be fought out in the contexts of industries' and individual firms' traditions and power configurations: "Constructing these solutions requires a process of organizational learning and political accommodation" (Child, 1987: 130).

Network analysts must get in on the ground floor of these changes, if they are to understand how restructuring comes about. Many experiments will be tried, from grafting Japanese-style practices onto Texan oil companies to wholly U.S. inventions constructed out of electronic gadgets and desperation. By concentrating on the twin power dimensions of influence communication and domination resources, structural analysts should be able to render a fair account of what works and what fails. Some of this research will be done largely within single firms, charting the consequences of internal rearrangements of positions from the executive suite to the loading dock. But an open-system conceptualization compels attention to interorganizational ties that transmit new ideas and the resources to implement them. In the brave new economic world hurtling into the twenty-first century, network tools will be vital both for comprehension and for action.

In conclusion, the accelerating revolutions in information technologies inexorably impose an uncontrolled agenda on macroeconomies and microeconomies. Confronting technical opportunities can only partially be a technical process. Adapting innovations in flexible work structures and versatile interorganizational relations offers a means to revive U.S. productivity and competitive standing in the world political economy. How workers and managers conduct their protracted struggle for autonomy and control depends greatly on using their positions within information exchange networks to define problems, identify solutions, and persuade the other significant participants to support their visions. These transformations will occur within a U.S. national polity where the procedures for accumulating and applying power also undergo major changes.

The changing polity

The 1988 presidential election marked the fifth time in six elections that the Republicans captured the White House. A national government divided between a Democratic Congress and Republican executive branch has taken on an air of permanence. This condition fosters policy deadlocks over serious national problems about the budget and trade deficits, economic stagnation, environmental deterioration, and a devastated underclass. To understand why the electorate splits its ballots among the candidates from different parties, analysts must probe the interaction between parties, campaigns, media, and voter networks.

When Joel Grey and Liza Minnelli sang in a Weimar cabaret that "money makes the world go 'round," they could not have been more prophetic about the American electoral system. The reason that, as Jesse Unruh observed, "money is the mother's milk of politics" is simply the cosmic cost of getting and staying elected. The eclipse of political parties as effective campaign vehicles means that candidates must establish their own identities (name recognition) with the voters. And that costs a lot. The 1984 presidential candidates together spent more than a third of a billion dollars, the typical 1986 Senate race ran $2.6 million per candidate, and even lowly representatives had to scrounge up at least a quarter of a million dollars (Loomis, 1988: 188). By the 1990s, the total bill for the presidential-year national elections will top $1 billion.

Such enormous funds are indispensable because elections have been overtaken by expensive new information technologies: instant telephone opinion polls; print, radio, and TV advertisements; press conferences and rallies staged to produce 15-second sound bites on local and national evening news shows (see Dye and Ziegler, 1986; Devlin, 1987; Vermeer, 1987; Armstrong, 1988). New networks of political organizations have become institutionalized. Pollsters and media consultants have superseded political parties as the mainstays for nominating candidates and conducting campaigns. The boundaries between entertainment, news, PR, advertising, and politics have been irrevocably blurred. No sharper symbol of the new system can be found than Vice-President Dan Quayle, who was inspired to go into politics by Robert Redford's movie, *The Candidate*.

Generating campaign funds to feed the media maw is simultaneously a fine art and a big business. Telecommunications, with their glitzy manipulation of political images, have captured most of the attention, but as devices for raising money, they are distinctly inferior to a preindustrial form of communication – the postal system. Richard Viguerie adapted direct-mail merchandising techniques for the authoritarian New Right. Starting in 1965 with the names of 12,500 donors to the defeated Goldwater presidential campaign, he ultimately compiled a computerized master file of 20 million prospects (Armstrong, 1988: 40–5; Schiller, 1986: 31). Pinpointing potential supporters and tailoring messages in direct-mail letters, he flooded the prospects with a combination of visceral political advertising and fund-raising solicitations on behalf of conservative Republican candidates. By plowing back most of the $25 and $50 contributions into new mailings to other prospects and to proven givers, even a 1 to 2 percent response rate could eventually yield a net of hundreds of thousands of dollars (Armstrong, 1988: 69–74). Soon mimicked by the major parties and hundreds of issue-oriented groups across the spectrum from civil libertarians to moral majoritarians, direct-mail methods have amplified the political voices of extremists beyond their numbers and given insurgent challengers such as Pat Robertson and Jesse Jackson new ammunition to fight the incumbents (Armstrong, 1988: 129). By connecting grass-roots passions directly to candidates, direct-mail technologies have helped redefine the U.S. political landscape as a more polarized battlefield where inflexibility and intolerance can rout compromise and consensus. The recent history of legalized abortion in the United States is undoubtedly the primary example.

Although direct mail raises substantial sums, these are small potatoes beside the funds channeled through political action committees (PACs). Initially a device favored by organized labor, the PAC was increasingly adopted by major corporations in the wake of the Watergate scandal reforms as a means to pool management contributions to preferred candidates. Business PACs now outspend all others in total donations. Despite a ceiling of $5,000 per candidate per election, in 1986 the 4,157 PACs gave $132 million to congressional candidates, according to Federal Election Commission (FEC) reports (Stern, 1988: 24–5). Politicians spend a substantial portion of their time, year in and year out, soliciting campaign donations from PAC lobbyists. Perhaps four-fifths of congressmen depend on PACs for 30 percent or more of their campaign money (Stern, 1988: 74). Participants may curse the system as a form of shakedown and for being one step away from bribery (Smith, 1988: 253), but it is the only game in town and the players cannot risk sitting on the sidelines (Loomis, 1988: 181–208).

The public availability of FEC contribution records has lifted the curtain on business funding of congressional campaigns (Handler and Mulkern, 1982; Malbin, 1984; Sabato, 1984; Masters and Keim, 1985; Maitland and Park, 1985; Stern, 1988: 203–80). The extent of corporate political unity is revealed in similarities of their PAC contributions. Firms operating in the same industries, although they compete with one another, are likely to share similar interests in regulatory conditions, tax laws, product markets, foreign competition, tariffs, labor problems, and the like. Hence, these businesses tend to target the same presidential and congressional candidates for donations, leading to structurally equivalent patterns of political behavior that indicate high levels of business cohesion (Mizruchi, 1984, 1987). Networks of direct interfirm communication may lead to purposefully coordinated contribution strategies:

> Whether or not the PACs "run in packs" in selecting candidates, they certainly share information freely with one another and use regular, organized meetings as well as informal consultants to do so. (Sabato, 1984: 44)

PAC officials mingle with politicians at the same fund-raisers, use the same polling services, overlap in boardrooms and on trade association advisory panels, and subscribe to the same candidate rating services. To expect that these multiplex networks would not shape PAC campaign financing decisions is naive.

However, independent decisions may also bring firms to support the same candidates without any overt collusion. Researchers are only beginning to investigate whether corporate unity results from coordination or whether firms appear to act together only because they share political objectives. For example, Clawson and colleagues (1986; Neustadtl and Clawson, 1988) identified corporate unity whenever one candidate in a 1980 congressional race received 90 percent or more of the money given to that race by business PACs. Despite following diverse pragmatic (giving to incumbents) or ideological (targeting the same recipients as the independent right-wing funders, such as the National Conservative Political Action Committee) donation strategies, unity among 243 business PACs occurred in almost three-quarters of the contests. Only in 7 percent of the races was the PAC money evenly divided. The researchers interpreted this pattern as evidence of "the possibility that corporations self-consciously avoid open conflict" (Clawson et al., 1986: 810).

A subsequent clique analysis based on structural equivalence in the corporation-to-candidate matrix found a single large subgraph consisting of half the business PACs (Neustadtl and Clawson, 1988). Its members operated mainly in unregulated industries and contributed heavily to conservative challengers. But these corporations also had fewer board of director interlocks than nonsubgraph firms, leaving unresolved the question of coordinated campaign giving (see also analyses by Kaufman, Karson, and Sohl, 1987; Mizruchi and Koenig, 1986, 1988; Burris, 1987, 1989). The secondary data from campaign documents must be supplemented by detailed survey and ethnographic studies of how PAC officers interact with their supporters, their donors, and their sister PACs. Only when the networks of information flow and money exchanges are carefully documented will we be able to conclude definitively that corporate political cohesion lies below the surface evidence of coordinated financing patterns.

What do lobbyists expect from politicians in exchange for their contributions? Curiously, campaign funds do not seem directly to buy congressional votes or presidential vetoes, despite the rhetoric of Common Cause and radical critics (e.g., Domhoff, 1983: 130). Careful multivariate studies have detected only limited effects of campaign contributions on legislative votes (e.g., Chappell, 1982; Welch, 1983). Legislators' ideologies and their constituencies' policy preferences seem to be far more important factors in officials' decisions. The most cautious observers argue that campaign donors only purchase the right to meet with the candidate or his staff after the election – in a word, *access* (Peters, 1980: 12; Smith, 1988: 256; Sabato, 1987: 202). In return for their contributions, lobbyists expect an opportunity to state their case for or against a legislative proposal or executive action. By bending the ears of officials, claimants hope to persuade the government to see things their way. In other words, the main consequence of the campaign contribution network is not PAC domination over the policy process, but a greasing of the skids under the influence process. Donations open doors, but interest groups must still convince policymakers on the merits of their proposals. Special-interest groups take pains to show that their proposals also have strong appeal to voters in a congressperson's home district (Smith, 1988: 240–51). Corruption creeps in when the messages heard by policymakers are mainly those that promote the PACs' interests over the interests of groups unable to play in the political money game. How else can we explain the lax oversight by public officials that allowed the savings and loans, nuclear fuel industry, and housing and urban development messes, whose multibillion-dollar cleanup bills will ultimately be picked up by the taxpayers?

The benign view of campaign money was echoed in recent interviews with government policy staff involved in national labor policymaking during the Reagan era. A White House official argued that campaign money bought only limited direct influence:

> The executive branch quickly learns it has to answer to all the
> people. We have to make the effort to hear all the many
> strongly held, conflicting points of view. Access around here is
> fairly open. We might have 30 meetings, each lasting just five
> minutes, where every group can state its case on a bill. So the
> *quality* of the information they provide is the key. A big
> campaign contribution might get you one meeting, but without
> honest information, you won't get a second meeting. Passionate
> displays of emotion don't help. What counts is factual
> information on a bill's impact and its implications: who else
> have you talked to and what position do they take? What's the
> downside – what arguments will I hear against your side?
> People who misrepresent what support they have in Congress
> will never get back into the White House. But, a lobbyist who

can state his side's weaknesses and fairly articulate others' views can continue to enjoy access. (Personal communication to author from White House policy official, June 1988)

Congressional staff members agreed that money was not a main consideration:

You seldom hear outright lies from lobbyists, usually just shallow analyses that overreach their expertise. One-sided analysis isn't effective – they need to present the counterargument. For example, in proposing to boost the minimum wage, what number of jobs will be lost, how much inflation produced? You do best by conceding your opponents' arguments when they are legitimate. (Personal communication to author from Republican counsel of House Education and Labor Committee, June 1988)

Money seems to count for a lot with some Senators, but only when it's backed by tangible evidence of grass-roots support. In most cases, we screen a proposal mainly on its merit. If it doesn't fly, we don't worry about interest groups' clout. Our task is to act as quasi-judicial dispute-resolvers between opposing groups, especially where well-defined rights to exercise property control are at issue. (Personal communication to author from Democratic counsel of Senate Labor and Human Resources Committee, June 1988)

Of course, no staffer who wants to keep his or her job will admit that the boss votes for or against a bill just to keep the $5,000 PAC donations flowing. For the few major legislative fights that become highly visible through the mass media, rational politicians will not risk their constituencies' wrath by openly opposing the public interest. However, most special interest legislation deals with esoteric matters of low visibility, and ample opportunities exist for special treatment during legislative drafting, mark-ups, and floor amendments. In some spectacular instances – the automobile domestic content, sugar and dairy subsidies, hospital cost containment bills – the circumstantial evidence was strong that PAC donations correlated with favorable votes in the Senate and House (Stern, 1988: 31–56, 137–45; Jackson, 1988).

The staff quotations above underscore the basic importance of *trust* in the social construction of interorganizational influence networks in national policy domains. Trust is information asserting that exchanges of political support for policy decisions will be completed in good faith (Zucker, 1987: 454). Because accurate, reliable information about both the technical content and the political popularity of policy proposals is often difficult to obtain, Congress and the executive branch frequently depend on experts and interest group proponents to vet them. Substantiated assertions that a proposal will accomplish its intended results form the basis for long-term trust relations between public officials and claimant organizations. Built up over years of recurrent transactions, reinforced by social similarity (homophily), sanctioned by formal structures and informal customs, these trustworthy links in policy networks are nevertheless susceptible to disruption by the vagaries of a miscalculation. Trust can evaporate overnight in a single exchange of mendacious or misleading information, intentional or not. Lobbyists are only as credible as the last datum they deliver. The rule of thumb for legislators is, "Fool me once, shame on you; fool me twice, shame on me."

The rapidly evolving networks of electronic-information-processing technologies render policymakers increasingly vulnerable to overload and disruption. As the twenty-first century dawns, new information technologies are fostering incredibly convoluted networks that link voters to candidates, corporations to bureaucrats, interest groups to officials, fundraisers to publicists, and pollsters to pundits. Congressional entrepreneurs are learning to use their expanded staffs and communication capacities to decentralize constituency services in ways reminiscent of old-line political machines (Loomis, 1988: 145–8). Constituent casework is intended to improve incumbent reelection prospects, which are already at exceptionally high historical levels, and only incidentally to reinvigorate policy initiatives. On the surface, the labyrinthine connections may resemble a coherent structure, but the underlying reality is composed of loosely knit fragments of ineffective political power. And as every labyrinth conceals a minotaur, the emerging polity is experiencing an enervating public policy paralysis, with competing factions failing to aggregate adequate resources for influencing, let alone dominating, the resolution of our pressing domestic and foreign relations problems. The demise of integrative national political policies has left a vacuum in which stalemate and drift insidiously corrode the nation's capacity to act collectively for the public good. Whether the very political structural relations that contributed to this paralysis might also be mobilized to reinvigorate public discourse and restore a sense of common purpose is an irony not yet seriously explored.

In one sense, the network analysis of the changing U.S. polity is now considerably more advanced than is the application of structural principles to the economy. Certainly, many overtly relational investigations have been performed and published. Yet in another sense, we are still in the infancy of structural politics. Many of the data are crude secondary measures that only hint at the grossest forms of political structures. We lack good longitudinal evidence about the formation and transformation of political networks. And we still only vaguely understand how information and money are translated into influence and domination. Network theorists and researchers must become increasingly sophisticated in teasing out the power connections that knit together constituents, parties, officials, bureaucrats, and interest groups. Fortunately, we live in a political culture that places a high value on openness, accessibility, and publicity, even if it does not always live up to those ideals. Thus, persistent network researchers can usually obtain high quality data directly from public policy participants.

The harder part is deciding what to ask in a way that reveals the inner workings of the system. For example, structuralists might want to consider how policy advice by experts from academic settings and think tanks is used in the policymaking process. Such allegedly disinterested information has justified everything from airline deregulation to Native American education, often with unintended or disastrous consequences. What could be very insightful is a structural investigation of the social production of policy knowledge, traced from its funding and sponsorship sources to its use in partisan debates. Network analysis is especially suitable for uncovering the long, twisting paths through which information is generated, transformed, and applied. Expert advisory networks, properly connected to other networks of policy advocacy, might prove to be a potent tracer of the deep structure of policy domains. Many such strands of policy analysis will have to be woven together before we can produce a clearer picture of the structural dynamics of the changing U.S. polity.

Restructuring the international order

The world system is moving relentlessly toward the new international order that is supplanting the United States' politicoeconomic domination in the same fashion that the United States dethroned Britain. Shifting networks of allies and clients are reshaping political, military, and economic relations into a more complex and ambiguous structure. The East-West military confrontations of midcentury are being superseded by West-West economic conflicts. Historian Paul Kennedy concluded his magisterial history of the past half-millennium by projecting a pentacentric future consisting of the United States, Japan, China, USSR, and an increasingly unified Western Europe (Kennedy, 1987: 536–40). Transformations in the structural relations among these major states and with the developing nations can be expected to continue at an accelerating pace. The core nations will garner the lion's share of total world product and military spending, but the balances among these five great powers are already tilting toward Japan and China. The bipolar military balance (United States-USSR) may erode at both the nuclear and the conventional levels of armament. Kennedy's insightful conundrum was that any great power's efforts to assure its prosperity and security inexorably lead to geographic and strategic overextension:

> If, even at a less imperial level, it chooses to devote a large proportion of its total income to "protection," leaving less for "productive investment," it is likely to find its economic output slowing down, with dire implications for its long-term capacity to maintain both its citizens' consumption demands and its international position. Already this is happening in the case of the USSR, the United States, and Britain; and it is significant that both China and West Germany are struggling to avoid an excessive investment in military spending, both suspecting that it would affect their long-term growth prospects. (Kennedy, 1987: 539)

The twin failed military adventures of the United States (in Vietnam) and the USSR (in Afghanistan) have shriveled their elites' appetites for world dominion. Strains from sustaining the production of both guns and butter have exacerbated the stagnation and deterioration in their populations' living standards. Recent joint U.S.-USSR steps toward a military entente suggest a growing awareness that the costs of victory in the ideological struggle would not be worth the trophy. By seeking to deescalate their ruinous arms race, these two stunted giants may yet buy enough time to restructure their internal and external political-economic networks to become more competitive in the emerging world system. Domination through control over military resources must be replaced with influence by moral suasion and mutual-benefit cooperation.

The situation is most parlous for the Soviet Union. As it declined precipitously to a third-rate economic and technological power, the brutal and cumbersome Leninist-Stalinist autarchy proved incapable of suppressing fractious national aspirations from Lithuania and Estonia to Armenia and Azerbaijan, let alone by its Czech, Hungarian, East German, and Polish allies. The Orwellian nightmare of total state domination was inverted; large segments of the population are now participating in proliferating networks of social, cultural, religious, and economic ventures outside the reach of the government (Muravchik, 1989). The apparatus of total control – party dictatorship, secret police, gulags, indoctrination – could no longer mask the obvious failure of state socialism to deliver the goods. In Eastern Europe, communism is proving to be the longest, most painful road to capitalism and democracy. In Poland, Solidarity reemerged from a long twilight struggle to take over the government from an exhausted dictatorship. Hungary reburied Imre Nagy with honors, tore down its barbed wire frontier, and is launching multiparty elections. The East Germans tore down the Berlin Wall and Romanians bloodily ousted the "butcher of Bucharest." The speed and turbulence of totalitarianism's transformation hinges in part on enlightened internal reforms and supportive external relations with the West. The Soviet leadership belatedly discovered the impossibility of creating a high-technology industrial society under the centralized control of a secretive, repressive political system. Scientific innovation and skilled technological production require both the continuous exchange of information and substantial worker autonomy. Borders open to travel and unfettered communication with noncommunist nations are essential to resuscitating the USSR's moribund factories and farms. The Soviet budget deficit, first publicly revealed in 1988, is almost three times the proportional size of the United States deficit. Soviet borrowing from the West now exceeds its financial ties to the developing world. Western aid may be Gorbachev's best hope for rapidly obtaining investment funds, debt restructuring, and consumer goods that Russian citizens want to buy (Shelton, 1989).

How to introduce the necessary internal reforms, particularly market pricing, entrepreneurial initiative, and responsive governance, is the crux of the Soviet problem. The effort to shift the economic base from military procurement to higher-quality consumer goods will require public candor by the Communist Party and popular compliance heretofore unseen in the Soviet experience. Gorbachev's *perestroika* and *glasnost* projects, partially relaxing central authority and information controls, have thus far succeeded only in fanning popular discontent with the shabby economy and inspiring new hope for autonomy among the restive Baltic, Armenian, Azerbaijani, Turkic, Kazakh, and other nationalities. His ultimate success may depend in part on how willing the West is to provide the trade credits, advanced technology, and breathing space the Soviets so desperately need. His plea at the United Nations in December 1988 was spoken like a true world-system network analyst:

> The world economy is becoming a single organism, and no
> state, whatever its social system or economic status, can
> normally develop outside it. This places on the agenda the need
> to devise a fundamentally new machinery for the functioning of
> the world economy.

To gain entry and acceptance by the liberal democracies, Gorbachev must sell his home constituents on making concessions toward democracy and property ownership that many comrades may find ideologically unpalatable. In spring 1989 the campaigns for the People's Congress featured limited competition resulting in election of reform candidates such as Andrei Sakharov and Boris Yeltsin, but the congress also placed extensive executive power in Gorbachev's hands. If a backlash from frustrated Stalinists and military cadres erupts on top of the mob violence sweeping the ethnic provinces, the domestic upheavals could shatter any Soviet aspirations to world system membership as surely as the Armenian earthquake shattered Yerevan's flimsy houses. The ghosts of Tiananmen Square are weighing like a nightmare on the brains of communist reformers everywhere.

Although less threatened by violent change, the United States' international position is also precarious. The enormous military buildup of the Reagan era was paid for by tripling the national debt and neglecting the worsening plight of the underclass. The steep erosion of the U.S.'s economic competitiveness has already been documented. But its military posture was no more secure than at the start of the buildup. Much of the money was spent hastily and foolishly. When not ripped off outright by contractors, it was squandered on guns, tanks, planes, and ships unable to perform to specification, and manned by soldiers, sailors, and airmen too ill-educated to operate the equipment properly. By pursuing the chimera of standing tall, the United States may have surrendered its position as undisputed political leader of the liberal democracies. Allies that formerly looked to the United States for moral inspiration now increasingly question whether we have anything valuable to contribute beyond our dubious nuclear umbrella. But Gorbachev's suit to end the Cold War presents the United States with a unique opportunity to reorient its global priorities around more sustainable relations with other nations. The election of a moderate Republican president who has serious international credentials augurs for revitalization.

The impending 1992 unification of the European Economic Community's currency and trade relations promises to forge a serious contender to the United States and Japan for world economic leadership. This event will be a momentous step towards transnational political sovereignty, comparable to the absorption of medieval duchies into the modern states. Unimpeded exchanges of capital, commodities, and cultural symbols across Europe's nation state borders will render unilateral politicomilitary decisions increasingly improbable. Their combined 320 million highly educated and affluent people will control a substantial portion of the world system's financial, scientific, and technological assets. What structural positions the separate states, especially a reunited Germany, will occupy within the unified European order and what role this new entity will play on the world stage have yet to emerge. New rules for the game of nations remain to be written. The European Parliament may gradually assume authority to set binding policies over the French, Germans, Britons, Spaniards, and Italians. New citizenship identities may materialize in consequence of personal networks that form within multinational corporations spanning previously territorial limits. Interests and passions unimagined today will restructure the European politics of tomorrow.

As Western Europe restructures its intranational relations, its international connections are being redrawn, especially its ties to Eastern Europe. Already West Germany is the largest trading partner of the Eastern bloc nations after the Soviet Union itself. As economic liberalism takes root in the East, the raw materials, cheap labor, and export markets of Poland, Hungary, Czechoslovakia, and even the Soviet Union become tempting zones into which Western European entrepreneurs may relocate their production processes (Wallerstein, 1982). Complex decisions about joint ventures, capital investment, and profit repatriation must be resolved. The three-sided political-economic relations among multinational companies, home nations, and host countries – already encountered in MNC dealings in developing countries (Evans, 1981) – will open up fascinating new research opportunities. The impending increase in European-Soviet bloc cooperation, while reinvigorating both sets of economies, poses formidable challenges to the United States and Japan. The ramifications for the North Atlantic Treaty alliance, premised on anticommunist ideology, may ultimately lead to its dismantling as Europe goes its own cultural, political, and military ways. The development prospects for the Middle Eastern, Chinese, Latin American, and other Third World components of the world system likewise will be altered by restructured relations among the industrial countries.

With the Cold War apparently winding down, instabilities within the emerging international system are now increasingly triggered by the smaller states of Asia, Africa, and Latin America that commit themselves to military buildups out of proportion to their economies' capacities to support such expenditures (Chan, 1985; Looney, 1988). High technology is coming to roost in these nations with a vengeance. Postage-stamp countries possess devastating war machines, ranging from poison gas and hand-held stingers to fighter planes and long-range missiles. Miniaturized nuclear devices are every tinhorn dictator's nightmare. The targets of choice are immediate neighbors (Garnham, 1976; Bueno de Mesquita, 1981; Most and Starr, 1980), but advanced societies are not immune to the terrorist spillovers from these postcolonial conflicts, as the Ayatollah Khomeini's death warrant on novelist Salman Rushdie dramatically underscored. The industrial nations are famous for practicing their own transnational forms of retaliatory terror (Herman, 1982). The developed nations' options for weaning their poorer cousins from military solutions are unclear. To the extent that bellicosity is a symptom of underlying poverty and stunted political institutions, more generous development aid and encouragement of meaningful democratic reforms may help. But for every successful Philippines or South Korea, there are likely to be many more Haitis and Chiles, Irans and Cubas. The United States' penchant for supporting repressive right-wing dictators who spout anticommunist rhetoric while torturing their own peasants is particularly dismaying.

The industrial democracies are too slowly realizing that a zero-sum approach to their relations with the Third World can be harmful to themselves. High tariff walls and the crushing debt run up in the 1970s and 1980s now block the advanced nations from exporting their goods and services to foreign markets. Propping up authoritarian elites may postpone but not prevent hostile revolutions, as in Iran and Nicaragua. Enlightened self-interest must direct international relations into more mutually beneficial channels. All nations have an unavoidable stake in the consequences of global environmental destruction – spewing chlorofluorocarbon gases into the atmosphere, dumping heavy metals into the oceans, and slash-burning tropical rain forests. These pollutants know no national boundaries and their externalities can only be eradicated or lessened by international cooperative arrangements. Bargaining between the planetary North and South will require some concessions on both sides that enable societal development to proceed without ruinous social inequities. Innovative policies can be implemented, for example, by retiring national debt in exchange for placing substantial wilderness acreage in nature preserves. To retard global warming, the advanced nations must lead by example in practicing energy conservation and substituting alternative technologies for fossil fuels. They may have to induce the developing nations to adopt renewable resources that skip the easy but harmful resort to the coal-burning and oil-burning technologies enjoyed during *their* own developmental era. The spy satellites used to count missile silos can be converted to monitor deforestation, oil spills, smokestacks, and lake desertification. Global networks for sharing research data are an essential first step in designing effective countermeasures, lest humanity itself become an endangered species.

Given all these current and impending transformations of relations among nation states, structurally oriented scholars of the international system should be falling all over one another in the scramble to apply network principles to the world political economy. That such a stampede is not taking place comprises both a problem and an opportunity. The problem is that network thinking has not yet penetrated very far into international relations research, which is still dominated by rational choice and historical approaches. The opportunity comes from the possibility to treat international relations from a truly *relational* perspective, meaning to show how the behavior of nations toward one another is conditioned by the structure of their multiplex exchanges. Much secondary data awaits careful analysis in the form of trade volumes, U.N. voting records, intergovernmental treaties, and related information and resource flows. Methodologically sophisticated network analysts should consider teaming with country and area specialists whose detailed knowledge of national politics will be indispensable for interpreting global structural patterns.

Because so little has yet been done using a genuine structural approach, the opportunity to make a major breakthrough is substantial and the rewards proportionately high.

Looking forward

Structural analysis forms the cutting edge of theory and research in many fields of political inquiry. The conceptual insights and methodological sophistication of network research are steadily contributing to a better understanding of power in its many guises. Whether investigating the socialization of political attitudes in the family or the diplomatic practices of nation states, network research offers a unique perspective on domination and influence processes. Exchanges of material resources and information among social actors generates complex social structures whose full impact on participants is often obscure. By uncovering these latent deep structures, political analysts can reveal the subtle ways that power relations shape perceptions, motives, thoughts, and actions. Once acquired, the conceptual reorientation required by network thinking about politics cannot be easily relinquished. Social scientists and policymakers alike will come to see the world as a fantastic web of strong and weak connections running from primary groups through organizations, communities, and nations. An accelerating invention and diffusion of communication technologies progressively binds the planetary population into a single global entity, where decisions taken in one arena have unanticipated consequences in physically distant but socially near locations. The new world political economy is at hand and we are struggling to understand its full implications.

Networking as a verb has gradually entered the popular vocabulary. It urges aspiring executives to create or tap into informal communication channels that can promote their chances within a corporate hierarchy at the very moment when such rigid conceptualizations of social structure are becoming outmoded. Embedded in relations rather than in actors, expertise becomes less a matter of what resides inside a head than how knowledge can be transmitted between heads. Power, like water, flows over and around formal constraints, seeking its own level. Formal authority relations and distinct organizational boundaries crumble as people discover that their fates are bound up in their connections to larger social entities. Power – the ability to produce intended and foreseen effects, to get things done – increasingly rests less on stocks of personally controlled resources for rewarding or punishing supporters and more on access to information storage and communication devices. Exchanging trusted, persuasive messages fosters intraorganizational and interorganizational cooperative interactions required to achieve collective goals. True networking rests on participants' understanding that their structural positions are everything. Occupying strategic locations provides the incumbents with opportunities to shape the political contents of their communications, not just to their personal advantages but to their mutual benefits as system participants. The unequal distributions of scarce resources among clusters of network positions, the decisions to pursue one line of action over another, the very subjective images we carry of the social worlds we live in – all stem from the shifting coalitions and alliances among individuals and groups made possible by the influence networks operating within families, neighborhoods, classes, firms, bureaucracies, and countless other formal enterprises.

This book describes the potential of structural analysis to pose and to answer questions about political behavior. The full realization of this power awaits the new generation of scholars for whom the network approach to politics will seem the natural and obvious choice. Our fondest hope is that this book will encourage that perception.

Appendix: some fundamentals of network analysis

The most important steps in any social network analysis are to delineate a concrete population of social objects and one or more types of relationships connecting them (Fararo and Skvoretz, 1986). The population may be all Fortune 500 corporations and the relations may be their interlocking directors and their product purchases from one another. Or the population is all capitalist industrial nations, with their trade ties and military alliances as the two relations of primary interest. Or the people in a social movement may comprise the population, with their coordinated participation in protests and demonstrations as the focal relation.

Analytic *boundary specification* of any social system is a crucial but poorly understood process (Laumann, Marsden and Prensky, 1983; Pappi, 1984). The realist assumption is that all member entities are consciously aware of who belongs and who does not. Inclusion may be based on a face-to-face primary relationship, such as friendship circle, or on a formal entrance qualification, as in joining a ward political organization. Alternatively, the nominalist assumption is that network closure can be imposed by the analyst's own requirements, with this specification conforming to reality. For example, a Marxist nominalist may define as working class all employees who do not own the means of production. Frequently, researchers combine subjective and objective criteria to stipulate network boundaries. Thus, studies of people who hold political power in cities (Hunter, 1953; Laumann and Pappi, 1976), invisible colleges of research scientists (Breiger, 1976), and national elites (Moore, 1979; Useem, 1983) used both formal authority positions and informants' reputational reports to identify the network members. Neither realist nor nominal approaches to boundary specification offer clear advantages, and both continue to be used according to different analysts' purposes.

In a network analysis, the objects of explanation are neither people, organizations, nor nations. Rather, the units of analysis are the varying interactions that link each pair (a *dyad* consisting of an *ego* and *alter*) of social actors in the system. A network thus consists of the set of all dyadic relations of a given type, whether baseball card trading or scientific col-

235

laboration. Relationships have both form and content. *Relational form* refers to the properties of connections between dyads, apart from their substantive meanings. Two basic forms are (1) *intensity,* the strength or frequency of the interaction and (2) the degree of *joint involvement* in activities, such as the reciprocal flow of information (Burt, 1982: 22). *Relational contents,* the substantive meanings of network connections, are as potentially diverse as the human mind: psychological-biological-sociological-sexual-financial-legal-artistic-athletic, ad infinitum. Fortunately, network analysts are typically interested in measuring only a small subset of the potential relational contents (Burt, 1983). Thus, most of the examples in this book draw on a small range of political relations, particularly varieties of power, conflict, and political information linkages.

Form and content are basic concepts in network analysis, because their variations are expected to explain observed behaviors of individual actors and entire social systems. Identifying appropriate relational forms and contents, measuring them properly, determining empirical equivalences, and eliminating redundant and ambiguous relations is an enormously complex methodological task to which this book contributes little (see, among others, Leinhardt, 1977; Holland and Leinhardt, 1979; Burt and Minor, 1983; Freeman et al., 1988). Rather, through the numerous substantive examples in this book, the range of operational procedures used by network analysts will become apparent.

A simple hypothetical example illustrates basic features of a social network. The example is designed to illustrate several distinct features of network social structure. Some of these features apply to the actors, others to the entire system. Figure A.1 displays a 10-actor network in both directed-graph and adjacency matrix representations. Assume that each actor, indicated by a capital letter, is a person and that the relational content is political discussion, that is, the transmission of information about political affairs (such as advising whom to vote for in an election). Perhaps this system resembles a small business with 10 coworkers who reported to a network analyst about their regular political discussion partners.

The arrow heads on the graph lines show the direction of information flow. Some of the 45 dyads reciprocally exchange advice, while others exhibit asymmetric ties (senders who do not receive and vice versa). In the 10×10 adjacency matrix representation, the senders comprise the rows and the receivers the columns (i.e., the cell entry in the ith row, jth column indicates the "from i to j" relation). In this example, only the presence or absence of a tie is indicated, using the binary (1-0) notion. Other numerical values might have been used, for example, the number of messages exchanged or the intensity of the discussion (e.g., a higher score for a hotter debate). Note the blank entries for the main diagonal elements (the 10 ith row, jth column cells); self-discussion is presumed to have no substantive meaning in this context.

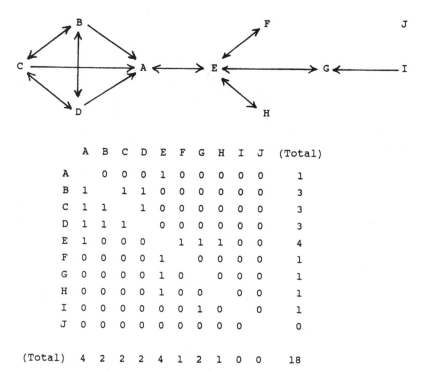

	A	B	C	D	E	F	G	H	I	J	(Total)
A		0	0	0	1	0	0	0	0	0	1
B	1		1	1	0	0	0	0	0	0	3
C	1	1		1	0	0	0	0	0	0	3
D	1	1	1		0	0	0	0	0	0	3
E	1	0	0	0		1	1	1	0	0	4
F	0	0	0	0	1		0	0	0	0	1
G	0	0	0	0	1	0		0	0	0	1
H	0	0	0	0	1	0	0		0	0	1
I	0	0	0	0	0	0	1	0		0	1
J	0	0	0	0	0	0	0	0	0		0
(Total)	4	2	2	2	4	1	2	1	0	0	18

Figure A.1. Directed-graph and matrix representations of hypothetical political discussion network.

An obvious global network property is its *density,* the ratio of the number of observed relations to the potential number. Of the 90 possible directed ties between pairs (i.e., $N(N - 1) = 10(10 - 1) = 90$), only 18 actually occur; thus, the network density is .20.

A *path* exists between a pair of actors if a sequence of directed ties links them through an intervening set of points. That is, all actors in the intervening set must be sequentially linked. A *path distance* between a pair is measured by the minimum number of links to connect that dyad. Thus, persons *I* and *A* have a path of length three because *I* can send a message to *G*, who in turn transmits to *E*, who then communicates with *A*. The full set of path distances can be calculated by multiplying the binary adjacency matrix by itself successively and observing the appearance of non-zero cell entries.

An actor is said to be *reachable* by another if a direct or indirect path connects them. Persons *A* and *E* are reachable by 8 of the 9 other network members; however, person J is an *isolate.* A network as a whole is *connected* to the extent that all actors can be joined by paths of particular types: *strongly connected* if every pair is reachable through mutual (bidirectional) ties; *unilaterally connected* if every pair is linked by a path in one direction but not the other; *weakly connected* if the points are joined by lines disregarding their direction; and *disconnected* if at least one point or subset of points is not tied to any of the others. Figure A.1 is obviously a disconnected graph, but if *J* is ignored, it is weakly connected. Among these 9 actors, 11 pairs are directly connected, 10 pairs are connected by weak paths of length two, 12 pairs are reachable in two-step paths, and only 3 dyads require weak paths of length three. Apparently, the content of political discussion would flow through much of this system with few disruptions.

The links are not randomly located; certain actors are better connected than others. These components reveal distinct network substructures and the roles (positions) occupied by specific actors. The row totals and column totals appended to the adjacency matrix for each actor reveal the numbers of others to whom he or she sends *(outdegree)* and receives *(indegree)* information, respectively. The two most prolific receivers are *A* and *E*, each the target of 4 persons, although all four of *E*'s ties are mutual while three of *A*'s ties are asymmetric. *E* is the largest sender, directing discussions to 4 others, followed by *B*, *C*, and *D* with three transmissions apiece.

Two additional concepts apply to the effects of single changes in elements. Removal of a point also deletes its associated lines. If a point removal results in a disconnected graph, that actor represents a *cut point* in the network, and the actor appears to play a liaison or *broker* role in the social system. Removal of a line without deleting its points may also disconnect a network. Such a line represents a *bridge* between system actors. In Figure A.1, actor *A* is a cutpoint because his deletion creates two disconnected subgraphs, while the line between *A* and E is a bridge whose removal also creates disconnected subgraphs. Granovetter (1973, 1982) discussed the importance of bridges as weak tie conduits that connect complex social systems in significant ways (see also Lin, Ensel, and Vaughn, 1981; Weimann, 1982, 1983). The strength of weak ties lies in their capacity to spread information beyond the insular boundaries of primary groups. The diffusion of innovations, cultural lore, and technical knowledge depends critically upon the existence of marginal actors, brokers, and bridges that sustain longer system reachabilities and thereby integrate distant network segments into a larger system. These configurations are an especially important consideration in investigating how an electorate decides to participate in political campaigns and elections, as discussed in Chapter 2.

One family of network measures of increasing importance is *prominence* (Knoke and Burt, 1983), defined as the extent to which an actor is visible within a system through direct and indirect ties to other actors. *Prestige prominence* takes into account the quality of such ties, so that an ego has greater prestige to the extent that he or she is the target of choices by alters who are themselves prominent. *Centrality prominence* emphasizes the volume of ties, so that central egos are those who receive many choices from alters, regardless of how prominent these alters are. Freeman (1977, 1979) and Bonacich (1987) have written extensively on the variety of centrality measures that can be calculated, both for individual actors and for whole networks, based primarily on the degree to which an actor lies on the pathways between others.

Subgroups of actors within a network can be identified by the patterns of their relations with other actors (Knoke and Kuklinski, 1982: 50–6). Two general principles can be used to aggregate actors into subgroups: *cohesion* and *structural equivalence* (Burt, 1978; Friedkin, 1984). To the extent that actors are directly linked to one another by intense, mutual, cohesive bonds, they comprise a *clique*. In Figure A.1, all six possible mutual ties occur among B, C, and D. They comprise a clique in the sense of a strongly connected set with path distances of one (a maximal complete subgraph). Such stringent definitions are typically difficult to obtain in real social systems of any great size. Instead, a modified clique concept, a *k-plex*, allows a subgraph with *n* points to have *k* mutually directly connected actors and *k* others. This form is consistent with the idea of a *social circle* in which a specified density of ties occur among a reachable set (see Alba and Moore, 1978). Thus, the subgraph *ABCD* contains .75 of possible ties, the subgraph *ABCDE* has a .55 density, but the subgraphs *EFGH*, *AEGH*, *AEFG*, and *AEFH* each have densities of only .50, possibly too low to be considered significant circles.

A second type of network subgroup, the *jointly occupied position*, consists of structurally equivalent actors. Two actors are structurally equivalent if, for a given relation, both relate to the other actors in exactly the same way (Lorrain and White, 1971: 63). If they have identical ties to the other $N - 2$ system actors, structurally equivalent actors are substitutable and hence can be aggregated into the same social position. In Figure A.1, actors B and D are equivalent because they both have reciprocal ties with C and asymmetric connections to A. Similarly, F and H are structurally equivalent in possessing only a mutual tie with E. Having exactly identical ties is a stringent criterion and, in most empirical uses, researchers require only a high degree of similar ties to others in order to place a pair into a jointly occupied position. Note also that the existence or absence of a direct link among actors jointly occupying a structurally equivalent position is irrelevant; F and H have no direct tie, but B and D do. The pattern of ties to other actors is the critical facet of structural equivalence, whereas the occurrence of direct ties is the central feature of cohesion. These two methods of identifying network subgroups are expected to have different consequences for attitudes and behaviors of network participants. Cohesion emphasizes mutual socialization and influence among clique members, whereas structural equivalence highlights emulation among position members as they compete for the attention of third parties (Burt, 1987b).

Empirical techniques too numerous to discuss here have been developed for identifying cliques and structurally equivalent groups of actors, based on computer analyses of graphs represented as algebraic matrices of network ties. Three of the most widely accessible computer packages, all available in PC versions, are GRADAP, UCINET, and STRUCTURE, discussed with source addresses listed by Freeman (1988). For this book, two of the most important techniques are *block-modeling* and structural equivalence based on *Euclidean distances*. In block-modeling methods, such as CONCOR (Arabie, Boorman, and Levitt, 1978), sets of actors are grouped into increasingly homogeneous positions (blocks) by a hierarchical clustering procedure that iteratively calculates Pearson product-moment correlations from the columns of an adjacency matrix. The larger the correlation, the more similar the pair of actors. Once a succession of blocks has been identified, the adjacency matrix can be permuted to reveal the within-block and between-block connections and a variety of descriptive and analytic procedures can be applied to the resulting reduced-form matrices (e.g., Boorman and White, 1976; White, Boorman, and Breiger, 1976).

The Euclidean distance approach to structural equivalence measures dissimilarity of a pair of actors as the discrepancy in the relational ties sent and received from all third actors in the adjacency matrix. The smaller the distance, the greater the structural equivalence. A hierarchical clustering routine is also used on the interactor distances to identify increasingly larger clusters whose members have smaller average distances to one another than to members of other position clusters. Because of the matrix nature of the distance measure, the Euclidean approach allows a variety of analytic techniques not possible with the discrete block-model analysis, most particularly the representation of social distances among actors and positions in a smallest space analysis (e.g., Burt 1976, 1977a, b). Comparable analyses can also be performed on the path distance measures described above (e.g., Laumann and Knoke, 1987: 226–48).

References

Abell, Peter, 1975. *Organizations as Bargaining and Negotiating Systems.* New York: Halstead.

Abernathy, William, Kim Clark, and Alan Kantrow, 1983. *Industrial Renaissance: Producing a Competitive Future for America.* New York: Basic Books.

Abrams, Floyd, 1983. "The new effort to control information." *New York Times,* September 25.

Abrams, Robert, 1980. *Foundations of Political Analysis: An Introduction to the Theory of Collective Choice.* New York: Columbia University Press.

Adorno, Theodore W., Else Frenkel-Brunswik, Daniel J. Levinson, and R. Sanford Nevitt, 1950. *The Authoritarian Personality.* New York: Harper & Row.

Agger, Robert E., 1956. "Power attributions in the local community." *Social Forces,* 34: 322–331.

Aiken, Michael, 1970. "The distribution of community power: structural bases and social consequences." In Michael Aiken and Paul Mott (eds.), *The Structure of Community Power.* New York: Random House, pp. 487–526.

Aiken, Michael, and Robert A. Alford, 1970. "Community structure and innovation: the case of urban renewal." *American Sociological Review,* 35: 650–65.

Alba, Richard D., 1972. "COMPLT – a program for analyzing sociometric data and clustering similarity matrices. *Behavioral Science,* 17: 566.

Alba, Richard D., 1973. "A graph-theoretic definition of a sociometric clique." *Journal of Mathematical Sociology,* 3: 113–26.

Alba, Richard D., and Gwen Moore, 1978. "Elite social circles." *Sociological Methods and Research,* 7: 167–88.

Alba, Richard D., and Gwen Moore, 1982. "Class and prestige origins in the American elite." In Peter V. Marsden and Nan Lin (eds.), *Social Structure and Network Analysis.* Beverly Hills, Calif.: Sage, pp. 39–60.

Alchian, A., A. Demsetz, and H. Demsetz, 1972. "Production, information costs, and economic organization." *American Economic Review,* 62: 777–95.

Aldrich, Howard E., 1979. *Organizations and Environments.* Englewood Cliffs, N.J.: Prentice-Hall.

Aldrich, Howard E., and Diane Herker, 1977. "Boundary spanning roles and organization structure." *Academy of Management Review,* 5: 217–30.

Aldrich, Howard E., and Peter V. Marsden, 1988. "Environments and organizations." In Neil Smelser (ed.), *Handbook of Sociology,* Newbury Park, Calif.: Sage, pp. 361–92.

Aldrich, Howard E., and Jeffrey Pfeffer, 1976. "Environments of organizations." *Annual Review of Sociology,* 2: 79–105.

Alexander, Jeffrey, 1978. "Formal and substantive voluntarism in the work of Talcott Parsons: a theoretical and ideological reinterpretation." *American Sociological Review,* 43: 177–98.

Alford, Robert R., and Roger Friedland, 1985. *Powers of Theory: Capitalism, the State, and Democracy.* Cambridge: Cambridge University Press.

Allen, Michael P., 1981. "Managerial power and tenure in the large corporation." *Social Networks,* 60: 482–93.

Allen, Michael P., and Sharon K. Panian, 1982. "Power, performance, and succession in the large corporation." *Administrative Science Quarterly,* 27: 538–47.

Allen, William, 1965. *The Nazi Seizure of Power.* Chicago: Quadrangle Books.

Almond, Gabriel, and Sidney Verba, 1963. *The Civic Culture: Political Attitudes and Democracy in Five Nations.* Princeton, N.J.: Princeton University Press.

Althusser, Louis, and Etienne Balibar, 1970. *Reading Capital.* London: New Left Books.

Aminzade, Ronald, 1981. *Class, Politics, and Early Industrial Capitalism: A Study of Mid-Nineteenth Century Toulouse, France.* Albany, N.Y.: State University of New York Press.

Andrews, Frank, James N. Morgan, and John Sonquist, 1967. *Multiple Classification Analysis.* Survey Research Center.

Arabie, Phipps, Scott Boorman, and Paul R. Levitt, 1978. "Constructing blockmodels: How and why." *Journal of Mathematical Psychology,* 17: 21–63.

Arendt, Hannah, 1958. *The Human Condition.* Chicago: University of Chicago Press.

Armstrong, Richard, 1988. *The Next Hurrah: The Communication Revolution in American Politics.* New York: Beech Tree Books.

Aveni, Adrian, 1977. "The not-so-lonely crowd: friendship groups in collective behavior." *Sociometry,* 40: 96–9.

Aveni, Adrian F., 1978. "Organizational linkages and resource mobilization: the significance of linkage strength and breadth." *Sociological Quarterly,* 19: 185–202.

Bacharach, Samuel B., and Edward J. Lawler, 1980. *Power and Politics in Organizations.* San Francisco: Jossey-Bass.

Bacharach, Samuel B., and Edward J. Lawler, 1981. *Bargaining.* San Francisco: Jossey-Bass.

Bachrach, Peter, and Morton Baratz, 1962. "The two faces of power." *American Political Science Review,* 57: 947–52.

Bakhash, Shaul, 1984. *The Reign of the Ayatollahs: Iran and the Islamic Revolution.* New York: Basic Books.

Barber, Benjamin, 1984. *Strong Democracy: Participatory Politics for a New Age.* Berkeley: University of California Press.

Barber, Bernard, 1983. *The Logic and Limits of Trust.* New Brunswick, N.J.: Rutgers University Press.

Barkan, Steven E., 1984. "Legal control of the southern civil rights movement." *American Sociological Review,* 49: 552–65.

Barry, Brian, 1978. *Sociologists, Economists and Democracy.* Chicago: University of Chicago Press.

Barton, Allen H., 1975. "Consensus and conflict among American leaders." *Public Opinion Quarterly,* 38: 507–30.

Barton, Allen H., 1985. "Determinants of economic attitudes in the American business elite." *American Journal of Sociology,* 91: 54–87.

Barton, Allen H., Bogdon Denitch, Charles Kadushin, Gwen Moore, Wayne Parsons, and Carol Weiss, 1981. "Backgrounds, attitudes, and activities of American elites." In Bogdon Denitch (ed.), *National Elites: What They Think, What They Do.* London: Sage.

Baumol, William J. and Kenneth McLennan, 1985. "U.S. productivity performance and its implications." In William J. Baumol and Kenneth McLennan (eds.), *Productivity, Growth, and U.S. Competitiveness.* New York: Oxford University Press, pp. 3–28.

Beardon, James, and Beth Mintz, 1987. "The structure of class cohesion: the corporate network and its dual." In Barry Wellman and S. D. Berkowitz (eds.), *Intercorporate Relations: The Structural Analysis of Business.* Cambridge, England: Cambridge University Press, pp. 187–207.

Becker, Gary S., 1976. *The Economic Approach to Human Behavior.* Chicago: University of Chicago Press.

Beller, Andrea H., 1982. "Trends in occupational segregation by sex and race, 1960–81." In Barbara F. Reskin (ed.), *Sex Segregation in the Workplace.* Washington, D.C.: National Academy of Sciences, pp. 11–26.

Bendix, Reinhard, 1960. *Max Weber: An Intellectual Portrait.* New York: Doubleday Anchor.

Benson, Kenneth J., 1975. "The interorganizational network as a political economy." *Administrative Science Quarterly,* 20: 229–49.

Berelson, Bernard, Paul F. Lazarsfeld, and William N. McPhee, 1954. *Voting: A Study of Opinion Formation in a Presidential Campaign.* Chicago: University of Chicago Press.

Berkowitz, Steven D., 1982. *An Introduction to Structural Analysis: The Network Approach to Social Research.* Toronto: Butterworths.

Bernard, H. Russell, Peter D. Killworth, and Lee Sailer, 1981. "Summary of research on informant accuracy in network data and on the reverse small world problem." *Connections,* 4: 11–25.

Berry, Jeffrey M., 1977. *Lobbying for the People: The Political Behavior of Public Interest Groups.* Princeton: Princeton University Press.

Berry, Jeffrey M., 1984. *The Interest Group Society.* Boston: Little, Brown.

Biddle, Bruce J., 1986. "Recent developments in role theory." *Annual Review of Sociology,* 12: 67–92.

Bielby, William T., and James N. Baron, 1986. "Men and women at work: sex segregation and statistical discrimination." *American Journal of Sociology,* 91: 759–99.

Black, Cyril, 1966. *The Dynamics of Modernization.* New York: Harper & Row.

Blalock, Hubert M., 1967. "Status inconsistency, social mobility, status integration, and structural effects." *American Sociological Association,* 32: 790–800.

Blau, Judith R., and Richard D. Alba, 1982. "Empowering nets of participation." *Administrative Science Quarterly,* 27: 363–79.

Blau, Peter M., 1964. *Exchange and Power in Social Life*. New York: Wiley.

Blau, Peter M., 1977. *Inequality and Heterogeneity*. New York: Free Press.

Blau, Peter M., and Richard A. Schoenherr, 1971. *The Structure of Organizations*. New York: Basic Books.

Blau, Peter M., and W. Richard Scott, 1962. *Formal Organizations*. San Francisco: Chandler.

Block, Fred, 1981. "The fiscal crisis of the capitalist state." *Annual Review of Sociology*, 7: 1–27.

Bluestone, Barry, and Bennett Harrison, 1982. *The Deindustrialization of America*. New York: Basic Books.

Blumer, Herbert, 1951. "Collective behavior." In Alfred M. Lee (ed.), *New Outline of the Principles of Sociology*. New York: Barnes and Noble, pp. 166–222.

Boissevain, Jeremy, 1974. *Friends of Friends: Networks, Manipulators, and Coalitions*. Oxford: Blackwell.

Boissevain, Jeremy, 1980. *A Village in Malta*. New York: Holt, Rinehart and Winston.

Boje, David M., and David A. Whetten, 1981. "Effects of organizational strategies and constraints on centrality and attributions of influence in interorganizational networks." *Administrative Science Quarterly*, 26: 378–95.

Bolland, John M., 1985. "Perceived leadership stability and the structure of urban agenda-setting networks." *Social Networks*, 7: 153–72.

Bollen, Kenneth A., 1983. "World system position, dependency, and democracy." *American Sociological Review*, 48: 468–79.

Bonacich, Phillip, 1972. "Techniques for analyzing overlapping memberships." *Sociological Methodology 1972*, 4: 176–85.

Bonacich, Phillip, 1987. "Power and centrality: a family of measures." *American Journal of Sociology*, 92: 1170–82.

Bonacich, Phillip, and G. William Domhoff, 1981. "Latent classes and group membership." *Social Networks*, 3: 175–96.

Boorman, Scott, and Harrison White, 1976. "Social structure from multiple networks. II. Role structure." *American Journal of Sociology*, 81: 1384–446.

Bornischier, Volker, and Christopher Chase-Dunn, 1985. *Transnational Corporations and Underdevelopment*. New York: Praeger.

Borus, Michael E., 1980. "Assessing the impact of training programs." In Eli Ginzburg (ed.), *Employing the Unemployed*. New York: Basic Books, pp. 25–40.

Bougon, Michael G., Karl Weick, and D. Binkhorst, 1977. "Cognition in organizations: an analysis of the Utrecht Jazz Orchestra." *Administrative Science Quarterly*, 22: 606–39.

Bradshaw, York W, 1988. "Reassessing economic dependency and uneven development: The Kenyan experience." *American Sociological Review* 53: 693–708.

Brams, Steven J., 1966. "Transaction flows in the international system." *American Political Science Review*, 60: 880–98.

Brass, Daniel J., 1984. "Being in the right place: a structural analysis of individual influence in an organization." *Administrative Science Quarterly*, 29: 518–39.

Breiger, Ronald L., 1974. "The duality of persons and groups." *Social Forces*, 53: 181–90.

Breiger, Ronald L., 1976. "Career attributes and network structure: a blockmodel study of a biomedical research specialty." *American Sociological Review*, 41: 117–135.

Breiger, Ronald L., 1979. "Toward an operational theory of community elite structure." *Quality and Quantity*, 13: 21–47.

Breiger, Ronald L., 1981. "Structures of economic interdependence among nations." In Peter M. Blau and Robert K. Merton (eds.), *Continuities in Structural Inquiry*. London: Sage, pp. 353–80.

Breiger, Ronald L., and Phillipa E. Pattison, 1978. "The joint role structure of two communities' elites." *Sociological Methods and Research*, 7: 213–26.

Brenner, Robert, 1977. "The origins of capitalist development: a critique of neo-Smithian Marxism." *New Left Review*, 104: 25–92.

Breton, Andre, 1974. *The Economic Theory of Representative Government*. Chicago: Aldine.

Broadbent, Jeffrey, 1985. "Social networks as transmitters of social control in local Japanese politics." *Hiroshima Shudo University Research Review*, 1: 29–36.

Bronfenbrenner, Martin, 1985. "Japanese productivity experience." In William J. Baumol and Kenneth McLennan (eds.), *Productivity, Growth, and U.S. Competitiveness*. New York: Oxford University Press, pp. 70–102.

Brown, Thad A., and Arthur A. Stein, 1982. "The political economy of national elections." *Comparative Politics*, 14: 479–97.

Browne, Eric C., 1973. *Coalition Theories: A Logical and Empirical Critique*. Beverly Hills: Sage.

Bueno de Mesquita, Bruce, 1981. *The War Trap*. New Haven: Yale University Press.

Bulmer, Martin, 1985. "The rejuvenation of community studies? Neighbours, networks, and policy." *Sociological Review*, 33: 430–48.

Burawoy, Michael, 1979. *Manufacturing Consent: Changes in the Labor Process Under Monopoly Capitalism*. Chicago: University of Chicago Press.

Burch, Philip, 1980. *Elites in American History: The New Deal to the Carter Administration*. New York: Holmes and Meier.

Burris, Val, 1987. "The political partisanship of American business: a study of corporate political action committees." *American Sociological Review*, 52: 732–744.

Burris, Val, 1989. "Director interlocks and corporate political behavior." Paper presented at first European Conference on Social Network Analysis, Groningen, The Netherlands.

Burstein, Paul, 1976. "Social networks and voting: some Israeli data." *Social Forces*, 54: 833–47.

Burt, Ronald S., 1976. "Positions in networks." *Social Forces*, 55: 93–122.

Burt, Ronald S., 1977a. "Power in a social topology." *Social Science Research*, 6: 1–83.

Burt, Ronald S., 1977b. "Positions in multiple networks. Part one: A general conception of stratification and prestige in a system of actors cast as a social topology." *Social Forces*, 57: 106–31.

Burt, Ronald S., 1978. "Cohesion versus structural equivalence as a basis for network subgroups." *Sociological Methodology and Research,* 7: 189–212.

Burt, Ronald S., 1982. *Toward a Structural Theory of Action.* New York: Academic Press.

Burt, Ronald S., 1983. *Corporate Profits and Cooptation.* New York: Academic Press.

Burt, Ronald S., 1986. "A note on sociometric order in the General Social Survey network data." *Social Networks,* 8: 149–74.

Burt, Ronald S., 1987a. "A note on the General Social Survey's ersatz network density item." *Social Networks,* 9: 75–85.

Burt, Ronald S., 1987b. "Social contagion and innovation: cohesion versus structural equivalence." *American Journal of Sociology,* 92: 1287–335.

Burt, Ronald S., 1987c. *STRUCTURE: Version 3.2.* New York: Columbia University Center for the Social Sciences.

Burt, Ronald S., 1988. "The stability of American markets." *American Journal of Sociology,* 94: 356–95.

Burt, Ronald S., and Michael J. Minor, 1983. *Applied Network Analysis: A Methodological Introduction.* Beverly Hills: Sage.

Butler, David, and Donald Stokes, 1974. "The influence of a local political environment." In David Butler and Donald Stokes (eds.), *Political Change in Britain.* New York: St. Martin's Press, pp. 144–50.

Cameron, David R., 1978. "The expansion of the public economy: a comparative analysis." *American Political Science Review,* 72: 1243–261.

Camic, Charles, 1987. "The making of a method: a historical reinterpretation of the early Parsons." *American Sociological Review,* 52: 421–39.

Campbell, Angus, Philip E. Converse, Warren E. Miller, and Donald E. Stokes, 1960. *The American Voter.* New York: Wiley.

Campbell, Angus, Philip E. Converse, Warren E. Miller, and Donald E. Stokes, 1964. *Elections and the Political Order.* New York: Wiley.

Campbell, Angus, Gerald Gurin, and Warren E. Miller, 1954. *The Voter Decides.* Evanston, Ill.: Row, Peterson.

Campbell, Ernest Q., 1969. "Adolescent socialization." In David A. Golsin (ed.), *Handbook of Socialization Theory and Research.* Chicago: Rand-McNally, pp. 821–60.

Caplow, Theodore, 1956. "A theory of coalitions in the triad." *American Sociological Review,* 21: 489–93.

Cardoso, Fernando Henrique, and Enzo Faletto, 1979. *Dependency and Development in Latin America.* Berkeley, Calif.: University of California Press.

Carlos, Manuel L., and Bo Anderson, 1981. "Political brokerage and network politics in Mexico: the case of a dominance system." In David Willer and Bo Anderson (eds.), *Networks, Exchange and Coercion.* New York: Elsevier, pp. 169–87.

Carnevale, Anthony P., 1987. *Statement before Subcommittee on Education and Health of the Joint Economic Committee, U.S. Congress.* October 29. Washington (mimeographed).

Carnevale, Anthony P., and Harold Goldstein, 1987. "Employee training: its changing role and an analysis of new data." Washington: American Society for Training and Development.

Carrol, Steven J., 1988. "Managerial work in the future." In Jerald Hage (ed.), *Future of Organizations: Innovating to Adapt Strategy and Human Resources to Rapid Technological Change*. Lexington, Mass.: Lexington Books, pp. 85–108.

Chan, Steve, 1985. "The impact of defense spending on economic performance: A survey of evidence and problems." *Orbis*, 29: 403–34.

Chappell, Henry W., Jr., 1982. "Campaign contributions and congressional voting: a simultaneous probit-tobit model." *Review of Economics and Statistics*, 64: 77–83.

Chase-Dunn, Christopher, 1988. *Structures of the World-Economy*, New York: Basil Blackwell.

Chase-Dunn, Christopher, and Richard Rubinson, 1977. "Toward a structural perspective on the world-system." *Politics and Society*, 7: 453–76.

Chilcote, Ronald, 1984. *Theories of Development and Underdevelopment*. Boulder, Colo.: Westview Press.

Child, John, 1977. *Organization: A Guide to Problems and Practice*. London: Harper & Row.

Child, John, 1987. "Organizational design for advanced manufacturing technology." In Toby D. Wall, Chris W. Clegg, and Nigel J. Kemp (eds.), *The Human Side of Advanced Manufacturing Technology*. Chichester, England: Wiley, pp. 101–34.

Chirot, Daniel, 1985. "The rise of the West." *American Sociological Review*, 50: 181–94.

Chirot, Daniel, 1986. *Social Change in the Modern Era*. New York: Harcourt Brace Jovanovich.

Chirot, Daniel, and Thomas Hall, 1982. "World system theory." *Annual Review of Sociology*, 8: 81–106.

Chisholm, Ruppert F., 1984. "A systems approach to organizational productivity." In Mark Holzer and Stuart S. Nagel (eds.), *Productivity and Public Policy*, Beverly Hills, Calif.: Sage, pp. 261–85.

Choate, Pat, 1982. *Retooling the American Workforce: Toward a National Strategy*. Washington: Northeast-Midwest Institute.

Clark, Peter B., and James Q. Wilson, 1961. "Incentive systems: a theory of organizations." *Administrative Science Quarterly*, 6: 129–66.

Clark, Terry N., 1968. "Community structure, decision-making, budget expenditures, and urban renewal in 51 American cities." *American Sociological Review*, 35: 576–93.

Clark, Terry N., 1973. *Community Power and Policy Outputs: A Review of Urban Research*. Beverly Hills: Sage.

Clark, Terry N., and Lorna C. Ferguson, 1984. *City Money: Political Processes, Fiscal Strain, and Retrenchment*. New York: Columbia University Press.

Clarke, Harold D., Richard G. Price, Marianne C. Stewart, and Robert Krause, 1978. "Motivational patterns and differential participation in a Canadian party: the Ontario Liberals." *American Journal of Political Science*, 22: 130–51.

Clawson, Dan, Alan Neustadtl, and James Bearden, 1986. "The logic of business unity: corporate contributions to the 1980 congressional elections." *American Sociological Review*, 51: 797–811.

Cobb, Robert W., and Charles D. Elder, 1972. *Participation in American Politics: The Dynamics of Agenda-Building.* Boston: Allyn and Bacon.

Cohen, Michael, James March, and Johan Olsen, 1972. "A garbage can model of organizational choice." *Administrative Science Quarterly,* 17: 1–25.

Cole, John W., and Eric R. Wolf, 1974. *The Hidden Frontier: Ecology and Ethnicity in an Alpine Valley,* New York: Academic Press.

Coleman, James S., 1957. *Community Conflict.* Glencoe: Free Press.

Coleman, James S., 1964. *Introduction to Mathematical Sociology.* New York: Free Press.

Coleman, James S., 1973. *The Mathematics of Collective Action.* Chicago: Aldine.

Coleman, James S., 1977. "Social action systems." In K. Szaniawski (ed.), *Problems of Formalization in the Social Sciences.* Wraclaw: Polskiej Akademij Nauk, pp. 11–50.

Coleman, James S., 1986. "Social theory, social research, and a theory of action." *American Journal of Sociology* 91: 1309–35.

Coleman, James S., Elihu Katz, and Herbert Menzel, 1966. *Medical Innovation: A Diffusion Study.* Indianapolis, Ind.: Bobbs-Merrill.

Comte, Auguste, 1855. *The Positive Philosophy of Auguste Comte,* translated by Harriet Martineau. New York: Calvin Blanchard.

Conger, Jay A., and Rabindra N. Kanungo, 1988. "The empowerment process: integrating theory and practice." *Academy of Management Review,* 13: 471–82.

Cook, Karen S., 1977. "Exchange and power in networks of interorganizational relations." *Sociological Quarterly,* 18: 62–82.

Cook, Karen S., 1982. "Network structures from an exchange perspective." In Peter V. Marsden and Nan Lin (eds.), *Social Structure and Network Analysis.* Beverly Hills, Calif.: Sage, pp. 177–99.

Cook, Karen S., and Richard M. Emerson, 1978. "Power, equity, and commitment in exchange networks." *American Sociological Review,* 43: 721–39.

Cook, Karen S., Richard M. Emerson, Mary R. Gillmore, and Toshio Yamagishi, 1983. "The distribution of power in exchange networks: theory and experimental results." *American Journal of Sociology,* 89: 275–305.

Crenson, Matthew, 1978. "Social networks and political processes in urban neighborhoods." *American Journal of Political Science,* 22: 578–94.

Crozier, Michel, 1964. *The Bureaucratic Phenomenon.* London: Tavistock.

Curtis, Russell L., and Louis A. Zurcher, Jr., 1973. "Stable resources of protest movements: the multi-organizational field." *Social Forces,* 52: 53–61.

Cyert, Richard M., and James G. March, 1963. *A Behavioral Theory of the Firm.* Englewood Cliffs, N.J.: Prentice-Hall.

Dahl, Robert A., 1957. "The concept of power." *Behavioral Science,* 2: 201–15.

Dahl, Robert A., 1958. "Critique of the ruling elite model." *American Political Science Review,* 52: 463–9.

Dahl, Robert A., 1961. *Who Governs? Democracy and Power in an American City.* New Haven: Yale University Press.

Dahrendorf, Ralf, 1959. *Class and Class Conflict in Industrial Society.* Stanford, Calif.: Stanford University Press.

Daniels, James (ed.), 1968. *The Complete Bolivian Diaries of Che Guevara and Other Captured Documents.* New York: Stein and Day.

Danzger, M. Herbert, 1964. "Community power structure: problems and continuities." *American Sociological Review,* 29: 707–17.

Davies, James C., 1969. "The J-curve of rising and declining satisfactions as a cause of some great revolutions and a contained rebellion." In Hugh D. Graham and Ted R. Gurr (eds.), *Violence in America.* Washington, D.C.: U.S. Government Printing Office, pp. 690–730.

Davis, James A., 1982. "Achievement variables and class cultures: family, schooling, job, and forty-nine dependent variables in the cumulative GSS." *American Sociological Review,* 47: 569–586.

Davis, Stanley, M., and Paul R. Lawrence, 1977. *Matrix.* Reading, Mass.: Addison-Wesley.

Debray, Regis, 1975. *Che's Guerilla War.* Baltimore: Harmondsworth.

De Graaf, Nan Dirk, and Hendrick Derk Flap, 1988. " 'With a little help from my friends': social resources as an explanation of occupational status and income in West Germany, the Netherlands, and the United States." *Social Forces,* 67: 452–72.

Deming, W. Edwards, 1985. "Transformation of western-style management." In Y. K. Shetty and Vernon M. Buehler (eds.), *Productivity and Quality Through People.* Westport, Conn.: Quorom Books, pp. 10–16.

Denemark, Robert A., and Kenneth P. Thomas, 1988. "The Brenner-Wallerstein debate." *International Studies Quarterly,* 32: 47–65.

Denison, E. F., 1979. *Accounting for Slower Economic Growth in the United States in the 1970s.* Washington: Brookings Institution.

De Swaan, Abram, 1973. *Coalition Theories and Cabinet Formations.* San Francisco: Jossey-Bass.

Deutscher, Isaac, 1966. *Stalin: A Political Biography.* New York: Oxford University Press.

Devine, Joel A., 1983. "Fiscal policy and class income inequality: the distributional consequences of governmental revenues and expenditures in the United States, 1949–76." *American Sociological Review,* 48: 606–22.

Devine, Joel A., 1985. "State and state expenditure: determinants of social investment and social consumption spending in the postwar United States." *American Sociological Review,* 50: 150–65.

Devlin, L. Patrick (ed.), 1987. *Political Persuasion in Presidential Campaigns.* New Brunswick, N.J.: Transaction Books.

DiMaggio, Paul, and Walter Powell, 1983. "The iron cage revisited: institutional isomorphism and collective rationality in organizational fields." *American Sociological Review,* 48: 147–60.

Domhoff, G. William, 1967. *Who Rules America?* Englewood Cliffs, N.J.: Prentice-Hall.

Domhoff, G. William, 1975. "Social clubs, policy-planning groups, and corporations: a network study of ruling-class cohesiveness." *Insurgent Sociologist,* 5: 173–84.

Domhoff, G. William, 1978. *Who Really Rules? New Haven and Community Power Reexamined.* New Brunswick, N.J.: Transaction.

Domhoff, G. William, 1979. *The Powers That Be: State and Ruling Class in Corporate America.* New York: Random House.

Domhoff, G. William, 1983. *Who Rules America Now? A View for the '80s.*

Englewood Cliffs, N.J.: Prentice-Hall.

Donnellon, Anne, Barbara Gray, and Michael G. Bougon, 1986. " Communication, meaning, and organized action." *Administrative Science Quarterly*, 31: 43–55.

Dos Santos, Theotonio, 1970. "The structure of dependence." *American Economic Review*, 60: 231–36.

Downing, John, 1986. "Government secrecy and the media in the United States and Britain." In Peter Golding, Graham Murdock, and Philip Schlesinger (eds.), *Communicating Politics: Mass Communications and the Political Process*. New York: Holmes and Meier, pp. 153–70.

Downs, Anthony, 1957. *An Economic Theory of Democracy*. New York: Harper & Row.

Duesenberry, James, 1960. "Comment on 'An economic analysis of fertility.'" In University-National Bureau Committee for Economic Research (ed.), *Demographic and Economic Change in Developing Countries*. Princeton, N.J.: Princeton University Press.

Dunn, William N., and Ari Ginsberg, 1986. "A sociocognitive network approach to organizational analysis." *Human Relations*, 40: 955–76.

Dye, Thomas R., 1976. *Who's Running America?* Englewood Cliffs, N.J.: Prentice-Hall.

Dye, Thomas R., 1978. "Oligarchic tendencies in national policy-making." *Journal of Politics*, 40: 309–31.

Dye, Thomas R., 1986. *Who's Running America: The Conservative Years*. Fourth Edition. Englewood Cliffs, N.J.: Prentice-Hall.

Dye, Thomas R., Eugene R. DeClercq, and John W. Pickering, 1973. "Concentration, specialization, and interlocking among institutional elites." *Social Science Quarterly*, 54: 8–28.

Dye, Thomas R., and John W. Pickering, 1974. "Governmental and corporate elites: convergence and specialization." *Journal of Politics*, 36: 900– 25.

Dye, Thomas R., and L. Harmon Ziegler, 1986. *American Politics in the Media Age*. Monterey, Calif.: Brooks/Cole.

Easton, David, 1965. *A Systems Analysis of Political Life*. New York: Wiley.

Eccles, Robert G., and Dwight Crane, 1987. "Managing through networks of investment banking." *California Management Review*, 30: 176–95.

Eckberg, Douglas Lee, 1988. "The physicians' anti-abortion campaign and the social bases of moral reform participation." *Social Forces*, 67: 378–97.

Eckstein, Harry, and Ted R. Gurr, 1975. *Patterns of Authority: A Structural Basis for Political Inquiry*. New York: Wiley.

Eckstein, Otto, Christopher Caton, Roger Brinner, and Peter Duprey, 1984. *The DRI Report on U.S. Manufacturing Industries*. New York: McGraw-Hill.

Eckstein, Susan, 1988. *Protest and Resistance in Latin America*. Berkeley: University of California Press.

Edwards, Richard, 1979. *Contested Terrain: The Transformation of the Workplace in the Twentieth Century*. New York: Basic Books.

Eisenstadt, S. N., and L. Roniger, 1984. *Patrons, Clients and Friends: Interpersonal Relations and the Structure of Trust in Society*. Cambridge: Cambridge University Press.

Eldersveld, Samuel J., 1964. *Political Parties: A Behavioral Analysis.* Chicago: Rand-McNally.

Emerson, Richard M., 1962. "Power-dependence relations." *American Sociological Review,* 27: 31–41.

Emerson, Richard M., 1972. "Exchange theory. Part II: Exchange relations, exchange networks, and groups as exchange systems." In Joseph Berger, Morris Zelditch, and Bo Anderson (eds.), *Sociological Theories in Progress, Vol 2.* Boston: Houghton Mifflin, pp. 58–87.

Emerson, Richard M., 1976. "Social exchange theory." *Annual Review of Sociology,* 2: 335–62.

Enelow, James M., and Melvin J. Hinich, 1984. *The Spatial Theory of Voting: An Introduction.* New York: Cambridge University Press.

Erickson, Bonnie, 1988. "The relational basis of attitudes." In Barry Wellman and S. D. Berkowitz (eds.), *Intercorporate Relations: The Structural Analysis of Business.* Cambridge: Cambridge University Press, pp. 99–121.

Esping-Andersen, Gosta, 1985. *Politics Against Markets: The Social Democratic Road to Power.* Princeton, N.J.: Princeton University Press.

Etzioni, Amitai, 1975. *A Comparative Analysis of Complex Organizations.* New York: Free Press.

Eulau, Heinz, 1980. "The Columbia studies of personal influence." *Social Science History,* 4: 207–28.

Eulau, Heinz, 1986. *Politics, Self, and Society: A Theme and Variations.* Cambridge, Mass.: Harvard University Press.

Evans, Peter B., 1979. *Dependent Development.* Princeton: Princeton University Press.

Evans, Peter B., 1981. "Recent research on multinational corporations." *Annual Review of Sociology,* 7: 199–223.

Evans, Peter, and Michael Timberlake, 1980. "Dependence, inequality, and the growth of the tertiary: a comparative analysis of less-developed countries." *American Sociological Review,* 45: 531–52.

Fairhurst, Gail T., and B. Kay Snavely, 1983. "Majority and token minority group relationships: power acquisition and communication." *Academy of Management Review,* 8: 292–300.

Fararo, Thomas J., and John Skvoretz, 1986. "E-state structuralism: a theoretical method." *American Sociological Review,* 51: 591–602.

Faulkner, Robert R., and Andy Anderson, 1987. "Short-term projects and emergent careers: evidence from Hollywood." *American Journal of Sociology,* 92: 879–909.

Feketekuty, Geza, and Johnathan D. Aronson, 1984. "Meeting the challenges of the world information economy." *The World Economy,* 7: 63–86.

Feld, Scott, 1981. "The focused organization of social ties." *American Journal of Sociology,* 86: 1015–35.

Fennell, Mary L., Christopher O. Ross, and Richard B. Warnecke, 1987. "Organizational environment and network structure." *Research in the Sociology of Organizations,* 5: 311–40.

Fennema, Meindart, and Huibert Schijf, 1978. "Analyzing interlocking directorates: theory and methods." *Social Networks,* 1: 297–332.

Fernandez, Roberto M., and Doug McAdam, 1988. "Social networks and social

252   *References*

movements: multiorganizational fields and recruitment to Mississippi Freedom Summer." *Sociological Forum,* 3: 357–82.

Fernandez, Roberto M., and Doug McAdam, 1989. "Multiorganizational fields and recruitment to social movements." In Bert Klandermans (ed.), *Organizing for Change: Social Movement Organizations in Europe and the United States,* Vol. 2. Greenwich, Conn.: JAI Press pp. 315–44.

Fernandez, Roberto M., and Lisa Rowe, 1988. "A micro model of activism in a social movement organization: differential activism in a women's center." Paper presented at the American Sociological Association meetings, Atlanta.

Field, G. Lowell, and John Higley, 1980. *Elitism.* London: Routledge and Kegan Paul.

Fieleke, Norman S., 1988. *The International Economy Under Stress.* Cambridge, Mass.: Ballinger.

Finifter, Ada W., 1974. "The friendship group as a protective environment for political deviants." *American Political Science Review,* 68: 607–25.

Fiorina, Morris P., 1977. *Congress: Keystone of the Washington Establishment.* New Haven: Yale University Press.

Fiorina, Morris P., 1981. *Retrospective Voting in American National Elections.* New Haven: Yale University Press.

Fireman, Bruce, and William A. Gamson, 1979. "Utilitarian logic in the resource mobilization perspective." In Mayer N. Zald and John D. McCarthy (eds.), *The Dynamics of Social Movements: Resource Mobilization, Social Control and Tactics.* Cambridge, Mass.: Winthrop, pp. 8–44.

Fiske, Edward B., 1984. "American students score average or below in international math exams." *New York Times,* September 23, p. 30.

FitzGerald, Frances, 1972. *Fire in the Lake: the Vietnamese and the Americans in Vietnam.* Boston: Little, Brown.

Fligstein, Neil, 1987. "The intraorganizational power struggle: rise of finance personnel to top leadership in large corporations, 1919–1979." *American Sociological Review,* 52: 44–58.

Fombrun, Charles J., 1983. "Attributions of power across a social network." *Human Relations,* 36: 493–508.

Fombrun, Charles J., 1986. "Structural dynamics within and between organizations." *Administrative Science Quarterly,* 31: 403–21.

Form, William, and William V. D'Antonio, 1959. "Integration and cleavage among community influentials in two border cities." *American Sociological Review,* 24: 804–14.

Forthal, Sonya, 1948. *Cogwheels of Democracy.* New York: Pamphlet Distributing.

Foss, Daniel A., and Ralph Larkin, 1986. *Beyond Revolution.* South Hadley, Mass.: Bergin and Garvey.

Frank, Andre G., 1967. *Capitalism and Underdevelopment in Latin America.* New York: Monthly Review Press.

Frank, Andre G., 1978. *World Accumulation, 1492–1789.* New York: Monthly Review Press.

Frank, Andre G., 1980. *Crisis in the World Economy.* New York: Holmes and Meier.

Freedman, Warren, 1987. *The Right of Privacy in the Computer Age.* New York: Quorom Books.

Freeman, Jo, 1979. "Resource mobilization and strategy: a model for analyzing social movement organization actions." In Mayer N. Zald and John D. McCarthy (eds.), *The Dynamics of Social Movements: Resource Mobilization, Social Control and Tactics.* Cambridge, Mass.: Winthrop, pp. 167–89.

Freeman, Jo, 1983. "On the origins of social movements." In Jo Freeman (ed.), *Social Movements of the Sixties and Seventies.* New York: Longman, pp. 8–30.

Freeman, Linton C., 1968. *Patterns of Local Community Leadership.* Indianapolis, Ind.: Bobbs-Merrill.

Freeman, Linton C., 1977. "A set of measures of centrality based on betweenness." *Sociometry,* 40: 35–41.

Freeman, Linton C., 1979. "Centrality in social networks: conceptual clarification." *Social Networks,* 1: 215–39.

Freeman, Linton C., 1988. "Computer programs and social network analysis." *Connections,* 11: 26–31.

Freeman, Linton C., Warner Bloomberg, Jr., Stephen P. Koff, Morris H. Sunshine, and Thomas J. Fararo, 1960. *Local Community Leadership.* Syracuse, N.Y.: University College of Syracuse University.

Freeman, Linton C., Douglas R. White, and A. Kimball Romney, 1989. *Research Methods in Social Network Analysis.* Fairfax, Va.: George Mason University Press.

Freitag, Peter, 1975. "The cabinet and big business: a study of interlocks." *Social Problems,* 23: 137–52.

French, John R. P., Jr., and Bertram Raven, 1959. "The bases of social power." In Dorwin Cartwright (ed.), *Studies in Social Power.* Ann Arbor, Mich.: Institute for Social Research, pp. 150–67.

Frey, Frederick W., 1971. "Comment: on issues and nonissues in the study of power." *American Political Science Review,* 65: 1081–101.

Friedell, Morris, 1967. "Organizations as semilattices." *American Sociological Review,* 32: 46–53.

Friedkin, Noah E., 1984. "Cohesion and structural equivalence explanations of social homophily." *Sociological Methods and Research,* 12: 235–61.

Friedman, Milton, 1953. "The methodology of positive economics." In Milton Friedman (ed.), *Essays in Positive Economics.* Chicago: University of Chicago Press, pp. 3–43.

Friedmann, Harriet, 1988. "Form and substance in the analysis of the world economy." In Barry Wellman and S. D. Berkowitz (eds.), *Intercorporate Relations: The Structural Analysis of Business.* Cambridge: Cambridge University Press, pp. 304–25.

Fromm, Erich, 1941. *Escape from Freedom.* New York: Rinehart.

Gais, Thomas L., Mark A. Peterson, and Jack L. Walker, 1984. "Interest groups, iron triangles, and representative institutions in American national government." *British Journal of Political Science,* 14: 161–85.

Galaskiewicz, Joseph, 1979a. "The structure of community interorganizational networks." *Social Forces,* 57: 1346–64.

Galaskiewicz, Joseph, 1979b. *Exchange Networks and Community Politics.* Beverly Hills, Calif.: Sage.

Galaskiewicz, Joseph, 1985. "Interorganizational relations." *Annual Review of Sociology,* 11: 281–304.

Galaskiewicz, Joseph, 1989. "Interorganizational networks mobilizing action at the metropolitan level." In Robert B. Perrucci and Harry R. Potter (eds.), *Networks of Power.* New York: Aldine de Gruyer, pp. 81–96.

Galbraith, Jay, 1977. *Organization Design.* Reading, Mass.: Addison-Wesley.

Galtung, Johan, 1970. "East-west interaction patterns." *Journal of Peace Research,* 2: 146–76.

Gambetta, Diego, 1988. *Trust: Making and Breaking Cooperative Relations.* New York: Basil Blackwell.

Gamson, William, 1964. "Experimental studies of coalition formation." In Leonard Berkowitz (ed.), *Advances in Experimental Social Psychology.* New York: Academic Press, pp. 81–110.

Gamson, William A., 1968. *Power and Discontent.* Homewood, Il.: Dorsey.

Gamson, William A., 1975. *The Strategy of Social Protest.* Homewood, Il.: Dorsey.

Gandy, Oscar H., Jr., 1982. *Beyond Agenda Setting: Information Subsidies and Public Policy.* Norwood, N.J.: Ablex.

Gant, Michael M., and Dwight F. Davis, 1984. "Mental economy and voter rationality: the informed citizen problem in voting research." *Journal of Politics,* 46: 132–53.

Garnham, David, 1976. "Dyadic international war 1816–1965: the role of power parity and geographical proximity." *Western Political Quarterly,* 29: 231–42.

Garrow, David J., 1978. *Protest at Selma.* New Haven: Yale University Press.

Geschwender, James A., 1967. "Continuities in theories of status consistency and cognitive dissonance." *Social Forces,* 46: 165–67.

Giddens, Anthony, 1979. *Central Problems in Social Theory: Action, Structure, and Contradiction in Social Analysis.* Berkeley: University of California Press.

Giddens, Anthony, 1984. *The Constitution of Society: Outline of the Theory of Structuration.* Berkeley: University of California Press.

Gilbert, Claire, 1968. "Community power and decision-making: a quantitative examination of previous research." In Terry N. Clark (ed.), *Community Structure and Decision-Making: Comparative Analyses.* San Francisco: Chandler, pp. 129–38.

Giles, Michael W., and Marilyn K. Dantico, 1982. "Political participation and neighborhood social context revisited." *American Journal of Political Science,* 26: 144–150.

Glass, Jennifer, Vern L. Bengston, and Charlotte Chorn Dunham, 1986. "Attitude similarity in three-generation families: socialization, status inheritance, or reciprocal influence?" *American Sociological Review,* 51: 685–99.

Godwin, R. Kenneth, and Robert C. Mitchell, 1982. "Rational models, collective goods and nonelectoral political behavior." *Western Political Quarterly,* 35: 161–81.

Gold, Thomas, 1986. *State and Society in the Taiwan Miracle.* New York: Sharpe.

Goldberg, Arthur S., 1969. "Social determinism and rationality as bases of party identification." *American Political Science Review,* 55: 5–25.

Goldstone, Jack, 1980. "The weakness of organization: a new look at Gamson's

The Strategy of Social Protest." *American Journal of Sociology*, 85: 1043–60.

Gordon, C. Wayne, and Nicholas Babchuk, 1959. "A typology of voluntary associations." *American Sociological Review*, 24: 22–29.

Gosnell, Harold F., 1937. *Machine Politics: Chicago Model.* Chicago: University of Chicago Press.

Gough, Ian, 1979. *The Political Economy of the Welfare State.* London: Macmillan.

Gould, Roger V., 1989. "Power and social structure in community elites." *Social Forces*, 68: 531–32.

Gould, Roger V., and Roberto M. Fernandez, 1989. "Structures of mediation: a formal approach to brokerage in transaction networks." *Sociological Methodology 1990*. San Francisco: Jossey-Bass pp. 89–126.

Gouldner, Alvin, 1960. "The norm of reciprocity: a preliminary statement." *American Sociological Review*, 25: 161–79.

Gramsci, Antonio, 1971. *Selections from the Prison Notebooks.* London: Lawrence and Wishart.

Granovetter, Mark, 1973. "The strength of weak ties." *American Journal of Sociology*, 78: 1360–80.

Granovetter, Mark, 1974. *Getting a Job: A Study of Contacts and Careers.* Cambridge, Mass.: Harvard University Press.

Granovetter, Mark, 1978. "Threshold models of collective behavior." *American Journal of Sociology*, 83: 1420–43.

Granovetter, Mark, 1982. "The strength of weak ties: a network theory revisited." In Peter V. Marsden and Nan Lin (eds.), *Social Structure and Network Analysis*. Beverly Hills, Calif.: Sage, pp. 105–30.

Granovetter, Mark, 1985. "Economic action and social structure: the problem of embeddedness." *American Journal of Sociology*, 91: 481–510.

Grayson, C. Jackson, Jr., and Carla O'Dell, 1988. *American Business: A Two-Minute Warning.* New York: Free Press.

Graziano, L., 1975. *A Conceptual Framework for the Study of Clientalism.* Ithaca, N.Y.: Cornell University Western Societies Program.

Griffin, Larry J., Michael Wallace, and Beth Rubin, 1986. "Capitalist resistance to the organization of labor before the New Deal: why? how? success?" *American Sociological Review*, 51: 147–67.

Grimes, Michael D., Charles M. Bonjean, Jerry L. Lyon, and Robert M. Lineberry, 1976. "Community structure and leadership arrangements: a multidimensional analysis." *American Sociological Review*, 41: 706–25.

Groennings, Sven, E. W. Kelley, and Michael Leiserson, 1970. *The Study of Coalition Behavior.* New York: Holt, Rinehart and Winston.

Guetzkow, Harold, 1965. "Communication in organizations." In James G. March (ed.), *Handbook of Organizations*. Chicago: Rand-McNally, pp. 535–72.

Gunn, Thomas G., 1987. *Manufacturing for Competitive Advantage: Becoming a World Class Manufacturer.* Cambridge, Mass.: Ballinger.

Gurr, Ted, 1970. *Why Men Rebel.* Princeton, N.J.: Princeton University Press.

Guterbock, Thomas, 1980. *Machine Politics in Transition: Party and Community in Chicago.* Chicago: University of Chicago Press.

Haas, Ernst B., 1964. *Beyond the Nation-State: Functionalism and International Organization.* Stanford, Calif.: Stanford University Press.

Hage, Jerald, 1974. *Communication and Organizational Control: Cybernetics in*

Health and Welfare Settings. New York: Wiley.

Hage, Jerald (ed.), 1988. *Futures of Organizations: Innovating to Adapt Strategy and Human Resources to Rapid Technological Change.* Lexington, Mass.: Lexington Books.

Haines, Valerie A., 1988. "Social network analysis, structuration theory, and the holism-individualism debate." *Social Networks* 10: 157–82.

Halebsky, Sandor, 1976. *Mass Society and Political Conflict: Towards a Reconstruction of Theory.* Cambridge: Cambridge University Press.

Halloran, R., 1984. "Pentagon forms war press pool; newspaper reporters excluded." *New York Times,* October 11.

Halpert, Burton P., 1982. "Antecedents." In David L. Rogers and David A. Whetten (eds.), *Interorganizational Coordination: Theory, Research, and Implementation.* Ames, Iowa: Iowa State University Press, pp. 54–72.

Handler, Edward, and John Mulkern, 1982. *Business in Politics.* Lexington, Mass.: Lexington Books.

Hanf, Kenneth, Benny Hjern, and David O. Porter, 1978."Local networks of manpower training in the Federal Republic of Germany and Sweden." In Kenneth Hanf and Fritz W. Scharpf (eds.), *Interorganizational Policy Making: Limits to Coordination and Central Control.* London: Sage, pp. 303–41.

Hanf, Kenneth, and Fritz W. Scharpf (eds.), 1978. *Interorganizational Policy Making: Limits to Coordination and Central Control.* London: Sage.

Hansen, John Mark, 1985. "The political economy of group membership." *American Political Science Review,* 79: 79–96.

Harper, Edwin L., 1984. "Do we need an industrial policy?" In Michael L. Wachter and Susan M. Wachter (eds.), *Removing Obstacles to Economic Growth.* Philadelphia, Penn.: University of Pennsylvania Press, pp. 457–69.

Harrison, Bennett, and Barry Bluestone, 1988. *The Great U-Turn.* New York: Basic Books.

Harsanyi, John C., 1969. "Rational-choice models of political behavior vs. functionalist and conformist theories." *World Politics,* 21: 513–38.

Harsanyi, John C., 1977. *Rational Behavior and Bargaining Equilibrium in Games and Social Situations.* Cambridge: Cambridge University Press.

Hart, Jeffrey, 1974. "Structures of influence and cooperation-conflict." *International Interactions,* 1: 141–62.

Hawkes, Terence, 1977. *Structuralism and Semiotics.* Berkeley: University of California Press.

Hawley, Amos, 1963. "Community power and urban renewal success." *American Journal of Sociology,* 68: 422–31.

Hayes, Michael T., 1978. "The semi-sovereign pressure groups: a critique of current theory and an alternative typology." *Journal of Politics,* 40: 134–61.

Hayes, Michael T., 1983. "Interest groups: pluralism or mass society?" In Allan J. Cigler and Burdett A. Loomis (eds.), *Interest Group Politics.* Washington, D.C.: CQ Press, pp. 110–25.

Hayes, Robert H., and William J. Abernathy, 1980. "Managing our way to economic decline." *Harvard Business Review* (July–August): 67–77.

Heath, Anthony, 1976. *Rational Choice and Social Exchange: A Critique of Exchange Theory.* Cambridge: Cambridge University Press.

Hechter, Michael (ed.), 1983. *The Microfoundations of Macrosociology.* Philadelphia: Temple University Press.

Heckathorn, Douglas D., 1984. "Mathematical theory construction in sociology: analytic power, scope, and descriptive accuracy as trade-offs." In Thomas J. Fararo (ed.), *Mathematical Ideas and Sociological Theory*. New York: Gordon and Breach, pp. 77–105.

Heckathorn, Douglas D., 1985. "Power and trust in social exchange." *Advances in Group Processes*, 2: 143–68.

Heclo, Hugh, 1978. "Issue networks and the executive establishment." In Anthony King (ed.), *The New American Political System*. Washington, D.C.: American Enterprise Institute, pp. 87–124.

Heims, Peter, 1982. *Countering Industrial Espionage*. Leatherhead, England: 20th Century Security Education.

Heinz, John P., Edward O. Laumann, Robert L. Nelson, and Robert H. Salisbury, 1988. "Inner circles or hollow cores? Elite networks in national policy systems." Chicago: University of Chicago unpublished manuscript.

Herman, Edward S., 1982. *The Real Terror Network: Terrorism in Fact and Propaganda*. Boston: South End Press.

Hess, Robert D., and Judith V. Torney, 1967. *The Development of Political Attitudes in Children*. Chicago: Aldine.

Hibbs, Douglas A., Jr., 1973. *Mass Political Violence: A Cross-National Causal Analysis*. New York: Wiley.

Hibbs, Douglas A., Jr., 1976. "Industrial conflict in advanced industrial societies." *American Political Science Review*, 70: 1033–58.

Hibbs, Douglas A., Jr., 1981. "Macroeconomic performance and mass political support in the United States and Great Britain." In Douglas A. Hibbs, Jr. and Heino Fassbender (eds.), *Contemporary Political Economy: Studies on the Interdependence of Politics and Economies*. Amsterdam: North-Holland, pp. 31–48.

Hicks, Alexander, Roger Friedland, and Edwin Johnson, 1978. "Class power and state policy: the case of large business corporations, labor unions, and governmental redistribution in the American states." *American Sociological Review*, 43: 302–15.

Hicks, Alexander, and Duane Swank, 1984. "On the political economy of welfare expansion: a comparative analysis of 18 advanced capitalist democracies, 1960–1971." *Comparative Political Studies*, 17: 81–119.

Hicks, Donald A., 1985. *Advanced Industrial Development: Restructuring Relocation and Renewal*. Boston: Oelgeschlager, Gunn and Hain.

Hickson, David J., 1987. "Decision-making at the top of organizations." *Annual Review of Sociology*, 14: 165–92.

Hickson, D. J., C. R. Hinings, C. A. Lee, R. E. Schneck, and J. M. Pennings, 1971. "A strategic contingencies theory of intraorganizational power." *Administrative Science Quarterly*, 16: 216–229.

Hickson, David J., Richard J. Butler, David Gray, Geoffrey R. Mallory, and David C. Wilson, 1986. *Top Decisions: Strategic Decision-Making in Organizations*. San Francisco: Jossey-Bass.

Higley, John, G. Lowell Field, and K. Groholt, 1976. *Elite Structure and Ideology*. New York: Columbia University Press.

Higley, John, and Gwen Moore, 1981. "Elite integration in the United States and

Australia." *American Political Science Review,* 75: 581–97.

Hiltz, Starr Roxanne, and Murray Turoff, 1978. *The Network Nation: Human Communication Via Computer.* Reading, Mass.: Addison-Wesley.

Hinckley, Barbara, 1981. *Coalitions and Politics.* New York: Harcourt Brace Jovanovich.

Hinings, C. R., D. J. Hickson, J. M. Pennings, and R. E. Schneck, 1974. "Structural conditions of intraorganizational power." *Administrative Science Quarterly,* 19: 22–44.

Hirsch, Paul M., 1986. "From ambushes to golden parachutes: corporate takeovers as an instance of cultural framing and institutional integration." *American Journal of Sociology* 91: 800–37.

Hoffer, Eric, 1951. *The True Believer.* New York: Harper & Row.

Holland, Paul W., and Samuel Leinhardt, 1979. *Perspectives on Social Network Research.* New York: Academic.

Holler, Manfred J. (ed.), 1984. *Coalitions and Collective Action.* Wuerzburg: Physica-Verlag.

Homans, George C., 1964. "Bringing men back in." *American Sociological Review,* 29: 809–18.

Hope, Keith, 1975. "Models of status inconsistency and social mobility effects." *American Sociological Review,* 40: 322–43.

Hopkins, Terence, 1978. "World-system analysis: methodological issues." In Barbara H. Kaplan (ed.), *Social Change in the Capitalist World Economy.* Beverly Hills, Calif.: Sage, pp. 199–217.

Hopkins, Terence, and Immanuel Wallerstein, 1982. *World-System Analysis: Theory and Methodology.* Beverly Hills, Calif.: Sage.

Horan, Patrick M., 1971. "Social positions and political cross-pressures: a re-examination." *American Sociological Review,* 36: 650–60.

Howard, Robert, 1985. *Brave New Workplace.* New York: Viking.

Hsaio, David K., Douglas S. Kerr, and Stuart E. Madnick, 1979. *Computer Security.* New York: Academic Press.

Hubbard, Howard, 1968. "Five long hot summers and how they grew." *Public Interest,* 12: 3–24.

Huckfeldt, Robert R., 1979. "Political participation and the neighborhood social context." *American Journal of Political Science,* 23: 579–92.

Huckfeldt, Robert R., 1984. "Political loyalties and social class ties: the mechanisms of contextual influence." *American Journal of Political Science,* 28: 399–417.

Huckfeldt, Robert R., and John Sprague, 1987. "Networks in social context: the social flow of political information." *American Political Science Review,* 81: 1197–216.

Huckfeldt, Robert R., and John Sprague, 1988. "Choice, social structure, and political information: the informational coercion of minorities." *American Journal of Political Science,* 32: 467–82.

Hunter, Albert, and Suzanne Staggenborg, 1988. "Local communities and organized action." In Carl Milofsky (ed.), *Community Organizations.* New York: Oxford University Press, pp. 242–76.

Hunter, Floyd, 1953. *Community Power Structure.* Chapel Hill, N.C.: University of North Carolina Press.

Hunter, Floyd, 1959. *Top Leadership, USA*. Chapel Hill, N.C.: University of North Carolina Press.

Hutt, Arthur E., Seymour Bosworth, and Douglas B. Hoyt, 1988. *Computer Security Handbook. Second Edition*. New York: Macmillan.

Hwang, Kwang-kuo, 1987. "Face and favor: the Chinese power game." *American Journal of Sociology*, 92: 944–74.

Jackson, Brooks, 1988. *Honest Graft: Big Money and the American Political Process*. New York: Knopf.

Jackson, Elton, and Richard F. Curtis, 1972. "Effects of vertical mobility and status inconsistency: a body of negative evidence." *American Sociological Review*, 37: 701–713.

Jenkins, J. Craig, 1983. "Resource mobilization theory and the study of social movements." *Annual Review of Sociology*, 9: 527–53.

Jenkins, J. Craig, and Craig M. Eckert, 1986. "Channeling black insurgency: elite patronage and professional social movement organizations in the development of the black movement." *American Sociological Review*, 51: 812–29.

Jenkins, J. Craig, and Charles Perrow, 1977. "Insurgency of the powerless: farm worker movements (1946–1972)." *American Sociological Review*, 42: 249–68.

Jennergren, L. Peter, 1981. "Decentralization in organizations." In Paul C. Nystrom and William H. Starbuck (eds.), *Handbook of Organizational Design, Vol. 2*. New York: Oxford University Press, pp. 39–59.

Jennings, M. Kent, and Richard G. Niemi, 1974. *The Political Character of Adolescence: The Influence of Families and School*. Princeton: Princeton University Press.

Jennings, M. Kent, and Richard G. Niemi, 1981. *Generations and Politics: A Panel Study of Young Adults and Their Parents*. Princeton, N.J.: Princeton University Press.

Jensen, M. and W. Meckling, 1976. "Theory of the Firm: Managerial Behavior, Agency, Costs and Ownership Structure," *Journal of Financial Economics*, 3: 305–360.

Johnson, Bryan, 1987. *The Four Days of Courage: The Untold Story of the People Who Brought Marcos Down*. New York: Free Press.

Johnson, William B., and Arnold E. Packer, 1987. *Workforce 2000: Work and Workers for the Twenty-First Century*. Indianapolis, Ind.: Hudson Institute.

Kadushin, Charles, 1968. "Power, influence, and social circles: a new methodology for studying opinion makers." *American Sociological Review*, 33: 685–698.

Kahneman, Daniel, Paul Slovic, and Amos Tversky (eds.), 1982. *Judgment Under Uncertainty: Heuristics and Biases*. New York: Cambridge University Press.

Kanter, Rosabeth Moss, 1977. *Men and Women of the Corporation*. New York: Basic Books.

Kappelhoff, Peter, 1989. "Power in exchange networks: An extension and application of the Coleman model of collective action." Paper presented at first European Conference on Social Network Analysis, Groningen, The Netherlands.

Kappelhoff, Peter, and Franz Urban Pappi, 1987. "The political subsystem of a community elite: blockmodelling the power structure." *Sosiologisk arbok for 1987*: 231–64.

Katz, Daniel, and Robert L. Kahn, 1978. *The Social Psychology of Organizations, Revised Edition.* New York: Wiley.

Katz, Daniel, and Paul F. Lazarsfeld, 1955. *Personal Influence: The Part Played by People in the Flow of Mass Communications.* Glencoe, Ill.: Free Press.

Katzenstein, Mary Fainsod, and Carole Mueller, 1987. *The Women's Movements of the U.S. and Western Europe.* Philadelphia: Temple University Press.

Kaufman, Allen, Marvin Karson, and Jeffrey Sohl, 1987. "Corporate factionalism and corporate solidarity in the 1980 and 1982 congressional elections." *Journal of Political and Military Sociology,* 15: 171–86.

Keller, Suzanne, 1963. *Beyond the Ruling Class: Strategic Elites in Modern Society.* New York: Random House.

Kelley, E. W., 1968. "Techniques of studying coalition formation." *Midwest Journal of Political Science,* 12: 62–84.

Kelley, Jonathan, and Ian McAllister, 1985. "Social context and electoral behavior in Britain." *American Journal of Political Science,* 29: 564–86.

Kendrick, John, 1980. "Productivity trends in the United States." In Shlomo Maital and Noah M. Meltz (eds.), *Lagging Productivity Growth.* Cambridge, Mass.: Ballinger.

Kennedy, Paul, 1987. *The Rise and Fall of the Great Powers: Economic Change and Military Conflicts from 1500 to 2000.* New York: Random House.

Kerlinger, Fred N., and Elazar J. Pedhazur, 1973. *Multiple Regression in Behavioral Research.* Holt, Rinehart and Winston.

Key, V. O., 1949. *Southern Politics in State and Nation.* New York: Knopf.

Kick, Edward L., 1980. "World system properties and mass political conflict within nations: theoretical framework." *Journal of Political and Military Sociology,* 8: 175–190.

Kick, Edward L., 1983. "World-system properties and military intervention-internal war linkages." *Journal of Political and Military Sociology,* 11: 185–208.

Kick, Edward L., 1987. "World-system structure, national development, and the prospects for a socialist world order." In Terry Boswell and Albert Bergesen (eds.), *America's Changing Role in the World System.* New York: Praeger, pp. 127–55.

Killian, Lewis, 1984. "Organization, rationality, and spontaneity in the civil rights movement." *American Sociological Review,* 49: 770–83.

Kim, Ilpyong J., 1969. "Mass mobilization policies and techniques developed during the period of the Chinese soviet republic." In A. Doak Barnett (ed.), *Chinese Communist Politics in Action.* Seattle: University of Washington Press, pp. 78–98.

Kingdon, John W., 1984. *Agendas, Alternatives, and Public Policies.* Boston: Little, Brown.

Kitschelt, Herbert P., 1986. "Political opportunity structures and political protest." *British Journal of Political Science,* 16: 57–85.

Klandermans, Bert, 1984. "Social-psychological expansions of the resource mobilization theory." *American Sociological Review,* 49: 583–600.

Klandermans, Bert, and Dirk Oegema, 1987. "Potentials, networks, motivations, and barriers, steps towards participation in social movements." *American*

Sociological Review, 52: 519–31.

Klein, Katherine J., and Rosalie J. Hall, 1988 "Innovations in human resource management: strategies for the future." In Jerald Hage (ed.), *Futures of Organizations: Innovating to Adapt Strategy and Human Resources to Rapid Technological Change*. Lexington, Mass.: Lexington Books, pp. 147–62.

Knoke, David, 1973. "Intergenerational occupational mobility and the political party preferences of American men." *American Journal of Sociology*, 78: 1448–68.

Knoke, David, 1976. *Change and Continuity in American Politics: The Social Bases of Political Parties*. Baltimore: Johns Hopkins University Press.

Knoke, David, 1981a. "Power structures." In Samuel Long (ed.), *The Handbook of Political Behavior Vol. 3*. New York: Plenum, pp. 275–332.

Knoke, David, 1981b. "Commitment and detachment in voluntary associations." *American Sociological Review*, 46: 141–58.

Knoke, David, 1982. "The spread of municipal reform: temporal, spatial, and social dynamics." *American Journal of Sociology*, 87: 1314–39.

Knoke, David, 1983. "Organization sponsorship and influence reputation of social influence associations." *Social Forces*, 61: 1065–87.

Knoke, David, 1986. "Associations and interest groups." *Annual Review of Sociology*, 12: 1–21.

Knoke, David, 1988. "Incentives in collective action organizations." *American Sociological Review*, 53: 311–29.

Knoke, David, 1989. "Fighting collectively: action sets and opposition networks in the U.S. labor policy domain." Paper presented at Sunbelt Social Networks Conference, Tampa, Fla.

Knoke, David, 1990a. *Organizing for Collective Action: The Political Economies of American Associations*. Hawthorne, N.Y.: Aldine de Gruyter.

Knoke, David, 1990b. "Networks of political action: toward theory construction." *Social Forces* (forthcoming).

Knoke, David, and Frank Burleigh, 1989. "Collective action in national policy domains: constraints, cleavages, and policy outcomes." *Research in Political Sociology*, 4: 187–208.

Knoke, David, and Ronald S. Burt, 1983. "Prominence." In Ronald S. Burt and Michael J. Minor (eds.), *Applied Network Analysis: A Methodological Introduction*. Beverly Hills, Calif.: Sage, pp. 195–222.

Knoke, David, and Natalie Kyriazis, 1977. "The persistence of the black-belt vote: a test of Key's hypothesis." *Social Science Quarterly*, 57: 899–906.

Knoke, David, and James H. Kuklinski, 1982. *Network Analysis*. Beverly Hills, Calif.: Sage.

Knoke, David, and Edward O. Laumann, 1982. "The social organization of national policy domains: an exploration of some structural hypotheses." In Peter V. Marsden and Nan Lin (eds.), *Social Structure and Network Analysis*. Beverly Hills, Calif.: Sage, pp. 255–70.

Knoke, David, and Franz Urban Pappi, 1989. "Fighting collectively: action sets and opposition networks in the U.S. and West German labor policy domains." Paper presented at American Sociological Association Meetings.

Knoke, David, and David L. Rogers, 1979. "A blockmodel analysis of inter-organizational networks." *Sociology and Social Research* 64:28-52

Knoke, David, and James R. Wood, 1981. *Organized for Action: Commitment in Voluntary Associations.* New Brunswick: Rutgers University Press.

Knoke, David, and Christine Wright-Isak, 1982. "Individual motives and organizational incentive systems." *Research in the Sociology of Organizations,* 1: 209–54.

Kornblum, William, 1974. *Blue Collar Community.* Chicago: University of Chicago Press.

Kornhauser, William, 1959. *The Politics of Mass Society.* New York: Free Press.

Krackhardt, David, 1987. "Cognitive social structures." *Social Networks,* 9: 109–34.

Krackhardt, David, and Lyman W. Porter, 1985. "When friends leave: a structural analysis of the relationship between turnover and stayers' attitudes." *Administrative Science Quarterly,* 30: 242–61.

Kruskal, Joseph B., and Myron Wish, 1978. *Multidimensional Scaling.* Beverly Hills, Calif.: Sage.

Lachman, Ran, 1989. "Power from what? A reexamination of its relationships with structural conditions." *Administrative Science Quarterly* 34: 231–51.

Laumann, Edward O, 1973. *Bonds of Pluralism: The Forms and Substance of Urban Social Networks.* New York: Wiley.

Laumann, Edward O., Joseph Galaskiewicz, and Peter V. Marsden, 1978. "Community structure as interorganizational linkages." *Annual Review of Sociology,* 4: 455–84.

Laumann, Edward O., John P. Heinz, Robert L. Nelson, and Robert H. Salisbury, 1985. "Washington lawyers and others: the structure of Washington representation." *Stanford Law Review,* 37: 465–502.

Laumann, Edward O., and David Knoke, 1986. "Social network theory." In Siegwart Lindenberg, James S. Coleman, and Stefan Nowak (eds.), *Approaches to Social Theory.* New York: Russell Sage Foundation, pp. 83–104.

Laumann, Edward O., and David Knoke, 1987. *The Organizational State: A Perspective on National Energy and Health Domains.* Madison, Wis.: University of Wisconsin Press.

Laumann, Edward O., David Knoke, and Yong-Hak Kim, 1985. "An organizational approach to state policymaking: a comparative study of energy and health domains." *American Sociological Review,* 50: 1–19.

Laumann, Edward O., and David Knoke with Yong-Hak Kim, 1987. "Event outcomes." In Edward O. Laumann and David Knoke, *The Organizational State.* Madison, Wis.: University of Wisconsin Press, pp. 343–73.

Laumann, Edward O., and Peter V. Marsden, 1979. "The analysis of oppositional structures in political elites: identifying collective actors." *American Sociological Review,* 44: 713–32.

Laumann, Edward O., Peter V. Marsden, and Joseph Galaskiewicz, 1977. "Community influence structures: replication and extension of a network approach." *American Journal of Sociology,* 31: 169–78.

Laumann, Edward O., Peter V. Marsden, and David Prensky, 1983. "The boundary specification problem in network analysis." In Ronald S. Burt and Michael J. Minor (eds.), *Applied Network Analysis: A Methodological Introduction.* Beverly Hills, Calif.: Sage, pp. 18–34.

Laumann, Edward O., and Franz Urban Pappi, 1973. "New directions in the study of community elites." *American Sociological Review*, 38: 212–30.

Laumann, Edward O., and Franz Urban Pappi, 1976. *Networks of Collective Action: A Perspective on Community Influence Systems.* New York: Academic Press.

Lawrence, Paul R., and Jay W. Lorsch, 1967. *Organization and Environment: Managing Differentiation and Integration.* Boston: Harvard University Graduate School of Business Administration.

Laws, Judith Long, 1975. "The psychology of tokenism: an analysis." *Sex Roles*, 1: 51–67.

Lazarsfeld, Paul F., Bernard Berelson, and Hazel Gaudet, 1948. *The People's Choice: How the Voter Makes Up His Mind in Presidential Campaigns.* New York: Columbia University Press.

Lazerson, Mark, 1988. "Organizational growth of small firms: an outcome of markets and hierarchies?" *American Sociological Review*, 53: 330–42.

LeBon, Gustave, 1896. *The Crowd.* London: Ernest Benn.

Ledyard, John, 1984. "The pure theory of two-candidate elections." *Public Choice*, 44: 1–60.

Lee, Sang M., Gerald L. Moeller, and Lester A. Digman, 1982. *Network Analysis for Management Decisions: A Stochastic Approach.* Boston: Kulwer-Nijhoff.

Lehmbruch, Gerhard, 1984. "Concertation and the structure of corporatist networks." In John H. Goldthorpe (ed.), *Order and Conflict in Contemporary Capitalism.* Oxford: Clarendon Press, pp. 60–80.

Leibenstein, Harvey, 1978. *General X-Efficiency Theory and Economic Development.* New York: Oxford University Press.

Leichter, Harold M., 1984. "National productivity: a comparative perspective." In Mark Holzer and Stuart S. Nagel (eds.), *Productivity and Public Policy.* Beverly Hills, Calif.: Sage, pp. 45–68.

Leinhardt, Samuel (ed.), 1977. *Social Networks: A Development Paradigm.* New York: Academic.

Leiserson, Michael, 1965. "Coalition in politics." Unpublished doctoral dissertation. New Haven: Yale University.

Lenski, Gerhard, 1954. "Status crystallization: a non-vertical dimension of social status." *American Sociological Review*, 19: 405–413.

Lerner, Barbara, 1982. "American education: how are we doing?" *Public Interest*, 69: 59–82.

Lévi-Strauss, Claude, 1952. "Social structure." In A. L. Kroeber (ed.), *Anthropology Today.* Chicago: University of Chicago Press, pp. 321–90.

Levy, Frank, 1987. *Dollars and Dreams: The Changing American Income Distribution.* New York: Basic Books.

Lewis, Gregory B., 1986. "Race, sex and supervisory authority in federal white collar employment." *Public Administration Review*, 46: 25–30.

Liebert, Roland, 1974. "Municipal functions, structure and expenditures: a reanalysis of recent research." *Social Science Quarterly*, 54: 765–83.

Lin, Nan, Walter M. Ensel, and John C. Vaughn, 1981. "Social resources and strength of ties: structural factors in occupational status attainment." *Amer-*

ican Sociological Review, 46: 393–405.

Lincoln, James R., 1982. "Intra- (and inter-) organizational networks." *Research in the Sociology of Organizations,* 1: 1–38.

Lincoln, James R., Mitsuyo Hanada, and Kerry McBride, 1986. "Organizational structures in Japanese and U.S. manufacturing." *Administrative Science Quarterly,* 31: 338–64.

Lincoln, James R., and Kerry McBride, 1987. "Japanese industrial organization in comparative perspective." *Annual Review of Sociology,* 13: 289–312.

Lincoln, James R., and Jon Miller, 1979. "Work and friendship ties in organizations: a comparative analysis of relational networks." *Administrative Science Quarterly,* 4: 181–99.

Lineberry, Robert L., and Edmund P. Fowler, 1967. "Reformism and public policies in American cities." *American Political Science Review,* 61: 701–16.

Linton, Ralph, 1936. *The Study of Man.* New York: Appleton-Century.

Lipset, Seymour Martin, 1964. *The First New Nation: The United States in Historical and Comparative Perspective.* London: Heinemann.

Lipset, Seymour Martin, Martin A. Trow, and James S. Coleman, 1956. *Union Democracy.* Glencoe: Free Press.

Lo, Clarence Y. H., 1982. "Countermovements and conservative movements in the contemporary U.S." *Annual Review of Sociology,* 8: 107–34.

Lofland, John, 1985. *Protest: Studies of Collective Behavior and Social Movements.* New Brunswick, N.J.: Transaction.

Loomis, Burdett, 1988. *The New American Politician: Ambition, Entrepreneurship, and the Changing Face of Political Life.* New York: Basic Books.

Looney, Robert E., 1988. *Third World Military Expenditures and Arms Production.* London: Macmillan.

Lorrain, Francois, and Harrison C. White, 1971. "Structural equivalence of individuals in social networks." *Journal of Mathematical Sociology,* 1: 49–80.

Lubben, Richard T., 1988. *Just-in-Time Manufacturing: An Aggressive Manufacturing Strategy.* New York: McGraw-Hill.

Luhmann, Niklas, 1979. *Trust and Power.* Chichester, England: Wiley.

Luker, Kristin, 1984. *Abortion and the Politics of Motherhood.* Berkeley: University of California Press.

Lukes, Steven, 1974. *Power: A Radical View.* London: Macmillan.

Lukes, Steven, 1977. *Essays in Social Theory.* New York: Columbia University Press.

Lyon, Larry, and Charles M. Bonjean, 1981. "Community power and policy outputs." *Urban Affairs Quarterly,* 17: 3–22.

McAdam, Doug, 1982. *Political Process and the Development of Black Insurgency 1930–1970.* Chicago: University of Chicago Press.

McAdam, Doug, 1986. "Recruitment to high-risk activism: the case of Freedom Summer." *American Journal of Sociology,* 92: 64–90.

McAdam, Doug, 1987. *The Idealists Revisited: The Personal and Societal Consequences of Mississippi Freedom Summer.* New York: Oxford University Press.

McAdam, Doug, and Roberto M. Fernandez, 1990. "Microstructural bases of recruitment to social movements." *Research in Social Movements, Conflict, and Change,* 12: (forthcoming).

McCall, Morgan, 1979. "Power, authority and influence." In Steven Kerr (ed.), *Organizational Behavior*. Columbus, Ohio: Grid, pp. 185–206.

McCarthy, John D., and Mayer N. Zald, 1973. *The Trend of Social Movements in America: Professionalization and Resource Mobilization*. Morristown, N.J.: General Learning Press.

McCarthy, John D., and Mayer N. Zald, 1977. "Resource mobilization and social movements: a partial theory." *American Journal of Sociology*, 82: 1212–41.

McElroy, James C., and Charles B. Shrader, 1986. "Attribution theories of leadership and network analysis." *Journal of Management*, 12: 351–62.

McFarland, Andrew S., 1983. "Public interest lobbies versus minority faction." In Allan J. Cigler and Burdett A. Loomis (eds.), *Interest Group Politics*. Washington, D.C.: CQ Press, pp. 324–53.

McKersie, Robert B., and Janice A. Klein, 1985. "Productivity: the industrial relations connection." In William J. Baumol and Kenneth McLennan (eds.), *Productivity, Growth, and U.S. Competitiveness*. New York: Oxford University Press, pp. 119–59.

McNeil, Kenneth, 1978. "Understanding organizational power: building on the Weberian legacy." *Administrative Science Quarterly*, 23: 65–90.

McPhail, Clark, and David Miller, 1973. "The assembling process: a theoretical and empirical examination." *American Sociological Review*, 38: 721–35.

McPhail, Clark, and Ronald T. Wohlstein, 1986. "Collective locomotion as collective behavior." *American Sociological Review*, 51: 447–63.

McPherson, J. Miller, 1982. "Hypernetwork sampling: duality and differentiation among voluntary organizations." *Social Networks*, 3: 225–50.

McPherson, J. Miller, 1983. "An ecology of affiliation." *American Sociological Review*, 48: 519–32.

McPherson, J. Miller, and Lynn Smith-Lovin, 1987. "Homophily in voluntary associations: status distance and the composition of face to face groups." *American Sociological Review*, 52: 370–79.

McQuail, Denis, and Karen Siune, 1986. *New Media Politics: Comparative Perspectives in Western Europe*. London: Sage.

Maitland, Ian H., and Dong Soo Park, 1985. "Campaign contribution strategies of corporate political action committees." Minneapolis: Strategic Management Research Center: (mimeographed).

Malbin, Michael J. (ed.), 1984. *Parties, Interest Groups and Campaign Finance Laws*. Washington: American Enterprise Institute.

Manigart, Philippe, 1986. "The Belgian defense policy domain in the 1980s." *Armed Forces and Society*, 13: 39–56.

Mansbridge, Jane J., 1980. *Beyond Adversary Democracy*. Chicago: University of Chicago Press.

Mansbridge, Jane J., 1986. *Why We Lost the ERA*. Chicago: University of Chicago Press.

March, James G., and Johan P. Olsen, 1976. *Ambiguity and Choice in Organizations*. Bergen, Norway: Universitetsforlaget.

March, James G., and Herbert A. Simon, 1958. *Organizations*. New York: Wiley.

Marchand, Donald A., 1980. *The Politics of Privacy, Computers, and Criminal Justice Records: Controlling the Social Costs of Technological Change*. Arlington, Va.: Information Resources Press.

Mariolis, Peter, 1975. "Interlocking directorates and control of corporations: the theory of bank control." *Social Science Quarterly,* 56: 425–39.

Markovsky, Barry, David Willer, and Travis Patton, 1988. "Power relations in exchange networks." *American Sociological Review,* 53: 220–36.

Markusen, Ann, Peter Hall, and Amy Glasmeier, 1986. *High Tech America: The What, How, Where, and Why of the Sunrise Industries.* Boston: Allen and Unwin.

Marsden, Peter V., 1981. "Introducing influence processes into a system of collective decisions." *American Journal of Sociology,* 86: 1203–35.

Marsden, Peter V., 1982. "Brokerage behavior in restricted exchange networks." In Peter V. Marsden and Nan Lin (eds.), *Social Structure and Network Analysis.* Beverly Hills, Calif.: Sage, pp. 219–34.

Marsden, Peter V., 1983. "Restricted access in networks and models of power." *American Journal of Sociology,* 88: 686–717.

Marsden, Peter V., 1987. "Core discussion networks of Americans." *American Sociological Review,* 52: 122–31.

Marsden, Peter V., and Jeanne S. Hurlbert, 1988. "Social resources and mobility outcomes: a replication and extension." *Social Forces,* 66: 1038–59.

Marsden, Peter V., and Edward O. Laumann, 1977. "Collective action in a community elite: exchange, influence processes, and issue resolution." In Roland J. Liebert and Alan Imershein (eds.), *Power, Paradigms, and Community Research.* London: Sage, pp. 199–250.

Marshall, Ray, 1986. "Working smarter." In David R. Obey and Paul Sarbanes (eds.), *The Changing American Economy.* New York: Basil Blackwell, pp. 180–202.

Martin, Patricia Yancey, 1985. "Group sex compositions in work organizations: a structural-normative model." *Research in the Sociology of Organizations,* 4: 311–49.

Marwell, Gerald, and Ruth E. Ames, 1979. "Experiments on the provision of public goods. I. Resources, interest, group size, and the free rider problem." *American Journal of Sociology,* 84: 1335–60.

Marwell, Gerald, Pamela Oliver, and Ralph Prahl, 1988. "Social networks and collective action: a theory of the critical mass. III." *American Journal of Sociology,* 94: 502–34.

Marx, Karl, 1852 [1978]. "The eighteenth Brumaire of Louis Bonaparte." In Robert C. Tucker (ed.), *The Marx-Engels Reader, Second Edition.* New York: Norton, pp. 594–617.

Marx, Karl, 1859 [1978]. "Preface to a contribution to the critique of political economy." In Robert C. Tucker (ed.), *The Marx-Engels Reader, Second Edition.* New York: Norton, pp. 3–6.

Masters, Marick F., and Gerald D. Keim, 1985. "Determinants of PAC participation among large corporations." *Journal of Politics,* 47: 1158–1173.

Mayhew, David R., 1974. *Congress: The Electoral Connection.* New Haven: Yale University Press.

Mechanic, David, 1962. "Sources of power of lower participants in complex organizations." *Administrative Science Quarterly,* 7: 349–62.

Menzies, Ken, 1977. *Talcott Parsons and the Social Image of Man.* London:

Routledge.

Merton, Robert, 1957. "The role-set: problems in sociological theory." *British Journal of Sociology*, 8: 106–120.

Meyer, John, and Bryan Rowan, 1977. "Institutional organizations: formal structure as myth and ceremony." *American Journal of Sociology*, 83: 340–63.

Michels, Robert, 1949. *Political Parties: A Sociological Study of the Oligarchical Tendencies of Modern Democracy*. Glencoe, Ill.: Free Press.

Michener, H. Andrew, Eugene D. Cohen, and Aage B. Sorenson, 1977. "Social exchange: predicting transactional outcomes in five-event, four-person systems." *American Sociological Review*, 42: 522–35.

Milani, Moshen M., 1988. *The Making of Iran's Islamic Revolution: From Monarchy to Islamic Republic*. Boulder, Colo.: Westview Press.

Miliband, Ralph, 1969. *The State in Capitalist Society*. New York: Basic Books.

Miller, Delbert C., 1970. *International Community Power Structures: Comparative Studies of Four World Cities*. Bloomington, Ind.: Indiana University Press.

Miller, Delbert C., 1975. *Leadership and Power in the Bos-Wash Megalopolis: Environment, Ecology, and Urban Organization*. New York: Wiley.

Miller, Jon, James R. Lincoln, and Jon Olson, 1981. "Rationality and equity in professional networks: Gender and race as factors in the stratification of interorganizational systems." *American Journal of Sociology*, 87: 308–35.

Miller, Nicholas, 1977. "Logrolling, vote trading, and the paradox of voting: a game theoretical overview." *Public Choice*, 30: 51–73.

Mills, C. Wright, 1956. *The Power Elite*. New York: Oxford University Press.

Milner, Murray, Jr., 1980. *Unequal Care: A Case Study of Interorganizational Relations in Health Care*. New York: Columbia University Press.

Mintz, Beth, 1975. "The president's cabinet, 1897–1972: a contribution to the power structure debate." *Insurgent Sociologist*, 5: 131–48.

Mintz, Beth, and Michael Schwartz, 1981. "Interlocking directorates and interest group formation." *American Sociological Review*, 46: 851–69.

Mintz, Beth, and Michael Schwartz, 1985. *The Power Structure of American Business*. Chicago: University of Chicago Press.

Mintzberg, Henry, 1979. *The Structuring of Organizations: A Synthesis of Research*. Englewood Cliffs, N.J.: Prentice-Hall.

Mintzberg, Henry, 1983. *Power In and Around Organizations*. Englewood Cliffs, N.J.: Prentice-Hall.

Mitchell, J. Clyde, 1969. *Social Networks in Urban Situations: Analysis of Personal Relationships in Central African Towns*. Manchester, England: Institute for Social Research of University of Zambia.

Mitchell, Robert C., 1979. "National environmental lobbies and the apparent illogic of collective action." In Clifford S. Russell (ed.), *Collective Decision-Making: Applications from Public Choice Theory*. Baltimore: Johns Hopkins University Press, pp. 187–221.

Mizruchi, Mark S., 1982. *The American Corporate Network 1904–1974*. Beverly Hills, Calif.: Sage.

Mizruchi, Mark S., 1983. "Who controls whom? An examination of the relation between management and boards of directors in large American corporations." *Academy of Management Review*, 8: 426–35.

Mizruchi, Mark S., 1984. "An interorganizational theory of class cohesion: incorporating resource dependence concepts into a social class model of inter-corporate relations." *Power and Elites,* 1: 23–36.

Mizruchi, Mark S., 1987. "Who does business stick together? An interorganizational theory of class cohesion." In G. William Domhoff and Thomas R. Dye (eds.), *Power Elites and Organizations.* Beverly Hills, Calif.: Sage, pp. 204–18.

Mizruchi, Mark S., and Thomas Koenig, 1986. "Economic sources of corporate political consensus: an examination of interindustry relations." *American Sociological Review,* 51: 482–91.

Mizruchi, Mark S., and Thomas Koenig, 1988. "Economic concentration and corporate political behavior: a cross-industry comparison." *Social Science Research,* 17: 287–305.

Mizruchi, Mark S., and Linda Brewster Stearns, 1988. "A longitudinal study of the formation of interlocking directorates." *Administrative Science Quarterly,* 33: 194–209.

Moe, Terry M., 1979. "On the scientific status of rational models." *American Journal of Political Science,* 23: 214–43.

Moe, Terry M., 1980. *The Organization of Interests: Incentives and the Internal Dynamics of Political Interest Groups.* Chicago: University of Chicago Press.

Moe, Terry, 1984. "The New Economics of Organization." *American Journal of Political Science,* 739–77.

Molm, Linda D., 1985. "Gender and power use: an experimental analysis of behavior and perceptions." *Social Psychology Quarterly,* 48: 285–300.

Molm, Linda D., 1986. "Gender, power and legitimation: a test of three theories." *American Journal of Sociology,* 91: 1356–86.

Molm, Linda D., 1989. "Punishment power: a balancing process in power-dependence relations." *American Journal of Sociology,* 94: 1392–418.

Moore, Barrington, Jr., 1966. *Social Origins of Dictatorship and Democracy: Lord and Peasant in the Making of the Modern World.* Boston: Beacon Press.

Moore, Gwen, 1979. "The structure of a national elite network." *American Sociological Review,* 44: 673–92.

Morgan, Gareth, 1988. *Riding the Waves of Change: Developing Managerial Competencies for a Turbulent World.* San Francisco: Jossey-Bass.

Morris, Aldon, 1981. "Black southern student sit-in movement." *American Sociological Review,* 46: 744–67.

Morris, Aldon, 1984. *The Origins of the Civil Rights Movement: Black Communities Organizing for Change.* New York: Free Press.

Morrissey, Joseph P., Mark Tausig, and Michael L. Lindsey, 1985. *Network Analysis Methods for Mental Health Service System Research: A Comparison of Two Community Support Systems.* Washington, D.C.: Government Printing Office.

Mosca, Gaetano, 1939. *The Ruling Class.* New York: McGraw-Hill.

Most, Benjamin, and Harvey Starr, 1980. "Diffusion-reinforcement, geopolitics, and the spread of war." *American Political Science Review,* 74: 932–46.

Mueller, Denis C., 1979. *Public Choice.* Cambridge: Cambridge University Press.

Muller, Edward N., and Karl-Dieter Opp, 1986. "Rational choice and rebellious collective action." *American Political Science Review,* 80: 471–87.

Mulford, Charles L., 1984. *Understanding Interorganizational Relations.* New York: Human Sciences Press.

Muravchik, Joshua, 1989. "Glasnostrums." *The New Republic,* January 30: 16–18.

Nadel, S. F., 1957. *The Theory of Social Structure.* Glencoe, Il.: Free Press.

Nelson, Reed E., 1986. "Social networks and organizational interventions: insights from an area-wide labor-management committee." *Journal of Applied Behavioral Science,* 22: 65–76.

Nelson, Robert L., John P. Heinz, Edward O. Laumann, and Robert H. Salisbury, 1987. "Private representation in Washington: surveying the structure of influence." *American Bar Foundation Research Journal:* 141–200.

Nemeth, Roger, and David Smith, 1985. "International trade and world-system structure: a multiple network analysis." *Review,* 4: 517–60.

Neustadtl, Alan, and Dan Clawson, 1988. "Corporate political groupings: does ideology unify business political behavior?" *American Sociological Review,* 53: 172–90.

Nie, Norman, and James Rabjohn, 1979. "Revisiting mass belief systems revisited: or, doing research is like watching a tennis match." *American Journal of Political Science,* 23: 139–75.

Nisbet, Robert, 1969. *Social Change and History.* New York: Oxford University Press.

Niskanen, William, 1975. "Bureaucrats and politicians." *Journal of Law and Economics,* 18: 617–43.

Nolan, Patrick D., 1983. "Status in the world system, income inequality, and economic growth." *American Journal of Sociology,* 89: 410–19.

Nordlinger, Eric, 1981. *On the Autonomy of the Democratic State.* Cambridge: Harvard University Press.

Norsworthy, J. R., and David H. Malmquist, 1985. "Recent productivity growth in Japanese and U.S. manufacturing." In William J. Baumol and Kenneth McLennan (eds.), *Productivity, Growth, and U.S. Competitiveness.* New York: Oxford University Press, pp. 58–69.

Obserschall, Anthony, 1973. *Social Conflict and Social Movements.* Englewood Cliffs, N.J.: Prentice-Hall.

Offerman, Lynn R., and Pamela E. Schrier, 1985. "Social influence strategies: the impact of sex, role and attitude toward power." *Personality and Social Psychology Bulletin,* 11: 286–300.

Office of Technology Assessment, 1984. *Computerized Manufacturing Automation: Employment, Education, and the Workplace.* Washington, D.C.: U.S. Government Printing Office.

Office of Technology Assessment, 1985. *Automation of America's Offices.* Washington, D.C.: U.S. Government Printing Office.

Oliver, Pamela, 1980. "Rewards and punishments as selective incentives for collective action: theoretical investigations." *American Journal of Sociology,* 85: 1356–75.

Oliver, Pamela, 1984. " 'If You don't do it, nobody else will': active and token contributors to local collective action." *American Sociological Review,* 49: 601–10.

Oliver, Pamela E., and Gerald Marwell, 1988. "The paradox of group size in collective action: a theory of the critical mass. II." *American Sociological Review,* 53: 1–8.

Oliver, Pamela E., Gerald Marwell, and Ruy Teixeira, 1985. "A theory of the critical mass. I. Interdependence, group heterogeneity, and the production of collective action." *American Journal of Sociology,* 91: 522–56.

Olmer, Lionel, 1986. "The competitive challenge." In David R. Obey and Paul Sarbanes (eds.), *The Changing American Economy.* New York: Basil Blackwell, pp. 66–72.

Olson, Mancur, Jr., 1965. *The Logic of Collective Action.* Cambridge: Harvard University Press.

Olson, Mancur, 1982. *The Rise and Decline of Nations: Economic Growth, Stagflation, and Social Rigidities.* New Haven: Yale University Press.

Opp, Karl-Dieter, 1986. "Soft incentives and collective action." *British Journal of Political Science,* 16: 87–122.

Opp, Karl-Dieter, 1988a. "Grievances and participation in social movements." *American Sociological Review,* 53: 853–64.

Opp, Karl-Dieter, 1988b. "Community integration and incentives for political protest." In Bert Klandermans, Hanspeter Kriesi, and Sidney Tarrow (eds.), *From Structure to Action: Comparing Social Movement Research across Cultures.* Greenwich, Conn.: JAI Press.

Ordeshook, Peter C., 1986. *Game Theory and Political Theory: An Introduction.* New York: Cambridge University Press.

Organski, A. F. K., 1965. *The Stages of Political Development.* New York: Knopf.

Ouchi, William G., 1981. *Theory X.* Reading, Mass.: Addison-Wesley.

Padgett, John F., 1980. "Managing garbage can hierarchies." *Administrative Science Quarterly,* 25: 583–604.

Paige, Jeffrey M., 1971. "Political orientation and riot participation." *American Sociological Review,* 36: 810–20.

Paige, Jeffrey, M., 1975. *Agrarian Revolution: Social Movements and Export Agriculture in the Underdeveloped World.* New York: Free Press.

Palfrey, Thomas R., and Howard Rosenthal, 1985. "Voter participation and strategic uncertainty." *American Political Science Review,* 79: 62–78.

Palmer, Donald, 1983. "Broken ties: interlocking directorates and intercorporate coordination." *Administrative Science Quarterly,* 28: 40–55.

Palmer, Donald, Roger Friedland, and Jitendra V. Singh, 1986. "The ties that bind: organizational and class bases of stability in a corporate interlock network." *American Sociological Review,* 51: 781–96.

Panitch, Leon, 1977. "The development of corporatism in liberal democracies." *Comparative Political Studies,* 10: 61–90.

Pappi, Franz Urban, 1984. "Boundary specification and structural models of elite systems: social circles revisited." *Social Networks,* 6: 79–95.

Pappi, Franz Urban (ed.), 1987. *Methoden der Netzwerkanalyse.* Munich, West Germany: R. Oldenbourg Verlag.

Pappi, Fraz Urban, and Peter Kappelhoff, 1984. "Abhaengigkeit, Tausch und kollektive Entsheidung in einer Gemeindeelite." *Zeitschrift fuer Soziologie,* 13: 87–177.

Pappi, Franz Urban, and Christian Melbeck, 1984. "Das Macht-potential von Organisationen in der Gemeindepolitik." *Kölner Zeitschrift für Soziologie und Sozialpsychologie,* 36: 557–84.

Pappi, Franz Urban, and Gunter Wolf, 1985. "The reliability and validity of statements about best friends in survey network data." New York: Columbia

University Center for the Social Sciences, mimeo.

Pareto, Vilfredo, 1968. *The Rise and Fall of the Elites.* Totowa, N.J.: Bedminster.

Parsons, Talcott, 1937. *The Structure of Social Action.* New York: Free Press.

Parsons, Talcott, 1963. "On the concept of influence." *Public Opinion Quarterly,* 27: 37–62.

Parsons, Talcott, 1966. *Societies: Evolutionary and Comparative Perspectives.* Englewood Cliffs, N.J.: Prentice-Hall.

Parsons, Talcott, 1969. *Politics and Social Structure.* New York: Free Press.

Parsons, Talcott, 1970. "Some problems of general theory in sociology." In John C. McKinney and Edward A. Tiryakian (eds.), *Theoretical Sociology: Perspectives and Developments.* New York: Appleton-Century-Crofts.

Parsons, Talcott, 1971. *The System of Modern Societies.* Englewood Cliffs, N.J.: Prentice-Hall.

Parsons, Talcott, 1974. "Social structure and the symbolic media of interchange." In Peter M. Blau (ed.), *Approaches to the Study of Social Structure.* New York: Free Press, pp. 94–120.

Parsons, Talcott, and Edward A. Shils, 1951. "Values, motives, and systems of action." In Talcott Parsons and Edward A. Shils, *Toward a General Theory of Action.* Cambridge: Harvard University Press, 47–275.

Pascale, Richard T., and Anthony G. Athos, 1981. *The Art of Japanese Management: Applications for American Executives.* New York: Simon and Schuster.

Pateman, Carole, 1970. *Participation and Democratic Theory.* Cambridge: Cambridge University Press.

Pennings, Johannes, and Arend Buitendam (eds.), 1987. *New Technology as Organizational Innovation.* Cambridge, Mass.: Ballinger.

Pennings, Johannes M., and Paul S. Goodman, 1977. "Toward a workable framework." In Paul S. Goodman and Johannes M. Pennings (eds.), *New Perspectives on Organizational Effectiveness.* San Francisco: Jossey-Bass.

Perrucci, Robert, and Marc Pilisuk, 1970. "Leaders and ruling elites: the interorganizational bases of community power." *American Sociological Review,* 35: 1040–57.

Peters, Charles, 1980. *How Washington Really Works. Revised Edition.* Reading, Mass.: Addison-Wesley.

Pettigrew, Andrew M., 1973. *The Politics of Organizational Decision Making.* London: Tavistock.

Pettigrew, Andrew M., 1975. "Towards a political theory of organizational intervention." *Human Relations,* 28: 191–208.

Pfeffer, Jeffrey, 1981. *Power in Organizations.* Marshfield, Mass.: Pitman.

Pfeffer, Jeffrey, 1982. *Organizations and Organization Theory.* Cambridge, Mass.: Ballinger.

Pfeffer, Jeffrey, 1987. "A resource dependence perspective on intercorporate relations." In Barry Wellman and S. D. Berkowitz (eds.), *Intercorporate Relations: The Structural Analysis of Business.* Cambridge: Cambridge University Press, pp. 25–55.

Pfeffer, Jeffrey, and A. Leong, 1977. "Resource allocations in United Funds: examination of power and dependence." *Social Forces,* 55: 775–90.

Pfeffer, Jeffrey, and Gerald Salancik, 1978. *The External Control of Organizations.*

New York: Harper & Row.

Piaget, Jean, 1971. *Structuralism.* London: Routledge and Kegan Paul.

Piore, Michael, 1986. "Beyond social anarchy." In David R. Obey and Paul Sarbanes (eds.), *The Changing American Economy.* New York: Basil Blackwell, pp. 156–66.

Piven, Frances, and Richard Cloward, 1977. *Poor People's Movements.* New York: Pantheon.

Polsby, Nelson W., 1980. *Community Power and Political Theory: A Further Look at Problems of Evidence and Inference.* New Haven: Yale University Press.

Popkin, Samuel, 1979. *The Rational Peasant: The Political Economy of Rural Society in Viet Nam.* Berkeley: University of California Press.

Porter, Michael E., and Victor E. Millar, 1985. "How information gives you competitive advantage." *Harvard Business Review* (July–August): 149–160.

Poulantzas, Nicos, 1975. *Classes in Contemporary Capitalism.* London: New Left Books.

Poulantzas, Nicos, 1978. *State, Power, Socialism.* London: New Left Books.

Powell, G. Bingham, 1986. "American voter turnout in comparative perspective." *American Political Science Review,* 80: 17–43.

Powell, Walter W., 1990. "Neither market nor hierarchy: network forms of organization." *Research in Organizational Behavior,* 12: (forthcoming).

Presthus, Robert, 1964. *Men at the Top: A Study in Community Power.* New York: Oxford University Press.

Prewitt, Kenneth, and W. McAllister, 1976. "Changes in the American executive elite 1930–1970." In Heinz Eulau and Moshe Czudnowski (eds.), *Elite Recruitment in Democratic Politics.* New York: Halstead Press, pp. 105–32.

Pridham, Geoffrey (ed.), 1986. *Coalition Behavior in Theory and Practice.* Cambridge: Cambridge University Press.

Provan, Keith G., Janice M. Beyer, and Carlos Krytbosch, 1980. "Environmental linkages and power in resource-dependence relations between organizations." *Administrative Science Quarterly,* 25: 200–25.

Putnam, Robert D., 1976. *The Comparative Study of Political Elites.* Englewood Cliffs, N.J.: Prentice-Hall.

Pye, Lucian W., 1985. *Asian Power and Politics: The Cultural Dynamics of Authority.* Cambridge: Harvard University Press.

Quadagno, Jill, 1987. "Theories of the welfare state." *Annual Review of Sociology,* 13: 109–28.

Rabinowitch, Alexander, 1976. *The Bolsheviks Come to Power: The Revolution of 1917 in Petrograd.* New York: Norton.

Raelin, Joseph A., 1980. "A mandated basis of interorganizational relations: the legal-political network." *Human Relations,* 33: 57–68.

Rakove, Milton, 1976. *Don't Make No Waves–Don't Back No Losers.* Bloomington, Ind.: Indiana University Press.

Ratcliff, Richard E., 1980a. "Capitalist class impact on lending behavior of banks." *American Sociological Review,* 45: 553–70.

Ratcliff, Richard E., 1980b. "Declining cities and capitalist class structure." In G. William Domhoff (ed.), *Power Structure Research.* Beverly Hills, Calif.: Sage, pp. 115–38.

Rees, John, 1986. *Technology, Regions, and Policy.* Totowa, N.J.: Rowman and Littlefield.

Reingen, Peter, 1988. "Individual influence within an organziational buying context: a structural and network perspective." San Diego, Calif. Paper presented to Sunbelt Social Network Conference.

RePass, David, 1971. "Issue salience and party choice." *American Political Science Review,* 65: 389–400.

Ricci, David, 1971. *Community Power and Democratic Theory.* New York: Random House.

Ricci, David, 1980. "Receiving ideas in political analysis: the case of community power studies, 1950–1970." *Western Political Quarterly,* 33: 451–75.

Richardson, Bradley M., 1974. *The Political Culture of Japan.* Berkeley: University of California Press.

Richardson, R. Jack, 1987. "Directorate interlocks and corporate profitability." *Administrative Science Quarterly,* 32: 367–86.

Riesman, David, 1961. *The Lonely Crowd.* New Haven: Yale University Press.

Riker, William H., 1962. *The Theory of Political Coalitions.* New Haven: Yale University Press.

Riker, William H., 1982. *Liberalism Against Populism: A Confrontation Between the Theory of Democracy and the Theory of Social Choice.* San Francisco: Freeman.

Riker, William H., and Peter C. Ordeshook, 1968. "A theory of the calculus of voting." *American Political Science Review,* 63: 25–43.

Riker, William H., and Peter C. Ordeshook, 1973. *An Introduction to Positive Political Theory.* Englewood Cliffs, N.J.: Prentice-Hall.

Ripley, Randall B., and Grace A. Franklin, 1978. *Congress, the Bureaucracy, and Public Policy.* Homewood, Il.: Dorsey Press.

Roethlisberger, Fritz J., and William J. Dickson, 1939. *Management and the Worker.* Cambridge: Harvard University Press.

Rogers, David L., and David A. Whetten, 1982. *Interorganizational Coordination: Theory, Research, and Implementation.* Ames, Iowa: Iowa State University Press.

Rogers, Everett M., and Rehka Agarwala-Rogers, 1976. *Communication in Organizations.* New York: Free Press.

Rogers, Everett M., and Dilip K. Bhowmik, 1971. "Homophily-heterophily: relational concepts for communication research." *Public Opinion Quarterly,* 34: 523–28.

Rogers, Everett M., and David L. Kincaid, 1981. *Communication Networks: Toward a New Paradigm for Research.* New York: Free Press.

Rogers, Everett M., and Frank F. Shoemaker, 1971. *Communication of Innovations.* New York: Free Press.

Rose, Arnold, 1967. *The Power Structure: Political Process in American Society.* New York: Oxford University Press.

Rosen, Ellen Doree, 1984. "Productivity: concepts and measurement." In Mark Holzer and Stuart S. Nagel (eds.), *Productivity and Public Policy.* Beverly Hills, Calif.: Sage, pp. 19–43.

Rosenberg, Shawn W., 1985. "Sociology, psychology, and the study of political behavior: the case of research on political socialization." *Journal of Politics,* 47: 715–31.

Rosenthal, Donald B., and Robert L. Crain, 1966. "Structure and values in local political systems; the case of fluoridation." *Journal of Politics,* 28: 169–96.

Rosenthal, Naomi, Meryl Fingrutal, Michele Ethier, Roberta Karant, and David McDonald, 1985. "Social movements and network analysis: a case study of nineteenth-century women's reform in New York state." *American Journal of Sociology,* 90: 1022–54.

Rossi, Peter H., 1960. "Power and community structure." *Midwest Journal of Political Science,* 4: 390–401.

Rossi, Peter H., and Robert L. Crain, 1968. "The NORC permanent community sample." *Public Opinion Quarterly,* 32: 261–72.

Rostow, Walt W., 1960. *The Stages of Economic Growth: A Non-Communist Manifesto.* Cambridge: Cambridge University Press.

Rubinson, Richard, 1976. "The world-economy and the distribution of income within states: a cross-national study." *American Sociological Review,* 41: 638–59.

Rummel, Rudolph J., 1963. "Dimensions of conflict within and between nations." *General Systems Yearbook,* 8: 1–50.

Rusk, Jerrold G., 1982. "The Michigan election studies: a critical evaluation." *Micropolitics,* 2: 87–110.

Russell, Bertrand, 1938. *Power: A New Social Analysis.* London: George Allyn and Unwin.

Russell, Diana E. H., 1974. *Rebellion, Revolution, and Armed Force.* New York: Academic Press.

Ryan, Mary P., 1979. "The power of women's networks: a case study of female moral reform in antebellum America." *Feminist Studies,* 5: 66–85.

Sabato, Larry J., 1984. *PAC Power: Inside the World of Political Action Committees.* New York: Norton.

Sabato, Larry, 1987. "PACs, parties, and presidents." In L. Patric Devlin (ed.), *Political Persuasion in Presidential Campaigns.* New Brunswick, N.J.: Transaction Books, pp. 197–204.

Sabel, Charles F., 1982. *Work and Politics: The Division of Labor in Industry.* New York: Cambridge University Press.

Salancik, Gerald R., and Jeffrey Pfeffer, 1977. "Who gets power and how they hold on to it: a strategic-contingency model of power." *Organizational Dynamics,* 6: 3–21.

Salancik, Gerald R., and Jeffrey Pfeffer, 1980. "Effects of ownership and performance on executive tenure in U.S. corporations." *Academy of Management Review,* 27: 199–226.

Salisbury, Robert H., 1984. "Interest representation: the dominance of institutions." *American Political Science Review,* 78: 64–76.

Salisbury, Robert H., John P. Heinz, Edward O. Laumann, and Robert L. Nelson, 1987. "Who works with whom? interest group alliances and opposition." *American Political Science Review,* 81: 1217–34.

Salzman, Harold, and G. William Domhoff, 1980. "The corporate community and government: do they interlock?" In G. William Domhoff (ed.), *Power Structure Research.* Beverly Hills, Calif.: Sage, pp. 227–254.

Samuelson, Paul A., 1954. "The pure theory of public expenditure." *Review of Economics and Statistics,* 36: 387–90.

Sartori, Giovanni, 1987. *The Theory of Democracy Revisited.* Chatham, N.J.: Chatham House.

Saussure, Ferdinand de, 1966. *Course in General Linguistics.* New York: McGraw-Hill.

Sayles, Leonard R., 1976. "Matrix organization: the structure with a future." *Organizational Dynamics,* 2–17.

Schapiro, Leonard, 1984. *The Russian Revolutions of 1917: The Origins of Modern Communism.* New York: Basic Books.

Schiffman, Susan S., M. Lance Reynolds, and Forrest W. Young, 1981. *Introduction to Multidimensional Scaling.* New York: Academic Press.

Schiller, Dan, 1986. "Transformations of news in the U.S. information market." In Peter Golding, Graham Murdock, and Philip Schlesinger (eds.), *Communicating Politics: Mass Communications and the Political Process.* New York: Holmes and Meier, pp. 19–36.

Schlesinger, Joseph A., 1984. "On the theory of party organization." *Journal of Politics,* 46: 369–400.

Schlozman, Kay L., 1984. "What accent the heavenly chorus? Political equality in the American pressure system." *Journal of Politics,* 46: 1006–32.

Schlozman, Kay L., and John T. Tierney, 1985. *Organized Interests and American Democracy.* New York: Harper & Row.

Schmitter, Philipp C., 1981. "Interest intermediation and regime governability in contemporary western Europe and North America." In Suzanne D. Berger (ed.), *Organizing Interests in Western Europe.* Cambridge: Cambridge University Press, pp. 287–330.

Schofield, Norman, and James Alt, 1983. "The analysis of relations in an organization." *Quality and Quantity,* 17: 269–79.

Schott, Thomas, 1986. "Models of dyadic and individual components of a social relation: applications to international trade." *Journal of Mathematical Sociology,* 12: 225–49.

Schott, Thomas, 1987a. "Scientific productivity and international integration of small countries: mathematics in Denmark and Israel." *Minerva,* 25: 3–20.

Schott, Thomas, 1987b. "Interpersonal influence in science: mathematics in Denmark and Israel." *Social Networks,* 9: 351–74.

Schott, Thomas, 1988. "International influence in science: beyond center and periphery." *Social Science Research,* 17: 219–38.

Schumpeter, Joseph A., 1943. *Capitalism, Socialism and Democracy.* London: Allen and Unwin.

Schwartz, Shalom, 1977. "Normative influences on altruism." In Leonard Berkowitz (ed.), *Advances in Experimental Social Psychology 10.* New York: Academic Press, pp. 221–79.

Scott, W. Richard, 1987. *Organizations: Rational, Natural, and Open Systems. Second Edition.* Englewood Cliffs, N.J.: Prentice-Hall.

Scott, W. Richard, 1988. "The adolescence of institutional theory." *Administrative Science Quarterly,* 32: 493–511.

Scott, W. Richard, and John W. Meyer, 1983. "The organization of social sectors." In John W. Meyer and W. Richard Scott (eds.), *Organizational Environments:*

Ritual and Rationality. Beverly Hills, Calif.: Sage, pp. 129–54.

Segal, David R., 1969. "Status inconsistency, cross pressures, and American political behavior." *American Sociological Review,* 34: 352–359.

Segal, David R., and Marshal W. Meyer, 1969. "The social context of political partisanship." In Mattei Dogan and Stein Rokkan (eds.), *Quantitative Ecological Analysis in the Social Sciences.* Cambridge, Mass.: MIT Press, pp. 217–32.

Seidman, Harold, 1980. *Politics, Positions, and Power: The Dynamics of Federal Organization. Third Edition.* New York: Oxford University Press.

Sheingold, Carl A., 1973. "Social networks and voting: the resurrection of a research agenda." *American Sociological Review,* 39: 712–20.

Shelton, Judy, 1989. *The Coming Soviet Crash: Gorbachev's Desperate Pursuit of Credit in Western Financial Markets.* New York: Free Press.

Shepsle, Kenneth, 1978. *The Giant Jigsaw Puzzle.* Chicago: University of Chicago Press.

Sherman, J. Daniel, Howard L. Smith, and Edward R. Mansfield, 1986. "The impact of emergent network structure on organizational socialization." *Journal of Applied Behavioral Science,* 22: 53–63.

Shubik, Martin, 1984. *A Game Theoretical Approach to Political Economy.* Cambridge Mass.: MIT Press.

Simmel, Georg, 1955. "The web of group affiliations." In Georg Simmel (ed.), *Conflict and the Web of Group Affiliations.* New York: Free Press, pp. 125–95.

Simon, Herbert A., 1957. *Models of Man.* New York: Wiley.

Simon, Herbert A., 1983. *Reason in Human Affairs.* Stanford: Stanford University Press.

Simon, Herbert A., 1985. "Human nature in politics: the dialogue of psychology with political science." *American Political Science Review,* 79: 293–304.

Singelmann, Joachim, 1978. *Agriculture to Services: The Transformation of Industrial Employment.* Beverly Hills, Calif.: Sage.

Skocpol, Theda, 1979a. *States and Social Revolutions.* Cambridge: Cambridge University Press.

Skocpol, Theda, 1979b. "Political response to capitalist crisis: neo-Marxist theories of the state and the case of the New Deal." *Politics and Society* 10: 155–201.

Smelser, Neil, 1963. *Theory of Collective Action.* New York: Free Press.

Smith, David, and Roger Nemeth, 1988. "An empirical analysis of commodity exchange in the international economy: 1965–1980." *International Studies Quarterly,* 32: 227–40.

Smith, David, and Douglas White, 1988. "Structure and dynamics of the global economy: network analysis of international trade 1965–1980." Paper presented at American Sociological Association, Atlanta.

Smith, Hedrick, 1988. *The Power Game: How Washington Works.* New York: Random House.

Snow, David A., E. Burke Rochford, Jr., Steven K. Worden, and Robert D. Benford, 1986. "Frame alignment processes, micromobilization, and movement participation." *American Sociological Review,* 51: 464–81.

Snow, David A., Louis A. Zurcher, Jr., and Sheldon Eckland-Olson, 1980. "Social networks and social movements: a microstructural approach to differential recruitment." *American Sociological Review,* 45: 787–801.

Snyder, David, and Edward Kick, 1979. "Structural position in the world system and economic growth, 1955–1970: a multiple-network analysis of transnational interactions." *American Journal of Sociology,* 84: 1096–126.

Snyder, David, and Charles Tilly, 1972. "Hardship and collective violence in France, 1830 to 1960." *American Sociological Review,* 37: 520–32.

Spencer, Herbert, 1910. *Principles of Sociology. Third Edition.* New York: Appleton.

Sprague, John, 1982. "Is there a micro-theory consistent with contextual analysis?" In Elinor Ostrom (ed.), *The Nature of Political Inquiry.* Beverly Hills, Calif.: Sage, pp. 99–121.

Stark, Rodney, 1985. *Sociology.* Belmont, Calif.: Wadsworth.

Stark, Rodney, and William S. Bainbridge, 1980. "Networks of faith: interpersonal bonds and recruitment to cults and sects." *American Journal of Sociology,* 85: 1376–95.

Steffens, Lincoln, 1931. *The Autobiography of Lincoln Steffens.* New York: Harcourt Brace World.

Stern, Philip M., 1988. *The Best Congress Money Can Buy.* New York: Pantheon.

Stinchcombe, Arthur, 1968. *Constructing Social Theories.* New York: Harcourt Brace.

Stokman, Frans N., Jan van den Bos, and Frans Wasseur, 1989. "A general model of policy analysis, with applications to the U.S. energy policy domain." Paper presented at first European Conference on Social Network Analysis, Groningen, The Netherlands.

Stokman, Frans N., Rolf Ziegler, and John Scott, 1985. *Networks of Corporate Power: A Comparative Analysis of Ten Countries.* Cambridge: Polity Press.

Streiber, Steven, 1979. "The world system and world trade: an empirical explanation of conceptual conflicts." *Sociological Quarterly,* 20: 23–36.

Sunkel, Osvaldo, 1972. "Big business and 'dependencia'." *Foreign Affairs,* 50: 517–31.

Tannenbaum, Arnold S., 1968. *Control in Organizations.* New York: McGraw-Hill.

Tanter, Raymond, 1966. "Dimensions of conflict behavior within and between nations, 1958–1960." *Journal of Conflict Resolution,* 17: 455–88.

Tarrow, Sidney, 1983. *Struggling to Reform: Social Movements and Policy Change During Cycles of Protest.* Ithaca, N.Y.: Cornell University Center for International Studies.

Tarrow, Sidney, 1988. "National politics and collective action: recent theory and research in western Europe and the United States." *Annual Review of Sociology,* 14: 421–40.

Tedin, Kent L., 1980. "Assessing peer and parental influence on political attitudes." *American Journal of Political Science,* 24: 136–54.

Therborn, Goran, 1976. "What does the ruling class do when it rules?" *The Insurgent Sociologist,* 6: 3–16.

Thomas, George M., and John W. Meyer, 1984. "The expansion of the state." *Annual Review of Sociology* 10: 461–82.

Thomas, William I., and Florian Znaniecki, 1918–20. *The Polish Peasant in Europe and America,* Boston: Badger.

Thompson, E. P., 1978. *The Poverty of Theory.* London: Monthly Review Press.

Thompson, James D., 1967. *Organizations in Action.* New York: McGraw-Hill.

Thurow, Lester, 1985. *The Zero-Sum Solution: Building a World-Class American Economy.* New York: Simon and Schuster.

Tichy, Noel, 1981. "Networks in organizations." In Paul Nystrom and William Starbuck (eds.), *Handbook of Organizational Design, Vol. 2.* London: Oxford University Press, pp. 225–49.

Tichy, Noel, and Charles Fombrun, 1979. "Network analysis in organizational settings." *Human Relations,* 32: 923–65.

Tichy, Noel, Michael Tushman, and Charles Fombrun, 1979. "Social network analysis for organizations." *Academy of Management Review,* 4: 497–619.

Tichy, Noel, Michael Tushman, and Charles Fombrun, 1980. "Network analysis in organizations." In Edward E. Lawler, David Nadler, and Cortland T. Commann (eds.), *Organizational Assessment.* New York: Wiley, pp. 372–98.

Tillock, Harriet, and Denton E. Morrison, 1979. "Group size and contribution to collective action: a test of Mancur Olson's theory on Zero Population Growth, Inc." *Research in Social Movements, Conflict, and Change,* 2: 131–58.

Tilly, Charles, 1978. *From Mobilization to Revolution.* Reading, Mass.: Addison-Wesley.

Tilly, Charles, 1985. *Big Structures, Large Processes, Huge Comparisons.* New York: Russell Sage.

Tilly, Charles, Louise Tilly, and Richard Tilly, 1975. *The Rebellious Century, 1830–1930.* Cambridge: Harvard University Press.

Timberlake, Michael, and Kirk R. Williams, 1987. "Structural position in the world system, inequality, and political violence." *Journal of Political and Military Sociology,* 15: 1–16.

Time, 1988. "$25,000,000,000." *Time* 132 (December 12): 56–7.

Tocqueville, Alexis de, 1945. *Democracy in America.* New York: Knopf.

Tolbert, Pamela, and Lynn Zucker, 1983. "Institutional sources of change in the formal structure of organizations: the diffusion of social service reform 1880–1935." *Administrative Science Quarterly,* 28: 22–39.

Trotsky, Leon, 1967. *The History of the Russian Revolution.* Ann Arbor, Mich.: University of Michigan Press.

Trounstine, Philip J., and Terry Christensen, 1982. *Movers and Shakers: The Study of Community Power.* New York: St. Martin's Press.

Trouwborst, A. A., 1973. "Two types of partial networks in Burundi." In Jeremy Boissevain and J. Clyde Mitchell (eds.), *Network Analysis: Studies in Human Interaction.* The Hague: Mouton, pp. 111–124.

Truman, David B., 1971. *The Governmental Process: Political Interests and Public Opinion. 2nd Edition.* New York: Knopf.

Tucker, Robert C., 1978. *The Marx-Engels Reader. Second Edition.* New York: Norton.

Tufte, Edward R., 1978. *Political Control of the Economy.* Princeton, N.J.: Princeton University Press.

Turk, Herman, 1977. *Organizations in Modern Life.* San Francisco: Jossey-Bass.

Turner, Ralph H., and Lewis M. Killian, 1972. *Collective Behavior*. Englewood Cliffs, N.J.: Prentice-Hall.

Tushman, Michael, 1979. "Work characteristics and subunit communication structure: a contingency analysis." *Administrative Science Quarterly*, 24: 82–98.

Tuttle, Thomas C., 1988. "Technology, organization of the future, and non-management roles." In Jerald Hage (ed.), *Futures of Organizations: Innovating to Adapt Strategy and Human Resources to Rapid Technological Change*. Lexington, Mass.: Lexington Books, pp. 163–180.

Ullman-Margalit, Edna, 1977. *The Emergence of Norms*. Oxford: Clarendon Press.

United Nations, 1983. *1983 International Trade Statistics Yearbook*. New York: United Nations.

Useem, Michael, 1979. "The social organization of the American business elite and participation of corporate directors in the governance of American institutions." *American Sociological Review*, 44: 553–72.

Useem, Michael, 1980. "Which business leaders help to govern?" In G. William Domhoff (ed.), *Power Structure Research*. Beverly Hills, Calif.: Sage, pp. 199–226.

Useem, Michael, 1981. "Business segments and corporate relations with American Universities." *Social Problems*, 29: 129–41.

Useem, Michael, 1982. "Classwide rationality in the politics of managers and directors of large corporations in the United States and Great Britain." *Administrative Science Quarterly*, 27: 199–226.

Useem, Michael, 1983. *The Inner Circle: Large Corporations and Business Politics in the U.S. and U.K.*. New York: Oxford University Press.

Useem, Michael, John Hoops, and Thomas S. Moore, 1976. "Class and corporate relations with the private college system." *Insurgent Sociologist*, 6(4): 27–35.

Useem, Michael, and Arlene McCormack, 1981. "The dominant segment of the British business elite." *Sociology*, 15: 381–406.

Van Velzen, H. U. E. Thoden, 1973. "Coalitions and network analysis." In Jeremy Boissevain and J. Clyde Mitchell (eds.), *Network Analysis: Studies in Human Interaction*. The Hague: Mouton, pp. 219–250.

van Winden, F., 1984. "Towards a dynamic theory of cabinet formation." In Manfred J. Holler (ed.), *Coalitions and Collective Action*. Würzburg, West Germany: Physica-Verlag, pp. 145–59.

Verba, Sidney, and Norman H. Nie, 1972. *Participation in America*. New York: Harper & Row.

Verbrugge, Lois M., 1977. "The structure of adult friendship choices." *Social Forces*, 56: 576–97.

Vermeer, Jan Pons (ed.), 1987. *Campaigns in the News: Mass Media and Congressional Elections*. Westport, Conn.: Greenwood Press.

Vogel, Ezra, 1979. *Japan as No. 1*. Cambridge: Harvard University Press.

Waldo, Charles N., 1985. *Boards of Directors: Their Changing Roles, Structure, and Information Needs*. Westport, Conn.: Quorum Books.

Walker, Jack L., 1983. "The origins and maintenance of interest groups in America." *American Political Science Review*, 77: 390–406.

Wallace, Michael, and Arne Kalleberg, 1982. "Industrial transformation and the decline of craft: the decomposition of skill in the printing industry, 1931–1978." *American Sociological Review*, 47: 307–24.

Wallerstein, Immanuel, 1974. *The Modern World System, I: Capitalist Agriculture and the Origins of the European World-Economy in the Sixteenth Century.* New York: Academic Press.

Wallerstein, Immanuel, 1980. *The Modern World System, II: Mercantilism and the Consolidation of the European World-Economy, 1600–1750.* New York: Academic Press.

Wallerstein, Immanuel, 1982. "The rise and future demise of the world capitalist system: concepts for comparative analysis." In Hamza Alavi and Teodor Shanin (eds.), *Introduction to the Sociology of 'Developing Societies'.* New York: Monthly Review Press, pp. 29–53.

Wallerstein, Immanuel, 1988. *The Modern World System, III: The Second Era of Great Expansion of the Capitalist World-Economy, 1730–1840.* Orlando, Fla.: Academic Press.

Walsh, Edward J., and Rex H. Warland, 1983. "Social movement involvement in the wake of a nuclear accident: activists and free riders in the TMI area." *American Sociological Review*, 48: 764–80.

Walton, John, 1966. "Discipline, method, and community power: a note on the sociology of knowledge." *American Sociological Review*, 31: 684–89.

Ward, Lester F., 1906. *Applied Sociology.* Boston: Ginn.

Warner, R. Stephen, 1978. "Toward a redefinition of action theory: paying the cognitive element its due." *American Journal of Sociology*, 6: 1317–49.

Warren, Roland L., Stephen Rose, and Ann Bergunder, 1974. *The Structure of Urban Reform.* Lexington, Mass.: Heath.

Waters, Malcolm, 1989. "Collegiality, bureaucratization, and professionalization: A Weberian analysis." *American Journal of Sociology* 94: 945–72.

Weber, Max, 1947. *The Theory of Social and Economic Organization.* New York: Free Press.

Weber, Max, 1968. *Economy and Society.* Vol. 2. New York: Bedminster Press.

Weimann, Gabriel, 1982. "On the importance of marginality: one more step into the two-step flow of communication." *American Sociological Review*, 47: 764–73.

Weimann, Gabriel, 1983. "The strength of weak ties in the flow of information and influence." *Social Networks*, 5: 245–67.

Weingrod, Alex, 1968. "Patrons, patronage, and political parties." *Comparative Studies in Society and History* 10: 377–400.

Weinstein, James, 1968. *The Corporate Ideal in the Liberal State, 1900–1918.* Boston: Beacon Press.

Weiss, Joseph W., 1981. "The historical and political perspective of Lucien Karpik." In Mary Zey-Ferrell and Michael Aiken (eds.), *Complex Organizations: Critical Perspectives.* Glenview, Ill.: Scott, Foresman, pp. 382–410.

Welch, W. P., 1983. "Do campaign contributions affect legislative voting? The case of the milk lobby." *Western Political Quarterly* 35: 478–95.

Whetten, David A., 1981. "Interorganizational relations: a review of the field." *Journal of Higher Education*, 52: 1–28.

Whetten, David A., and Howard Aldrich, 1979. "Organization set size and diversity: people-processing organizations and their environments." *Administra-*

tion and Society, 3: 251–81.

Whisler, Thomas, 1970. *Information Technology and Organizational Change*. Belmont, Calif.: Wadsworth.

White, Douglas, and Karl Reitz, 1983. "Graph and semigraph homomorphisms on networks of relations." *Social Networks*, 5: 193–234.

White, Harrison C., Scott Boorman, and Ronald L. Breiger, 1976. "Social structure from multiple networks. I. Blockmodels of roles and positions." *American Journal of Sociology*, 81: 730–80.

White, Robert W., 1989. "From peaceful protest to guerilla war: micromobilization of the Provisional Irish Republican Army." *American Journal of Sociology*, 94: 1277–302.

Whitt, Allen, 1982. *Urban Elites and Mass Transportation: The Dialectics of Power*. Princeton: Princeton University Press.

Wilensky, Harold, 1975. *The Welfare State and Equality*. Berkeley: University of California Press.

Wiley, Mary Glenn, and Arlene Eskilson, 1982. "Coping in the corporation: sex role constraints." *Journal of Applied Social Psychology*, 12: 1–11.

Wiley, Mary Glenn, and Arlene Eskilson, 1983. "Scaling the corporate ladder: sex differences in expectations for performance, power and mobility." *Social Psychology Quarterly*, 46: 351–59.

Willer, David, 1967. "Max Weber's missing authority type." *Sociological Inquiry*, 37: 231–39.

Williamson, Oliver, 1975. *Markets and Hierarchies*. New York: Free Press.

Williamson, Oliver, 1981. "The economies of organization: the transaction cost approach." *American Journal of Sociology*, 87: 548–577.

Williamson, Peter J., 1985. *Varieties of Corporatism: A Conceptual Discussion*. London: Cambridge University Press.

Wilson, James Q., 1973. *Political Organizations*. New York: Basic Books.

Wilson, Kenneth, and Tony Orum, 1976. "Mobilizing people for collective political action." *Journal of Political and Military Sociology*, 4: 187–202.

Wolf, Wendy, and Neil D. Fligstein, 1979. "Sex and authority in the workplace: the causes of sexual inequality." *American Sociological Review*, 44: 235–52.

Wolfinger, Raymond E., 1960. "Reputation and reality in the study of community power." *American Sociological Review*, 25: 636–44.

Wolfinger, Raymond E., 1971. "Nondecisions and the study of local politics." *American Political Science Review*, 65: 1063–80.

Wolfinger, Raymond E., and Steven J. Rosenstone, 1980. *Who Votes?* New Haven: Yale University Press.

Wolff, Edward N., 1985. "The magnitude and causes of the recent productivity slowdown in the United States: a survey of recent studies." In William J. Baumol and Kenneth McLennan (eds.), *Productivity, Growth, and U.S. Competitiveness*. New York: Oxford University Press, pp. 29–57.

Wright, Erik Olin, 1978. *Class, Crisis and the State*. London: New Left Books.

Wright, Erik Olin, and Bill Martin, 1987. "The transformation of the American class structure." *American Journal of Sociology*, 93: 1–29.

Wright, Erik Olin, and Joachim Singelmann, 1982. "Proletarianization in the changing American class structure." In Michael Burawoy and Theda Skocpol (eds.), *Marxist Inquiries: Studies of Labor, Class, and States*. Chicago: University of Chicago Press, pp. 176–209.

Wright, Gerald C., Jr., 1976. "Community structure and voting in the South." *Public Opinion Quarterly*, 40: 201–215.

Wrong, Dennis, 1979. *Power: Its Forms, Bases and Uses*. Oxford: Basil Blackwell.

Yamagishi, Toshio, Mary R. Gillmore, and Karen S. Cook, 1988. "Network connections and the distribution of power in exchange networks." *American Journal of Sociology*, 93: 833–51.

Yates, Douglas, 1985. *The Politics of Management: Exploring the Inner Workings of Public and Private Organizations*. San Francisco: Jossey-Bass.

Zald, Mayer N., 1969. "The power and functions of boards of directors: a theoretical synthesis." *American Journal of Sociology*, 75: 97–111.

Zald, Mayer N., and Michael Berger, 1978. "Social movements in organizations: coup d'etat, insurgency, and mass movements." *American Journal of Sociology*, 83: 823–61.

Zald, Mayer N., and David Jacobs, 1978. "Compliance/incentive classifications of organizations: underlying dimensions." *Administration and Society*, 9: 403–24.

Zeitlin, Maurice, 1978. "Who owns America?" *The Progressive* 42: 14–19.

Zey-Ferrell, Mary, 1981. "Criticisms of the dominant perspective on organizations." *Sociological Quarterly*, 22: 181–205.

Zimmer, Lynn, 1988. "Tokenism and women in the workplace: the limits of gender-neutral theory." *Social Problems*, 35: 64–77.

Zinnes, Dina, 1970. "Coalition theories and the balance of power." In Sven Groennings, E. W. Kelley, and Michael Leiserson (eds.), *The Study of Coalition Behavior*. New York: Holt, Rinehart and Winston, pp. 351–68.

Zucker, Lynne G., 1977. "The role of institutionalization in cultural persistence." *American Sociological Review*, 42: 726–43.

Zucker, Lynne G., 1986. "Networks for evaluation: reputation in economic life." Los Angeles: University of California at Los Angeles (mimeographed).

Zucker, Lynne G., 1987. "Institutional theories of organization." *Annual Review of Sociology*, 13: 443–64.

Index

283

in, 49–50; political networks, 51–4; radial, 48; social mobility and, 46
elections: cost of, 220; realigning, 36; *see also* voting
electronic information revolutions, 205–9
electronic tribes, 206
elite democratic theory, 29
elite theory, 149
Elmira, New York, 34–5, 44–5
Emerson, Richard, 2, 15, 98
employment, 214–15
Engels, Friedrich, 152
environmental destruction, 231
Equal Employment Opportunities Commission (EEOC), 166
Equal Rights Amendment, 75, 80
equity, *see* norms
Erie County, Ohio, 34, 44
ersatz network, 34
ethnic conflict, 147
Euclidean distance, 240
European Economic Community, 229
Evans, Peter, 181–2
events, 123; outcome of, in community, 137–8
evolution of societies, 176–7
exchange: international trade, 190, 191–2, 195, 196–9; media of, 129; among organizations, 109; and policy outcomes, 171–3; social, 98–101

Fairhurst, Gail, 102
Faletto, Enzo, 180–1
Federal Election Commission (FEC), 221
Fennell, Mary, 111–12
Fennema, Meindart, 113
Fernandez, Robert, 73, 145–6
Field, G., 153, 162
Finifter, Ada, 42
Fiorina, Morris, 31–3
"first order zone,"40
fiscal sociology, 151
Fligstein, Neil, 101
Florida A&M University, 80
form, concept of, in network analysis, 236
frame alignment, 71
France, 61, 66, 71, 153, 192, 211
Frank, Andre, 178–9
Freeman, Jo, 74
Freeman, Linton, 240
free-riding, 62, 64
funnel of causality, 30

Galaskiewicz, Joseph, 132, 136–8
game theory, 25, 38–9, 155–6
Gamson, William, 75
garbage can model, 155
gender in organizations, 101–3

General Social Survey (GSS), 50–4, 56
German Socialist Party, 130
Germany, 57, 66, 163, 171, 192, 197, 211, 229
Giddens, Anthony, 16–17
Godwin, Richard, 64
Gold, Thomas, 182
Goldwater, Barry, 220–1
Gorbachev, Mikhail, 228–9
Gould, Roger, 145–6
GRADAP computer program, 240
Granovetter, Mark, 25–6, 108, 238
Grey, Joel, 220
Groholt, K., 153
Group of Seven, 175
Guevara, Che, 82
Guterbock, Thomas, 140

Haas, Ernst, 187
Hall, Thomas, 183, 185
Hamburg, West Germany, 64
Hansen, John, 64
Hart, Jeffrey, 191–2
Heclo, Hugh, 155
hegemony, definition of, 114
Herrschaft, 2
hierarchies, 107–8
Higley, John, 153–4, 162–3
hishinter influence structure, 192
Hobbes, Thomas, 20
homophily, 70, 225
Hopkins, Terence, 182–3
Huckfeldt, Robert, 47–8, 55
Hungary, 227, 230
Hunter, Floyd, 120–2

imperceptible effect, 62
imports-exports, 187, 190
incentives: soft, 64; typologies of, 63
indegree, 238
industrial relations, 216–17
industrialization, 231
influence, 5; definition of, 3; networks of, 11, 13, 26
influence reputation: of community organizations, 130–3; definition of, 133
informants: in community power research, 120–1; in network studies, 112
information: exchange of, 12–13; perfect, 24; political, 34
inner circle, 159
innovations, diffusion of, 70, 111
institutional theory, 110–11
intercorporate relations, 113–15
intergovernmental organizations (IGOS), 190, 191, 196
interlocking directors, 113–15, 159–60
international Monetary Fund, 175